Perennials

Designing, Choosing, and Maintaining Easy-Care Plantings

Perennials

Designing, Choosing, and Maintaining Easy-Care Plantings

Sally Roth and Jane Courtier

Reader's Digest

The Reader's Digest Association, Inc.
Pleasantville, New York/Montreal

A Reader's Digest Book

This edition published by
The Reader's Digest Association, Inc.
by arrangement with Toucan Books, Ltd.

For Toucan Books
  Design: Nigel Soper
  Editor: Theresa Bebbington
  Managing Editor: Ellen Dupont
  Index: Lina Burton
  Photo Research: Sharon Southren
  Photo Manager: Christine Vincent
  Proofreader: Jill Anderson
  Special Photography: Mark Winwood and
  Neil Hepworth

For Reader's Digest
  U.S. Project Editor: Marilyn Knowlton
  Canadian Project Editor: Pamela Johnson
  Canadian Consulting Editor: Trevor Cole
  Project Designer: Jennifer Tokarski
  Associate Art Director: George McKeon
  Executive Editor, Trade Publishing:
  Dolores York
  Associate Publisher, Trade Publishing:
  Rosanne McManus
  President & Publisher, Trade Publishing:
  Harold Clarke

Library of Congress Cataloging-in-
Publication Data
Roth, Sally.
  Perennials : designing, choosing, and
  maintaining easy-care plantings /
  by Sally Roth and Jane Courtier.
      p. cm
  Includes index.
  ISBN-13: 978-0-7621-0841-1
  ISBN-10: 0-7621-0841-X
  1. Perennials. 2. Gardening. I. Courtier,
  Jane. II. Reader's Digest
  Association. III. Title.
  SB434.R68 2008
  635.9'32--dc22   2007023658

We are committed to both the quality of
our products and the service we provide to
our customers. We value your comments,
so please feel free to contact us:

The Reader's Digest Association, Inc.
Adult Trade Publishing
Reader's Digest Road
Pleasantville, NY 10570-7000

For more Reader's Digest products and
information, visit our website at:

www.rd.com (in the United States)
www.readersdigest.ca (in Canada)

NOTE TO OUR READERS
No garden center carries every species,
much less every cultivar, of plant included
in the book, so in some instances you may
have to make substitutions. Ask a
knowledgeable salesperson at your local
garden center to help select plants with
both a similar appearance and cultural
requirements to those in the book.

When buying perennials, check to see
whether they are hardy in your climate.
The suggested U.S.D.A. Hardiness Zone
given for each plant is a general
recommendation based on cold-hardiness
and is to be used only as a general guide.
Hardiness may vary depending on the
microclimate in your own garden, as well
as on variations in weather from one year
to the next. Other conditions, such as
humidity, drought, and soil type, also
affect plants.

Printed in China
3 5 7 9 10 8 6 4 2

CONTENTS

3 Plant Care 72

A–Z Plant Directory 108

Introduction

For a garden full of summer color, you just can't beat border perennials—which is why they have been among our favorite plants for many years. Easy to grow, they will often reward you with a brilliant display—requiring little effort on your part. And it's simple to make that display even better when you know how. Behind the glorious, seemingly chaotic "riot of color" of the best summer borders, there is always a guiding hand, gently but firmly orchestrating the show, providing the unseen backstage support that makes everything run smoothly.

With so many beautiful plants to choose from, it's all too easy to get carried away, picking the most spectacular and appealing plants without stopping to think about how they will work together in your garden. Remember, just as every production has to have its supporting roles as well as its star performers, for a successful garden filled with perennials, some plants need to play a background role, while others shine in the starring role. In *Designing with Perennials* we'll guide you through the complete process of designing stunning perennial beds and borders, whether you are starting from scratch or trying to breathe new life into a worn-out garden.

You'll also need just a little knowledge of what each plant can offer so you'll be able to assemble the perfect cast, which you'll find in *Choosing the Right Plants*. Is your garden in a problem area? From drought-stricken plots to seaside gardens, we will help you find the most suitable plants. And while perennials are certainly a feature of the summer garden, it does not need to end there—we provide ideas for extending the season all the way through from early spring to late fall.

You'll need to coax the best performance from your plants, and it will be vital to provide them with the conditions they need to help them be at their best. From preparing the soil and buying the plants to caring for them through the year, in *Plant Care* we'll guide you

every step of the way, supplying practical advice on what to plant and why. In all of these chapters, you'll find tips and hints along the way to help you design your perennial garden and care for your plants. You'll also find plenty of charts and boxes that recommend plants for different features, including color, texture, height, foliage, and fragrance, as well as suggestions for plants that are at their peak in spring, summer, and fall.

A–Z OF PERENNIALS

As well as practical advice on designing with and growing your perennials, there's a colorful, photo-filled directory of more than 100 of the top perennials, with entries chock-full of fun facts about a plant's history, lore, or idiosyncracies, providing you with an insight into the plant not just as a pretty flower but as a real garden character. The directory includes a bounty of new cultivars and hybrids, as well as the best of the old reliables, and it

points out trends that have revamped the perennials scene. There are perennials for all regions, no matter what kind of climate or conditions you're blessed with. Of course, the usual facts on growing habits, hardiness, and other need-to-know information are included, too.

A few perennials are a little more demanding, so you'll also find suggestions on ways to avoid difficulties with them. Special features include the Perfect Partners sidebars—to get you excited about actually using the plants in your own garden, envisioning them as part of a bigger picture and soaking up design basics without being intimidated. We've also picked 20 truly outstanding perennials and dedicated extra pages to show you how spectacular they can be.

Whether you already garden with perennials or you're just beginning, *Perennials* provides you with everything you need to be successful—except the shovel and the plants. Happy gardening!

The Perennial Garden

1

Designing with Perennials

Designing a garden is like creating a work of art. A great painting starts with an artist taking a pencil and sketching the main outlines of the picture. For the gardener that pencil sketch is formed by placing fences and hedges, laying paving and grass, cutting and shaping beds and borders—forming the basic shapes of the finished garden.

Once the artist is satisfied with his sketch, it's time to take the paints and fill in the penciled outlines with color, carefully blending hues and adding textures to bring the picture to life. What is the gardener's paint palette? Plants, of course. With their endless subtle shades, shapes, and textures, a gardener can create a living picture that will give just as much pleasure as the greatest old masterpiece.

In this chapter we take a look at the two main elements of design— the overall shape of the garden and its features, and the effective and harmonious combination of plants to fill it with life.

This stunning summer border uses a combination of shrubs and perennials, such as basket-of-gold (*Aurinia* spp.) and catmint (*Nepeta* spp.), to acheive its effects. When designing this border, the gardener thought about how the colors would work together and about the plants' heights and shapes.

Planning Your Garden

The best way to create the garden of your dreams is to plan it right from the beginning—before you sow the first seeds or set out the first plant.

Perennials add not only flowers and color to a garden but also attractive foliage, architectural shapes, intriguing textures, and beautiful fragrances. No longer are these outstanding plants restricted to the "herbaceous border"—now they are grown among shrubs, under trees, mixed with bulbs and rock-garden plants, and in containers.

Whether you are planning a new garden entirely from scratch, adding new beds and borders to an existing design, or simply want to incorporate more perennials among the plants you are growing already, you will need to think carefully about where each plant will be going and what part it will play in the overall effect. Drawing up a plan will help you decide what plants to use and where to position them. You'll need to know the height, flower color,

and season of interest—the time of year when it will be most attractive—of each of the plants you choose for your garden.

Make sure you allow enough room for each plant to show off its features as it matures, and think about whether or not the plant will complement the plants around it. It is easy to be seduced by the many magnificent varieties of perennials that are available, with glowing flower colors, strikingly handsome foliage, or delicious fragrances, making plant after plant a "must" on your plant list. Be careful that you don't end up with a mismatched assortment that will never form a satisfying overall design.

GARDEN STYLES

Make sure you have a clear idea of the style of garden that you want to create. You'll need to

Even a small city garden can be transformed into a formal garden with simple lines and shapes. This split-level garden has a pink-purple flowering theme, which includes hosta, bugleweed (*Ajuga* spp.), bleeding heart (*Dicentra* spp.), and iris.

The riot of color in this cottage-style garden was planned from the beginning. The white flowers were deliberately planted to break up the vibrant colors so they didn't become overwhelming.

gardenTIPS

For inspiration to help you design your garden, try the following:

- Look at pictures in gardening books and magazines.
- Visit local gardens that are open to the public.
- Think about how the style of your house will work with a particular garden style.

ask yourself what kind of garden you like. Are you attracted to the straight lines and simple geometric shapes of a formal design or the gentle flowing edges and seemingly haphazard planting of an informal cottage-style garden? A garden that gives its all in a fantastic burst of short-lived color during only the summer months or one that will provide interesting features over a longer period? A design that uses refined and relaxing pastel shades or a bright, unrestrained kaleidoscope of color?

Don't be fooled by the gloriously informal appearance of a traditional cottage-style garden or the apparently random riot of color of a perennial bed at its peak—both of these were meticulously designed. Sometimes the most informal garden style takes the most careful planning of all!

Tulips (*Tulipa* spp.) and other bulbs are a wonderful way to add early color to a spring garden that is otherwise dominated by foliage.

A Garden through the Seasons

When designing your garden, think about how it will look in all the seasons—spring, summer, fall, and winter—not just in summer when most gardens are at their peak. Take monthly photographs of your existing garden throughout the year or at least between early spring and late fall. These pictures will be helpful when it comes to deciding which features of the current design are worth preserving. They will also help you identify the times when the performance doesn't live up to your standards. Visiting a large garden open to the public in all the seasons is a good way for you to see how a garden's appearance can change throughout the year.

What Is a Perennial?

Plants are divided into different groups, such as annuals, perennials, and bulbs, or trees and shrubs. However, the definition of "perennial" seems to have become something of a minefield.

The normal definition of "perennial" is a plant that lives for more than two seasons. This definition distinguishes a perennial from an annual or biennial, both of which die after flowering (an annual within one growing season and a biennial in its second season, after overwintering). However, such a definition would also include trees and shrubs—which is not what most gardeners mean when they talk about perennials. Trees and shrubs are correctly known as woody perennials, but for most gardeners "perennial" means herbaceous, or nonwoody, plants that die down in fall and produce new shoots from the underground rootstock each spring.

But hold on—that's not right, either. What about Italian arum (*Arum italicum*), a perennial valued for its glossy, arrowhead-shaped leaves and upright stems of bright red berries? Arum produces its leaves not in spring but in fall; it hangs on to them over winter and lets them die away in spring. And there are some perennials, including bloodroot (*Sanguinaria* spp.) and bleeding heart (*Dicentra* spp.) that die down right after flowering in spring or early summer, not in fall—not to mention the evergreen perennials, such as spurge (*Euphorbia* spp.), bergenia, and bugleweed (*Ajuga* spp.), that keep their leaves throughout the year.

OTHER TYPES OF PERENNIALS

There are other groups of plants that are usually treated separately, but some of these are considered as perennials. Bulbs form underground storage organs from their stems or leaf bases, but they certainly fit into the definition of "plants that live for more than two seasons," and alliums, lilies (*Lilium* spp.), and camas (*Camassia* spp.) are familiar plants in perennial borders. Irises and dahlias are rhizomes, gladiolus are corms, and agapanthus can't decide what it is—sometimes sold as a bulb, others as perennials, and occasionally (by those who've given up trying to decide) as "bulbous perennials." Alpines are plants that have adapted to growing in mountainous regions above the tree line; here is another specialized group that contains familiar perennials, such as varieties of geranium, campanula, and phlox.

Most gardeners think of perennials as plants that carry on for years, needing only a little care and attention now and then to keep

Bulbs fit happily among perennials, as shown in this mixed springtime border featuring tulips (*Tulipa* spp.) and globe-shaped alliums.

The striking red-leaved canna adds an exotic touch to this border. It is not a hardy perennial—it won't survive frosts—but it makes a good temporary summer resident.

A traditional border planted with groups of flowers is at its best in the summer. In this type of border, annuals are sometimes interspersed among perennials.

in today's gardens. Such plants certainly have the potential to survive for several years, but if you live in a cold area, you will need to protect them over winter (see pages 106–7). Certain varieties of salvia and exotic-looking cannas have become favorites, however dahlias are perhaps more familiar tender perennials.

So where does this leave us? As far as this book is concerned, we won't be too strict about definitions. "Hardy herbaceous perennials" is a term that will accurately describe most of the plants found in these pages—but be prepared for a few departures, too!

them looking their best. However, not all are long-lived; there are several plants that are usually described as "short-lived perennials," and these have a habit of turning up their toes after a few years for no good reason at all. Rose campion (*Lychnis coronaria*), wallflower (*Erysimum* 'Bowles Mauve'), pinks (*Dianthus* spp.), and the blue poppy (*Meconopsis* spp.) are all among that frustrating group of plants that may appear to be thriving one year but simply fails to appear the following spring. So while some perennials can indeed keep going strong for 20 years or so, 4 or 5 years is all you can expect from others.

HARDY OR TENDER?

A few years ago the word "perennial" nearly always had "hardy" tacked onto the front, and it was taken for granted that a perennial plant would be tough enough to survive frosts or even prolonged freezing spells. However, more tender perennials are making an appearance

Beds and Borders

Whether you prefer a traditional border with straight lines or one with flowing curves, beds, and borders—and the plants that can be grown in them—today's gardener have a number of choices.

It's not so long ago that for many people the backyard consisted of a rectangular lawn surrounded on three sides by straight-edged, formal, perennial flower borders. The depth of these borders depended on how large your garden was—and how much time you were prepared to spend weeding and staking. Then this formal, straight-laced garden evolved into something different.

Flowing curves took over from straight edges, giving the garden a relaxed atmosphere. New, stockier, more compact varieties of plants were bred that didn't need so much staking. While traditional flower borders had nearly always contained only herbaceous perennials, mixed plantings of shrubs, perennials, bulbs, and annuals have become more popular, providing a longer season of interest and reducing the amount of maintenance required. And today "borders" are no longer always on the edge—island beds, which can be viewed from all angles, have taken their place in the center of the lawn.

As the years have gone by, the size of the average garden has shrunk considerably. This suits many busy, working garden owners, who know that they won't have enough time to maintain a large garden. Nevertheless, they demand that their smaller gardens work hard, providing them with color and interest, and a

Sweeping curves help to create a relaxing style in a perennial border, making the garden a more inviting place to visit.

gardenTIPS

You are the person who knows best what you want from your garden, but remember that good garden designs will:

- Divide the garden into different areas that cannot be seen all at once, which will create a sense of mystery and inspire curiosity.

- Make use of strong shapes that will interlink well.

- Lead the eye to the best views by careful positioning of focal points.

- Keep things simple!

place to relax through all the seasons. Getting maximum value out of a small space means that good design is more important than ever.

DRAWING UP THE DESIGN

If you are planning your garden from scratch, you can design it exactly the way you want. However, most people have to work with an existing layout. Before starting your plan, decide where you will be most often when you want to view your garden. During the summer you might find you spend most of your time enjoying the garden from a patio or other outdoor sitting area. The main summer show might, therefore, be best seen from the patio. However, the view from the kitchen window should provide interest in spring, fall, and winter. If you won't be outdoors in the garden during wintertime, you won't mind a bare section if you can't see it from the house. However, if a large living-room window looks out onto your garden, you'll want to add a special feature to make the garden more interesting in winter, such as a deciduous tree that looks striking without its leaves.

The next stage is to draw a rough sketch of the garden. It doesn't have to be artistic—it's just a way of keeping track of your ideas. Mark existing beds and borders, trees, shrubs,

major plants, and any other large features on your sketch. You can use month-by-month photographs (see page 15) to help you decide which of these you want to keep and which you want to get rid of or move to a different position. You now have a basic garden plan.

This bench is in a hidden area and provides a relaxing place to sit and admire the garden.

Perennials in Containers

There are a number of benefits to growing plants in containers. They are mobile, so a container-grown plant in its full glory can be moved to center stage and then returned to the wings once its performance is over, while tender perennials can be taken under cover before a frost destroys them. Containers help to raise plants off the ground and closer to eye level, allowing their finer points to be appreciated; mud splashes are kept off foliage and flowers, and pests, such as slugs and snails, are easier to keep at bay. The containers themselves are often decorative and can be used as ornamental focal points in the garden.

Not all perennials are suitable for growing in containers. (See page 59 for ideas for those that are.) They need frequent watering in summer and regular feeding. If they remain outdoors all winter, they may need extra protection because the roots are more exposed to cold than when planted in the ground. And like most perennials, they will benefit from division to keep them healthy and growing strongly.

Herbaceous Borders

"Herbaceous" means that a plant has soft stems that die back in winter, and classic herbaceous borders contain only this type of plant. This is the traditional way to grow perennials—in wide, straight borders.

In large gardens wide, straight herbaceous borders are magnificent in their summer glory, often stretching for many feet into the distance and packed with plants 10 feet (3 m) deep or more. However, in most people's gardens, herbaceous borders have been scaled down to a more manageable size.

Traditional herbaceous borders are truly spectacular during their flowering season, but once the summer flowers have faded, there is little to provide interest during the winter and spring months. Dead stems are usually cut back severely in the fall, leaving a bare and unappealing border until the following spring.

Maintaining a traditional herbaceous border involves plenty of hard work. The bare soil in early spring can be quickly colonized by weeds, which will need constant attention to keep them under control. And once the herbaceous plants start to grow in spring, their shoots may need thinning to encourage the production of strong flowering stems. Tall varieties need staking from an early stage to prevent their shape from being ruined by wind and rain, and the staking needs to be done carefully so that it remains unobtrusive.

All through the summer, weeds have to be kept under control and stems need regular tying to their supports. The plants also need to be checked for dead flower heads, which should be removed to keep the display attractive and to encourage more flowers to form to keep the display going.

A CHANGE IN FASHION

For these reasons traditional herbaceous borders became unfashionable. Beautiful as they looked in their season, most people demanded a greater return for their labors than a brief few weeks of summer color. They were replaced by shrubs, which require less maintenance and provide a permanent framework for the garden—some even provide year-round interest. With the emphasis on easy care, perennial border plants almost completely disappeared for a while. Fortunately, it wasn't long before perennials found their way back into favor. Although they once again play a major role in the border, they usually share the stage with other top performers.

MODERN HERBACEOUS BORDERS

You can still enjoy the glory of the true herbaceous border in your garden but with

When planning borders, include paths or other types of access to allow you to reach the plants for maintenance.

gardenTIPS

Visit several large gardens famous for their traditional herbaceous borders in summer, and see if you can incorporate some of their best features into a smaller border for your own garden.

- **Pay particular attention to the way they use different heights and textures, and how they achieve good color combinations.**

- **Take plenty of photographs; they will help you plan how to scale the ideas down for use in your own garden.**

less work and a longer season of interest. Start by choosing plant varieties carefully and using slightly different gardening techniques. Both can make a big difference in the amount of time you will need to maintain the garden.

Select modern varieties of perennials that have been bred for their shorter stems and sturdier shape, because these will need less staking. Set plants close together so that they help support one another and cover the ground more quickly, which will give weeds less opportunity to become established.

Choose a mixture of plant varieties to create a long season of interest, from early spring to late fall, and allow some seed heads and sculptural stems to remain through the winter to provide out-of-season interest. *Choosing the Right Plants* (see pages 46–71) provides more ideas on extending the seasons.

Another important step is to keep your borders at a size that you can easily manage. Instead of having a long, narrow border, try a shorter, deeper border, which usually creates more impact but with the same number of plants and same amount of work. Make sure you plan access to the border from both sides to make maintenance easier. There are plenty of other time- and labor-saving ideas in *Plant Care* (see pages 72–107); employ as many of these as possible to keep your work to a minimum.

At the same time that you make these changes, remember to keep the best features of traditional herbaceous borders. For example, use a plain background, such as a wooden fence, dark evergreen hedge, or a wall, so that the flowers will stand out, and grade the heights of plants from the tallest ones at the back of the bed to the shortest in the front.

Modern borders can be only a few feet wide, but plan to keep shorter plants near the front, where they can be seen.

A large, traditional herbaceous border is outstanding in the summer, providing a variety of colors, shapes, and textures.

Island Beds

Instead of displaying perennials in a traditional herbaceous border, they can be shown off in an island bed—a great way to see perennials at every angle.

Traditional herbaceous borders were invariably rectangular, with completely straight edges, and as their name implies, they were normally situated at the edges of a garden. Originally called a "flower bed," the round "island bed" was first used in the 1930s and was popularized in the mid-1950s by British perennial specialist Alan Bloom.

These island beds were simply cut out of the center of a lawn instead of being positioned along the edges, and they provided a number of benefits. Traditional borders usually had a fence, hedge, or wall running along one side, and while this provided shelter, it also cast shade and prevented free movement of air. The island bed allowed far more light and air to reach the plants, with the result that they

grew more sturdily and needed less staking. The beds could be viewed from every side, adding much more interest and variety to the garden. They were particularly suited to the more informal styles of garden design that were becoming popular at that time and were versatile; they could be made in an infinite range of different shapes and sizes. Island beds made it easy to divide the garden up and keep some "hidden" areas to be discovered on a garden walk—always an important feature of good design.

PLANNING THE BEDS

Be careful when planning your island bed—there are some traps into which it is too easy to fall. The most common one is the temptation to make the shape of the bed too complex, with a lot of fussy curves and indentations. Not only is this more difficult to mow and edge around, it never looks as successful in reality as it does on paper. Keep to simple, flowing lines—kidney shapes, crescents, and comma shapes work well—or for a slightly more formal effect try using geometric shapes.

Whatever shape you decide to create, mark it out on the lawn, preferably with a long piece of rope or hose, which is easy to adjust. Look at it from a lot of different angles and, if relevant, from an upstairs window in your house, then make any necessary adjustments until you are completely satisfied with the result.

Be careful that you don't make any part of the bed too narrow—plants need room to grow and spread without spoiling the design. The overall size of each bed is important; it must be in scale not only with the rest of the yard—a big bed in a small yard will make the

In a large garden, island beds planted with a variety of perennials chosen for their shape, texture, and color break up what would have otherwise been a huge monotonous lawn.

Geometric shapes, such as triangles, diamonds, and ovals, make interesting island beds. This bed uses a geometric shape for a mixed border that includes allium, iris, poppy (*Papaver* spp.), and mullein (*Verbascum* spp.).

space feel crowded, while a small bed will appear too tiny—but also with the plants you are intending to grow there. It should not be so large that access to the center is difficult; it helps to be able to reach the middle of the bed with a hoe from every side. If you are planning a really large bed, place some stepping stones at strategic points to allow access to the center for routine maintenance. And if you intend to cut out several island beds, remember to leave plenty of space between them. Not only will you have to walk between the beds, but you will need to get the mower between them, too.

When you have finalized the shape of the bed, place garden stakes in the lawn every few inches along the edge of the rope or hose. (If the rope is accidentally knocked askew, you won't lose your shape.) You are now ready to cut out the bed and prepare it for planting (see *Plant Care,* pages 72–107).

While most island beds are created in lawn—grass provides a perfect background to show off the flowers—they can be surrounded by other surfaces, such as gravel or chipped bark. In this case you'll need some type of raised edging to keep the outline of the beds crisp and neat.

greenTHUMBS

When drawing up a planting plan for an island bed, remember that it will be viewed from all sides, so the tallest plants must go in the center of the bed, with heights gradually decreasing toward the edges. The plants will be more exposed than in a traditional border, so make use of sturdy, medium-tall varieties for island beds.

A raised edging around an island bed helps to maintain its shape and keep a crisp line between the bed and lawn. The gravel border makes it easier to mow the lawn.

Mixed Borders

Growing perennials among other types of plants doesn't dilute their impact—it enhances it. So mixed borders provide us with the best of all worlds.

Giant feather grass (*Stipa gigantea*) makes a striking background for flowers, such as helenium and coreopsis.

Black-eyed Susan (*Rudbeckia* spp.), marigold (*Tagetes* spp.), geranium (*Pelargonium* spp.), and dahlia are stunning against dark foliage.

Growing different types of plants together in a mixed border helps to overcome many of the drawbacks associated with the traditional herbaceous border. Using a combination of plant types can extend the season of interest, reduce the amount of maintenance required, and provide shelter and support for plants so that less staking is needed.

The mixed border allows the use of more types of foliage to provide a good background for (and contrast to) colorful flowers; evergreen foliage is particularly valuable because relatively few perennial plants are green year-round. The range of plant colors, shapes, forms, and textures available is also greater, allowing for some stunning combinations. A mixed border might contain a large number of different types of plants or just one or two—there are plenty of options.

SHRUBS

A popular way to provide a year-round framework for the border is to plant shrubs. Evergreen shrubs have the advantage of keeping their foliage throughout the winter. However, deciduous shrubs, such as the frantically twisted corkscrew hazel (*Corylus avellana* 'Contorta') or the fiery red-stemmed dogwood (*Cornus alba* 'Sibirica'), have striking branches that will provide winter interest. Fragrant flowers from viburnum and witch hazel (*Hamamelis* spp.) will brighten up the winter and early spring, while the spectacular leaf colors of Japanese maple (*Acer palmatum*) or deciduous barberry (*Berberis* spp.) varieties bring a touch of fire to the border in late fall.

Shrubs that perform well in spring, fall, or winter can often appear dull through the summer months when grown alone, but this can be a positive advantage in the mixed border. In summer their plain foliage provides a calming touch and effective contrast to the brilliant colors of the perennials, allowing the flowers to take pride of place.

Be careful to choose varieties of shrubs that will remain in scale with the perennial plants—they shouldn't swamp the perennials with vigorous growth as they reach their mature size. You will probably need to prune shrubs each year to keep them in shape. Shrubs often form the backbone of the design, so plot their positions first when planning a mixed border.

TREES

A small tree can look great when combined with perennials in a border, but it can also make conditions difficult for perennials to thrive. A tree will cast shade, which many

perennials dislike. Tree roots are greedy, sucking up soil moisture and nutrients at a rate that leaves perennials, with their shallower root systems, struggling to cope. In fall leaves falling from deciduous trees can smother low-growing perennials and encourage pests and diseases.

However, a small-to-medium or slow-growing tree with an open habit of growth can be successful in a mixed border. In a reasonably large border try paperbark maple (*Acer griseum*), with its lovely, peeling, coppery bark; honey locust (*Gleditsia triacanthos* 'Sunburst'), with its lacy golden leaves; or crab apple (*Malus* 'Golden Hornet'), with its white flowers followed by yellow crab apples. Any of these can form a beautiful focal point.

ANNUALS AND BIENNIALS

Invaluable for providing quick and easy color, bedding plants are widely available from garden nurseries in spring and summer. They are useful if there is a lull in perennial flowers or for filling in gaps in the border, perhaps where a perennial has died or failed to fill its allotted space. They can also fill in spaces in newly planted areas, where there are relatively large gaps between the plants before they reach their mature size. Annuals can be grown from seed sown directly where they are to flower.

CLIMBERS

For punctuation points in a border, plant climbers and train them up tripods or tepees of bamboo sticks to add height and sculptural interest. You can also plant them to scramble through shrubs or up trees, or into a hedge behind the border. However, allowing them to twine through the perennials is not usually a good idea—perennials are not strong enough to take their weight and tend to be pulled out of shape. Clematis, honeysuckle (*Lonicera* spp.), and climbing and rambling roses (*Rosa* spp.) combine well with perennials, as do annual climbers, such as sweet peas (*Lathyrus* spp.) and nasturtiums (*Tropaeolum* spp.).

BULBS

Old favorites, such as daffodil (*Narcissus* spp.), crocus, and tulips (*Tulipa* spp.), provide early spring interest, and when their show is over, the developing perennials help to disguise the bulbs' foliage. Use bulbs to extend the season at the other end, too, with autumn crocus (*Colchicum* spp.), cyclamen, and fall-flowering crocus. There are also many summer-flowering bulbs that are so much at home among perennials that they tend to be thought of as perennials, including crocosmia, lilies (*Lilium* spp.), and gladiolus.

Orange and yellow tulips (*Tulipa* spp.) mimic the new shrub foliage in this border.

Shell pink roses (*Rosa* spp.) echo the color theme of the flowering perennials.

greenTHUMBS

Once the bulbs' foliage dies down, it can be difficult to remember where they were planted. Mark the bulbs' planting positions clearly to avoid damaging them when cultivating between perennials.

Backgrounds for Perennials

The flowers of perennial plants are best appreciated when they are displayed against a plain background. For this reason traditional herbaceous borders were often backed by tall, dark evergreen hedges—but these are by no means the only option.

Hedges make a satisfying background for many flowers, particularly if a dark-leaved evergreen, such as privet or yew, is used. A dense hedge will shelter your perennials from cold winds, which encourages sturdy growth. Deciduous hedges are another option, but the cleanup job necessary when they shed their leaves makes them less popular.

Hedges have their drawbacks. They usually shade the plants for at least part of the day, and most perennials prefer full sun. Hedges will compete with the perennials for soil nutrients and water. (The hedge has size on its side, so it will usually win.) For this reason it's a good idea to plant perennials about 2 to 3 feet (60 to 90 cm) away from hedges. Hedges also need clipping two or three times a year—and reaching them can be difficult when you need to avoid trampling plants underfoot.

Fences and walls can be a good choice for a plain background against which to display perennial flowers, but make sure they don't create wind damage or frost pockets (see *Wind Damage and Frost Pockets,* opposite page). Like hedges, they may cast shade, but at least they do not compete with the plants for food and water. Take the color of the background into account when planning your planting; for

Below left:
Red brick walls and brown wooden fences make an ideal background for many colors, including white flowers—but not red and orange flowers.

Below right:
Stone walls or hedges help red and orange flowers to look their best.

example, orange and red flowers will have far less impact against a red brick wall than against a dark green hedge, and white flowers and silver foliage will be lost against gray stone.

GROUND LEVEL

Low-growing plants at the front of a border will usually spill over the edges and be displayed against the ground, so the ground-covering material chosen is important in the overall design. Grass is the favorite choice, and there is no doubt that the rich green of a well-kept lawn makes the perfect foil for border plants. However, it needs to be well kept—a scruffy lawn will ruin the whole effect. To keep the grass a rich emerald green color during the summer, mow it frequently throughout the growing season but set the blades high, at about 3 inches (8 cm). Feed the grass and treat lawn weeds as necessary. You can also maintain neat edges around the borders by using plastic lawn edging strips to help prevent grass from invading the flower beds.

LAWN ALTERNATIVES

Perennial beds and borders are not only made in grass. Bricks and other paving materials, gravel, and shredded bark are other options for surfacing materials. They are useful in areas where grass is too labor-intensive, or where access for mowing is difficult. If you use bricks and paving materials, don't be tempted to make complex patterns using different colors; these

will only detract from the perennials' display. A plain background is best.

Loose materials, such as gravel and bark, will invade the beds if they are not restrained—this is also true if bark or woodchips are used in the bed as a mulch (see page 91). You will need to use some type of raised edging around the borders to keep their edges neat.

These conifers provide a plain background for purple and yellow flowers. The gravel also provides a background for the low-growing plants.

Following pages:
Bright yellow lilies (*Lilium* spp.) stand out among crocosmia and poppies (*Papaver* spp.).

Wind Damage and Frost Pockets

A solid barrier, such as a fence or wall, can cause problems in windy gardens. When fast-moving air hits such a barrier, it is deflected up over the top. Once on the other side of the barrier, it drops quickly and forms unpredictable swirls and eddies, which can cause a lot of damage to plants. Where strong winds are a problem, a semipermeable barrier, such as a hedge or slatted fence, is best. This will slow down and filter winds to reduce their impact without producing damaging turbulence.

Walls at the base of a slope can also cause frost pockets. Because cool air sinks, on a cold night it will flow down a slope like water. If the cold air hits a solid barrier at the bottom of the slope, it will form a growing pool where the temperature will be significantly colder than in other areas. These pockets are often subjected to damaging and prolonged frosts. Solid barriers should be above the plants on a slope, not below them.

Height, Shape, and Texture

Flowers are not the whole story when creating a perennial garden—you should consider the height, shape, and texture of the plants when planning your garden and how they will work together.

You'll need to arrange border plants by their height if you want to see each plant, so taller plants won't hide shorter neighbors in front of them. However, ranks of plants lined up strictly by size have an uncomfortable appearance. Try putting lower-growing subjects between groups of taller plants, or try setting the occasional tall specimen near the front of the border to break up the outline. Large plants, such as pampas grass (*Cortaderia selloana*)—only plant it if it's not invasive in your area (see p. 148)—yucca, and feather grass (*Stipa gigantea*) as well as bold architectural subjects, such as New Zealand flax (*Phormium tenax*), are imposing enough to be planted as specimens. These can make an attractive feature in a border.

The height of the tallest plants should be in proportion to the size of the border, particularly its depth—a pampas grass at more than 6 feet (2 m) high or an even taller yucca would look out of place towering over a narrow bed. A useful rule of thumb is that the depth of the border should be at least equal to the height of its tallest plants, preferably more.

Remember the varying seasons of plants when you are planning their positions, too. For example, set the Lenten rose (*Helleborus orientalis*) where its cup-shaped blooms can be viewed in spring; by midsummer its flowers are long over, and it doesn't matter if the plant is hidden by a summer-flowering neighbor. At the other end of the season, perennials that have passed their peak in early summer can be cut down to reveal fall-flowering specimens, such as sedum or Joe Pye weed (*Eupatorium* spp.).

PLANT SHAPES

Plant height and flower color are often the only attributes considered when making a planting plan for perennials, but the outline of the mature plant is an important feature in the design, too. Perennials have many forms, from the spiky phormium to the soft, low mounds of perennial geraniums, tight cushions of blue fescue (*Festuca* spp.), and delicate, airy drifts of yarrow (*Achillea* spp.) or baby's breath (*Gypsophila* spp.). Good design uses the different shapes to complement and contrast with each other.

Softly flowing, rounded forms and delicate arching plants have a gentle, soothing effect, while bold, upright, and spiky shapes are more stimulating. Often the best way to use strong shapes is as accents—the spiky silver-blue heads of sea holly (*Eryngium* spp.), for

A well-designed border will have shorter plants at the front and taller plants at the back, so all the plants will get a chance to show off their graceful display of blooms.

Planting in Groups

Nearly all perennials are best planted in groups. Odd numbers of plants are always more appealing to the eye than even numbers; groups of three or five plants are common, depending on the size of the mature plants and the border. You can temporarily fill in areas around slow-growing species with extra plants; once the slow-growing plants become mature, the place-fillers can be moved elsewhere. In bigger gardens you can try using a large number of plants to create spreading drifts of color.

The bold leaves of variegated hostas contrast effectively with the feathery plumes of astilbe flowers.

example, make a dramatic exclamation mark rising out of gentle hummocks of more rounded plants. An unexpected bold shape can help to concentrate the eye on a planting.

Shapes become more important in winter, when the perennial border is usually thought to have little that is interesting. Instead of cutting down all dead plant material in fall, try leaving dead stems and flower heads in place, perhaps just tidying them a little to improve their shape. They'll look especially attractive when outlined in silver by a heavy frost or topped with snow.

TEXTURE

Plant texture refers to the surface quality of the plant—not just the physical feel of it but also its visual quality. The texture may be created by its foliage, flowers, or both. Textures vary from fine to coarse. Finely textured plants are those with small or finely cut leaves or flowers; when

Finely textured plants can appear to have a hazy quality and can make the border seem longer than it is.

viewed from a distance, they add a delicate hazy appearance to a border and can make it appear to stretch farther away than it does in reality.

Coarse-textured plants are those with large, bold leaves, such as hosta and bergenia. Many of these show another layer of texture when the surface of the leaves is ribbed, quilted, or heavily veined, and these textures change subtly according to the quality of light and the time of day.

Many finely textured plants simply ask to be touched, their feathery, fernlike leaves

running pleasingly through the fingers. Other plants are even more obviously tactile; the silky soft fur of lamb's ears (*Stachys* spp.) and mullien (*Verbascum* spp.) leaves are almost irresistible. The marble-smooth, succulent leaves of plants, such as sedum, are also pleasant to stroke.

PLANT HEIGHT

The following charts will help you to choose plants for their height and ground-covering abilities. Also included are some plants known for their interesting textures and bold shapes.

Tall Plants

Name	Description	Height
Alcea rosea (hollyhock)	Spires of funnel-shaped, double or single flowers; available in a range of colors.	Up to 6 feet (1.8 m)
Calamagrostis × acutiflora 'Karl Foerster' (feather reed grass)	Bold, upright spikes of silvery gold, feathery flower heads, which remain attractive throughout the winter.	Up to 4 feet (1.2 m)
Cortaderia selloana (pampas grass)	Large, arching, serrated leaves and towering plumes of silky flower heads.	Up to 10 feet (3 m)
Delphinium elatum hybrids	Deeply cut leaves and tall spikes of densely packed, cup-shaped flowers in a range of colors.	Up to 6 feet (1.8 m)
Digitalis purpurea (purple foxglove)	Long spikes of tubular flowers in shades of pink and yellow, often with attractively spotted throats.	Up to 5 feet (1.5 m)
Echinops ritro (globe thistle)	Tight, drumstick flower heads of steely silver-blue are borne over thistlelike leaves.	Up to 4 feet (1.2 m)
Eryngium giganteum (giant sea holly)	Showy silver bracts surround a long central cone on tall, stiff stems.	Up to 6 feet (1.8 m)
Euphorbia sikkimensis (spurge)	Bright pink new shoots in winter and early spring, with foliage turning yellow in fall; lime-green flowers bloom in late summer.	Up to 4 feet (1.2 m)
Helianthus maximiliani (Maximilian's sunflower)	Willowy stems carry numerous bright yellow sunflowers with a brown central disk.	Up to 12 feet (3.6 m)
Rudbeckia 'Herbstsonne'	Yellow, reflexed petals show off the prominent, greenish brown central cone; showy in late summer.	Up to 6 feet (1.8 m)
Verbascum olympicum (Olympic mullein)	Large mound of tactile, woolly silver leaves with tall spikes of golden flowers.	Up to 6 feet (1.8 m)

Low-Growing Plants

Name	Description	Height
Ajuga reptans (common bugleweed)	Glossy evergreen leaves often turn bronze in winter; short spikes of blue flowers appear in spring.	12 inches (30 cm)
Bergenia 'Abendglut'	Large, robust "elephant's ear" leaves turn reddish bronze in fall.	12 inches (30 cm)
Festuca glauca (blue fescue)	Slender, gray-blue leaves form a neat, rounded tuft; likes well-drained soil.	up to 10 inches (25 cm)
Geranium spp. (hardy geranium)	Many varieties form mounds of soft, rounded leaves with blue or pink cup-shaped flowers in summer.	8–48 inches (20–120 cm)
Heuchera 'Palace Purple' (coral bells)	The deep plum-red leaves have finely cut margins; sprays of delicate pink flowers appear in summer.	18 inches (45 cm)
Pulmonaria longifolia 'Little Star'	Bristly, lance-shaped leaves are freely splashed with silver; small, bright blue flowers appear in spring.	10 inches (25 cm)
Stachys byzantina (lamb's ears)	Silver, woolly "lamb's ears" form a dense carpet in a sunny spot; withstands dry soils.	Up to 6 inches (15 cm)

Astilbe spp.

Plants with Texture

Adiantum pedatum (northern maidenhair fern): Delicate, slender fronds on dark, wiry stems create a light, lacy effect.

Alchemilla mollis (lady's mantle): Lobed, lightly hairy leaves with a froth of yellow flowers in summer.

***Allium* 'Globemaster':** Silvery, pinkish purple flower heads on long stalks give a dramatic touch.

***Artemisia* 'Powis Castle':** Lacy, silvery leaves form a rounded hummock.

***Astilbe* spp.:** Panicles of fluffy, rosy pink flowers form a soft drift in the border.

Carex buchananii (leatherleaf sedge): Delicate cinnamon brown leaves arch upward with curling tips.

Gypsophila paniculata (baby's breath): Small white flowers are held on slender stems and float in a filmy cloud above the foliage.

Stachys byzantina (lamb's ears): Dense silver hairs make these leaves irresistibly furry.

Plants with Bold Shapes

Acanthus mollis, A. spinosus (bear's-breeches): Mounds of deeply lobed, dark green leaves and stately purple and white flower spikes.

Cortaderia selloana (pampas grass): Big clumps of arching foliage and silky flower plumes—it is invasive in certain regions.

Echinops ritro (globe thistle): Drumstick clusters of blue flowers held high over lobed gray-green leaves; also good for texture.

***Eryngium* spp.** (sea holly): Spiky, ruffed, silver-blue flowers above sharp, thistle-type leaves; also good for interesting texture.

Euphorbia characias* subsp. *wulfenii (spurge): Lax, candelabra-like stems thickly clothed with narrow leaves and topped with large, dense, cylindrical flowers.

Phormium tenax (New Zealand flax): Large clumps of striking, sword-shaped leaves in a variety of colors.

Eryngium spp.

Using Color

Whether you want to create an exuberant explosion of color or a restrained monochromatic planting scheme, you'll be using color in your design. To create the best effect, you'll need to understand how color design works.

No matter what color scheme you choose, a little knowledge of the theory of color is useful, so let's take a look at the basics. The color wheel (left), which shows the color spectrum in a circular form, is a helpful planning tool and also helps to explain color theory.

Primary colors are those colors that cannot be created by mixing other colors together; they are red, yellow, and blue. Secondary colors are obtained by mixing equal amounts of two primary colors; they are orange (red and yellow), green (yellow and blue), and purple (blue and red). There are also tertiary colors, which are a mixture of primary and secondary colors; red-orange, yellow-green, blue-purple, and so on.

Colors that don't appear on the wheel—because theoretically they are not colors at all—

The complementary colors of purple Russian sage (*Perovskia* spp.) and yellow-flowered redhot poker (*Kniphofia* spp.) provide a lively palette. The hint of red anchors the purples and yellows together.

are black and white. If you mix a color with black, this produces what is known as a tone of that color. Mix the color with white, and you produce a tint of the color; mix it with gray, and the result is known as a shade. Also absent from the color wheel is brown, produced by mixing all three primary colors or by mixing red, yellow, and black. It's easy to see how altering the proportions of colors (or of the black, white, or gray) in the mix can produce an almost infinite number of variations.

COMBINING COLORS

Colors that are directly opposite each other on the color wheel are known as complementary colors—for example, purple and yellow or red and green. Those that are next to each other are called analagous—orange and red are an example.

Happy combinations of three colors can be obtained by cutting out a triangle that will fit over three neighboring colors on the color wheel; rotate the triangle for different combinations. The three colors it highlights are known as a triad, and they will always look appealing together. You can also try the same with a square to pick out four color partners (a tetrad).

PUTTING THEORY INTO PRACTICE

The color wheel will help you to see which colors combine harmoniously. A combination of analagous colors creates a restful effect, while pairing up complementary colors is more stimulating. The sparing use of a complementary color—for example, a single dash of red among a sea of green—is an effective way of preventing the eye from

becoming so used to the dominant shade that it no longer sees it properly.

Understanding warm and cool colors is important if you want to create a certain type of atmosphere in your garden. Cool colors—green, blue, purple, and white—are calming, relaxing, and soothing. Warm colors—red, orange, and yellow—are exciting, stimulating, and arousing. (On the 12-color wheel you will find red-purple and yellow-green, which are neither clearly warm nor cool and can be used in either scheme.)

Warm colors impress themselves on the eye and can look closer than they are. However, cool colors will seem to retreat into the distance (think of distant blue hills) and give the impression of being farther away. You can use this to trick the eye when planning your garden, particularly if you combine it with plant texture (fine-textured plants imply distance, while bold-textured ones come to the foreground).

CALMING INFLUENCES

Where you have neighboring groups of plants whose colors do not harmonize successfully, use neutral colors between them to form a smooth transition. White is invaluable for this, but so is gray or silver foliage, or even plain green. A scheme composed entirely of warm colors, such as vibrant reds and bold orange shades, can be wearying, and here again the occasional touch of white or gray has a welcome calming and cooling effect.

SINGLE-COLOR BORDERS

Vita Sackville-West's white garden at Sissinghurst Castle in Great Britain is one of the most famous single-color planting schemes. However, a monochromatic scheme is difficult to carry off, and it can become boring. If you want to try it, use the full range of shades and tints for the color you choose; for example, yellow can include pale lemon, deep gold, cream, beige, apricot, primrose, and mustard, with even a touch of neighboring orange.

FOLIAGE OR FLOWERS?

Flowers have the largest number of colors, but don't forget to factor foliage into the equation. Perennials have leaves in all shades of green, as well as some in purple, red, blue, steely gray, and even black. Don't forget variegated foliage, in varying striped and marbled patterns in shades of green, cream, yellow, and white.

When planning the colors, take flowering time into account. The effect may be spoiled if one of your selected varieties does not come into flower until after its neighbor has faded.

White flowers are invaluable for separating colors that would otherwise clash.

Try sneaking in another color to break up a monotonous single-color border.

COLORS IN NATURE

Although we talk about "all the colors of the rainbow," the seven rainbow colors are only a tiny proportion of the range of different hues, shades, and tints that occur in nature. For example, the boundaries between purple and blue are sometimes blurred, as are those between pink and purple, red and orange, and yellow and green. The subtle differences in colors found in plants are difficult to describe in words, and even photographs cannot be relied on to reproduce a color accurately. The same photograph of a plant in bloom may appear a different color when printed in different books or catalogs.

Flowers come in an amazing number of different colors, varying not only from one variety to another, but also with the growing conditions. The climate and position, even the nutrients available to the plant, can all affect the shade and intensity of a flower's color. For example, the flowers of daylilies (*Hemerocallis* spp.) will fade to a lighter color in reaction to the sun's intensity, as will hostas' blooms.

The varieties you have chosen may not always turn out exactly the shade you expected. And if you grow perennials from seeds that you gather from your own garden, chances are that the offspring will not be the same color as the parent plant.

Choosing Flowers by Color

The following charts highlight some of the best and most reliable perennials in various color ranges to start you off when planning the colors for your borders.

RED	Name	Description	Flowering Season
	Bergenia cordifolia **'Rotblum'**	Deep red flowers carried in large clusters; the red theme is continued in the foliage, which takes on bronzy tints in winter.	Early spring
	Dahlia **'Bishop of Llandaff'**	Glowing scarlet daisy-type flowers contrast magnificently with deep bronze-purple foliage.	Summer to fall
	Lobelia cardinalis	Tall stems lift bright scarlet flowers above striking purple-red foliage; likes moist soil.	Summer to early fall
Dahlia 'Bishop of Llandaff'	*Monarda didyma* **'Gardenview Scarlet'**	Bee balm has striking, shaggy-petaled flower heads in shades of deep pink and red; foliage is pleasantly aromatic.	Summer
	Paeonia **'Felix Crousse'**	Large, fully double carmine flowers are sweetly fragrant; flowering stems need staking.	Summer
	Papaver orientale **'Brilliant'**	Striking, fiery red blooms of this classic poppy have a contrasting black center.	Early summer
ORANGE	*Achillea* **'Marmalade'**	Flattened heads of long-lasting flowers in a beautiful shade of warm, tawny orange, carried above fernlike, finely cut leaves.	Summer through fall
	Crocosmia × **'Emily McKenzie'**	Swordlike foliage with long wands of bright orange, open-faced flowers.	Summer

Orange (cont'd)	Name	Description	Flowering Season
Crocosmia × 'Emily McKenzie'	*Euphorbia griffithii* 'Fireglow'	Long, ribbed leaves topped with bracts of fiery orange, long-lasting flowers.	Early summer
	Hemerocallis 'Indian Paintbrush'	Daylily with well-shaped blooms of an intense tangerine shade; each petal has a ruffled edge.	Summer
	Kniphofia 'Royal Standard'	Stately torchlike flower heads of densely clustered, brilliant orange, yellow-tipped flowers.	Mid- to late summer
	Verbascum 'Helen Johnson'	Tall flower spikes carrying blooms of variable, subtle shades— tawny orange, apricot buff, copper-pink, or pinkish peach.	Summer
YELLOW *Anthemis tinctoria*	*Achillea* 'Coronation Gold'	Large, flat flower heads of a deep golden orange, above ferny, aromatic silver-gray foliage.	Summer through fall
	Alchemilla mollis	Low-growing plant with rounded, scalloped leaves and foamy heads of tiny greenish yellow flowers.	Early to late summer
	Anthemis tinctoria	Pale lemon yellow daisy blooms with deep gold centers; flowers profusely.	Summer to fall
	Oenothera fruticosa	Deep yellow flowers borne on leafy, reddish stems, often in clusters of at least three blooms.	Late spring to late summer
	Rudbeckia laciniata	Large, pale yellow daisy flowers with a prominent, greenish cone-shaped center.	Summer to fall
	Solidago sempervirens	A tall clump-forming plant with individual yellow blossoms tightly packed into plumes.	Late summer to fall
BLUE *Echinops ritro*	*Agapanthus* 'Blue Heaven'	Tall stems bear rounded heads of tubular dark blue flowers.	Early summer to early fall
	Camassia quamash	Spikes of saturated deep blue flowers are held above slim, pointy, grasslike foliage.	Early summer
	Echinops ritro	Drumstick heads of spiky, steely blue flowers above thistle-like foliage; attractive both in tight bud and full bloom.	Summer
	Meconopsis betonicifolia	Nodding, poppylike flowers of an intense, brilliant blue with a central golden boss of stamens; likes cool, moist conditions.	Summer
	Scabiosa caucasica 'Perfecta Blue'	Pretty, lavender-blue pincushion flowers that are attractive to butterflies and bees.	Summer to fall
	Veronica peduncularis	Masses of blue flowers appear in loose clusters on this mat-forming plant.	Spring to early summer

(continued)

PURPLE	Name	Description	Flowering Season
	Aconitum napellus	Deep purple-blue, hooded flowers in tall spikes over a dome of deeply cut, dark green leaves.	Late summer through fall
	Allium christophii	Huge globes of starry, purple-pink flowers; very spectacular.	Spring to late summer
	Aster novae-angliae **'Purple Dome'**	Michaelmas daisy with a profusion of rich, bright purple flowers almost completely covering the foliage.	Early to midfall
Aconitum napellus	*Campanula glomerata*	Dense, rounded heads of purple, bell-shaped flowers; can be invasive.	Spring to summer
	Nepeta × *faassenii*	From a mound of aromatic gray-green foliage rise numerous spikes carrying whorls of lavender flowers.	Early summer to fall
	Verbena **'Homestead Purple'**	Clusters of vibrant purple, primroselike flowers on trailing stems; attractive to bees and butterflies.	Summer to fall
PINK	*Astilbe chinensis* **'Finale'**	Fluffy plumes of soft pink flower spires over fernlike foliage.	Summer to fall
	Centranthus ruber	Erect panicles of deep pink, starlike flowers on a sprawling plant.	Spring through summer
	Dianthus × *allwoodii* **'Doris'**	Delicate, pale pink flowers with a deeper pink stain at the center; fragrant and free flowering.	Late spring into summer
Dicentra spectabilis	*Dicentra spectabilis*	Charming, rose-pink and white, heart-shaped flowers on graceful, arching stems.	Spring to summer
	Liatris spicata	Sturdy, fluffy spikes of tiny, deep pink flowers stand erect above the foliage; good for cutting.	Mid summer to early fall
	Sedum spectabile	Large, flat, platelike heads of small pink flowers carried over blue-green, succulent foliage; a magnet for butterflies.	Summer
WHITE	*Anemone* × *hybrida* **'Honorine Jobert'**	Large, pure white, cup-shaped flowers with a central boss of golden stamens, carried on tall, slender stems.	Fall
	Convallaria majalis	Arching stems carrying nodding heads of fragrant creamy bells push their way through midgreen leaves.	Spring
	Gypsophila paniculata	A foam of small, starry, white flowers on branching, wiry stems; delicate.	Summer
Anemone × *hybrida* **'Honorine Jobert'**	*Helleborus niger*	Large, saucer-shaped white flowers with golden stamens are borne over evergreen, fingered leaves.	Winter to spring

White (cont'd.)	Name	Description	Flowering Season
	Iberis sempervirens 'Schneeflocke'	A spreading, low-growing, evergreen plant, studded with a profusion of flat, shining white flower heads.	Early to late spring
	Lilium regale 'Album'	Beautiful, stately, pure white, trumpet-shaped blooms with an intense, sweet fragrance.	Midsummer
OTHER COLORS *Alcea rosa* 'Nigra'	*Alcea rosea* 'Nigra'	Deep red—almost black—cup-shaped blooms.	Summer
	Aquilegia vulgaris 'Black Barlow'	Double, nodding flowers without spurs, dark purple-black.	Spring to summer
	Euphorbia characias subsp. *wulfenii*	Tall, cylindrical heads of green flowers contrast well with blue-green foliage.	Early spring to summer
	Geranium phaeum 'Samobor'	The reflexing petals vary from deep maroon to chocolate brown and echo a dark purplish blotch on the foliage.	Late spring to fall
	Helleborus foetidus	Nodding, pale green flowers with red margins.	Winter to spring
	Iris × *louisiana* 'Black Gamecock'	A vigorous, clump-forming plant with dark purple-black flowers accented with a thin band of yellow.	Midspring
PLANTS IN MANY SHADES *Lupinus* spp.	*Aquilegia* spp.	Blue, white, red, yellow, green, and mixed shades.	Spring to early summer
	Aster spp.	Red, blue, pink, purple, violet, cream, and white.	Summer to fall
	Chrysanthemum spp.	Red, orange, yellow, pink, and white.	Summer and fall
	Geranium spp.	Blue, purple, pink, red, and white.	Early to late summer
	Helleborus spp.	Green, white, cream, purple, and pink.	Winter to spring
	Hemerocallis spp.	Red, orange, yellow, cream, pink, lavender, and white.	Late spring to late summer
	Lupinus spp.	Red, yellow, blue, lavender, pink, and cream.	Late spring to early summer
	Papaver spp.	Red, orange, pink, purple, and white.	Early summer

Foliage Effects

The size, shape, color, and surface finish of leaves can provide a palette that is as rich and exciting as a rainbow of blooms.

Many perennials are grown especially for their decorative foliage—for example, hostas, coral bells (*Heuchera* spp.), and many ferns and grasses—but even plants that are grown mainly for their flowers can contribute to the foliage tapestry. Bleeding heart (*Dicentra spectabilis*) is loved for its dainty blossoms, but its delicate leaves are also attractive. Once the ivory bells of lily of the valley (*Convallaria majalis*) are over, the neatly unfurling tongues of midgreen leaves continue to provide pleasant ground cover for weeks. The humble geraniums form nicely shaped hummocks of cut-edged foliage even when no flowers hover above them.

Many perennials have a gently rounded outline, and occasional clumps of the swordlike leaves of iris or New Zealand flax (*Phormium tenax*) punching their way through the border provide a welcome contrast. Leaf colors range from ice blue to deep purple, bright silver to almost black, deep green to gold—and there are the many variegated varieties, with splashes and stripes of yellow, cream, white, or red.

But even the plainest of green leaves have a valuable role to play in the perennial border, providing a tranquil background and helping to calm and cool brilliant flower colors that might otherwise be in danger of clashing.

Foliage shapes are variable. Leaves can be grassy, such as in the miscanthus and blue fescue (*Festuca* spp.), or lacy, filmy, upright, arching, rounded, or spearlike.

Combining a mixture of foliage shapes that includes broad leaves, mounds, and arching leaves can create an interesting border.

Perennials for Foliage Effects

Acanthus mollis, A. spinosus (bear's-breeches): Large, deep green, shiny leaves that are deeply divided.

Achillea (yarrow): Ferny, feathery, divided leaves that are softly hairy and gray-green; they are aromatic when touched.

Adiantum (maidenhair fern): Delicate ferny leaves on dark stems, with a pretty, arching habit.

Ajuga reptans (common bugleweed): Rounded leaves; particularly good colors include 'Atropurpurea' in shiny purple-bronze and 'Burgundy Glow' in rose red, bronzy green, and cream.

Alchemilla mollis (lady's mantle): Rounded, soft green, downy leaves, which hold drops of water on their surface, making them sparkle in the sunlight.

Bergenia: Large, rounded, glossy leaves form a low mound; they are often tinted red in winter.

Cerastium tomentosum (snow-in-summer): Small, pointed, silver leaves on a low, spreading plant that forms a gray mat; can be invasive.

Convolvulus cneorum (silverbush): Narrow, evergreen leaves are covered with silky hairs to give them an intense silvery appearance.

Coreopsis verticillata (thread-leaved coreopsis): Threadlike, bright green foliage creates an attractive ferny effect.

Echinops ritro (globe thistle): Bold, divided, steely blue thistle leaves.

Euphorbia amygdaloides 'Purpurea' (wood spurge): One of many euphorbias with good foliage, it has whorls of linear, purple-red leaves.

Festuca glauca (blue fescue): Neat hummocks of fine, threadlike, bright blue leaves.

Hakonechloa macra 'Aureola' (Japanese forest grass): Its narrow leaves are marked with green and gold and have an elegant arching habit; they turn a rusty bronze in fall.

Helleborus foetidus (hellebore): Evergreen palmate leaves, often a bronzy purple shade, have slender, toothed leaflets.

Heuchera (coral bells): Low mounds of lobed, rounded leaves are strikingly colored in shades of burgundy, purple, pink, and silver, as well as green, often with contrasting veining.

Hosta: King of the foliage perennials, with leaves in an enormous variety of shapes, sizes, textures, and colors.

Pulmonaria (lungwort): The low-growing, pointed leaves are often spotted or speckled with white or pale green; good as ground cover.

Sedum spectabile (showy sedum): Thick, succulent, bluish green leaves add substance to a flower border; 'Purple Emperor' has dark purple leaves.

Verbascum olympicum (Olympic mullein): Bold rosettes of large leaves are densely covered in silver felt.

Hosta spp., *Hakonechloa macra* 'Aureola', and *Euphorbia* spp.

Special Features

While plants are the most important element in most gardens, other features and structures can be used to enhance the plant display and form a significant part of the overall design.

Garden ornaments form attractive focal points through the summer months, and they provide interest in the off-season, too. There are plenty to choose from at any good garden center; pick a piece that blends well with your garden style and forms an integral part of the display.

SCULPTURES

Animal subjects have a natural appeal, while figures can give the garden a classical touch. Traditional materials are bronze or stone but plastic resin and concrete subjects are also popular, or you may want to choose a more unusual material, such as wire or woven willow. Large planters, sundials, and birdbaths are both attractive and practical.

Whatever ornament you choose, remember that planning its position is important. Think about how its size will work with the mature plants, and consider texture, shape, and color. Ornaments should develop organically from the surrounding planting.

FURNITURE

Strategically placed seats create a relaxed air in a garden and invite you to pause for a while to enjoy the view and the atmosphere. Furniture can range from a single seat, perhaps with a small table for a drink or a book, to tables and chairs that will accommodate the whole family for alfresco dining. Garden furniture should be attractive as well as functional.

Treated hardwood, cast iron, and resin-coated steel and aluminum are suitable materials for furniture that will be left outside year-round. For furniture that will be packed up

A carved spiral sculpture echoes the natural shapes of leaf whorls and snail shells, complementing this planting with strong vertical stems.

and put away once the summer is over, use materials such as canvas and wicker. Outdoor sitting areas should be in a sheltered spot, preferably secluded and not visible to neighbors, and should make the most of the view.

GARDEN LIGHTING

People who work away from home all day must regret that they cannot spend longer in the garden after work before darkness descends. Garden lighting offers a way around this problem, making the garden an inviting place to relax on a warm summer evening. Lighting can make a garden a magical place, providing an air of mystery and enchantment.

The object of garden lighting is not to turn night into day with powerful floodlights, but to softly highlight some of the garden's best features. Spotlights can be directed up or down to create different effects, and colored lenses can alter the mood. Use spotlights to pick out individual plants or trees, or to light up a statue or other garden feature. You can use medium-height and low-level lamps to light a path or steps, encouraging you to venture farther into the garden, and lamps are a good safety feature, too. They can also be used for backlighting plants to illuminate dramatic silhouettes or to softly shine through colored foliage.

Garden lighting can run off the main electricity supply to your house, or you can use a transformer to lower the voltage. Low-voltage lighting is safer and easier to install, but it will not create really bright lighting if you want to illuminate a sitting area. Solar-powered lights store power from the sun in the daytime and light up at night. These provide a low level of lighting. Ask advice from a qualified electrician about installing lights since some types must be installed by a professional.

Remember that intrusive light is a form of pollution. Keep your garden lighting soft and atmospheric so that it does not upset your neighbors or disturb wildlife that might visit the garden after dusk. Turn the lights on only

when you want them on instead of having them turn on automatically at dusk.

WATER FEATURES

Water is always a delightful addition in a garden, particularly when it is moving, such as in a waterfall or fountain, where its sparkle catches the eye and its gentle splashing sound soothes the ear. The mirrored surface and dappled reflections of a still pool of water are attractive, too. Water adds a delicious sense of coolness to a garden on a hot summer day, and it will also help to attract birds.

While a pool with a fountain or waterfall can be incorporated into a larger perennial border, there are a lot of smaller, self-contained water features that will make perfect focal points—and double as sculptures, too—in even the smallest garden. Any water garden specialist will be able to show you a selection of attractive designs from which to choose.

The tranquil sound of gurgling water is an appealing feature in most gardens—even a small fountain adds a magical touch. Here a fountain is surrounded by plants with attractive foliage.

Plants for Fragrance and Wildlife

No garden should be without the extra dimension added by sweet-scented plants. Another important element in any garden is wildlife, and by attracting animals and insects to your garden, you'll also be attracting some natural pest controllers.

Keeping fragrant plants in containers enables you to move them around the garden as desired.

The scents of flowers come in many forms, including honey, citrus, musky, and spicy ones. Yet what is beautifully fragrant to one person may be overpowering or unpleasant to another, while someone else might not be able to detect a scent at all. The scents themselves may vary according to the weather and the time of day. All these aspects make fragrance mysterious and elusive—and add to its charm.

PUTTING FRAGRANCE IN ITS PLACE

We are probably most familiar with fragrance from flowers, produced to attract pollinating insects, but several plants have scented foliage, too. The fragrance of leaves is usually fresher, cleaner, and more aromatic than flower scents, but the leaves need to be brushed against or squeezed before they release a scent. Perennials with aromatic leaves include yarrow (*Achillea* spp.), artemisia, bee balm (*Monarda didyma*), catmint (*Nepeta* spp.), and salvia.

Place fragrant plants where their scent can be appreciated. A favorite position is near a seating area or under a window, where the scent can drift up into the house on a summer evening. Plants with fragrant foliage can be set at the edges of paths where they are most likely be brushed against or even on the path itself so that the leaves can be crushed underfoot.

Be careful not to overdo fragrant plantings, because scents can clash with each other and become overwhelming. Space them throughout the garden, so that you come across new and delicious wafts of scent as you walk along.

Fragrant Flowers

Name	Description	Flowering Season
Convallaria majalis	"ily of the valleys are one of the best-loved fragrant flowers; 'Rosea' is a pink form, while 'Flore Pleno' is a double form.	Spring
Dianthus spp.	Among the many fragrant varieties of pinks are cherry red *D. deltoides* 'Zing Rose' and *D. gratianopolitanus* 'Firewitch', with magenta flowers.	Spring or summer
Bearded iris hybrids	Bearded iris hybrids, such as 'Cantina', 'Mary Frances', 'Old Black Magic', 'Orange Harvest', and 'Pacific Mist', are good choices.	Spring or summer
Lilium spp.	Avoid the Asiatic lilies and go for Oriental hybrids, such as 'Black Beauty', 'Journey's End', and 'Star Gazer'.	Midsummer
Paeonia spp.	'Afterglow', 'Alexander Fleming', 'Bowl of Beauty', and 'Eden's Perfume' are just a few gloriously fragrant peonies.	Summer
Phlox paniculata	Blue and white varieties are often particularly fragrant. 'Blue Paradise', 'David', and 'Natural Feelings' are reliable.	Summer

Plants to Attract Butterflies and Bees

Name	Description	Flowering Season
Agastache spp.	Spikes of tubular blossoms are borne above the foliage.	Midsummer through fall
Aster novae-angliae	New England aster has daisylike blue, pink, red, white, or purple flowers.	Summer to fall
Centranthus ruber	Jupiter's beard has upright panicles of starry, deep pink or red flowers.	Spring through summer
Echinacea spp.	Coneflowers have prolific rosy pink daisylike flowers.	Early summer to fall
Echinops ritro	Spiky, steely blue buds in a drumhead open to tubular, bright blue flowers.	Summer
Eryngium spp.	Sea holly has blue cone-shaped flower heads surrounded by a ruff of bracts.	Summer to early fall
Hemerocallis spp.	Daylilies have grassy foliage and lilylike flowers in a range of colors.	Late spring to late summer
Liatris spicata	Fluffy, bright pink flowers open from the top down on spike gayfeather.	Summer
Monarda didyma	Bee balm has shaggy, rose-red flower heads and citrus-scented foliage.	Summer
Nepeta × *faassenii*	Catmint bears spikes of lavender-blue, tubular flowers and gray-green foliage.	Early summer to fall
Phlox paniculata	Loose panicles of open-faced flowers in white, red, lavender, pink, and rose.	Summer
Rudbeckia spp.	Brownish black central cones are typical of daisylike black-eyed Susans.	Summer to fall
Scabiosa spp.	Pincushion flowers have delicate blue-lilac petals and a pincushion center.	Summer to fall
Sedum spectabile	Sedums carry large, flat heads of small, bright pink flowers for a long period.	Summer to fall
Solidago spp.	Goldenrod has feathery sprays of yellow flowers on tall, graceful stems.	Late summer to fall
Verbena bonariensis	Purple-pink, tubular flowers are borne on Brazilian verbena's tall stems.	Summer to midfall

ATTRACTING WILDLIFE

Birds and butterflies are colorful, bees and other insects help to pollinate plants, and frogs and toads dine on slugs, so it is worth thinking about wildlife when planning your garden.

Instead of cutting perennial plants back in fall, leave those with seed heads through the winter. They will provide winter interest, and many, such as evening primrose (*Oenothera* spp.), coneflowers (*Echinacea* spp.), wallflowers (*Erysimum* spp.), and sunflowers (*Helianthus* spp.), also supply food for birds. The dead stems and top growth of border plants provide shelter to small mammals, reptiles, and insects, so don't be in a hurry to tidy up. To avoid a messy garden, set aside a small, tucked-away portion as a wildlife area.

A pond is a useful source of water and is one of the best features for attracting wildlife to the garden, even if it is only a small pool. Encourage birds by providing a reliable supply of food and water and nest boxes for breeding. There are specialized suppliers that sell a whole range of boxes for different species of birds, as well as habitats for other forms of wildlife.

The indiscriminate use of garden pesticides will not be helpful to wildlife. If you adopt a nonorganic approach to gardening, make sure you use chemicals only when it is absolutely necessary, and always observe the relevant precautions and directions completely. A chemical-free garden will be home to a much wider variety of wildlife—although, of course, not all species may be as welcome as others!

Sedum (*Sedum spectabile*) is a popular choice to attract butterflies to the garden.

2 Choosing the Right Plants

Choosing plants for your garden is one of the most exciting aspects of gardening, but it can also be one of the most difficult and confusing. This is because there are so many wonderful plants to choose from. You can pore through books, magazines, and catalogs filled with enticing descriptions and mouthwatering photographs and feverishly write down a list of "must-haves." However, the list will often simply grow longer and longer and be difficult to whittle down!

Choosing the right plants involves knowing about what the plants will need from you, and what you want from them. You'll need to know about the conditions your garden provides and have a clear idea of the style of garden you want to create. These are the first steps to making plant choices that will please you for many years to come.

The bright yellow flowers of black-eyed Susan (*Rudbeckia* spp.) stand out in this perennial border that includes complementary purple asters. The rosy heads of sedum help to calm down the palette.

Selecting Plants for Your Garden

The key to growing perennials that will give a great performance is to choose plants that will thrive in the conditions your garden can provide.

Gardens can vary in many ways. For example, you'll need to consider the climate—whether you have early springs and long, hot summers, or whether winter keeps an iron grip for months at a time, with short, unreliable summers in between. The garden may be exposed to cold and drying winds, or perhaps it bakes in scorching sun with little rain. Or then again, it may be partially shaded by high walls or overhanging trees. Each of these sets of conditions may rule out a number of different types of plants, while at the same time they can make your garden particularly suitable for others.

YOUR GARDEN SOIL

Soil is one of the most important aspects of growing any type of plant successfully. You'll need to go out with a trowel and get closely acquainted with the particular soil type in your garden. You can tell a lot about soil by simply grabbing a handful of it, but chemical testing will give you a whole lot more invaluable information about its acidity and nutrient status (see pages 76–77). Perennials will generally grow in most types of soil, but some species do have definite preferences and will give a much better show if the soil meets their needs.

Below left:
The astilbe and lady's mantle (*Alchemilla mollis*) in this border thrive in shade or sun.

Below right:
White flowers will help to make a shady garden seem brighter than it is.

Test your soil every year or so. After a while its character can change considerably, particularly if you are looking after it by adding copious amounts of organic matter. Poor, sandy soil that is prone to drying out can be transformed by regular additions of compost and manure into a rich, moisture-retentive loam. Suddenly you'll find you no longer need to limit your choice of plants to those that will put up with dry, hungry conditions.

CHANGING CONDITIONS

Remember that different areas of your garden will vary. It is unlikely that your whole garden will be plunged in deep shade all day, and an otherwise exposed garden will probably have one or two corners sheltered by walls or hedges. Even the quality of the soil can change from one end of the garden to another, and most gardeners will probably be able to grow a wide range of plants.

On the following pages you will find a lot more detail about the different aspects of your garden that could affect your choice of plants, with plenty of help to make good decisions. Remember that all gardens are different, and a degree of trial and error may be necessary before you find the perfect plant for a particular place.

If you have a real hankering for a particular plant or group of plants that are not ideally suited to your conditions, you can make some adjustments that will enable you to try them— for example, growing lime-hating plants in a raised bed or a container of lime-free soil in an otherwise alkaline garden. However, try to make these the exception instead of the rule. It's much easier and more successful to work with your natural conditions than to try to battle against them.

EXTENDING THE SEASON

The traditional herbaceous border is definitely a feature of the summer garden—its season may be glorious, but it is often all too brief for

most gardeners. However, it is not too difficult for perennial borders to provide interest at other times of the year, too. With a little planning, you can find ways to bring a border to life early in the spring and keep it colorful well into fall. In this chapter we feature three borders at their best at different times of the year to show you how it's done.

Attractive foliage is highlighted by late-season blooms and allium seed heads, creating a garden that will stay interesting into the fall.

greenTHUMBS

While you should make choices that fit your garden conditions, by all means experiment with one or two more challenging subjects— it's always fun to try to push the boundaries. However, don't make these experimental plants the keystone of your display. That's a role for traditional plants that you can rely on.

Plants for Dry Soil and Alkaline Soil

Most gardens will have some problem areas, and to achieve success, you must choose plants to suit those particular conditions. Two such conditions are dry soil or alkaline soil.

The soil in your garden can have an effect on the type of plants that will thrive in it, and some plants have adapted to certain soil conditions. You can learn a lot about your soil by looking at it, but you also need to do a soil test (see pages 76–77).

DRY SOIL

Free-draining soils are easy to dig and warm up quickly in spring, but they can leave the plants thirsty and hungry because nutrients drain away with the water. Dry soils are usually sandy or gravelly, and they can be improved by adding organic matter. Seasonally droughts can also be an issue—if so, consider a xeric garden, where the garden is designed to use water as efficiently as possible.

Plants that have adapted to growing in dry, impoverished conditions include species

Lupines are a good choice for a tall plant that will grow in dry soil conditions.

Plants for Dry Soil

The following perennials will all do well grown in dry soil conditions:

Achillea spp. (yarrow)
Ajuga reptans (common bugleweed)
Arabis spp. (rock cress)
Artemisia spp. (sagebrush)
Aurinia saxatilis (basket-of-gold, golden alyssum)
Bergenia cordifolia (heartleaf bergenia)
Centranthus ruber (Jupiter's beard)
Cerastium tomentosum (snow-in-summer)
Convolvulus cneorum (silverbush)
Coreopsis verticillata (thread-leaved coreopsis)
Corydalis ochroleuca (white cordalis)
Dianthus spp. (pinks)
Echinacea purpurea (purple coneflower)
Echinops ritro (globe thistle)
Euphorbia spp. (spurge)
Festuca glauca (blue fescue)
Geranium sanguineum (cranesbill)
Helianthemum spp. (rock rose)
Helleborus foetidus (stinking hellebore)
Lupinus spp. (lupine)
Oenothera macrocarpa (Ozark sundrops)
Salvia spp. (sage)
Sedum spectabile (showy sedum, showy stonecrop)
Verbascum olympicum (Olympic mullein)

native to mountainous regions and coastal areas. They reduce the amount of water lost from leaves to the air in several ways. The leaves are often slender or covered with fine hairs or a waxy bloom. Silver foliage is usually a sign that the plant will tolerate dry conditions. Plants that are best adapted to dry soils will often do poorly in wet conditions, particularly silver-leaved types, which may need protection from damp through the winter.

Improve dry soils with organic matter before planting, and be careful to keep newly planted specimens moist while they are getting established. Mulching the soil (see page 91) will improve its water-holding capacity, but make sure the soil is thoroughly moist before mulching, and keep mulching material away from the necks of the plants.

ALKALINE SOIL

Most perennials grow best in neutral or slightly acid soil. There are certain plants, known as ericaceous plants, that prefer acid soil, but most of these are shrubs, such as heathers, rhododendrons, and camellias. Fortunately, few perennials are bothered by acid soils.

However, if you live in the arid Southwest, your soil is probably alkaline. (If there is limestone rock in your area, it could indicate neutral to alkaline soil.) A proper soil test will give you a more accurate picture, telling you exactly how alkaline it is. Soil is measured on a pH scale, with pH 14.0 being highly alkaline (see page 77 for more on soil acidity).

Some perennials, such as pinks (*Dianthus* spp.), baby's breath (*Gypsophila* spp.), and scabiosa, prefer alkaline conditions. Alkaline soils are often shallow, free draining, and low in nutrients, and like dry soils, they can be improved by adding plenty of organic matter. Applying an occasional application of liquid fertilizer containing trace elements (see pages 88–89) will help to supply nutrients that may otherwise be inaccessible to plants because of the alkalinity of the soil.

Plants for Alkaline Soil

The following perennials will all do well grown in alkaline soil conditions:

Achillea filipendula (yarrow)
Aurinia saxatilis (basket-of-gold, golden alyssum)
Bergenia spp.
Campanula spp. (bellflower)
Dianthus spp. (pinks)
Dicentra spectabilis (bleeding heart)
Echinops ritro (globe thistle)
Gypsophila paniculata (baby's breath)
Helenium spp. (sneezeweed)
Helianthemum spp. (rock rose)
Helleborus spp. (hellebore)
Bearded iris hybrids
Paeonia spp. (peony)
Platycodon grandiflorus (balloon flower)
Rudbeckia fulgida (black-eyed Susan)
Scabiosa caucasia (scabiosa)
Verbascum spp. (mullein)

For a bold statement in a garden with alkaline soil, why not consider globe thistle (*Echinops ritro*)?

Plants for Clay Soil and Shade

Clay soil and shady areas can be two of the most problematic areas for gardeners, but there are plenty of perennials that will cope well.

Plants that grow well in shade are often those that occur naturally in woodland conditions. Perennials for clay need a strong root system to penetrate the soil, and they should not be prone to rotting at the neck and crown. For this reason some plants, such as alpine perennials, are not suitable for growing in these conditions.

Hosta is truly stunning when in bloom and will stand out in a garden with clay soil.

greenTHUMBS

In very heavy clay soil, grow young plants in pots so that they can be planted in the garden with a good root-ball of soil to sustain them until they get established.

Plants for Clay Soil

The following perennials will do well grown in clay soil conditions:

Aconitum napellus (monkshood)
Anemone nemorosa (wood anemone)
Asclepias tuberosa (butterfly weed)
Aster novae-angliae (New England aster)
Aster novi-belgii (Michaelmas daisy)
Astilbe × arendsii (astilbe)
Campanula latiloba (bellflower)
Carex spp. (sedge)
Crocosmia × crocosmiiflora (montbretia)
Echinacea purpurea (purple coneflower)
Eupatorium spp. (Joe Pye weed)
Helenium spp. (sneezeweed)
Heliopsis helianthoides (heliopis)
Helleborus orientalis (Lenten rose)
Hemerocallis spp. (daylily)
Hosta spp.
Iris ensata (Japanese iris)
Liatris spicata (spike gayfeather)
Lobelia cardinalis (cardinal flower)
Monarda fistulosa (wild bergamot)
Penstemon digitalis (foxglove penstemon)
Pulmonaria spp. (lungwort)
Rudbeckia hirta (gloriosa daisy)
Solidago spp. (goldenrod)

The delicate flowers of columbine (*Aquilegia* spp.) will add color to any shady garden situation.

Following pages:
The cheerful yellow mound of thread-leaved coreopsis (*Coreopsis verticillata*) anchors the tall daisylike coneflowers (*Echinacea* spp.) and the pink, spike gayfeather (*Liatris spicata*) on its left.

CLAY SOIL

A potential nightmare for gardeners, clay soil clings stickily to boots and shovels, is slow to drain, and often remains waterlogged for long periods. It is slow to warm up and become workable in spring. In long periods of drought, it can dry out and bake hard as a brick, defying all attempts at cultivation. However, clay soil does have its good points: It is usually rich in nutrients and remains moist even in dry spells.

Adding copious quantities of organic matter to clay will greatly improve the soil texture and drainage. The plants themselves will also improve the aeration of the soil as they penetrate it with their roots.

SHADY AREAS

While all plants need sunlight in order to grow, a number of woodland plants have adapted to low levels of light and thrive in shade. However, the degree of shade is important. Light, dappled shade is far more plant friendly than dense shade that persists throughout the entire day.

Shade in gardens may be cast by trees and hedges, or by solid objects such as walls, fences, and buildings. Shade cast by deciduous trees and hedges is more likely to be dappled as the leaves move in the breeze. Plants below them can also produce good growth early in the year, before the leaves on the trees are fully out. However, the roots of trees and hedges remove nutrients and moisture from the soil, so that plants can sometimes struggle to grow beneath them.

As the sun's position changes through the day, the pattern of shade in the garden will alter. An area in deep shade in the morning could be in bright sunshine by the afternoon. However, there may be parts of the garden that remain untouched by sun all through the day. It is often helpful to take photographs of the garden every few hours during a day to see exactly where the shade lies at different times.

Hot and Sunny Sites

Most gardeners would be only too pleased to have a sunny garden, but as far as plants are concerned, it is possible to have too much of a good thing.

Whether or not excess heat is a problem depends on where you are gardening, but even cool, temperate regions can increasingly find conditions becoming too hot for the optimum growth of some plants. Those plants listed as suitable for dry soil (see page 50) are also likely to do well in hot and sunny sites.

Plants that have delicate leaves can be scorched by strong sunshine, and flowers may have a short life. The fine white hairs that give silver- and gray-leaved plants their color not only cut down moisture loss but reflect sunlight to avoid tissue damage, making them ideal for growing in sunny sites.

If a hot, sunny site is also dry, water is lost rapidly from both the soil and from the plants' leaves. However, some hot, sunny sites are not dry, but humid. You'll need to choose a different selection of plants if you live in such an area.

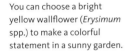

You can choose a bright yellow wallflower (*Erysimum* spp.) to make a colorful statement in a sunny garden.

Plants for Hot, Sunny Sites

These will do well in a hot, sunny dry site:

Acanthus spp. (bear's-breeches)
Allium spp. (ornamental onion)
Anthemis tinctoria (golden marguerite)
Erysimum spp. (wallflower)
Gaillardia spp. (blanket flower)
Helianthus spp. (sunflower)
Papaver orientale (Oriental poppy)
Phormium tenax (New Zealand flax)
Salvia spp. (sage)
Verbascum spp. (mullein)

These will do well in a hot, sunny humid site:

Agastache spp. (anise hyssop)
Anemone × *hybrida* (Japanese anemone)
Baptisia spp. (false indigo, wild indigo)
Coreopsis spp. (tickseed)
Kniphofia spp. (red-hot poker)
Leucanthemum × *superbum* (Shasta daisy)
Paeonia spp. (peony)
Phlox spp. (phlox)
Solidago spp. (goldenrod)

Exposed Gardens

Exposed gardens are those that have little shelter from the wind, which can cause a variety of problems for plants.

Wind exposure can have a number of effects on a garden plant that hasn't adapted to this condition. If the plant's stem is not sturdy, it can break or the plant can be blown down. Wind originating from a colder region will lower the temperature in a garden, too. Although, fortunately, plants are not affected by "windchill" as people are, the lower temperatures might mean choosing plants that are more hardy if you have a garden in an exposed site. In addition, plants are affected by wind scorch, where fast-moving air blowing over plant tissues whips away moisture, causing leaves, buds, and flowers to shrivel up in no time.

For plants that cope well with these rough conditions, look for ones that have waxy leaves, which do not give up their moisture readily. Finely cut or slender leaves can filter the wind, so they are less likely to be damaged than leaves that present a large, flat surface area. Low-growing plants present less of a target than taller specimens, so look for shorter, stockier varieties of susceptible plants, such as delphiniums, as well as making the most of ground-cover perennials. Many flowers, such as yarrow (*Achillea* spp.), will tend to sway in a breeze rather than snap. Trial and error will tell you which are best for your particular conditions.

greenTHUMBS

You can consider setting up windbreaks and screens (see page 27) if you want to grow plants that aren't suitable for an exposed site.

Plants for Exposed Sites

The following perennials will do well grown in exposed situations:

Allium spp. (ornamental onion)
Anemone × hybrida (Japanese anemone)
Astilbe × arendsii (astilbe)
Bergenia spp.
Centranthus ruber (Jupiter's beard)
Carex spp. (sedge)
Dianthus spp. (pinks)
Echinacea purpurea (purple coneflower)
Echinops ritro (globe thistle)
Eryngium spp. (sea holly)
Euphorbia characias (spurge)
Hemerocallis spp. (daylily)
Kniphofia uvaria (red-hot poker)
Miscanthus sinensis (eulalia grass)
Stachys byzantina (lamb's ears)
Veronica spicata (spike speedwell)

Not only does it have pretty round globes of flowers, but ornamental onions (*Allium* spp.) are a good choice for a garden in an exposed site.

Seaside Gardens

A garden near the sea can be a dream come true, but there are several conditions that will need to be considered when planning it.

On the positive side of having a seaside garden, the sea has a moderating effect on winter temperatures, so that gardens near the coast can be several degrees warmer than those farther inland, increasing the range of plants that can be grown and prolonging their season. However, coastal gardens also have to put up with strong winds blowing in from the ocean—and those winds are often laden with salt, which is even more damaging to plants.

Some plants are naturally adapted to coastal conditions and have their own way of coping with salt spray and wind. These plants have a waxy leaf covering, finely

The warm glow of the blooms from evening primrose (*Oenothera* spp.) will be stunning in a seaside garden.

Plants for Seaside Gardens

The following plants are suitable for growing in a garden near the sea:

Achillea **spp. (yarrow)**
Agapanthus africanus **(African lily)**
Anthemis tinctoria **(golden marguerite)**
Artemisia **spp. (sagebush)**
Campanula poscharskyana **(Serbian bellflower)**
Coreopsis verticillata **(thread-leaved coreopsis)**
Dianthus **spp. (pinks)**
Echinops ritro **(globe thistle)**
Erigeron **spp. (fleabane)**
Eryngium **spp. (sea holly)**
Euphorbia characias **(spurge)**
Festuca glauca **(blue fescue)**
Iberis sempervirens **(candytuft)**
Kniphofia **spp. (red-hot poker)**
Oenothera **spp. (evening primrose)**
Penstemon **spp. (beard tongue)**
Phormium tenax **(New Zealand flax)**
Sedum spathulifolium **(stonecrop)**
Solidago sempervirens **(seaside goldenrod)**
Veronica spicata **(spike speedwell)**

dissected or needlelike leaves, or a covering of silvery hairs. For plants that will thrive near the sea, consider those with "maritima" in their botanical names, such as *Armeria maritima* (common thrift), *Lavatera maritima* (tree mallow), and *Crambe maritima* (sea kale). Common names might give clues, too— for example, sea lavender (*Limonium platyphyllum*), sea holly (*Eryngium* spp.), and sea spurge (*Euphorbia paralias*).

Perennials in Containers

Containers are more often planted with annuals (or at least plants that are treated as annuals) than perennials, but many perennial plants make excellent container subjects.

Growing perennials in containers has some advantages. They can be moved to a sunroom or greenhouse for the winter, enabling you to grow tender subjects in cool regions. If you want a plant that is known to be invasive, you can safely confine it to a pot without having to worry about it overrunning your borders. Some pests are easier to control on container-grown plants, too—for example, hostas in a flowerpot are far less likely to be reduced to lacework by slugs than when grown in the open ground.

Use as large a container as practical, and fill it with good-quality loam-based potting soil, which will provide a long-lasting supply of nutrients and has good water-retaining qualities. Look for reasonably compact plant varieties, and balance the height of the plant to the depth of the container. Remember that staking can be difficult for container plants, so try to grow self-supporting varieties as much as possible.

Plants can be grown as single specimens or as a mixed planting. Whichever you choose, both will need dividing and repotting after a while, but the mixed plantings are likely to need attention more quickly.

Luscious lilies (*Lilium* spp.) are ideal for a container that can be moved around to make a corner of your patio more exotic. Their fragrance will be an added bonus.

Plants for Containers

The following plants are suitable for growing in a container:

Adiantum pedatum (common maidenhair fern)
Agapanthus africanus (African lily)
Ajuga reptans (common bugleweed)
Alchemilla mollis (lady's mantle)
Artemisia 'Powis Castle' (sagebrush)
Campanula carpatica (Carpathian harebell)
Coreopsis verticillata (thread-leaved coreopsis)
Dryopteris erythrosa (Japanese autumn fern)
Geranium spp. (cranesbill)
Hakonechloa macra 'Aureola'
   (Japanese forest grass)
Helleborus spp. (hellebore)
Hemerocallis spp. (daylily)
Heuchera spp. (coral bells)
Hosta spp.
Lilium spp. (lily)
Salvia spp. (sage)
Verbena spp.

A Spring Border

It is a joy to see the fresh green shoots of perennial plants thrusting through the soil in early spring.

Even a border that has been planned to provide as much out-of-season interest as possible will still look a little dull during the winter months, and the appearance of new growth is always eagerly awaited as the first sign of spring. This border shows that spring need not merely be a time of promise for the approaching perennial summer border—it can be a beautiful season in its own right. Here, it is not flowers that take center stage, but beautiful spring-fresh foliage that provides a palette of bright colors.

All too often when we think of perennial plants we think only of their flowers and neglect the wonderful foliage that many of them display. Spring is often the best time to appreciate this, when foliage is fresh and bright, before it has had a chance to become spoiled by the wear and tear that comes with being exposed to weather conditions or due to pests and diseases.

This border of moisture-loving plants has been carefully planned to provide a contrast of shapes and textures, as well as a harmonious palette of spring greens and golds. The lush, deeply veined leaves of a variegated hosta provide the anchor at the front of the border, while an unfurling royal fern (*Osmunda regalis*) and dark-leaved

▲ *Carex oshimensis* '**Evergold**'
Grasses add interesting textures with their narrow leaves and arching habit of growth. Evergreen varieties, such as this sedge, will maintain interest all year round; variegated or golden-leaved varieties will add a bright note.

◀ *Astilbe* × *arendsii*
The glossy, deep green, fingered foliage adds a note of contrast to the lighter spring greens in this border. The dark-stemmed flower spikes add interest even while they are still tightly in bud, but by late spring they will have opened out into fuzzy heads of tiny flowers in pink, red, or white shades.

▶ *Iris ensata*
The upright spikes of iris foliage are like a miniature echo of the phormium towering behind them. The Japanese iris produces attractive flowers of unusual form; there are many cultivars, mainly in shades of blue, but also some with pinkish lavender tones.

◀ *Osmunda regalis*

The royal fern is a statuesque plant with a beautiful spreading vase shape and sturdy yet lacy foliage. It adds real substance to this border.

◀ *Carex elata* 'Aurea'

This golden sedge dies down in winter, but in spring it produces wonderfully vibrant new foliage. It's perfect for a shady site, where the golden color is richest.

◀ *Persicaria amplexicaulis*

This mountain fleece has lush, heart-shaped foliage. The red flower spikes that are just appearing here will become much more prominent as spring moves into summer.

PLANTING PLAN

Iris ensata
Position three plants 10 in. (25 cm) apart and expect them to grow up to 5 ft. (1.5 m) high.

Carex elata 'Aurea'
Set three plants 6 in. (15 cm) apart near the back. They'll reach 15 in. (38 cm) high and 6 in. (15 cm) tall.

Persicaria amplexicaulis
Place the three plants 9 in. (23 cm) apart. They eventually grow 3–4 ft. (90–120 cm) tall and up to 3 ft. (90 cm) wide.

Astible × *ardenii*
This plant spreads to 2 ft. (60 cm).

Carex oshimensis 'Evergold'
Set three plants 9 in. (23 cm) apart; they'll grow 8 in. (20 cm) tall and 6–8 in. (15–20 cm) wide.

Hosta spp.
Set five plants 18 in. (45 cm) apart and expect the clumps to grow up to 2 ft. (60 cm) wide.

▲ *Origanum vulgare* 'Variegata'

The creamy variegation of these fragrant oregano leaves helps lift the center of the border. Clusters of pink flowers will follow later in the season.

▲ *Hosta spp.* foliage

The creamy yellow edges add a crispness to the broad, heart-shaped variegated leaves, making them refreshing in springtime. Flower stalks will follow in summer.

A Spring Border (cont'd)

phormium provide height with strong upright shapes. The narrow, arching foliage of golden-leaved sedges (*Carex* spp.) provide an effective contrast to the lush solidity of the hosta leaves, while a further change of texture is provided by the fingered foliage of astilbe. The astilbe is still in tight bud, but the dark flower stems and buds give further vertical emphasis to the overall design.

While foliage provides the main interest in this spring border, flowers have their part to play, too. Iris blooms lighten the effect of the greenery with their pale, purple-pink shade and interesting form. Little red spikes of mountain fleece (*Persicaria amplexicaulis*) add a contrasting red tone, like miniature red-hot pokers. As the spring progresses toward summer, the tall, fluffy spires of astilbe flowers and the delicate bells of hosta will add further interest, though the strong foliage shapes will continue to carry this border right through the seasons.

◄ **Pastels**

The delicate pastel colors of these flowers form a harmonious late spring scene. The lavender-blue of the bearded iris picks up the tones of blue false indigo (*Baptisia australis*) in the background and the geranium in the foreground, while the full blooms of a shell pink peony (*Paeonia* spp.) hold sway in the center of the group.

▲ **Framing a focal point**

This mixed spring border uses a golden-leaved maple as a focal point, framed by the delicate flowers of bleeding heart (*Dicentra spectabilis* 'Alba'), whose green and white tones are echoed in the variegated foliage of hostas and pulmonaria. Extra color is provided by early poppies (*Papaver* spp.) and pansies (*Viola* spp.).

▲ **Bright colors**

Spring is the season of bulbs, which add bright color to the perennial border. Here majestic crown imperials (*Fritillaria imperialis*) take pride of place, but the dramatic green heads of spurge (*Euphorbia characias*) form the perfect background.

Spring Flowering Plants

Name	Description	Height
Aquilegia vulgaris (columbine, granny's bonnet)	Nodding, spurred flowers in shades of red, purple, yellow, and blue. McKana hybrids are some of the best strains.	1½–2 ft. (45–60 cm)
Aurinia saxatilis (basket-of-gold)	Dense heads of small, bright golden flowers cover the plant in spring. Good for the front of a border.	1 ft. (30 cm)
Cerastium tomentosum (snow-in-summer)	A mat-forming plant with branching stems topped by an abundance of dainty, snowy white flowers.	6–12 in. (15–30 cm)
Convallaria majalis (lily-of-the-valley)	Nodding, creamy bells held on arching stems; very sweetly scented. 'Fortin's Giant' is a large-flowered variety.	8 in. (20 cm)
Dicentra spectabilis (bleeding heart)	Pretty, heart-shaped, rose-pink flowers with a contrasting white center dangle from elegant arching stems.	18–30 in. (45–75 cm)
Erysimum spp. (wallflower)	Spikes of four-petaled flowers over gray-green, lance-shaped leaves. 'Bowles Mauve' and pale yellow 'Moonlight' are popular. Tend to be short lived.	1½ ft. (45 cm)
Helleborus orientalis (Lenten rose)	Nodding, saucer-shaped flowers with golden stamens from early spring. Many varieties in shades of white, pink, purple, and plum.	1½–2 ft. (45–60 cm)
Iberis sempervirens (candytuft)	A spreading mat of deep green, evergreen leaves, smothered by flat heads of pure white flowers.	8 in. (20 cm)
Iris ensata (Japanese iris)	Usually flat-faced, beardless iris in a wide range of colors with yellow streaks on the petals. Likes moist, lime-free soil.	2–5 ft. (60–150 cm)
Paeonia tenuifolia (fernleaf peony)	A handsome, rounded plant with delicate, feathery foliage topped with single, deep red flowers.	1–1½ ft. (30–45 cm)
BULBS		
Crocus chrysanthus (crocus)	Short-stemmed, cup-shaped flowers in a wide range of colors, appearing from late winter onward.	3 in. (8 cm)
Hyacinthus spp. (hyacinth)	Densely clustered spikes of sweetly scented flowers in a wide range of shades of red, blue, pink, and white.	6–9 in. (15–23 cm)
Muscari spp. (grape hyacinth)	Spikes of bright blue bells on a fleshy stem. The slender, bright green leaves appear well before the flowers and add winter interest.	4–10 in. (10–25 cm)
Narcissus spp. (daffodil)	One of the best-known, best-loved spring bulbs. Flowers in various shades of cream and yellow usually have a central cup or trumpet, but come in many different forms and sizes.	6–18 in. (15–45 cm)
Tulipa spp. (tulip)	Typically, brightly colored cup-shaped blooms are held on elegant stems, but like *Narcissus* spp. (daffodil), a vast range of forms, sizes and colors exists.	4–24 in. (10–60 cm)

A Peak Summer Border

Summer is *the* season for perennials—when every gardener expects the border to be at its best.

Although pastel shades and muted colors form a restful oasis in the summer heat, it is the bold, bright, hot colors that really sing out "summer" for most people. Here is a border that is uncompromising in its use of color. Vivid golds and yellows and glowing reds give a fiery warmth that radiates against the cool green of the lawn. Even on a dull day, this is a border that conjures up thoughts of sunshine and summer heat.

The plants have been carefully positioned to give unity to the border. The dominant brilliant yellow of the goldenrod (*Solidago* spp.) in the center of the border is reinforced by clumps of golden helenium at the front and side, while the intense red of dahlias and phlox to the right has an echo in tawny orange heleniums. Green foliage helps to separate the blocks of color and prevent them from becoming overwhelming— the spiky, swordlike leaves of red-hot pokers (*Kniphofia* spp.) and crocosmia on either side of the goldenrod are valuable even when the plants are not in flower. A touch of purple from the common heliotrope (*Heliotropium arborescens*) at the front adds a cooling note for contrast.

The foliage of the rose (*Rosa* spp.) toward the back of the border forms a good background for the bright

▶ **Kniphofia spp.**
The tall spires of red-hot poker flowers, which come in reds, oranges, and yellows, will fit into this color scheme perfectly—but the clumps of swordlike foliage will play a valuable role even before the flowers make an appearance.

▲ **Heliotropium arborescens**
Valued for its lovely "cherry pie" fragrance, this easy-to-grow plant provides a cooling touch with its lilac flowers and deep green, crinkled leaves.

▲ **Rosa 'Golden Years'**
This is a position for a strong-growing rose with healthy foliage. There are dozens of excellent new varieties being introduced every year; look for a disease-resistant, vigorous grower.

◀ *Dahlia* cv.
There are hundreds of dahlia cultivars to choose from, in a whole range of shades and flower forms. This bright scarlet ball type could be the cultivar 'Red Balloon', but there are many others to choose from.

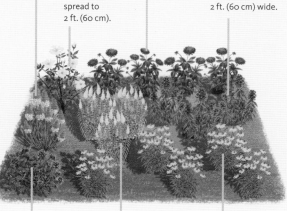

◀ *Solidago* 'Strahlenkrone' (Crown of Rays)
The brilliant yellow, fluffy spires of goldenrod form the focal point in this border. This cultivar is shorter than many and is noninvasive.

▲ *Helenium*
Pipsqueak ('Blopip')
At 18 inches (45 cm) tall, this bright-colored sneezeweed is ideal for the front of the border. The golden flowers with their prominent cones are long lasting.

▲ *Phlox paniculata*
'Red Riding Hood'
The cherry red blooms of this phlox are fragrant, and the plant stands up well without staking.

PLANTING PLAN

Kniphofia spp.
This plant will spread 1½–2 ft (45–60 cm).

Rosa 'Golden Years'
Set at the back of the border, where this plant will spread to 2 ft. (60 cm).

Dalia cv.
Set four plants 18 in. (45 cm) apart.

Phlox paniculata
Set three plants 18 in. (45 cm) apart. They grow up to 3 ft. (90 cm) tall and 2 ft. (60 cm) wide.

Heliotropium arborescens
Set three plants at the front of the border 10 in. (25 cm) apart; they grow 1 ft. (30 cm) tall and wide.

Solidago 'Strahlenkrone'
Position three plants 1½–2 ft. (45–60 cm) apart.

Helenium Pipsqueak
Place five plants 12–18 in. (30–45 cm) apart. They grow up to 18 in. (45 cm) tall.

A Peak Summer Border (cont'd)

flowers of goldenrod with its abundant foliage, and the yellow roses with their hint of apricot shades help to draw together the reds and yellows of the planting. The plants have been carefully graded by height without giving too formal an appearance, ensuring each group of plants can have its effect. This is a lesson in the importance of the careful choice of cultivars of border plants. The low-growing heleniums at the front of the border are the perfect height for their position, but many helenium cultivars grow to 5 feet (1.5 m) or more and would be completely out of place here.

This peak summer border will not only look good at the height of the summer season, the plants it contains will keep its interest going until the fall. Deadheading and unobtrusive staking, plus watering during dry periods, will help to ensure the plants remain in top condition for the longest possible time.

◄ **Cool tones**

If you want to tone down a hot summer border, the addition of cool flower colors, such as white and pale pink, plus silver foliage, does the job admirably. This style of border is more restful and relaxing than one composed entirely of vibrant colors.

▲ **Bicolor border**

This gentle, misty border shows how effective it can be to use just a few colors—these blue and yellow tones create a wonderfully ethereal air. Purple-blue asters, catmint (*Nepeta* spp.), and tall spires of delphinium contrast with yellow mullein (*Verbascum* spp.), coreopsis, daylilies (*Hemerocallis* spp.), and giant yellow scabiosa.

▲ **Bright hues**

This is every gardener's idea of a delightful, colorful summer border. Brilliant blue agapanthus, pink asters, yellow coreopsis, and yellow and orange daylilies (*Hemerocallis* spp.) are just a few of the plants jostling for your attention in this informal bed.

Summary Flowering Plants

Name	Description	Height
Acanthus spinosus (bear's-breeches)	A mound of glossy, dark green, deeply cut leaves topped by stately spires of blue and white flowers.	3–4 ft. (90–120 cm)
Agapanthus campanulatus (African lily)	Rounded heads of trumpet-shaped flowers in intense blue shades; it prefers a sheltered spot.	3–5 ft. (90–150 cm)
Astilbe spp. (astilbe)	Tall, fluffy plumes of tiny flowers in shades of pink, red, and white add an interesting texture to the border; requires moist soil.	up to 5 ft. (up to 150 cm)
Campanula persicifolia (peach-leaved bellflower)	Bell-shaped flowers in clear shades of blue on tall, delicate stems; a white variety is also available. It prefers well-drained conditions.	2–3 ft. (60–90 cm)
Delphinium spp. (delphinium)	Tall spires of open-faced flowers in shades of blue and white, often with a contrasting eye. Needs staking.	4–6 ft. (1.2–1.8 m)
Gaillardia × grandiflora (blanket flower)	Large, showy, daisylike flowers have a red center surrounded by a ring of golden petal tips; dwarf varieties such as 'Goblin' are available.	up to 2 ft. (up to 60 cm)
Geranium spp. (hardy geranium, cranesbill)	Many species and varieties available, most making a low mound of attractive foliage studded by saucer-shaped blue or pink summer flowers.	8–24 in. (20–60 cm)
Gypsophila paniculata (baby's breath)	Airy panicles of tiny, white, starry flowers form a white mist of bloom, delicate and ethereal; double and pink forms are also available.	3–4 ft. (90–120 cm)
Heliopsis helianthoides (heliopsis, false sunflower)	Bright golden, shaggy daisylike flowers provide a long-lasting splash of color on a sure-to-please plant.	3–5 ft. (90–150 cm)
Hemerocallis spp. (daylily)	Large, trumpet-shaped flowers are produced in great profusion all through the summer; there are many hybrids in a wide range of striking colors.	up to 3 ft. (up to 90 cm)
Lilium regale (regal lily)	Intensely fragrant, funnel-shaped flowers are glistening white, flushed with gold at their centers, and have rosy backs to the petals.	up to 4 ft. (up to 120 cm)
Lupinus spp. (lupine)	Pea-type flowers are arranged in dense, pyramid-shaped spires. Color range includes blue, white, pink, cream, and yellow, and flowers are often bicolored.	up to 3 ft. (up to 90 cm)
Papaver orientale (oriental poppy)	Bold clumps of deeply cut, bristly leaves and bowl-shaped, brilliant scarlet, black-blotched flowers on long stems. There are also pink and double varieties.	up to 3 ft. (up to 90 cm)
Phlox paniculata (phlox)	Flat-faced, sweetly scented flowers in red, pink, purple, or white shades are carried in loose trusses on tall stems; 'Harlequin' and 'Norah Leigh' have variegated leaves.	3–4 ft. (90–120 cm)
Scabiosa columbaria (small scabiosa)	Slender, bare stems support prolific blue-lilac flowers above a mound of basal foliage; cultivars are smaller than the species.	1–1½ ft. (30–45 cm)
Veronica spicata (spike speedwell)	Graceful, tall spikes of bright blue spires of blooms appear above a mound of leaves.	1–2 ft. (30–60 cm)

An End-of-Season Border

Color and movement make this border
a delight from late summer to winter.

Wild and natural-looking, this border is actually the result
of careful planning. There are not many plants: just two
kinds of grasses, two masses of purple-violet perennials,
a pink-rose, and the uprights of red-hot pokers (*Kniphoria
rooperi*). Each element has been planted in a large group,
allowing it to have the greatest possible impact. The
grasses wave in unison at the back and sides, the violet
asters form a pool of vibrant color in the foreground, while
the soft pink of the roses (*Rosa* 'Sally Holmes') provides an
oasis of calm in the center.

Color plays a major role in unifying the planting.
The violet petals and yellow centers of the aster are the
key. The color is picked up and intensified by the tall,
stately purple aconites at the rear and the purple-tinged
seed heads of the grass on the right. The asters' yellow
centers are echoed by the bleached blond grass at the
rear and the vivid yellow of the red-hot pokers at the
front of the bed.

The main photograph shows the border in late
summer just as it is coming into flower. However, even
after the rose has lost its petals, the asters, aconites
(*Aconitum carmichaelii* 'Arendsii'), and red-hot pokers

◄ *Kniphofia rooperi*

It holds its own because of its height,
at 4 feet (1.2 m) and by virtue of its
yellow-red torches. This red-hot
poker has sturdier stems than many
varieties. The arching grasslike
leaves are attractive even when the
plant is not in flower.

▶ *Calamagrostis* × *acutiflora*
'Karl Foerster'

A tall, pale reed grass , its seed heads
become ever more bleached by the
sun and wind as fall turns to winter.
The soft pink-bronze plumes fade to
a pale buff color in winter.

◀ *Aconitum carmichaelii* **'Arendsii'**

This plant bears tall upright spikes with deep blue, almost purple, flowers. The leaves are glossy and dark green. These late-flowering aconites are at their best in early fall. This plant needs plenty of moisture and is happiest in woodland settings; however, it can tolerate full sun.

◀ *Rosa* **'Sally Holmes'**

Here is a shrub rose that flowers from summer through fall. Its single scented flowers have ivory white petals with a delicate pink flush at the edges. Prune it in late winter or early spring, when the grasses are cut back.

PLANTING PLAN

Miscanthus sinesis
Position in full sun and moist soil. It grows 4 ft. (120 cm) tall and 18 in. (45 cm) or more wide.

**Calamagrostis ×
acutiflora 'Karl Foerster'**
Position one plant at the back of the bed. It grows to 5 ft. (150 cm) tall and 2 ft. (60 cm) wide.

Aconitum carmichaelli
Set the three plants 18 in. (45 cm) apart. They will reach 3 ft. (90 cm) tall and 2 ft. (60 cm) wide.

Kniphofia rooperi
Space the three plants 18 in. (45 cm) apart. By the end of summer, each plant will reach 4 ft. (120 cm) tall and 2 ft. (60 cm) wide.

Rosa 'Sally Holmes'
At planting time, improve poor or free-draining soil by digging in organic matter. It grows to 4 ft. (120 cm) high.

Aster amellus
Plant in a triangle with two at the front, one at the back, 15 in. (38 cm) apart. They will grow 2 ft. (60 cm) tall and 18 in. (45 cm) wide.

▲ *Aster amellus* **'Veilchenkönigin' (Violet Queen)**

The purple-blue blooms fit perfectly in the front of the border. This upright aster does not need staking and forms large, bushy clumps. The hairy leaves are lance shaped.

▲ *Miscanthus sinensis* **'Silberspinne' (Silver Spider)**

Planted in a wide clump, its arching leaves and flowers curve outward and move with the wind. This elegant perennial grass should be cut down before spring. Avoid the wild species, which is invasive.

An End-of-Season Border (cont'd)

will provide a splendid show of color far into fall, while the grasses will keep the border alive into the dead of winter.

The year-round interest provided by grasses has led to them becoming a staple of modern gardens. As they change color with the seasons, grasses make a subtle yet spectacular show, turning from spring's pale green to summer's emerald, from fall's bronze to winter's pale, glistening silver. And they retain their spiky shapes and contours as they stand against the winter sky, whether barely brushed by frost or rising out of a blanket of snow. Tossed by the winds of fall, grasses give a natural, almost wild, appearance to the garden.

This border seems to merge into the woods and fields behind it. Here, the border becomes not just a formal part of the garden but an intermediate staging post between the garden and the landscape around it.

Of course, there are alternative choices for plants in a late-season border. The photographs below and opposite and the chart on page 71 will provide extra inspiration.

◄ **Seed heads**

After the flowers fade from ornamental onion (*Allium* spp.), the drumstick seed heads continue the season of interest into fall. Here they contrast well with the feathery seed heads of feather grass (*Stipa pulcherrima*).

▲ **Bright late-season color**

This group shows the effective use of contrasting colors, with bright black-eyed Susans (*Rudbeckia fulgida* 'Goldsturm') singing out near purple and violet asters.

▲ **Fiery farewell to summer**

The glowing reds and pinks of border phlox are set off by tall russet plumes of *Macleaya* 'Spetchley Ruby' in the background. The flat heads of sedum at the front of the border will develop to a rich red as the season progresses into fall.

Perennials for Late-Season Interest

Name	Description	Height
Achillea filipendula **'Gold Plate'** (yarrow)	Spreading, flat yellow flower heads turn to an "old gold" shade in fall and look particularly attractive when rimmed with frost.	4 ft. (120 cm)
Anemone × hybrida (Japanese anemone)	Open-faced white or pink flowers with fluffy gold stamens continue from midsummer until the first hard frost.	3–4 ft. (90–120 cm)
Artemisia **'Powis Castle'** (sagebrush)	Finely cut, strikingly silver leaves form a neat mound that shines out brightly as other flowers die away in fall.	2–3 ft. (60–90 cm)
Bergenia cordifolia (heartleaf bergenia)	Large, evergreen, roughly heart-shaped leaves are often tinted red in fall and winter, making good ground cover; pink flowers appear in early spring.	8–12 in. (20–30 cm)
Chrysanthemum **cultivars** (chrysanthemum)	Well-known flowers in a wide range of shades and forms that are very showy; flowers persist until a hard frost.	3–4 ft. (90–120 cm)
Cortaderia selloana (pampas grass)	Majestic, fluffy silver plumes last from late summer through fall and into winter in reasonably sheltered gardens.	up to 10 ft. (up to 3 m)
Dahlia **hybrids** (dahlia)	Colorful flowers in a wide range of shades and forms make a valuable contribution through summer until the first frosts of fall.	1–4 ft. (30–120 cm)
Epimedium acuminatum (arrow-leaved barrenwort)	Elongated, glossy evergreen leaves have a reddish tint when they first emerge; excellent winter ground cover.	9–12 in. (23–30 cm)
Eryngium **ssp.** (sea holly)	Sea holly has deeply cut, spiny leaves and thistlelike flower heads with a striking silver-blue ruff; great architectural value.	up to 3 ft. (up to 90 cm)
Festuca glauca (blue fescue)	This ornamental grass forms neat, tufted mounds of slender, bright steely blue, evergreen leaves.	6–10 in. (15–25 cm)
Helenium autumnale (sneezeweed)	Bold daisylike flowers in a range of yellow, bronze, and red shades are carried well into the fall.	3–5 ft. (90–150 cm)
Helleborus niger (Christmas rose)	Lobed, deep green, leathery leaves provide year-round interest; saucer-shaped white flowers extend the season into winter and early spring.	12 in. (30 cm)
Papaver orientale (Oriental poppy)	The rounded, flat-topped seed heads of poppies stand tall in the fall border and look particularly attractive when silvered by frost.	2–3 ft. (60–90 cm)
Rudbeckia **spp.** (black-eyed Susan, coneflower)	Yellow, tawny, or orange daisylike flowers with a dark central cone make a good late display.	2–4 ft. (60–120 cm)
Sedum spectabile, **S. 'Autumn Joy'** (sedum)	Succulent, gray-green leaves and flat heads of tiny pink flowers attract late-summer butterflies. 'Autumn Joy' has flower heads that turn to rusty red in late fall.	1–2 ft. (30–60 cm)
Solidago **spp.** (goldenrod)	Dense, branching sprays of tiny yellow flowers are produced from late summer onward; 'Golden Wings' is a good late-flowering variety.	up to 5 ft. (up to 1.5 m)

3 Plant Care

Fortunately, most perennials are easy plants to grow—there are few temperamental prima donnas among them. However, there's no doubt that the better the conditions and care you provide, the more your plants will reward you. From preparing the soil before planting to cleaning up the established flower bed in the fall, this chapter will take you through all the care your plants will need. And if you don't have as much time as you would like to work in the garden, you'll find plenty of tips on ways to cut down on time-consuming tasks while still getting fantastic results.

When provided with the proper care, perennials will thrive and display a plethora of flowers, such as these lupines (*Lupinus* Russell hybrids) planted next to daylilies (*Hemerocallis lilioasphodelus*).

Getting Started

Thorough preparation is the key to getting the best from your perennials. Your perennial border will be a feature of your garden for many years to come—so it's worth investing some time and effort at the start.

Before you do anything else, you'll need to get rid of any perennial weeds in the area to be planted. This is one of the most important jobs because if you don't tackle these right away, they will become a nuisance for years to come. If the weeds are not too numerous, you can simply remove them while digging. However, some of the more persistent offenders, such as couch grass and bindweed, are difficult to eradicate like this, because even a tiny portion of broken-off root left behind will grow back.

If the area is weedy and you have no objection to using chemicals, you can spray it with a weed killer, such as glyphosate. This is a translocated weed killer, which is delivered through the whole plant so there is no new growth, even from stubborn, deep-rooted weeds. If you prefer to avoid using a weed

killer, you can burn off the weeds' top growth with a flame gun, but repeated treatments will be necessary to deal with new growth from problem weeds. Alternatively, you could cover the area tightly with black plastic sheeting for a whole growing season to starve weeds into submission.

MAKING A NEW BED

New beds and borders are often cut out of an existing lawn. For a large area, consider renting a sod-lifting machine; otherwise, you will need to sharpen your spade and half-moon edger and prepare for some healthy exercise. As you strip off the layer of sod, you will have the satisfaction of exposing perfectly clean, weed-free soil.

Once the bed is cleared, turn the soil thoroughly. Double-digging, which is also known as trenching, involves digging a trench the depth of a spade's blade, then forking over the base of the trench another spade-depth deep. Make the trenches 2 feet (60 cm) wide. After you dig the first trench, pile soil from the adjacent trenches into the previously dug trench. You can put the soil from the first trench into a wheelbarrow, and use it to fill the last trench. Double-digging is ideal for breaking up the soil, but it is hard work, especially if you

Use a hose to outline the shape of a new bed or island, then use a half-moon edger to create the outline in the lawn.

greenTHUMBS

If you need to remove grass sod to create a bed or border, you may be able to use it elsewhere. If not, stack the strips of sod upside down in a pile and wait for them to be transformed into useful compost.

are not physically fit. You may choose to compromise by using a rotary tiller; it won't dig as deeply but it will certainly save you a lot of time and effort.

RENOVATING AN EXISTING BORDER

You won't necessarily be starting your perennial bed entirely from scratch—you might have an existing border that needs some attention. Perhaps it's been neglected and is overgrown; perhaps it is poorly planned and doesn't provide flowers over a long season; or perhaps it's just an unsatisfactory mess of border plants, shrubs, and trees that doesn't really work. Whatever the reason, you've decided that improvements are necessary—but where should you start?

The first step is to take a look at the overall shape of the bed or border and see if the shape can be improved. Then take a long, hard look at the plants that are already there and decide which are worth keeping. Existing shrubs and trees may help to provide structure and out-of-season interest to a mixed border, and perennial plants that look tired and overgrown can often be rejuvenated by being divided and replanted (see pages 102–3). There may be some plants you want to keep, but that would be better transferred to another position in the garden. And don't be afraid to get rid of plants that don't fit in with your plans.

One of the benefits of perennial plants growing in an existing border is that they can be dug up and moved around while dormant without being damaged. This allows you to

reposition the plants if you change your mind, and it also makes it easier to deal with any weeds that have established themselves among the plants. Add organic matter such as compost to the soil before replanting, and mulch around any plants that are not going to be moved.

In an established border you can use a plank to reach areas to plant or reposition perennials—the plank will help you avoid compacting the soil.

Preparing an Existing Bed

1 An existing bed will also need digging. Dig down to the depth of a spade's blade, turning over and breaking up the soil.

2 If you have only a few weeds, use a garden fork to remove them as you dig. Make sure you get the fork under the roots and remove as much as you can.

3 Improve the soil by adding an organic material, such as compost, after digging.

Understanding Soil

Without good soil, it will be difficult to grow good, healthy plants. Remember that soil is not only the provider of a plant's food and water supply, it is also its support system—so improving your soil is always important.

There are several types of soil, which is basically composed of weathered rock. Soil type depends on local geography and, to an extent, how the soil has been treated over the years of cultivation.

Once the compost is a brown, crumbly material, add it to your soil to help improve its texture and nutrient level.

Clay soil has tiny particles packed tightly together with few air spaces between them. This makes it is difficult for water to find a way through, so clay soil does not drain freely and is prone to waterlogging. It is slow to warm up in spring, sticky and heavy, and difficult to cultivate. However, clay soil usually contains good nutrient supplies.

In contrast sandy soil has large particles that create plenty of air spaces between them, so water can drain through this type of soil freely. Sandy soil is light and easy to dig, and it warms up quickly in spring. However, it is also prone to drying out and often is not fertile, because its soluble nutrients drain away with the water.

Silt is a type of soil with particles that are a little larger than clay, but much smaller than sand. Silt soil is moisture-retentive but does not waterlog as easily as clay. It is also usually fertile with good quantities of nutrients.

Garden soil is composed of a mixture of clay, sand, and silt in varying proportions, and this mixture is known as loam. You can classify soil according to the different proportions of its constituents—sandy clay loam, silt loam, silty clay, and so on.

TESTING SOIL TEXTURE

A simple "touch test" will usually give you a good idea of what type of soil you have. Take a small handful of moist soil, and rub a little between your fingers. Sandy soil will feel gritty, silt will feel smooth and slippery, and clay will be sticky.

Next, squeeze the handful of soil into a ball. Soil with a high proportion of clay will form a tight ball and can be rolled into a

Homemade Compost

Most garden waste and fruit and vegetable trimmings, such as peels, from the kitchen can be converted to valuable compost easily. Stack the waste up in a pile or in a special compost container (a container keeps the garden tidy and speeds up composting), trying to get a good mix of different textures by interspersing dense items, such as lawn clippings, with more open material. Add a layer of garden soil after every 18 inches (45 cm) or so of waste, and continue until the container is full. Then cover it to keep the heat in and leave it until it has decomposed— it will then be ideal for adding to the soil or using as a mulch. Avoid adding perennial weeds; invasive plants, such as bindweed; diseased plants; the first three grass clippings from lawns treated with a selective weed killer; and dairy and meat products.

long snake without breaking. The more easily it can be molded and the longer the snake, the higher the clay content. Soil with a high proportion of sand may form a ball when squeezed, but it will fall apart easily, and the soil cannot be molded into other shapes. The ideal soil for perennials is a sandy clay loam, which can be molded into a ball that clings together reasonably well and will roll into a short snake.

SOIL ACIDITY

Soil acidity varies according to the amount of lime present. Alkaline soil (high in lime) can be problematic because the alkalinity makes some nutrients unavailable to plants, although perennials are not as affected by this as shrubs. A simple soil test uses the pH scale to tell you your soil acidity: pH 7.0 is neutral, pH 7.0–14.0 is alkaline, and pH 1.0–7.0 is acid. Most soil is between pH 4.0 and 8.5, and the ideal for the majority of plants is around pH 6.5—although many perennials will grow well on soil that is the alkaline side of neutral. You can easily make acid soil more alkaline by adding garden lime; however, it is not practical to try to make alkaline soil more acid. Plants in very alkaline soil may need feeding with special fertilizers (see pages 88–89).

ORGANIC MATTER

The other major constituent of good soil is organic matter—decomposed plant and animal matter that improves the soil texture and often provides high levels of nutrients. Organic matter is added naturally to soil when plants die and are left to rot away; good gardeners also add it to the soil in the form of compost or composted manure. The fibrous texture of organic matter will greatly improve both clay soil and sandy soil. It opens up heavy clay and allows it to drain more freely, while its spongelike texture absorbs and holds onto moisture in free-draining sand.

The large particles in sandy soil (top) allow water to drain freely, while the tiny ones in clay soil (center) trap water. Loam (bottom) is a crumbly mixture that has the good qualities found in clay and sandy soil.

Obtaining Plants

Filling a large border with perennial plants can be an expensive proposition, but there are ways of keeping the costs down. The best season to buy plants is in time for spring planting, or in warmer areas for a fall planting.

You can purchase perennials as container-grown plants, or bare rooted. Container-grown plants have been raised for sale in pots of various sizes—the larger the pot, the more expensive the plant. You can leave these plants in their containers for a few weeks if you are not ready to plant them as soon as they arrive in your garden—as long as you make sure they don't dry out. In addition, root disturbance is kept to a minimum so the plants will grow quickly when they are planted. You can get container-grown plants all year round. However, the cost of the container and soil

makes these plants more expensive, and if they are delivered, delivery costs will be high due to the extra weight.

Bare-root plants are grown in fields and lifted from the open ground as required. They are less expensive to produce and transport, which helps to keep prices down. Because bare-root plants take up less space, their producers can grow a wider range of varieties. However, they can be shipped to your home only during their dormant season, and they must be planted or potted shortly after you receive them. You'll need to handle the plants carefully

A good nursery specializing in perennials will have a wider and more interesting variety of plants to choose from.

gardenTIPS

If you are buying mail-order plants, consider the following:

- **Plants can be subject to damage and delays in transit, so always check the plants immediately on arrival.**

- **If the roots are dry when the plants arrive, leave them in water for several hours.**

- **Make sure you order your plants early so they will arrive in plenty of time to plant them at the appropriate time in your garden.**

- **Get your order in early if you want scarce or popular varieties.**

- **Check the last order dates and shipping times for individual catalogs.**

advice. If you have a nursery within reasonable traveling distance, you can inspect the plants before you buy, although the nurseries may not be open during the summer season.

Many specialist nurseries sell their plants by mail order, and larger seed companies also often sell young plants this way. Specialist nurseries tend to sell larger, bare-root plants or plants in 3½-inch (9-cm) containers. Shipping costs are calculated by weight or charged a flat rate, based on the value of the order. Young plants from seed companies may range from mini plug plants—grown in special plugs of soil and measuring 3 inches (7.5 cm) high or less—to larger, garden-ready plants 6 inches (15 cm) tall. Plants are shipped in lightweight plastic cell flats and travel well. Because the plants are small, shipping costs are reasonable.

to avoid damaging their roots, and they can dry out if they are not carefully packed.

WHERE TO OBTAIN PLANTS

The least expensive way to start your perennial collection is to swap divisions or cuttings with friends and neighbors, but check the plants carefully for pests or diseases before planting them in your garden. You can also grow many perennials from seed (see page 98), although you may have to wait one or two years for them to reach flowering size, and you'll need a little skill to nurse them through their early stages.

You can buy plants from garden centers. These plants will be container grown and often available in a range of sizes. You can see exactly what you are getting and choose the best plants available. However, in most garden centers choices are limited to the most popular species and varieties.

Another option is to visit specialist nurseries. They usually sell both container-grown and bare-root plants and have a good range of varieties, often including more rare plants. The staff should have a good knowledge of perennials and will be able to offer you good

How to Select a Healthy Plant

Make sure leaves are a rich green and healthy, with no obvious signs of pests or diseases. Inspect the drainage holes in container-grown plants—they should not have a thick mat of roots growing through them. The root-ball should slide out of the pot in one piece. Choose plants that are labeled, and with weed-free soil in the pots. Dormant plants should have a good fibrous root system and a healthy crown, preferably with a number of growing points visible.

Planting Perennials

The best time to plant perennials is normally in spring, or in warmer areas in fall. Although they can be planted any time in the dormant season, plants will not do well if they are planted in freezing weather in the middle of winter.

When you plant young perennials, make sure you allow enough space around them so they can reach their mature size without becoming crowded.

In most areas early spring is usually the prime time for planting perennials. Although—in theory—container-grown perennials can be planted all year round, a spring or fall planting will still provide better results than planting in summer. Because the plants are in full leaf in summer, it can be difficult for them to get their roots established if they are also coping with heat and drought. In winter a particularly harsh cold spell can damage the roots of newly planted specimens, so choose a mild period of weather for winter plantings.

PLANTING BASICS

The first step is to prepare the soil by digging and turning over the planting area as deeply as possible, making sure you remove all weeds and, if possible, incorporating well-rotted organic matter such as garden compost. Tread lightly over the soil after digging to firm it. Ideally, you should do this soil preparation a couple of weeks before planting to allow the soil to settle.

The ideal time for planting perennials is during a cool, cloudy, and still day. Avoid bright sunshine and windy conditions, which will rob the plants of moisture and make it more difficult for them to become established in the crucial first few days. Make sure the soil is moist; if the weather is dry, water the planting area thoroughly several days in advance. You should water container-grown plants the evening before planting, and bare-root plants will benefit from a soaking for several hours to ensure the roots have plenty of moisture.

If you are planting more than just a few plants, a planting plan is always a good idea. If your plants are in containers, you can place them in their planting positions on top of the soil before you start digging any planting holes—this will allow you to see how they look and make any adjustments necessary. However, don't do this with bare-root plants, because their roots will dry out.

Once you are satisfied with the positioning of your new plants, you can begin planting. A sturdy trowel is the best tool to use, although a small spade will be useful if you have some large plants. The planting technique for container-grown plants is slightly different than that for bare-root plants.

PLANTING CONTAINER-GROWN PERENNIALS

Leave a container-grown plant in its container while you prepare the planting site. Start by digging a planting hole that is wide enough to fit the root-ball comfortably. Make sure you also make it deep enough for the crown of the plant—where the stem exits the soil—to remain at the same position in the soil as it is in the container.

Break up the soil at the bottom of the planting hole. If the soil is either heavy or light, it is a good idea to add a few handfuls of a special planting mix. Remove the plant from its container and set the root-ball firmly in the center of the planting hole, making sure you are happy with how it is positioned. Refill around the edges of the plant with soil and firm gently.

Make sure you do not set the plant too deeply; its crown should be level with the soil surface, not buried—otherwise it may rot. Finally add an unobtrusive label—you might think you'll remember the variety name, but it's surprising how easy it is to forget it. Or draw up a little plan showing the plants and label them. You can also make any care notes, such as if they need deadheading or cutting back, on the plan.

PLANTING BARE-ROOT PLANTS

The planting holes for bare-root plants do not need to be as big as those for container-grown plants. Again, the crown of the plant should be just level with the soil surface. For fibrous-root plants—where there are a lot of fine roots—dig a suitable size hole and pile up the soil slightly to create a small mound at the bottom. Remove the plant from its covering of soil or plastic and carefully spread the roots out, then

Planting a Container-Grown Plant

1 To remove the plant from its pot, spread fingers on either side of the plant's crown and turn the pot upside down. A couple of sharp taps on the bottom of the pot with the handle of the trowel will enable the root-ball to slide out.

2 As you fill in around the edges of the planting hole, firm down the soil with your fingers. You can sprinkle in a little slow-release fertilizer to help keep the plants fed all through the growing season.

3 Finish off by just covering the top of the root-ball with a thin layer of soil, and firm down the soil around the plant with your knuckles.

set them firmly on the mound of soil so that there is good contact between the soil and the roots. Holding the plant in position, fill in over and around the roots with the soil dug out from the hole, mixing in a little slow-release fertilizer if desired. Firm the soil all the time you are filling in the hole, and give a final firming with your knuckles when you are finished.

Plants with long taproots will obviously need slightly different treatment. The object is to make sure the soil makes good, firm contact all around the root system, without any air pockets. Remember that some perennials have brittle roots, which are easily snapped off, so treat them gently.

greenTHUMBS

Keep the roots of bare-root plants covered with soil or plastic at all times while they are out of the ground and keep in the shade.

Planting Depths for Bulbs

The depths given below all refer to the depth of soil over the tip of the bulb, not the depth of the planting hole.

Agapanthus spp.: 4 inches (10 cm)

Allium spp. (ornamental onion):
3–6 inches (7.5–15 cm)

Amaryllis belladonna (belladonna lily): 6 inches (15 cm)

Anemone blanda (Grecian windflower): 2–3 inches (5–7.5 cm)

Anemone nemorosa (wood anemone):
2 inches (5 cm)

Camassia spp. (cama): 4 inches (10 cm)

Colchicum autumnale (autumn crocus): 3 inches (7.5 cm)

Convallaria majalis (lily of the valley):
1 inch (2.5 cm)

Crinum powellii (swamp lily):
6 inches (15 cm)

Crocosmia spp.: 3 inches (7.5 cm)

Crocus spp.: 3 inches (7.5 cm)

Cyclamen hederifolium, C. coum
(cyclamen): 1–2 inches (2.5–5 cm)

Dahlia spp.: 3 inches (7.5 cm)

Eremurus spp. (foxtail lily):
3 inches (7.5 cm)

Eucomis comosa (pineapple lily):
level with surface

Fritillaria imperialis
(crown imperial): 8 inches (20 cm)

Fritillaria meleagris (checkered lily, snakes head): 4 inches (10 cm)

Galanthus nivalis (common snowdrop):
4 inches (10 cm)

Gladiolus spp.: 4 inches (10 cm)

Hyacinthus (hyacinth):
6 inches (15 cm)

Iris spp.: 3–6 inches (7.5–15 cm)

Lilium (lily), basal rooting:
(*L. canadense, L. candidum,
L. martagon*): 2 inches (5 cm)

Lilium (lily), stem-rooting:
(*L. auruatum, L. bulbiferum,
L. hansonii, L. henryi, L. lancifolium,
L. regale, L. speciosum*):
6–8 inches (15–20 cm)

Narcissus spp. (daffodil): 4–6 inches
(10–15 cm)

Tulipa spp. (tulip): 4–8 inches (10–20 cm)

A bulb planter makes digging holes for large bulbs an easier and faster job.

When planting a bulb, make sure the side from which the shoots will grow is facing up.

PLANTING BULBS

A useful rule of thumb for the planting depths for bulbs is to cover the top of the bulb with two to three times its own height in soil. However, you should plant the bulbs more deeply in light, sandy soil; more shallowly in heavy clay soil.

Dig holes for the bulbs to the required depth (see *Planting Depths for Bulbs,* above), using a trowel, dibble, or other specialized bulb-planting tool. It is not always clear which way up a bulb should go in the ground—if in doubt, plant it on its side. Cover the bulbs with soil, and label their positions.

PLANTING CONTAINERS

When planting perennials, if you use a large container, make sure it is in its final position before you fill it with soil and plants—it will be surprisingly heavy and difficult to move once it is filled. For any size container, use good-quality potting soil, either soil-based or soil-less, according to your preference. Soil-based potting soil is more appropriate if you want your container to last for several seasons. If you use a soil-less mix, add water-retaining granules to reduce the frequency of watering required. Use special pot feet, or small wooden or stone blocks, to raise the container a few inches off the ground so that it can drain freely. Rember that containers are prone to becoming waterlogged in wet weather, as well as drying out in summer. For suitable perennials that will grow in a container, see page 59.

To plant the perennials, fill the bottom of the container with a layer of coarse drainage material, such as broken clay pots, rough stones, or coarse gravel. If there is a single large drainage hole, cover it with a piece of weed control fabric or netting to prevent the soil from being washed out. Add the soil mix to the pot until it is one-half to two-thirds full. Set the plants in their position, filling in around them with more of the soil mix and firming it down well as you work. Water the completed container well, then finish off with a layer of mulch, such as shredded bark or gravel.

CARING FOR YOUR NEW PLANTS

After planting, water the bed to help the plants settle in. Use a watering can fitted with a fine watering head, or a sprinkler that breaks the water up into fine drops so that you don't disturb the soil around the plants. Then mulch around the plants with shredded bark or a similar material to help keep the moisture in the ground (see pages 90–91). Competition from weeds will rob newly planted perennials of vital soil moisture, so make sure you keep weeds under control. A mulch will help to achieve this, but you should also hoe away any weeds that do poke their heads through the soil. If you are planting in fall, a mulch will help to protect the plant roots from freezing temperatures, and it can help prevent the "soil heave" that might disturb the roots in a heavy frost.

Finally, stake the plants at an early stage (see pages 94–95). It is particularly important to stake perennials that have been only recently planted. Their roots will not have had a chance to get a firm grip on the soil, so they will be more susceptible to movement in windy conditions. This movement, or wind rock, sets up a vicious circle. The movement tears

the delicate root hairs as soon as they form, perpetuating the problem.

SPRINGTIME PLANTINGS

Perennials planted in spring usually begin to grow before the roots have a chance to become fully established. Once the leaves develop, plants will start to lose water from the foliage, and because the roots are not fully established, the plant can have trouble replacing this water. This makes it particularly important to protect these plants from excess water loss while the roots are still developing. Keep the soil moist—not wet—at all times, and protect the plants from strong sun or drying winds for several weeks after planting. A floating row cover provides shade and wind protection, but it needs to be firmly anchored.

Bark mulch will help this young hosta to become firmly established.

Watering Your Plants

In many areas rain will supply all the water that perennials need—the only additional watering necessary will be shortly after planting, while the roots are becoming established. However, in other areas the amount of rain may not be sufficient.

Plants need water for many reasons: to enable photosynthesis to take place; to transport nutrients around the plant; to keep the plant erect; and to provide cooling by transpiration. If sufficient water is not available to the roots, these processes are impaired. Eventually the effects of the water shortage will become obvious as plants wilt—but long before this visible stage is reached their performance will have been adversely affected.

Ideally you should provide plants with water before they start showing signs of stress, but it is not always easy to know when it is the right time. Your common sense will tell you when conditions are drier than normal, and the best way to see whether this might be affecting plants is to dig a hole in the flower bed with a trowel. Often the soil is only dry on the surface; as long as it is moist a few inches below, the plants will be fine for the time being. However, if it is still dry more than a few inches down, it's time to start watering.

The amount of water a plant needs will vary according to the weather conditions; hot, sunny, or windy weather increases the amount of moisture required because it increases the rate at which water evaporates from the leaves. The drying effect of wind is

A gentle spray of water is best for newly planted perennials, especially seedlings.

garden TIPS

Water is becoming an increasingly scarce resource in many areas, so it is vital to avoid wasting it.

- Improve the moisture-holding capacity of the soil by adding plenty of composted organic matter.

- Mulch the soil surface when the soil is thoroughly moist to help slow down the evaporation of water.

- Grow drought-tolerant plants in dry areas.

- Control weeds, which will compete with plants for water.

- Collect rainwater in a rain barrel and use it for watering plants.

- In hot, dry areas water plants in the evening, when water evaporation is at its slowest.

- Use soaker hoses or similar devices instead of sprinklers.

Watering Equipment

Buy the right watering equipment and use it wisely.

CANS: For small areas, watering cans are fine. Use a coarse head on the spout to break the water up into large droplets that will avoid washing away soil, and direct the water flow straight to the base of individual plants.

HOSE: Labor-saving for a larger garden, avoiding all those trips back and forth to the faucet with a heavy, awkward watering can. If possible, attach an "on-off" device at the end of the hose farthest from the faucet to allow fine control and avoid wasting water.

SPRINKLER: An easy way to apply large volumes of water but also a wasteful method. Much of the water is lost by evaporation, and there is also a tendency to leave the sprinkler running longer than is strictly necessary.

SOAKER HOSE: Lengths of special hose are perforated with small holes. Water sprays or oozes through the holes in a narrow band, which allows water to be applied precisely and avoids waste through evaporation. The hoses are flexible so that they can be twisted through the bed just where they are needed. In areas where water restrictions apply, these hoses are classified as sprinklers.

often not appreciated by gardeners. In exposed positions protect vulnerable plants, such as newly planted specimens, with a temporary windbreak, or spray the leaves with an antitranspirant spray to cut down water loss.

HOW TO WATER PLANTS

When it comes to watering, "little and often" is a bad idea. Small quantities of water moisten only a shallow area of soil just below the surface. This encourages plants to form the majority of their roots in that area—just the region that is most subject to drying out. Deep-rooted plants are much better able to withstand dry conditions, so encourage deep, moisture-seeking roots by giving plants an occasional thorough soaking instead of frequent sprinklings. A few hours after watering, get the trowel out again and dig another hole to check that the soil is moist at least a few inches down.

Following pages:
By taking care of your plants, you're bound to have a lush garden, such as this one with bee balm (*Monarda* spp.), yarrow (*Achillea* spp.), sunflowers (*Helianthus* spp.), phlox, and coneflowers (*Echinacea* spp).

Below:
For a larger garden, a sprayer nozzle attached to a hose will be less time-consuming than using a small watering can.

Feeding Your Plants

Plants have the amazing ability to obtain all the energy they need from sunlight, which they convert to a usable form by the process of photosynthesis. However, to carry out photosynthesis, and a range of other functions, they also need minerals.

The minerals your plants need are taken up in a solution, usually by the roots—although occasionally they are absorbed through the leaves. The main nutrients they require are nitrogen, which helps to promote leafy growth; phosphorus, which is essential for healthy root development; and potassium, which promotes flower formation and helps to harden plants against disease and cold weather. These three nutrients are needed in the largest quantities by plants, but there is also a whole range of other minerals that are needed in much smaller amounts, including calcium, magnesium, sulfur, iron, manganese, boron, copper, zinc, and molybdenum.

The minerals needed by perennials are naturally available in garden soil, but the quantities in the soil vary according to the soil type and its treatment. Plants take minerals out of the soil, but in nature these minerals are returned when the plants die down and decompose—or, if animals eat the plants, the minerals are returned to the soil in the form of manure. However, in a garden setting not only do we pack a lot more plants to a square yard than would occur naturally, we whisk away dead stems and leaves before they have a chance to rot, so the soil soon becomes depleted of nutrients. This means we need to increase the supply by adding plenty of organic matter, such as well-rotted manure, but it's often necessary to add nutrients in the more concentrated form of fertilizers.

GARDEN FERTILIZERS

Fertilizers usually contain a mixture of the major plant nutrients in varying proportions. A package of fertilizer will normally be labeled with the proportions of nitrogen, phosphorus, and potassium (usually abbreviated to NPK) that it contains—for example, NPK 7-7-7 is a balanced fertilizer with equal quantities of nitrogen, phosphorus, and potassium, while bonemeal, at 4-20-0, is high in phosphorus with a little nitrogen and no potassium. Fertilizers containing a mixture of nutrients are called compound fertilizers; "straight" fertilizers contain just one nutrient, such as the nitrogen fertilizer ammonium nitrate.

Garden fertilizers come in a variety of different forms. Powders are usually dissolved in water before application, but you can sometimes sprinkle them directly onto the soil, where the rain will take them down to the roots. If rain does not fall within a day or two of application, you should water them in.

Granules are easier to handle than powders, especially in windy conditions. Liquid fertilizers are faster acting than granules or dry powders, and there is less risk of scorching plants by applying too much fertilizer. Keep dry fertilizer, such as powders and granules, off plant foliage to avoid leaf scorch. Growing points can easily be killed by a carelessly applied fertilizer that lodges in the leaf bases.

Slow-release fertilizers usually come in the form of granules, which are broken down at different rates by warmth and moisture. This means that the nutrient content is released gradually over an extended period from a single application. Trace element fertilizers contain the minerals that plants need in only tiny amounts, but which, nevertheless, are still sometimes in short supply, especially in alkaline soils. Foliar feeds are specially

Granule fertilizers are easy to spread, especially in windy conditions. If rain does not fall within a few days, water them in, as you would powdered fertilizers.

formulated so they can be absorbed by the plants' leaves. They usually contain trace elements and are fast acting. They are particularly useful on alkaline soils, where the lime content can sometimes "lock up" particular nutrients, making them unavailable to the plants.

WHEN TO FEED

In most gardens perennials will benefit from a fertilizer application each year in early spring, using a compound fertilizer that has slightly more potassium than nitrogen or phosphorus. Richly colored flowers and plenty of them is usually the main objective for perennials, and

a high potassium content will help to ensure this. However, if plant growth is slow and leaves are small and pale, tip the balance slightly in favor of nitrogen in your fertilizer brand. But remember that too much nitrogen will result in a jungle of lush, leafy plants with few flowers—so be careful you don't overdo it.

Plants can have a trace element deficiency. Symptoms include a marked yellowing between the veins of the leaves, or browning around the leaf edges. An application of a foliar feed containing trace elements will soon correct the balance, but fortunately perennials are rarely bothered by this type of deficiency.

If you are unsure of the nutrient content of your soil or are having particular problems with your plants, it is often worth sending a soil sample away for a complete analysis. A professional soil-testing laboratory will give a more accurate result than home-testing kits, and will advise on any measures necessary to return the soil to a better balance.

A late summer border of helenium, crocosmia, goldenrod (*Solidago* spp.), sunflowers, (*Helianthus* spp.), yarrow (*Achillea* spp.), and sedum has a bright display of flowers, thanks to plenty of care and the careful application of fertilizer.

Left:
Liquid fertilizers are normally diluted with water before applying with a watering can. Some can be measured by using the container's cap.

Winning the Weed Battle

A weed is a plant in the wrong place. Although we tend to think of weeds as being wild plants, perennials can become weeds, too—invasive species that overrun the border or self-seeders can be just as infuriating as chickweed or shepherd's purse.

Why do weeds matter? Not only do they spoil the appearance of the garden, but they also compete with cultivated plants for nutrients, light, moisture, and space—and because weed species are tough characters, they usually win. It's true that weeding can be a chore, but there are ways to keep the upper hand and make the job of banishing weeds easier.

STARTING EARLY ON

Make sure you begin your war on weeds right from the start, when preparing the ground for planting (see pages 74–75). If the area is weedy, get rid of them with a translocated weed killer (see *Chemical Weed Control,* opposite page), scorch them off with a flame gun, or cover the area for several months with plastic sheeting or a thick layer of newspapers or cardboard, depriving the weeds of light and starving them into submission. Then you'll need to dig the soil deeply and remove all traces of perennial weed roots. However, cultivation will bring weed seeds up near the surface where they can germinate, so after digging, allow a few weeks for weed seedlings to appear and deal with them before planting.

DIGGING UP WEEDS

Weeds are much easier to deal with when they are young, so be vigilant. Always take a hoe with you when you stroll around the garden—it only takes a few minutes to decapitate newly germinated weed seedlings, or you can simply pull them up by hand. However, if you allow them a few weeks to become established, they will become much harder to deal with, entwining themselves among garden plants and sending their roots threading through the borders so that pulling the weed up loosens half a dozen border plants, too.

Larger weeds with a well-established root system may send up new shoots even after the top growth is removed, but if you continue to hoe off new growth as soon as it appears, the roots will eventually run out of steam. Or you can dig up the weed with a garden fork, roots and all, and remove it. (Don't add perennial

Below left:
A well-sharpened hoe is one of the best ways of dealing with weeds, but don't use it to dig the weed up—slide it across the soil surface so that it slices off weed stems.

Below right:
Annual weeds have a weak root system and can be pulled up by hand.

greenTHUMBS

If you leave a weed complete with its roots lying on a moist soil surface, it will often be able to reroot itself and grow again.

You can use manure or garden compost that has been well-rotted beforehand as a mulch, but there is a risk that they might contain weed seeds that were not killed by the composting process. Commercial compost- or manure-based mulches are more likely to be sterile so that weeds will not be a problem.

Straw can be used as a mulch but it looks untidy, tends to blow around, and will rob soil of nitrogen as it rots. Another, more attractive option is pine needles; but because they can make the soil more acidic, avoid using them around plants that don't love acidic soil. Alternatively, you can pack down grass clippings to form a thick blanket that suppresses weed growth well, but it may also be impenetrable to rain. Although fresh grass clippings look reasonably pleasant, they will soon turn an unattractive yellowish brown. Like straw, they use up soil nitrogen as they rot.

Cocoa-shell mulch makes an attractive addition to this border of primroses (*Primula* spp.), columbine, (*Aquilegia* spp.), and yarrow (*Achillea* spp).

weeds or weeds that have gone to seed to the compost pile—they will spread.)

MULCHING MATERIALS

Weeds need light and air to grow, so covering a clean soil surface with a mulch about 2 inches (5 cm) deep will prevent weed seedlings from getting established—and those weeds that do grow through the mulch will be easier to pull out of the loose material.

Bark and wood chips come in a wide range of different particles, sizes, and colors. They look attractive, stay in place well, and allow moisture through to the plants. Crushed cocoa shells also make an excellent weed-suppressing mulch; they are attractive, clean to handle, and smell deliciously of chocolate. However, dog owners should be aware that dogs have been poisoned by cocoa-shell mulch. Similar by-products from other crops—pecan shells, for example—may be available in areas where they are grown. Spent mushroom compost is another useful mulching material available from commercial mushroom growers.

A Low-Maintenance Garden

It pays to be honest about the amount of time and effort you are able (or prepared) to give to your plants. If you don't have plenty of extra time for your garden, there are ways to still have a nice garden—without dedicating a lot of time.

Below left:
Choose easy-to-maintain plants, such as blue globe thistle (*Echinops* spp.), with interesting seed heads that won't need deadheading. It is planted here with crocosmia.

Below right:
Choose perennials with flower heads that remain attractive for a long period, such as sedum and grasses.

Although there are some lucky people who have the luxury of being able to spend hours caring for their gardens—and many people find doing simple, repetitive gardening jobs both relaxing and satisfying—this is not often the case. If you lead a busy working and family life, you will probably have to grab an hour in the garden here or there whenever you can. Unfortunately, gardening in this manner is often not relaxing, but filled with frantic hand weeding and deadheading, which is perhaps not the most appealing way to garden.

TIME-SAVING TECHNIQUES

Low-maintenance plants and techniques can help provide the time-saving answer. The type of chores required by perennials include weeding, staking, deadheading, watering, and feeding, but there are some general time-saving techniques you can use to deal with many of these tasks. Mulching will greatly reduce the amount of both weeding and watering required. If you live in a dry area and need to water plants frequently, it may be worth investing in an automatic irrigation system.

By using slow-release fertilizers, you will need to make only one application at the beginning of the season.

To reduce some of the other chores, choose your plants carefully. If you want to cut down on work, these are some of the plants to avoid:

• Self-seeding plants, such as columbine (*Aquilegia* spp.), tickweed (*Coreopsis lanceolata*), and Brazilian verbena (*Verbena bonariensis*). The numerous self-sown seedlings quickly become weeds.

• Plants that need dividing frequently, such as bellflower (*Campanula* spp.), iris, and phlox.

These deteriorate unless they are regularly split and replanted, while others, such as bergenia, spurge (*Euphorbia* spp.), hosta, and peonies (*Paeonia* spp.), can be left alone for years.

• Plants that are prone to pests and diseases. Asters, for example, are ruined by any mildew in many areas, while hollyhocks (*Alcea* spp.) can be disfigured by rust disease.

• Plants that need staking, such as tall varieties of delphiniums.

• Plants that need deadheading to continue blooming, such as yarrow (*Achillea* spp.), or to look good, such as daylilies (*Hemerocallis* spp.).

Low-Maintenance Plants

Name	Description	Flowering Season
Acanthus mollis (bear's-breeches)	Large, bold, dark green foliage with tall flower spikes that need no staking; hardy and generally trouble-free.	Late spring to early summer
Achillea filipendula (yarrow)	Flat, bright gold, long-lasting flower heads and fernlike gray-green foliage; it is self-supporting and suitable for most soils and positions.	Summer through fall
Aurinia saxatilis (basket-of-gold)	A low-growing, nonaggressive plant that is easy to care for, even in poor soil, with prolific golden flowers in spring; shear off top growth when it gets untidy.	Spring
Coreopsis verticillata '**Moonbeam**' (tickweed)	Fine, fernlike foliage and small, daisylike, pale lemon flowers; 'Moonbeam' is sterile, so self-sown seedlings are not a problem; suitable in sun or light shade.	Early summer to fall
Dicentra spectabilis (bleeding heart)	Heart-shaped pink and white flowers dangle from arching stems; attractive leaves are divided. No staking or deadheading needed; no pest and disease problems.	Spring to summer
Echinops ritro (globe thistle)	A showy, thistlelike plant with striking globular flower heads that look good through the winter, too, so there's no need to deadhead; suitable for most soils.	Summer
Heuchera '**Palace Purple**' (coral bells)	Rich purple, shapely leaves form neat mounds that are spangled with delicate pale pink flowers in early summer; trouble-free.	Late spring to summer
Liatris spicata (spike gayfeather)	Spikes of bright purple, densely packed flower heads are produced on neat, compact plants that grow just about anywhere.	Summer
Nepeta × faassenii (blue catmint)	Gray-green, aromatic leaves with a toothed margin and heads of lavender-blue flowers, it grows well in most soils, but is particularly good on poor, dry sites.	Early summer to fall
Sedum '**Autumn Joy**' (sedum)	Fleshy, gray-green leaves and heads of reddish pink flowers; the dead flower heads add structure to the winter garden. It's easy to please, but prefers full sun.	Summer

Staking and Supporting Your Plants

Many perennial plants will need staking to show their blossoms at their best. Although plants growing in the wild may thrive well enough without staking, garden varieties are different.

Below left:
Cut stems to make twig supports during winter, before they come into leaf.

Below right:
Push the supports into the ground around the plant. As the plant grows, it will obscure the supports.

Well-grown garden plants are taller and more lush than wild varieties, which makes them more prone to toppling over. Garden varieties have often been bred to produce larger, more numerous flowers, and double-flowered varieties have particularly heavy flower heads, which may droop or snap their stems.

Even those plants that seem sturdy enough to be able to manage well without supports can be knocked over by a gust of wind or a sudden heavy downpour. Flowering stems of some plants, such as lupines (*Lupinus* spp.) and delphiniums, do not need to be lying flat for long before the tips of the flower stalks start to turn upward, and this means that even if you manage to pick up the flattened stems and stake them, the shape of the flowers is ruined.

SECRET STAKING

If stakes and supports in the perennial border are used carefully, they should not be obtrusive. Once plants have reached the flowering stage, you shouldn't be able to see that the supports are there—the plants should appear to be holding themselves up as if by magic. Few things look more dispiriting than a perennial

that has been trussed to a single stake by a piece of string lashed tightly around its middle. Whatever type of supports you decide to use, the key is to get them in place early—long before the plants actually need them. The shoots will then grow up through the supports naturally, instead of having to be pulled out of position to be tied up.

TYPES OF SUPPORT

You can choose from a whole variety of both natural and commercial products to keep your perennials in shape. Twig sticks are the time-honored way of staking plants, using lengths of twig stems (hazel stems are perfect) pushed in among the growing shoots. The sticks are completely natural, so they blend in beautifully, and as long as they have plenty of branching, twig portions, they will provide great support. They can be difficult to obtain unless you have suitable bushes or hedges in your own garden. It is also sometimes difficult to find suitable stems long enough to support tall plants. You can also insert garden stakes in a circle around the plants, and loop twine around the stakes to keep the plant stems in place as they grow. Individual stems can be tied to stakes as necessary. This support system is not as easy to disguise as twig sticks, but it can work well. Green plastic "stakes" are available and are slightly less obvious than natural bamboo.

Grow-through rings are among the commercial supports available. They consist of a ring of broadly spaced metal mesh on legs. They are positioned over young plants so that the shoots grow up through the mesh. On some products, the ring slides up and down

the legs so that you can adjust the support height as the shoots grow, but it is easy to snap plant stems when moving the ring. There are also L-shaped metal stakes that link together at their tops to form a continuous ring around plants. Their advantage is that you can easily vary the size of the ring to suit the size of the plant clump.

There are many types of supports available, including this wire ring held on a stake.

To reduce the risk of stakes causing eye injuries when you are working among plants, attach special safety tops over them. They are available from garden centers, or you can make your own from a piece of Styrofoam.

Pests and Diseases

Fortunately, perennial border plants are not too often troubled by pests and diseases, particularly when they are well grown and given conditions that suit them. However, always keep an eye open for the first signs of trouble.

It's much easier to deal with a problem in its early stages. Diseased or pest-infested shoots or leaves can often simply be pinched off and destroyed, and handpicking of pests, such as caterpillars, is surprisingly effective.

If you feel that pesticides are necessary, there are plenty of organic products, such as insecticidal soap or sulfur powder, which you can use as a first resort. Nonorganic chemical pesticides are rigorously tested for safety and can be used with confidence—but you must ensure that you follow the directions for their use, storage, and disposal absolutely, and that you keep them away from children.

Insect Pests

Name	Description	Treatment
Aphids	Small, black or green, soft-bodied creatures cluster in large numbers, mainly on young shoots. They suck sap, weakening the plant, spreading viruses, and exuding sticky substances on which sooty molds may grow.	Inspect plants frequently and act quickly. Knock off aphids with a forcible spray of water, or pick off heavily infested shoots where possible. Spray with insecticidal soap or a contact insecticide.
Caterpillars	Larvae of various moths and butterflies, which may be solitary or occur in groups. They have voracious appetites, feeding on leaves, buds, and shoots.	Handpicking can be effective. Spraying forcibly with water may dislodge caterpillars, but they often find their way back on the plant. *Bacillus thuringiensis* (Bt) is a natural bacterial control. Organic and nonorganic insecticides can be used.
Japanese beetle	Small, shiny brown beetles, which occur in large numbers, feeding from the tip of a plant downward, skeletonizing and destroying leaves.	Check plants regularly and deal with outbreaks promptly—established beetles give off a scent that attracts others. Handpicking or shaking beetles off into a bucket of soapy water works well, as does spraying with insecticidal soap.
Leaf miner	These larvae of various flies tunnel into leaves, leaving winding or blotchy discolored mines visible. Plants can be weakened. Chrysanthemums, columbines (*Aquilegia* spp.), and pinks (*Dianthus* spp.) are often affected.	Pick off and destroy affected leaves as soon as they are seen.
Slugs and snails	Well-known, slimy, nocturnal feeders particularly attracted to young shoots in spring but capable of causing severe damage to a wide number of plants, especially hostas.	Trap in beer traps or grapefruit skins, or handpick at night. Surround plants with deterrents, such as crushed eggshells, diatomaceous earth, or copper bands, or use slug pellets. Remove habitats, such as damp leaf litter, from near plants.
Thrips	Tiny, black, flying insects, also known as thunder flies. They are particularly troublesome on dadyliles (*Hemerocallis* spp.), where they damage the buds before they open, leaving corky scars.	Difficult to deal with because they are hidden within the flower buds and leaf joints. Insecticidal soaps can reduce damage; systemic insecticide can also be used.

Diseases

Name	Description	Treatment
Crown rot and root rot	These rots may be caused by a variety of soil-living bacteria or fungi; they cause rotting of the roots and/or of the plant's crown at soil level. First symptoms are usually wilting and yellowing of the leaves, followed eventually by the collapse of the plant. Delphiniums, bellflowers (*Campanula* spp.), and hostas are among likely victims.	These rots are usually a sign of poorly drained soil, so improving drainage will help. Affected plants should be removed and destroyed, although fungicides can sometimes halt progress of the disease in its earliest stages.
Leaf spots	Widespread and numerous, caused by fungi or bacteria, leaf spots appear as spots or holes in leaves, regular or irregular in shape, black or pale brown in color. Plants affected include delphinium, columbine (*Aquilegia* spp.), anemone, chrysanthemum, and bellflower (*Campanula* spp.), among others.	Symptoms are often mild, and picking off affected leaves is usually all that is necessary. While some leaf spots will respond to fungicide treatment, it is almost impossible for gardeners to identify those caused by fungi and those caused by bacteria.
Mildew	Downy mildew and powdery mildew are different diseases; downy mildew affects few border plants, but powdery mildew is common and serious. It occurs mainly in hot, dry weather, covering foliage and stems in a powdery white mold; leaves yellow and droop. It can affect many plants; asters and phlox are prone to it.	Avoid mildew by keeping the soil moist but not waterlogged and thinning shoots in spring to prevent overcrowding of stems. Plants can be sprayed with fungicide at the first signs of the disease but it is difficult to control.
Rust	Fungus that causes characteristic spots on foliage, usually yellow on the upper side of the leaf with a ring of orange or brown pustules on the underside. Plants can be severely weakened. Hollyhocks (*Alcea* spp.) are commonly affected; primroses (*Primula* spp.), pinks (*Dianthus* spp.), lilies (*Lilium* spp.), and irises can also suffer.	Remove and destroy affected leaves or whole plants if greatly affected. Clear away all plant debris to prevent infection from remaining over the winter. Fungicides may help as a preventive treatment or in the early stages of the disease.
Viruses	Viruses cause many symptoms, including mottling and streaking of the foliage, malformation and strange colors in flowers, distorted growth, and stunting. They are often spread by aphids and other insects. Plants affected include bellflower (*Campanula* spp.), dahlia, columbine (*Aquilegia* spp.), delphinium, and pinks (*Dianthus* spp.).	Affected plants should be destroyed. Keeping aphids under control will help to prevent the spread of viral diseases.

ANIMAL PESTS

While the main foes attacking your perennials will probably be insects, animals can be a problem, too. Rabbits will eat almost anything that grows, and rodents will nibble, dig up, or disturb plants with shallow roots. Depending on where you live, deer can be a disaster for gardens, grazing on your carefully tended borders until there's almost nothing left.

These animals pests are difficult to control. Repellents—either commercial products or homemade remedies, including human hair and cayenne pepper—have a poor success rate, although they might be worth a try. Physical barriers work better. For smaller animals, surround vulnerable plants with sharp twigs or cover them with cloches or mesh while they are young, enabling them to get established.

For rabbits and deer, fencing is the only answer. Rabbits and other burrowing animals need fencing that extends well below soil level, while deer (prodigious jumpers) require 8-foot (2.4-m)-high fences to keep them out. Some plants are said to be deer-resistant, but hungry deer will eat almost anything. Favorite deer food varies according to region, so seek advice from your local authority on the best species to plant to avoid deer damage.

Aphids often cluster together in large groups.

Propagating Your Plants

Increasing your stock of plants by seed, cuttings, or division will not only save you money, but is fun to do. It doesn't need any special equipment—or even particularly green thumbs.

As well as providing you with new plants to fill your own beds and borders, increasing your stock will allow you to give plants away to friends, neighbors, or charity sales, or to negotiate plant swaps with other gardeners for some of their perennial treasures.

SEXUAL OR NONSEXUAL?

There are a number of ways in which plants can reproduce themselves, but only one of them is sexual—the production of seed. Sexual reproduction can introduce variety into the plant's family line by mixing the different genes through cross-pollination. This variety provides the resulting plants with the widest opportunity for survival, so it's an advantage for the plants. However, for gardeners it is a nuisance because the feature you most admire in a plant may not appear in its seedling offspring. A relatively small number of varieties will "breed true"— where the majority of their seedlings will exhibit the same characteristics as the parents. A few of these are listed in *Plants from Seed* on the opposite page. The advantage of growing plants from seed is that it is a relatively cheap way of obtaining a lot of plants.

To be certain of obtaining a new plant that is exactly the same as its parent, you usually need to reproduce the plant vegetatively—in other words, by cuttings (see pages 100–1) or division (see pages 102–3). Many named varieties are selections that have been propagated in this way for many generations.

GROWING PLANTS FROM SEED

Raising plants from seed requires a modicum of skill, plus suitable space to grow the seedlings. Some varieties also take several seasons to reach flowering size. Most of the major seed companies list a number of perennials in their catalogs (but remember that many popular perennial varieties do not come true from seed, so you will need to buy these as plants). You can also save seed from plants in your own garden, although these will often have cross-pollinated so the seedlings will not

Right:
To gather seeds from plants, such as this columbine (*Aquilegia* spp.), carefully place a small paper bag over the seed pods to catch the seeds as they fall free from the plant.

Far right:
When watering seedlings, make sure you use a watering can with a rose (spout head) to create a fine spray.

be true to variety. However, this can make it fun—some plants, such as hellebores, often interbreed with abandon, and you can produce some excellent new hybrids that will be absolutely unique.

You can sow seeds thinly by scattering them over the top of a seed flat filled with moist, lightly firmed seed-starting mix. Make sure you check individual sowing instructions because some seeds will need to be covered with a layer of the mix, while some are best left uncovered. Cover the flat with a clear propagator top and leave it in an evenly warm place out of direct sun. Alternatively, sow the seed outside in a patch of finely cultivated soil.

Plants from Seed

Below are some perennial varieties that breed true from seed—the offspring will look like their parents:

Aquilegia vulgaris 'Nora Barlow'
Aurinia saxatilis 'Gold Dust'
Campanula persicifolia 'Telham Beauty'
Coreopsis 'Sunburst'
Delphinium 'Blue Bird'
Digitalis 'Giant Primrose'
Gaillardia × *grandiflora* 'Kobold' (Goblin)
Helleborus foetidus 'Wester Flisk'
Heuchera 'Palace Purple'
Lupinus 'Chandelier'
Papaver orientale 'Royal Wedding'
Penstemon digitalis 'Husker Red'
Rudbeckia vulgida var. *sullivantii* 'Goldsturm'
Scabiosa caucasica 'Fama'

Sow in short rows, cover lightly with soil, and pat firm. Water them using a watering can with a fine spray or a hose with a fine nozzle.

Once the seedlings are growing strongly, prick them out of the seed flat into individual pots, or transplant them a few inches apart if they are being grown in the open garden. Transfer into larger pots or space further apart as they develop. Set the plants in their final growing positions in fall or spring once they are large enough.

PROPAGATING BULBS, CORMS, AND TUBERS

You can increase bulbs and corms in a number of different ways. Bulbs, such as daffodils (*Narcissus* spp.), develop smaller bulbs around their bases as they grow. You can detach these new bulbs from the parents to grow them separately as soon as they are large enough. Treat corms, such as gladiolus, in a similar way.

Some bulbs, such as lilies (*Lilium* spp.) and fritillaries (*Fritillaria* spp.), have overlapping scales. Two or three of these scales can be carefully pulled away from the outside of the bulb, making sure each scale includes some of the base. Place in a plastic bag of moist potting soil and keep in a warm place; tiny bulblets will form at the base of the scales within a few weeks and can eventually be potted individually.

Some species of lilies, including tiger lilies (*Lilium lancifolium*), produce bulbils in the leaf axils on the stems. When the bulbils ripen, you can detach them from the stem easily. Pot four bulbils in a 3½-inch (9-cm) pot, just covering their tips with sandy seed-starting mix, and they will soon produce shoots. Grow them in their pots for a year or so before potting them individually in larger pots or moving to a nursery bed outside to reach flowering size.

Dahlias are unusual because they produce tuberous roots. New growth appears on the tubers from eyes at the base of the previous year's stem. Each plant produces a cluster of roots; these can be divided into single tubers.

Store dahlia tubers over winter in a box of potting soil after cutting back the stems.

If you have several dahlias of different varieties, you should store them in separate pots. Make sure you label them.

In early spring give the dahlia tubers a drink, whether in a pot or a box. When 3- to 4-inch (7.5- to 10-cm)-high shoots appear, you can take cuttings.

Taking Cuttings

There are two main methods of taking cuttings that are used to increase herbaceous plants: stem cuttings and the less common root cuttings. A third method is by taking basal cuttings.

Unlike plants raised from seed, you can rely on plants raised from cuttings being identical to the parent plant from which they were taken. Because of this, you should always select the strongest, best-performing plants from which to take cuttings.

TAKING STEM CUTTINGS

The best time to take soft stem cuttings is in mid- to late spring, when the shoots are growing strongly and before they have started to form flower buds. Select cuttings material in the morning, when the plants are refreshed and filled with moisture. Place the stems you pick straight into a plastic bag and keep it out of the light to prevent the stems from wilting before they are prepared.

Choose strong, vigorous growth and remove a shoot tip about 3 inches (8 cm) long. You'll need to reduce the length of the stem to about 2 inches (5 cm) and remove the lower leaves. Insert several cuttings around the edge of a pot filled with moist seed-starting mix, and firm them in well.

Cover the pot with a plastic propagator top and keep in a shaded place, or cover with a sheet of newspaper until the cuttings have recovered from their initial wilting, then they can be brought out into the light (although not strong, direct sun). After a few weeks you should see signs of the shoot tips growing; once they are growing strongly, the rooted cuttings can be carefully tipped out of the pot and potted individually.

TAKING ROOT CUTTINGS

Root cuttings are less common than stem cuttings, but in many ways they are easier. They are taken in the dormant season and they don't need any special aftercare. There's

Taking a Stem Cutting

1 To take a stem cutting, either snap it cleanly at a leaf joint or cut it with a sharp knife.

2 To reduce the length of the stem, cut directly beneath a node (leaf joint) with a sharp knife or razor blade.

3 Keep potted stem cuttings moist at all times, and keep the atmosphere around the cuttings humid.

no problem with the cuttings wilting, and they don't need warmth or humidity.

Choose a period when the soil is workable and not waterlogged or frozen. Lift the plant and gently wash some soil off the roots so you can see what you are doing. If you don't want to disturb a plant by lifting it, dig down carefully and scrape away the soil on one side to expose some suitable roots for cuttings. Pick medium-size, firm, sturdy roots and cut them with a sharp knife; take only two or three from each plant to avoid weakening it. Place the roots in a plastic bag so they don't dry out, and replant the parent as soon as possible.

Cut the roots you have taken into 2-inch (5-cm) sections, trimming off any whiskery side roots first if necessary. Make a straight cut across the top of each section (the end nearest the plant's crown) and a sloping cut at the base so that you know which way up they should go, then simply push them into a pot of moist seed-starting mix until the tops are just below the soil surface. (If you forget which end is which, or the roots are thin, lay the sections horizontally instead, and lightly cover them with the mix.) Then all you need to do is put the pot in a cold frame or a sheltered place

Plants for Stem Cuttings

Almost all perennials that produce leafy stems can be propagated from stem cuttings but these are particularly successful:

Ajuga reptans
Artemisia spp.
Aster spp.
Centranthus ruber
Chrysanthemum spp.
Dahlia spp.
Delphinium spp.
Dianthus spp.
Helianthemum spp.
Iberis spp.
Origanum spp.
Phlox spp.
Salvia spp.
Sedum spp.
Tradescantia spp.

Dahlia spp.

outside, and keep it moist. Shoots will start to grow in spring, but leave the cuttings where they are until the following dormant season to be sure they have developed a good root system, then pot them individually.

BASAL CUTTINGS

In spring, when plants are producing basal shoots just a couple of inches tall, scrape a little soil away from the crown of the plant and tug away one of these shoots complete with a few roots. Pot it in the same way as a root cutting, but take a little more care to keep it moist and humid for the first few days after potting.

Basal cuttings are an easy way to propagate plants.

Plants for Root Cuttings

Take root cuttings from these plants:

Aconitum spp.
Anemone × hybrida
Anemone pulsatilla
Campanula spp.
Dicentra spectabilis
Echinacea spp.
Echinops ritro
Eryngium spp.
Papaver orientale
Phlox paniculata
Primula spp.
Verbascum spp.

Campanula spp.

greenTHUMBS

Plants with variegated foliage, such as *Phlox* 'Nora Leigh', will revert to plain green leaves if you propagate them by root cuttings. Increase these by division or stem cuttings instead.

Dividing Your Plants

Division has to be one of the easiest of all methods of propagation—it really is difficult to make a mistake. Almost all border plants can be divided, and not only does it increase your number of plants, it helps to rejuvenate your stock.

The main seasons for division are fall and spring, but you can divide plants at any time in the dormant season when the weather is suitable (not soaking wet or freezing cold). Although the majority of plants don't mind too much when they are divided, most border plants seem to prefer early spring, which allows their roots to start getting established right away. However, there are one or two spring and early summer flowering plants, such as Bearded iris hybrids, rock cress (*Arabis* spp.), and primroses (*Primula* spp.) that buck the trend. These do best when they are divided as soon as they finish flowering in early summer.

DIVIDING THE PLANTS

How you tackle division depends on the size of the plant. The first step is to dig the plant up by using a garden fork underneath it, being careful to avoid damaging the roots as much as you can. It is usually a good idea to place the plant on a sheet of plastic so that you can see what you are doing; this also helps to avoid getting the lawn covered in soil.

Small plants with fibrous roots are usually easy to divide by hand, teasing the roots apart gently. Each portion should have a good supply of roots and some healthy growth buds. As far as size is concerned, the portions should be at

method is to place two garden forks back to back through the center of the clump, and push the fork handles backward and forward to pry the clump apart. Some big, established plants are real brutes, and here you'll need to get tough. A few swift, downward blows with a well-sharpened spade will usually do the trick, but remember to keep your feet out of the way!

Old, established clumps often have a lot of weak, woody material in the center, with stronger growth around the edges. Use these vigorous outer portions for your divisions, and throw the worn-out centers onto the compost pile. Even if you don't want to increase your plants, it's worth replacing established clumps every few years; it will give the whole border a new lease on life.

least the size of your fist, or a little bigger. If they are smaller, you will need to plant them in a nursery bed to allow them to reach a healthy size before they are planted in their final positions. If the plant won't pull apart easily by hand, cut it into suitable-size sections with a sharp knife, again making sure each section has buds and roots. Slightly larger plants may need a little more brute force; try using a hand fork (or two) to persuade them into portions.

More stubborn plants, and really large specimens, can need a lot of effort to split. One

CARING FOR DIVISIONS

Get the divided portions back into the ground promptly. Make sure the soil is moist but not waterlogged, and firm them in place thoroughly with your knuckles. If they have growing shoots, keep the plants shaded from strong sun for a few days with black plastic netting or a similar material. Otherwise they are remarkably trouble-free; just treat them as you would any newly planted specimen, keeping the soil around them moist at all times.

Dividing Irises

Bearded irises have thick, fleshy rhizomes that tend to spread outward year by year, and after four or five years the center of the clump is often bare. Once all the flowers have died, in early summer, lift the shallowly rooting rhizomes with a garden fork. The swordlike leaves arise from the rhizome in fans, and each fan of leaves will make a new plant.

Cut the rhizome at each side of a strong, healthy leaf fan with a sharp knife, and then cut the fan of leaves itself back to about 4 inches (10 cm). This may seem drastic, but don't worry; it does not harm the plant and prevents it from being top heavy. Replant the new sections of rhizome shallowly, so the tops are just covered by soil, and firm them in. Make sure you keep them moist during the summer, and they will grow into strong flowering plants next spring.

Bearded iris hybrid

Thinning, Pinching, and Deadheading

Are you one of those gardeners who becomes nervous at the mere mention of pruning? Then you'll probably be relieved to learn that ever-obliging perennials require no complicated pruning techniques at all.

To thin a plant in spring, use a sharp knife, or simply snap the shoots off at ground level with your fingers.

Pinching off growing tips is simple, using your index finger and thumb.

Branching perennials that respond well to pinching include chrysanthemums (right), asters, coneflowers (*Echinacea* spp.), Joe Pye weed (*Eupatorium* spp.), bee balm (*Monarda* spp.), phlox, and sedum (*Sedum spectabile*).

Although perennials don't normally require much pruning, don't think that means your pruners can remain idle, hanging up in the shed. The appearance and performance of many perennial plants can often be greatly enhanced by just a little judicious snipping and snapping of shoots.

THINNING YOUR PLANTS

In spring, when most perennials start to come to life, they often send up a thicket of shoots. If you allow all of these to develop, the plants can become overcrowded. Stems may flop because they don't get sufficient light to strengthen them; diseases, such as mildew, are encouraged by the lack of air circulation; and flowers may be fewer and smaller. When the shoots are just a few inches high, you should thin them out to leave the strongest ones 2 to 3 inches (5 to 8 cm) apart.

PINCHING AND DISBUDDING

This is another technique for improving a plant's performance. When the shoots have reached about one-third of their final height, pinch off the growing tips. This prevents the stems from becoming too tall, and it encourages the production of sturdy, free-flowering side shoots. It is also a technique that delays flowering slightly, so you can use it on some shoots and not others to prolong the flowering season.

If you want to encourage a single, large flower at the end of a stem, remove the rest of the buds when they are tiny. They will be growing in the leaf axils down the stem and you can simply push them off with your thumb. Alternatively, you may want the opposite effect—a spray of smaller flowers instead of a single large one. In this case you should simply pinch out the terminal bud. Disbudding is most often used on chrysanthemums and dahlia, although peonies (*Paeonia* spp.) and pinks (*Dianthus* spp.) can benefit from it, too.

DEADHEADING

Removing faded flower heads not only improves the appearance of a plant, it can also help to encourage further blooms. Plants produce flowers in order to set seeds; if you remove spent flower heads before seeds have a chance to form, the plant will often carry on blooming in its effort to reproduce.

Faded flowers can be pinched off individually (peonies and dahlias, for example), or a whole spike can be removed (delphiniums and acanthus), or if the flowers are numerous and fiddly (such as alchemilla, geraniums, or coreopsis), you can trim the whole plant with pruners when the majority of the flowers are done. Plants that are regularly deadheaded may continue to produce flowers

over an extended period, or they may have a second flush of bloom later in the season.

Plants that self-seed freely often produce numerous seedlings that can swiftly become weeds. Deadheading the flowers before they set seed can save weeding later on. Columbine (*Aquilegia* spp.), Brazilian verbena (*Verbena bonariensis*), coneflowers (*Echinacea purpura*), pampas grass (*Cortaderia* spp.), and coreopsis are all candidates for early deadheading.

Plants with Decorative Seed Heads or Berries

While most plants look better when they are deadheaded, flowers that go on to produce attractive seed heads or berries can be left in place. Here is a selection to choose from:

Plant	Common Name	Description
Actaea spp.	baneberry	Clusters of glossy red or white berries are showy but they are also poisonous, so be careful to grow them safely if you have children.
Baptistia spp.	false indigo	Spikes of pealike blossoms create a casual effect above a big, branching mound of stems bearing cloverlike leaves; the seedpods will stay on the stems.
Calamagrostis × *acutiflora*	feather reed grass	Tall, elegant stems topped with fluffy pinkish plumes turn to pale gold.
Cortaderia selloana	pampas grass	Fantastic fluffy plumes tower above the plant at up to 10 feet (3 m) tall. More compact varieties, such as 'Pumila', are also available for smaller gardens.
Crocosmia 'Lucifer'	crososmia, montbretia	Branching stems carry twin rows of knobby seed capsules, which look particularly striking when silvered by frost.
Echinacea purpurea	purple coneflower	As well as being decorative, the spiky central cones that are left when the petals fall are popular with seed-eating birds.
Echinops ritro	globe thistle	The silvery blue, spiky drumsticks persist long after the blue flowers have fallen.
Eryngium spp.	sea holly	Tall spiky cones surrounded by a papery bract turn from steely blue to tan and deep brown in winter.
Iris sibirica	Siberian iris	Clumps of narrow, swordlike foliage remain attractive in winter; the flowers bloom in summer, leaving behind seedpods that are decorative in winter.
Miscanthus sinensis	miscanthus, eulalia grass	Gracefully arching, silver plumes turn to golden tan shades through fall and winter. Some varieties of this plant can be invasive.
Papaver spp.	poppy	Round, "pepperpot" seed heads are topped with a little crown and carried on erect stems.
Rudbeckia spp.	black-eyed Susan, coneflower	Spiky round cones persist through the winter, holding frost and snow.
Sedum 'Autumn Joy'	sedum, stonecrop	The flat heads of tiny pink flowers dry to rich mahogany brown in fall and winter and are especially attractive in frost.

Winter Care

Some perennials provide interest into fall, but the main flowering season is over by late summer. Besides tidying up the remnants of the summer's glory, if you live in an area with cold winters, think about helping the plants through the colder months.

At one time mid- to late fall saw plants in the perennial border receiving ruthless treatment. Virtually everything was cut back "tidily" to the ground, usually leaving a lifeless, soul-less area of almost bare soil through the winter months. Fortunately, most gardeners now plan for a more extended season of interest, and most also realize the benefits of leaving stems in place through the cold weather. The skeletons of summer stems have a beauty all their own, particularly when they are dusted with snow or heavy frost. They also provide food and shelter for wildlife, and help to protect the roots of plants that are sensitive to cold conditions.

However, some plants do need cleaning up in fall. Lush leaves and stems turn to a damp, decaying mass in wet weather, and not only does this look unattractive, it encourages disease and harbors pests, such as slugs and snails. Soft-leaved plants, such as hostas, collapse into mush at the first touch of a cold frost, so it is usually best to clear away the dying foliage before a severe frost strike.

A variety of short and tall grasses covered in frost can make a garden more interesting in the winter.

Cloches

Cloches are usually made from glass or plastic, and are either bell shaped (*cloche* is French for "bell") or shaped like tents. You can use them to protect individual plants or groups of plants by keeping off cold winds and winter rain and making the most of warmth from the sun. Remember that ventilation is necessary to allow moisture to escape, otherwise plants will tend to rot in the wet conditions.

Use your judgment to decide which plants need to be cut back to ground level and which might look good if their stems are left in place through the winter—you can always cut them down later if you are wrong. Obviously you shouldn't cut down evergreen plants or plants that flower in the winter or early spring; also leave those plants with decorative seed heads or berries (see page 105). All the debris can be put on the compost pile unless it is diseased.

ON THE TENDER SIDE

Some plants are often called "dubiously hardy." This means that they may come through an average winter with absolutely no problem—but you just can't depend on it. Dahlia, some of the exotic sages (*Salvia* spp.), penstemon, and agapanthus are among those that may or may not survive the winter outdoors, depending on where you garden. You can help them by applying a good mulch of well-rotted compost, peat moss, or a similar material over their roots (see page 91). The insulation can keep the soil temperature that vital few degrees higher. Further protection is given by dry leaves and stems piled over the growing area, heaps of straw held in place by a cage of chicken wire, or a covering of horticultural fleece. It pays to get all these in place before the temperature has dropped too much and there is still some residual summer heat left in the soil.

There are increasing numbers of truly tender perennials available, and these will not survive any degree of frost at all. They make a valuable contribution to the summer garden, but they must be taken under cover to a frost-free place to spend the winter. They include coleus (*Coleus × hybridus*), begonia, heliotrope (*Heliotropium arborescens*), and in warm areas, caladium; put them in pots and take them into a greenhouse, sunroom, or other frost-free place well before the first frost is due. They do not need a lot of heat over the winter, just to be kept safe at a few degrees above freezing.

Perennials for Winter Interest

The following plants will bring some life to what might be an otherwise boring winter garden:

Bergenia cordifolia (heartleaf bergenia): The foliage develops a burgundy or bronze color in the winter months. The cultivar 'Winterglut' (Winter Glow) has bronze-red leaves.

Calamagrostis × acutiflora 'Karl Foerster' (feather reed grass): Feathery plumes turn a tawny gold and will stand up well to winter weather.

Carex elata 'Aurea' (Bowles' golden sedge): A sedge with bright golden, grassy foliage, which should be cut back in early spring. It needs moist soil.

Epimedium × perralchicum 'Frohnleiten' (barrenwort): This popular cultivar has heart-shaped leaves tinted bronze-red in winter, with a marbling

Epimedium × perralchicum 'Frohnleiten'

of contrasting green veins. Semievergreen in cold areas.

Festuca glauca (blue fescue): Neat, tufted clumps are formed from brilliant silver-blue, grassy leaves. 'Elijah Blue' is the bluest of the fescues.

Helleborus foetidus, H. niger, H. orientalis (stinking hellebore, Christmas rose, Lenten rose): With only their attractive fingered foliage, hellebores would provide appeal for the winter garden—however, it's their flowers in shades of white, green, purple, pink, and red that make hellebores the real winner in wintertime.

Heuchera hybrids (coral bells): There are many varieties to choose from that have colorful winter foliage, including 'Winter Red', 'Chocolate Veil', 'Purple Petticoats', and 'Molly Bush'.

Miscanthus sinensis 'Strictus' (porcupine grass): Bronze plumes that eventually fade to silvery white rise above striped leaves with golden yellow bands.

Phormium tenax: (New Zealand flax): A bold, architectual shape for the winter garden. It will need a sheltered spot to stay in good condition.

A–Z Plant **Directory**

Acanthus ah-KAN-thus • acanthus, bear's-breeches

This robust plant adds dramatic character to either containers or garden beds if you have the space. Its 3- to 4-foot (90- to 120-cm) clump of magnificent shiny leaves—with each leaf 1 to 2 feet (30 to 60 cm) long—is bold enough to catch the eye from across the yard. The stout, rigid, 3- to 6-foot (1- to 1.8-m) spikes of pale, purplish white hooded flowers heighten the effect. Acanthus, from the plant family Acanthaceae, has been embraced for ages, beginning with the ancient Greeks and Romans, who used the leaves as a motif in stone carvings and pottery. A single specimen is all you'll need for an accent or focal point.

Acanthus hungaricus This is a big, tough, hardy plant that is more cold tolerant than other species. It has long, deeply lobed leaves and abundant flowers that continue into fall. It grows to 4 feet (120 cm) tall and 3 feet (90 cm) wide.

A. mollis *Mollis* means "soft," which in the case of acanthus is a matter of degree: The wide, deep green leaves of this species have fewer spines. The broad, shining leaves are a perfect complement to soft, lacy ferns. 'Hollard's Gold' is a cultivar with glossy foliage that emerges golden yellow, then softens to chartreuse as it ages.

A. spinosus On the opposite end of the spiny spectrum from *A. mollis*, this species is prickly enough to make anybody pause in his tracks. The leaves are narrower and more erect than the arching mound of other species. This species will spread quickly by underground stems, forming dense clumps.

THE BASICS

Plant acanthus in a permanent spot, away from paths or play areas, and keep in mind that this is a big plant: That little plant you bring home is going to be a major shrub-sized clump in a couple of years. Acanthus will take a year or two to become established, then it grows fast. It spreads by thick tuberous roots, which are difficult to eradicate.

Growing Conditions: Acanthus is evergreen in mild climates. The leaves die back in cold winters. The plant thrives in average well-drained garden soil; it does well in dry conditions. Wear gloves to protect

Acanthus spinosus

against spines when working with this plant. Clip off the finished flower spikes and dead leaves in late fall. Or clip the flowers when fresh and put the stems in a vase without water; they dry easily.

Propagation: Seed, root cuttings, or division in winter or early spring.

▶ **Bloom Time** Late spring to late summer

▶ **Planting Requirements** Full sun to part shade

▶ **Zones** 7 to 10; *A. hungaricus*, 6 to 9

Perfect Partners

You can combine bold acanthus with plants that don't fight for attention, but allow about 12 inches (30 cm) of space between the acanthus and its partners, so it has room to show off. Balance the size of the clump with a generous group of velvety coleus or plectranthus, all of the same kind and color. In shade the delicacy of corydalis, the lacy fronds of lady fern (*Athyrium* spp.), or the taller cinnamon fern (*Osmunda cinnamomea*) add a softening effect to macho bear's-breeches. Small-leaved ground covers, such as ajuga, are surprisingly effective, too. You can also try deep purple or blue petunias and a mass of soft, fluffy, pale blue annual ageratum with golden cultivars.

A

Achillea *ak-kill-EE-uh* • yarrow

One of the most reliable workhorses in the garden, yarrow blooms for months and thrives on neglect. It looks good with most plants, especially those with daisylike flowers, such as coneflowers (*Echinacea* spp. and *Rudbeckia* spp.) and dahlias, which contrast with yarrow's clusters of tiny flowers and soft, filigreed foliage.

With dozens of cultivars available, including some with silvery leaves and stems, you can find a plant from this member of the Asteraceae family to match any color scheme. The flowers change color as they age, paling to softer shades that provide a gentle multicolored effect. Yarrow's foliage has a pungent, slightly bitter scent, revealing its heritage as a medicinal herb. Butterflies often visit the flowers.

Achillea filipendula This species and its cultivars have better posture than other yarrows, standing upright without staking. *A. filipendula* has flat, 4-inch (10-cm)-wide heads of golden flowers. It's the parent of some popular golden cultivars, including tall 'Gold Plate', a good choice with 6-inch (15-cm) flower heads. If your

Achillea millefolium 'Cerise Queen'

garden is subject to wind, try 'Parker's Gold', which has stiff, strong stems. Most grow 3 to 5 feet (1 to 1.5 m) tall.

A. millefolium (common yarrow) This white species is found alongside many roads in North America and is at home in cottage gardens. Red, pink, and white cultivars, such as cherry red 'Cerise Queen' and deep red 'Fire King', improve on the wild version. They quickly form dense clumps 3 feet (90 cm) wide, so you'll get fast coverage from a few plants—and a bonus of babies when you divide the clump. Most are 1½ to 2 feet (45 to 60 cm) tall.

A. ptarmica A whole different look than typical yarrows: upright, with narrow leaves and open clusters of small ball-like double flowers in snow white. 'Angel's Breath', shorter 'Ballerina', and 'The Pearl' look more like open, airy baby's-breath than the usual flat-headed clusters of yarrow.

A. tomentosa (woolly yarrow) This yarrow has a ground-hugging habit that makes it ideal for a fast-growing ground cover, especially in dry gardens. It's perfect in rock gardens or along sidewalks, which give it extra heat. In summer, it is covered with flat heads of yellow flowers on 6- to 10-inch (15- to 25-cm) stems. For a change of pace, try bright yellow 'Maynard's Gold'. Shear off any faded flowers to keep the mat of woolly silver foliage looking good.

THE BASICS

Yarrow is easy to grow, but too much kindness can kill it. Keep it on the lean side, and it will reward you with abundant flowers and butterflies.

Achillea millefolium

Growing Conditions: Yarrow is at its prime in poor soils. Give it average-to-dry garden soil, and avoid fertilizer. Rich soil will make it floppy, so it will require staking. Summer storms may cause flowering stems to keel over; avoid this by placing a grow-through wire grid support over the plant in spring. For more compact plants cut back by one-third after the first flush of flowers. Older plants may die out in the center; divide and replant the more vigorous outer parts of the clump. Too much humidity in summer can cause mildew; cut the plant back to the ground, and it will quickly regrow. Grows well in sand and in seaside gardens. Those with woolly foliage do not do well in humid summer areas. Silver-foliage varieties are drought tolerant and flourish in xeric gardens.

Propagation: Spreads by fibrous roots; propagate by division. Or take cuttings of stem tips, before buds form, and root in moist soil. May self-sow.

▶ **Bloom Time** Summer through fall; snip off faded blooms to keep fresh flowers coming

▶ **Planting Requirements** Full sun

▶ **Zones** 3 to 9

Glowing Achilleas

Until recently, yarrows were grandma's garden plants, a handful of background characters that were passed along by friends and neighbors. Then along came a riveting group of hybrids from Germany in warm shades of orange, salmon, brick red, and terra-cotta, plus a palette of pinks. That was enough to bring yarrows back to center stage, and with a constant parade of new cultivars, they haven't left. These mouthwatering colors are hybrids that take advantage of the strengths of more than one species to add great color, vigor, and improved form. Most are 1½ to 2 feet (45 to 60 cm) tall.

◀ *A.* **'Marmalade'**
Another beauty for the warm-colored garden, this deep golden orange cultivar gleams like a sunlit jar of marmalade.

▲ *A.* **'Coronation Gold'**
Although not a German hybrid, we couldn't resist including this outstanding variety. It puts on a superb show, with large clusters of golden flowers above deep green foliage. It's taller than the German hybrids, reaching 3 feet (90 cm). Clip fresh flowers and dry for everlasting bouquets.

▶ *A.* **'Paprika'**
Add a little spice with deep orange-red 'Paprika' yarrow, a modern cultivar that mellows to pale salmon pink as the blossoms age, giving the entire plant a soft multicolored effect as fresh flower heads emerge among older blooms. Contrast with sulfur yellow or blue to blue-purple perennials, or you can increase the heat by combining it with vivid dahlias.

▼ *A.* **'Walther Funcke'**
These warm copper-colored flowers soften to a pastel shade of salmon pink.

▲ *A.* **'Moonshine'**
Sulfur yellow flowers and silver foliage. Humid summers are not kind to the foliage; try a cultivar with green leaves instead.

▶ *A.* **'Feuerland' (Fireland)**
Fire-engine red is just the beginning: The flowers turn to toasty orange and apricot, and finally to gold, like a warm fire.

113

❧ Aconitum *ah-koe-NY-tum* • monkshood, wolfsbane

Aconitum napellus

Rich, deep blue is a rare color in perennials, and this tall, handsome plant, with its generous display of branching spires, is one of the best at supplying it. With a little imagination the unusual flowers resemble a lineup of monks with cowls thrown over their heads. Monkshood, from the Ranunculaceae family, looks similar to delphinium at first glance, but it is a tougher plant. It's a strong, sturdy perennial that can live for decades. Because this perennial waits until late in the season to bloom, it is not as well known as many other plants in the garden.

Aconitum × cammarum (bicolor monkshood) Many cultivars spring from this hybrid, a dependable performer that may bloom blue, blue-violet, pink, or white. This stalwart plant can reach 3 to 4 feet (90 to 120 cm) tall and up to 2 feet (60 cm) wide and has lobed leaves. Although staking is necessary for most tall monkshoods, the deep blue cultivar 'Bressingham Spire' has rigid stems that top out at 3 feet (90 cm), so it can stand alone. The cultivar 'Stainless Steel' is tinged with gray, from the glossy leaves to the smoky, steel blue stems. The flowers are pale violet-blue, almost whitish from a distance, with a silver sheen.

A. carmichaelii (azure monkshood) These flowers are a lighter blue than most monkshoods. The lobed leaves show the relation of monkshoods to their cousins, the buttercups. The foliage of this species has a leathery look and feel. 'Arendsii' is a deservedly popular cultivar with masses of abundant blue-violet flowers on 3½-foot (105-cm) stems. It blooms for months, from July to October.

A. lycoctonum 'Ivorine' This short, white-blooming plant is a cultivar of the yellow-flowered species, which blooms from a basal rosette of leaves weeks earlier than other types. It grows 1 to 3 feet (30 to 90 cm) tall.

A. napellus This old-fashioned favorite has been superseded by *A. × cammarum*, but it is still worth a place in the garden. Its branching spikes of blue-purple flowers can reach up to 4 feet (120 cm) tall. The variety 'Rubellum' has pink flowers.

THE BASICS

Monkshood is sturdy and tough, and makes for a long-lived member of the garden. Its dramatic color is rare, and it will even bloom in shade. It takes a few years to form a large clump.

Perfect Partners

In a sunny garden monkshood's beautiful hues of blue and blue-purple are gorgeous behind a spill of pale blue asters and a fireworks display of goldenrod. Add textural appeal to the group with the airy sprays of switchgrass flowers (*Panicum* spp.). The cheerful yellow daisies of heliopsis and rock rose (*Helianthemum* spp.), and the russet tones of helenium, are other late-blooming options, with dahlias for a punch of bright color. In shadier spots you can brighten that blue with white or pink Japanese anemones (*Anemone × hybrida*).

Monkshood contains the toxic alkaloid aconitine, so wear gloves when handling this plant and do not touch your skin, mouth, or eyes. Do not eat any part of it, and plant it in the back of the garden, where it won't be a temptation to others, especially children. By taking these sensible precautions, you can enjoy its dependable beauty for years.

Growing Conditions: Select a permanent place where the plant can grow into its full glory undisturbed. It flourishes in fertile, moist soil. Make sure you are careful when handling the roots because they are brittle. Plant them just below the surface of the soil. Space plants about 2 feet (60 cm) apart for a bigger display. Fertilize yearly. Stake taller varieties to keep the dramatic branching spires upright.

Propagation: Divide the roots when the plant is dormant.

▶ **Bloom Time** Late summer through fall
▶ **Planting Requirements** Full sun to part shade in cool climates; afternoon shade in warmer regions
▶ **Zones** 3 to 8; *A. lycoctonum*, 4 to 8

Actaea *ak-TEE-uh* • baneberry

Baneberries add a decorator's touch to a shady garden. The stout, bushy plants from the Ranunculaceae family have showy, white spring-blooming flowers, which form a fuzzy globe or cylinder. The sprays of red or white berries make baneberry a real showpiece.

Actaea pachypoda (white baneberry, white cohosh, doll's eyes) The cluster of ivory white berries, each marked by a dot to make the "doll's eye," gleam in the shade. Berries are held on red stems.

A. rubra (red baneberry) This species has bigger, bright red berries that create an eye-catching display. The berries are held at the tips of the stems, emerging at the leaf axils. The heavy berries can bend the stems.

THE BASICS

Baneberries grow fast to form a leafy clump 2 feet (60 cm) tall and wide. Use them as a background plant or as an accent among other shady flowers, such as hepatica, and to add textural contrast to ferns and hostas. These species are attractive into fall. Baneberries are toxic if eaten. Make sure children don't sample the berries.

Growing Conditions: Plant in moist, humus-rich soil, and supply regular water. Set the roots just below the surface of the soil.

Actaea rubra

Propagation: Carefully divide the fleshy roots in early spring.

▶ **Bloom Time** Blooms in spring; berries mature in summer to late summer
▶ **Planting Requirements** Part to full shade
▶ **Zones** 4 to 8

Adenophora *ah-den-OFF-for-uh* • adenophora, ladybells

Adenophora can be tricky to track down at nurseries, but this member of the Campanulaceae family is worth the hunt. Its rich, amethyst blue color and bell-shaped flowers make it look like a campanula, but this plant blooms longer, lives longer, and adapts to adverse conditions better than most campanulas. In a casual garden its spreading roots can weave their way among other perennials, pausing to raise pretty spires of purple bells. Or grow it in a large mass, as you would grow bee balm (*Monarda* spp.) or other enthusiastic spreaders. The soft hue of the long-blooming flowers combines easily with warm or cool pastels or with hot colors.

Adenophora confusa Whether you call it blue or purple, the signature color of ladybells is welcome in the garden, where it lasts for months. This is the most common species. Its spires stretch to 2½ feet (75 cm) tall.

A. liliifolia This hard-to-find species is a shorter version, to 1½ feet (45 cm), with paler flowers.

THE BASICS

Adenophora is simple to grow and spreads gratifyingly fast to give you more purple bells. The longevity of this perennial is legendary. Colonies of plants still persist around old homesteads abandoned 50 years ago. It's easy to keep in boundaries if you prefer; just pull up any strays by hand.

Growing Conditions: Average-to-rich garden soil, with regular to moderate water, are all you need to

Adenophora liliifolia

grow ladybells. It adapts to clay soils but won't tolerate sogginess.

Propagation: Use a trowel or your hands to divide pieces for replanting.

▶ **Bloom Time** Early to late summer
▶ **Planting Requirements** Full sun to light shade
▶ **Zones** 3 to 8

Adiantum *ay-dee-AN-tum* • maidenhair fern

The maidenhair fern, *Adiantum pedatum,* and its relative *A. aleuticum,* produce a circlet of delicate fronds that looks like a cascade of long, wavy hair. These deciduous ferns from the Adiantaceae family are instantly recognizable. The tall, dark, wiry stems are crowned by an 8- to 10-inch (20- to 25-cm) horseshoe-shaped fan of lacy fronds held horizontally. The fragile appearance of these beauties belies their hardy character. In a garden they'll live for many years, expanding by creeping rootstocks into a graceful colony.

Adiantum aleuticum (western maidenhair fern) This species is native to the West, as far north as Alaska. Similar to *A. pedatum,* it is usually tucked into rocky crevices near

waterfalls or where water spills down the rock. It thrives in acid soil and also grows well in serpentine soil.

A. capillus-veneris (Venus maidenhair fern) It forms a cascade of lacy, drooping fronds of delicate leaflets and is often sold as a small potted houseplant. It is less cold hardy than other species; Zones 7 to 10.

A. pedatum (common maidenhair fern, northern maidenhair fern, five-finger fern) The classic maidenhair, this is an outstanding plant, with shiny black stems 16 inches (40 cm) tall and a large circlet of fronds held almost horizontally on each stem. It spreads moderately quickly in moist, rich soil but is never a pest. The cultivar 'Miss Sharples' (golden maidenhair fern) has large chartreuse leaflets that will bring a glow to shady nooks. It is beautiful planted with red- or pink-flowered heucheras.

A. venustum (Himalayan maidenhair fern) It forms a small waterfall of overlapping triangular fronds, as delicate as any in this genus. Pair this 4- to 8-inch (10- to 20-cm) fern with woodland wildflowers, such as Virginia bluebells *(Mertensia virginica).* Hardy in Zones 4 to 8.

THE BASICS

Maidenhair ferns are native across almost the entire United States, which shows how adaptable they can be. In the wild they're often found springing out of a rocky crevice near a waterfall or in shaded ravines, yet they are easy to grow in moist garden soil.

Growing Conditions: Maidenhair ferns prefer moist soil, but they will do

Adiantum pedatum

well in average garden conditions. In fertile, humus-rich soil, the creeping rootstocks spread more quickly. They are drought tolerant once established. In areas with dry summers, the ferns go dormant in summer, then send up fresh fronds when rain returns. In cold-winter regions, the fronds die back in fall, then emerge anew in spring. They are perfect around waterfalls or garden pools but avoid constantly soggy sites.

Propagation: Divide established plants in spring, before new fronds emerge. Slice deep with a small spade to be sure of getting both creeping rootstocks and fibrous roots below.

▶ **Bloom Time** Foliage is green from spring to fall in cold regions; winter through late summer in dry-summer areas

▶ **Planting Requirements** Light to full shade; also locations with morning sun and afternoon shade

▶ **Zones** 3 to 8 unless otherwise noted

Perfect Partners

The delicate grace of maidenhair ferns is an ideal contrast to plants of simpler or bolder leaf form. For strong contrast, try hostas (*Hosta* spp.) or the substantial foliage of hellebores (*Helleborus* spp.). The lovely foliage of lady's mantle (*Alchemilla* spp.) or neat clumps of coral bells (*Heuchera* spp.) or foam-flower (*Tiarella* spp.) give a softer look. Near water, the pointed spears of Japanese, Siberian, or Louisiana iris (*Iris ensata, I. sibirica,* Louisiana iris hybrids) are pleasing partners. Planted among rocks along a pool or tucked into niches along a man-made waterfall, maidenhair ferns soften the scene.

A

Agapanthus

ag-uh-PAN-thus • agapanthus, African lily, lily of the Nile

Stunning blue-flowered agapanthus from the Alliaceae (Amaryllidaceae) family are South African natives. Today agapanthus is often grown in mild-winter areas of the United States. Long-blooming flower heads are usually the size of softballs, but they can reach immense size in some cultivars. Use it as a dramatic accent in the garden or in containers. Flowers are sky blue to rich blue-purple or white, depending on the cultivar.

Agapanthus africanus (African lily) A big, tough, beautiful plant, it reaches 3 to 5 feet (90 to 150 cm) tall and wide. Substantial strappy leaves make the plant more emphatic. It is usually deciduous. 'Alba' has white flowers.

A. orientalis (lily of the Nile) This species is nearly as tall as *A. africanus* but narrower in form, about 2 feet (60 cm) wide. It is usually evergreen in mild climates and relatively cold hardy; worth a try in Zone 7. Many

Agapanthus cv.

popular cultivars are downsized plants that don't demand as much space. Try dwarf cultivars as a ground cover. The 'Headbourne' hybrids are smaller than the species. They form a leafy clump to 2½ feet tall (75 cm) with mostly dark violet-blue flowers. These are vigorous plants and may live in Zone 7 gardens if deeply mulched over winter. The cultivar 'Peter Pan' forms a small, leafy evergreen clump that can reach 12 inches (30 cm) high; the blue flowers rise to 18 inches (45 cm). 'Tinkerbell' is a cultivar that has variegated leaves striped with white; blue flowers are held above the foliage.

A. 'Blue Globe' Dark blue 5-inch (12.5-cm) flower heads form on 3-foot (90-cm) stems. You can use several plants to create a calming effect in a hot-colored garden.

A. 'Blue Heaven' This dark blue cultivar grows 1 to 2 feet (30 to 60 cm) tall and is cold tolerant in Zones 7 to 10; it may survive even in Zone 6 if mulched deeply over winter.

A. 'Blue Triumphator' Here is an old reliable with soft violet-blue flowers and delicate, darker stripes.

A. 'Elaine' Huge 8-inch (20-cm) globes of blue-violet flowers form on stems up to 4 feet (120 cm) tall. This fast-growing plant is evergreen in mild climates. Plant with silvery foliage plants, such as artemisia and lamb's ears *(Stachys byzantina)*.

A. 'Getty White' It forms a clump of foliage 2 feet (60 cm) tall, with white flower stems to 4 feet (120 cm).

A. 'Storm Cloud' Magnificent bluish purple, double flower heads form on sturdy 6-foot (1.8-m) stems.

Agapanthus orientalis

A. 'White Heaven' The 10-inch (25-cm) pure white flower heads may be the biggest in this genus. Flowering stems grow to 2½ feet (75 cm).

THE BASICS

In California, Florida, and other areas with mild winters, agapanthus is easy to grow. In colder climates growth is slower and the plant may be smaller, with shorter flower stems. Good drainage is a must. Agapanthus takes a few years to reach full size.

Growing Conditions: It grows in moist, fertile soil but also tolerates drought well once established. Water new plants about every 10 days when weather is dry. Agapanthus leaves serve as hiding places for slugs and snails; they don't trouble this plant but will come out to forage on other perennials. Place slug traps or other deterrents nearby to control.

Propagation: Divide large, well-established clumps in early spring.

▌ **Bloom Time** Early summer to early fall
▌ **Planting Requirements** Part to full sun
▌ **Zones** 8 to 11 unless otherwise noted

A

Agastache
ay-guh-STAY-key • agastache, anise hyssop, hummingbird mint

Spotlight this pretty perennial by planting it near the front of a bed or in a container, where you can enjoy its fragrance as you admire the butterflies, hummingbirds, and bumblebees it attracts. The tubular blossoms are held above the foliage in a narrow, blunt-tipped spike. Easy-to-grow agastache is from the Labiatae family and comes in warm sunset colors and cool blue-purple. The flowers are long-blooming, but the plants can be short-lived.

***Agastache aurantiaca* 'Apricot Sunrise'** A variable type, but it has beautiful hues of soft orange flowers. Its parent is a Southwest native, but this proficient bloomer thrives in midwestern and southeastern gardens, as well as in the West. It grows up to 2½ feet (75 cm) tall and 1½ feet (45 cm) wide and is suitable for Zones 6 to 10.

A. cana (Texas hummingbird mint) The large, curving spikes of raspberry-colored flowers are spaced just right for hummingbirds. It reaches 3 feet (90 cm) tall and blooms last into fall. Hardy in Zones 5 to 9.

Perfect Partners

Try a complementary color of yarrow (*Achillea* spp.) for an easy-care companion. Let warm-colored agastaches show off with silver or gray partners, including lavenders (*Lavandula* spp.), or pair them with flowers in similar hues but with different shapes, such as butterflyweed (*Asclepias tuberosa*), geum, or red-hot poker (*Kniphofia* spp.) Blue-flowered varieties will cool down bright dahlias or crocosmia.

A. foeniculum (anise hyssop) This upright 1- to 3-foot (30- to 90-cm) clump of scented foliage is topped by spikes of densely packed, small blue-violet flowers on stiffly upright stems. Crush and sniff a leaf for a licorice aroma, or snip a few flowering stems for a scented bouquet. The species self-sows and is cold hardy in Zones 3 to 8. The cultivar 'Golden Jubilee' has golden green foliage with compact lavender-blue flower spikes. It is hardy in Zones 6 to 10; with deep winter mulch, it may survive to Zone 4. The flowers of the species vary in color from dark to paler blues, but 'Licorice Blue' is a blue-lavender cultivar. 'Licorice White' has creamy white flowers and grows in Zones 3 to 8.

A. rupestris One of the parents of many warm-colored hybrids, this Southwest native grows 2 to 4 feet (60 to 120 cm) tall and has lovely bicolored flowers in a melange of rosy pink and orange. The plant has a more relaxed attitude than *A. foeniculum,* with a more open form and gracefully bending stems. The gray-green foliage is covered with a soft nap to help it withstand water loss during hot, dry summers. Reliable in Zones 5 to 8.

A. 'Black Adder' You can't get much darker than these deep twilight-blue flowers, making them the perfect punctuation for sunny goldenrods (*Solidago* spp.) and asters (*Aster* spp.) in fall. Hardy in Zones 6 to 9.

A. 'Blue Fortune' This hybrid has dramatic, deep blue-violet flowers held in branching candelabra spikes. It is tall and robust, with flowering stems reaching to 3 feet (90 cm).

Agastache 'Globetrotter'

A. 'Desert Sunrise' The prolific, multicolored blossoms in shades of pink, lavender, and orange create a rosy pink effect in any garden from midsummer well into fall. It is highly adaptable in Zones 5 to 10.

A. 'Globetrotter' Lavender with a hint of pink, it grows 2 to 3 feet (60 to 90 cm) tall in Zones 7 to 9.

THE BASICS

All you need is well-drained soil to grow adaptable agastache. Many flourish in xeric gardens as well as gardens with regular water. Warm-colored species and cultivars are generally more drought tolerant. Cold-hardiness varies.

Growing Conditions: Plant in average, well-drained soil. Clip the plants back once or twice a season if you want them to be compact.

Propagation: Cuttings will give quick results. The species and 'Golden Jubilee' are easy to grow from seed.

▶ **Bloom Time** Midsummer through fall
▶ **Planting Requirements** Full sun to part shade
▶ **Zones** Hardiness varies; choose one that's suited for your zone

Ajuga
ah-JOO-ga • ajuga, bugleweed, carpet bugle

Ajuga spreads quickly to form a solid mat of ground-hugging, evergreen foliage in sun or shade. The glossy, dark green or bronze leaves from this member of the Lamiaceae family are pretty, and the display of clear blue flower spikes in spring is a bonus.

***Ajuga pyramidalis* 'Metallica Crispa'** This cultivar has dense, deep bronze foliage crinkled like a prune, with spikes of blue flowers in spring.

A. reptans (common bugleweed) Plant this tough ground cover beneath shrubs or in places too shady for lawn grass. It quickly spreads up to 3 feet (90 cm) across. The foliage often turns ruddy bronze in winter. 'Bronze Beauty' has short blue flower spikes, and its bronze leaves keep their color. 'Burgundy Glow' is not as vigorous as the species, but the leaves are splashed with pink, green, and white. 'Catlin's Giant' is a large cultivar, with 12-inch (30-cm)-tall blue flower spikes. 'Purple Torch' has striking 12-inch (30-cm)-tall pinkish lavender flower spikes.

THE BASICS

Young plants will cover the ground quickly. Weeds cannot compete with ajuga's thick overlapping foliage.

Growing Conditions: Plant in well-drained soil, with 12 inches (30 cm) between plants. Water regularly until established. Dense foliage can impede air circulation, causing crown rot. If this happens, clip off dead or withered leaves at the crown; apply a fungicide.

Propagation: Use a trowel to take divisions for transplanting.

Ajuga reptans 'Catlin's Giant'

- **Bloom Time** Early to late spring
- **Planting Requirements** Sun to shade
- **Zones** 3 to 9

Alcea
al-SEE-uh • hollyhock

Old-fashioned hollyhocks have tall spikes of flowers that add height to gardens. Years ago, single hollyhocks were the rule, but today double types abound. Hollyhocks, members of the Malvaceae family, are long-blooming, but they live only a few years and are often classed as biennials.

Alcea ficifolia (Antwerp hollyhock) This species has deeply lobed leaves. It grows 6 feet (1.8 m) tall, in a clump 3 feet (90 cm) wide. Flowers come in warm shades, from clear yellow to golden orange.

A. rosea (common hollyhock, hollyhock) The cultivar 'Crème de Cassis' has pinkish maroon flowers that fade to a whitish edge; it often blooms the first year from seed. 'Nigra' has deep red flowers. Both have single flowers, as does 'Old Barnyard Mix'. 'Chater's Double' and 'Powder Puffs' have a charming color mix of yellow, red, pink, apricot, rose, and white.

A. rugosa (yellow hollyhock) A group of these soft yellow plants is a superb backdrop. It is rust resistant and is cold hardy in Zones 4 to 8.

THE BASICS

Hollyhocks are easy to start from seed and easy to grow. They form a huge clump, so give them breathing room.

Growing Conditions: Plant in well-drained, average-to-fertile soil. Water regularly in the first year if planting in sandy or dry conditions. Watch out for spider mites, rust, and

Alcea rugosa

anthracnose, as well as the caterpillars of painted lady butterflies.

Propagation: Seed sown in spring or late summer. It takes two years from seed to see a flower.

- **Bloom Time** Summer through early fall
- **Planting Requirements** Full sun
- **Zones** 3 to 8

Alchemilla *al-kuh-MILL-uh* • lady's mantle

It's hard to resist touching the oh-so-soft leaves of lady's mantle, especially when beads of water spangle the surface like droplets on a lady's velvet cape (or mantle). And the sharply pleated fan of newly emerged leaves will invite a careful inspection. This is a superb foliage plant from the Rosaceae family, but it also boasts generous, fine-textured sprays of tiny, greenish yellow flowers. Use it for an accent, flank a garden bench, line a path or wall, or let it billow forth from a cobalt-blue pot on your front step. It's elegant wherever it finds a home.

Alchemilla alpina (mountain lady's mantle) More than 300 species of lady's mantle grow wild around the world, but only a few have made it to the nursery. This one is a diminutive species that's popular with rock gardeners because of its small scale. The clump grows to about 8 inches (20 cm) high and 10 inches (25 cm) wide. The leaves are gray below, green above, and more deeply lobed than those of more familiar *A. mollis.* It is not good in areas with hot, steamy summers. Plant in Zones 3 to 7; to Zone 8 in the Pacific Northwest.

A. erythropoda (red-stemmed lady's mantle) Lady's mantle hardly needs more embellishment, but rock gardeners and plant aficionados appreciate the red leaf stems of this smaller species, which grows to about 8 inches (20 cm) tall and 12 inches (30 cm) wide. Try it in a pot raised on a pedestal, where you can see the details. Flower clusters are more restrained than *A. mollis,* and the small leaves are gray-green.

A. mollis (lady's mantle) This perennial lives up to every word of praise given to it. Its beauty is legendary, but it's also a hearty, trouble-free plant. It slowly expands by creeping roots into an enticing clump. Be sure to admire it after rain, when the foliage is dotted with water drops that shine like silver beads.

THE BASICS

Lady's mantle is tougher than it looks. It's easy to grow in most areas except the steamy South, where fungal problems may attack the foliage. If summers are hot in your region, plant it in shade, where it's sheltered from the full brunt of afternoon sun. Snip

Alchemilla mollis

a few flowering stems when they first open to use in dried bouquets.

Growing Conditions: Alchemilla is best in moist, humus-rich, well-drained soil, with regular water. If you notice the leaves wilting, give the plant a good drink of water; it will probably perk right up. Clip off flowering stems when finished for another round of bloom. If leaves begin to look shabby, cut the entire plant to ground level; it will rapidly regrow. For a grand display plant *A. mollis* in groups of three, spaced 2 feet (60 cm) apart, so that they soon form a solid mass.

Propagation: Division in early spring, before leaves unfold.

▶ **Bloom Time** Summer; may rebloom
▶ **Planting Requirements** Sun to shade; plant where there is afternoon shade in hot-summer areas
▶ **Zones** *A. mollis,* 4 to 8; *A. alpina* and *A. erythropoda,* 3 to 7

Perfect Partners

Blue or blue-purple flowers, such as those of campanulas, columbines (*Aquilegia caerulea* and other spp.), and hardy geraniums (*Geranium* 'Johnson's Blue' and other cvs.), look great with the chartreuse sprays of lady's mantle. Contrast the softness of lady's mantle with the upright form of Siberian iris (*Iris sibirica*), bearded iris (*Iris* × *germanica*), or perennial salvias, including 'Mainacht' and 'Caradonna'. The velvety foliage and fine-textured flowers work well against bricks, walls, or rocks. In shady nooks combine it with hostas, ferns, and other foliage plants. In sunny spots lady's mantle increases the romance of roses, such as 'New Dawn', a fragrant blush pink climber.

Allium *AL-lee-um* • allium, ornamental onion

Who would ever think that onions have so much to offer the garden? These ornamental onions from the Alliaceae (Amaryllidaceae) family are a big notch above those bulbs in your vegetable patch. They come in all sizes and characters, from dainty and diminutive to robust, shoulder-high giants, and they bloom in starbursts of yellow, white, purple, pink, or blue. Those with tiny flowers tightly compressed into a large round head are known as globe alliums.

Many allium bulbs have been around long enough to be called heirloom garden plants, but their popularity waxes and wanes. Maybe it's because they're often sold in fall, when our thoughts are preoccupied with daffodils and tulips. You'll find scores of alliums for sale; this is just a sampling to whet your appetite. Many members of this genus have a faint scent of onion. Appreciate them in the garden, though, not on that burger! The sweet-smelling blossoms are popular with butterflies.

Allium 'Globemaster'

Allium aflatunense 'Purple Sensation' This is a globe allium, with tiny purple flowers in a baseball-sized head atop a 1½- to 2½-foot (45- to 75-cm)-tall stem. Grow it with euphorbias and pale pink roses. It is hardy in Zones 3 to 8.

A. atropurpureum This globe allium has dark purple, almost black, flower heads the size of a tennis ball. Hardy in Zones 4 to 7.

A. caeruleum (blue allium) A small species, its round, quarter-sized heads of clear flax-blue flowers are held on 12- to 18-inch (30- to 45-cm)-tall stems. It naturalizes well in lawn or garden; hardy in Zones 4 to 7.

A. christophii Large, starry, silvery purple flowers are supported on 12- to 20-inch (30- to 50-cm)-tall stems. Hardy in Zones 3 to 8.

A. flavum This species has drooping, lemon yellow flowers on stems 10 to 12 inches (25 to 30 cm) tall. It is suitable for growing in Zones 4 to 8. *A. moly* is similar but has golden yellow flowers.

A. giganteum The round, softball-sized, lilac purple flower heads appear on stems that reach 4 feet (1.2 m). Hardy in Zones 4 to 8.

A. karataviense The smaller, golfball-size pale lilac flowers are held 8 to 10 inches (20 to 25 cm) above broad leaves; these have a grayish cast and often reddish margins. Hardy in Zones 4 to 9.

A. pulchellum This more casual species has a loose, quarter-sized cluster of dangling, reddish purple flowers on 2-foot (60-cm)-tall stems. 'Album' is white. Hardy in Zones 4 to 8.

Allium aflatunense 'Purple Sensation'

A. **'Globemaster'** The silvery, pinkish purple flower heads of this vigorous hybrid can become almost as big as a volleyball. Flowers produce secondary blooms that extend the flowering period. The plant grows 2½ to 3 feet (75 to 90 cm) tall. Hardy in Zones 4 to 8.

THE BASICS

Buy bulbs in early fall, when selection is at its peak. Like many other bulbs, alliums go dormant when they're done blooming. Plant them where other perennials, such as hardy geraniums or dianthus, can disguise the ripening foliage. Alliums look best in groups. Space the bulbs according to size: For giant alliums, plant 1 bulb per square foot (30 cm sq); large alliums, 5 per square foot (30 cm sq); small species, 10 per square foot (30 cm sq).

Growing Conditions: Plant in average-to-fertile, well-drained soil.

Propagation: Most are easy to grow from seed; small species often self-sow.

▶ **Bloom Time** Spring through late summer, depending on species

▶ **Planting Requirements** Full sun

▶ **Zones** 3 to 9; varies according to species

Anemone *uh-NEM-o-nee* • anemone, windflower

Elegant, yet diverse, anemones from the Ranunculaceae family glow in the garden. Wildflower types grow close to the ground in a shady garden. Larger species offer flowers like a wild rose.

Anemone blanda (Grecian windflower) Blue starry flowers are borne on 6-inch (15-cm)-tall stems. Plant them beneath trees in Zones 4 to 8, or plant in drifts in fall. 'Charmer' and 'Pink Star' are pink.

A. coronaria (poppy anemone) The large, showy flower has colors of blue, purple, mauve, white, and scarlet. Plant in fall in Zones 7 to 10. Plant in spring in Zones 3 to 6.

A. hupehensis A late summer to early fall bloomer, rose-pink or white flowers are held on 2½- to 3-feet (75- to 90-cm)-tall stems; grow in Zones 5 to 8.

A.* × *hybrida (Japanese anemone) Add color to the late-season garden with this fall bloomer; flowers rise on stems 3 to 4 feet (90 to 120 cm) tall. 'Honorine Jobert' has pure white flowers. Hardy in Zones 5 to 8.

A. nemorosa (wood anemone) This plant is up to 10 inches (25 cm) tall with white blooms. Hardy in Zones 4 to 8.

THE BASICS

Treat *A.* × *hybrida* and *A. hupehensis* like any hardy perennial. *A. nemorosa* will take a few years to get established.

Growing Conditions: Plant in well-drained, humus-rich, fertile soil.

Anemone nemorosa

Propagation: Divide *A.* × *hybrida* and *A. hupehensis* in spring.

▶ **Bloom Time** Spring, summer, or fall, depending on species
▶ **Planting Requirements** Sun to shade
▶ **Zones** 4 to 8, depending on species

Anthemis *AN-them-is* • golden marguerite, marguerite

These big plants are smothered all summer in small, buttery yellow daisies. However, golden marguerite, from the Asteraceae family, tends to sprawl unless you stake it or clip it back to keep it compact. Left to its own devices, it will spill among other plants. It's best for casual gardens.

Anthemis tinctoria The abundant butter yellow daisies with button centers bloom for several weeks. The clump can reach 3 feet (90 cm) tall and wide in fertile soil—until it falls over. 'E. C. Buxton' is a shorter cultivar, 2 to 2½ feet (60 to 75 cm), with bountiful pale yellow daisies. 'Kelwayi' has more profuse flowers than the species, with wider petals. 'Sauce Hollandaise' forms a compact mound, to 2 feet (60 cm) tall, cloaked in ivory daisies with yellow centers.

THE BASICS

One of the most floriferous perennials, marguerites are easy to grow.

Growing Conditions: To fend off floppiness, plant in lean-to-average garden soil and do not fertilize. Cut back by one-third when stems reach 12 inches (30 cm) tall to encourage branching and a compact form; cut back again by one-third after flowering. Or stake in early spring, using a grow-through grid that will help the branching stems stand up. Water every 7 to 10 days when rain is scarce. After a few years, plants may become leggy and bare at the bottom;

Anthemis tinctoria 'E. C. Buxton'

slice back to near ground level in early spring to reinvigorate the clump.

Propagation: Cuttings root in two weeks. Or divide clumps in early spring.

▶ **Bloom Time** Summer to fall
▶ **Planting Requirements** Full sun
▶ **Zones** 3 to 8

A

Aquilegia *ack-wi-LEE-gee-uh* • columbine

Columbines are a garden must. These outstanding plants, which are members of the Ranunculaceae family, put on a show of dainty, dancing flowers that you'll look forward to every spring. The unusual shape of the blossoms, with long spurs extending from the petals, will attract hummingbirds. Their clump of rounded leaflets makes columbines superb partners for most perennials of mounding or vertical form. All of the varied species and cultivars are easy to grow. Columbines of mixed parentage exhibit an immense diversity of color and form, proving that it's hard to go wrong with these plants.

Aquilegia alpina (alpine columbine) A columbine from the Swiss Alps, it is at home in American gardens. A bouquet of lovely blue flowers appears on 1- to 2-foot (30- to 60-cm) stems. Hardy in Zones 3 to 8.

A. caerulea (Rocky Mountain columbine) Enjoy one of the Rockies' most beautiful wildflowers with these long-spurred 2-inch (5-cm) blue flowers with a refreshing white center. Hardy in Zones 3 to 8.

A. canadensis (wild columbine) This grand plant bears long-spurred red-and-yellow blossoms on graceful, 2- to 3-foot (60- to 90-cm) stems in either sun or shade. *A. formosa* is similar but a little taller. Both are hardy in Zones 3 to 8.

A. chrysantha (golden columbine) Although a southwestern native, it adapts to other climates, too. The large yellow flowers reach 3 inches (7.5 cm) across, and the plant is taller and looser. A 4-foot (120-cm) plant in full bloom is quite a sight. 'Swallowtail' has spectacular, 4-inch (10-cm)-long curving spurs. Hardy in Zones 4 to 8.

A. flabellata (fan columbine) A plant of compact habit, it has blue-green fans of leaves. Stems of blue-to-lilac flowers with hooked spurs reach 1½ feet (45 cm). 'Mini-Star' is an 8-inch (20-cm) blue-and-white dwarf.

A. vulgaris (Granny's bonnet) This species has been livening up gardens for years. There's plenty of variation in the color, the shape of the flower and spurs, and the height of the plants. Flowers may be fluffy double forms, such as crimson 'Nora Barlow'; 'Black Barlow' is purple-black. 'Variegata' has golden-marbled leaves and blue flowers.

A. 'Crimson Star' One of the Star series, this is a ruby-red version with a yellow center.

A. 'Fairyland Mix' Short-spurred flowers face upright above a dwarf clump of tidy foliage.

A. McKana hybrids Popular since the 1950s, these large-flowered hybrids are still wonderful plants.

A. Songbird hybrids A more modern group of hybrids, including light blue-and-white 'Bluebird' and intense crimson-and-white 'Cardinal'.

Aquilegia chrysantha cv.

Aquilegia canadensis

All are 2 to 3 feet (60 to 90 cm) tall. These colors are some of the richest in the columbine kingdom.

THE BASICS

Columbines are undemanding plants. Each plant lives only a few years, but most reseed themselves freely; the self-sown progeny of a hybrid usually doesn't look like its parent plant.

Growing Conditions: Plant in loose, well-drained, average-to-fertile soil. Tuck seedlings or young plants into niches among rocks, too, where their taproot can reach down to get a roothold. Leaf miners may disfigure the foliage; remove the affected leaves. Sometimes an entire plant suddenly keels over due to a borer; remove the plant, root and all, and dispose of it in a closed trash bag. Clip off bloom stalks when flowers are finished, or allow seedpods to ripen and self-sow.

Propagation: Propagate species by seed. Gently lift self-sown seedlings with a trowel to transplant them.

▶ **Bloom Time** Spring to early summer
▶ **Planting Requirements** Sun to part shade, depending on species
▶ **Zones** 3 to 9 unless otherwise noted

A

Arabis *AR-a-bis* • rock cress

Early spring bloomers are dear to our hearts, brightening the garden with welcome splashes of color after a drab winter, so rock cress will certainly be appreciated. It will form a low, solid mat of tiny flowers, which can be grown to create a dainty, pristine white collar around daffodils, tulips, and other spring bulbs. If you lean close, you'll be able to sniff the plant's sweet scent. Rock cress, which is from the Brassicaceae family, blooms for weeks, from the first crocuses to tulip time. Blue and pink cultivars add more possibilities for spring color.

Once the flowers are gone, the leaves provide a calm green carpet throughout the summer. Even bare rocks will look better with a froth of rock cress softening their edges, making this ground-cover plant an execellent choice for a rock garden.

Arabis × arendsii 'Rosabella' (pink rock cress) Add a happy note to your spring garden with this cheerful pink cultivar, which can sometimes be found at the garden center labeled as *A. caucasica* 'Rosabella'.

A. caucasica (wall rock cress) Snowy white flowers appear in small upright clusters, which form a ground-hugging drift among tiny, woolly leaves. The flowers reach to 6 to 10 inches (15 to 25 cm), and each plant will spread to about 12 inches (30 cm) wide. Plant several of them in a group for an eye-catching spill on a slope or along a walk. This species can spread vigorously, but it is easy to uproot if necessary.

For a more dramatic display, try 'Flore Plena', a double-flowered cultivar; it is also a more compact plant. The slow-growing cultivar 'Variegata' has white-edged leaves, which will be a bonus after the flowers finish. 'Pink Charm' is a reliable cultivar with pink flowers; 'Compinkie' is a similar cultivar but more compact.

THE BASICS

Rock cress hails from mountains and the seaside, which is a clue that it prefers good drainage and cool temperatures. The plant will spread fast into a solid mat. Give rock cress room to spread, where it won't be buried by later perennials when its flowers give way to a calming green-gray mat of leaves.

Arabis caucasica

Growing Conditions: Rock cress prefers light-to-average, well-drained soil. It will sulk in areas with long, humid summers; if that's your garden, plant it in a spot with afternoon shade and allow plenty of elbow room for air circulation. Rock cress tolerates drought moderately well. Shear back to half its height immediately after blooming, which will keep the plants compact and vigorous; kitchen shears make fast work of the task.

Propagation: Start taking cuttings in early spring, before the plants begin to flower. Divide clumps frequently to keep them vigorous and extend your planting.

▶ **Bloom Time** Early to midspring

▶ **Planting Requirements** Full sun to light shade, such as beneath a spring-flowering ornamental cherry tree

▶ **Zones** 3 to 7

Perfect Partners

Rock cress is a great excuse to indulge in the more unusual spring bulbs, which often get overlooked in the rush to plant tall daffodils or stately tulips. You can't beat species tulips with rock cress, such as stoplight-red *Tulipa greigii*, flamelike *Tulipa acuminata*, or romantic *Tulipa bakeri* 'Lilac Wonder'. For more variety, plant rock cress with miniature daffodils, brilliant blue scilla (*Scilla siberica*), grape hyacinths (*Muscari* spp.), or other small bulbs. In a partly shady spot, pink rock cress is irresistible next to delicate maidenhair ferns (*Adiantum pedatum*). In sun use pink rock cress with white or creamy miniature daffodils 'Minnow', 'Snipe', or 'Tête à Tête'.

Artemisia *ar-te-MEES-ee-uh* • artemisia, sagebrush

Gallop your mustang through the cowboy country of the American West, and you'll be riding through artemisia. Reined in for the garden, cultivated species of these silvery gray foliage plants from the Asteraceae family are worth their weight in gold. Most are robust plants with woody stems, but they're cloaked in fine foliage that creates instant romance among bolder perennials or roses. Grow these plants for their foliage, not their flowers; individual blossoms are tiny and inconspicuous, although the sprays of bloom do add height and texture. The foliage is strongly aromatic, with a medicinal aroma that hints at the herbal history of these plants.

Artemisia abrotanum (southernwood) A feathery, delicately textured plant that spreads by creeping roots. It grows to 3 feet (90 cm) tall and wide; but you can keep it sheared to a smaller size. Cut back to 4 inches (10 cm) from the ground in early spring to keep it shaped, or it will get "leggy," with bare lower stems.

A. absinthium (wormwood) This is the source for absinthe, a French drink immortalized in Edgar Degas' *The Absinthe Drinker* and other artwork of the day, which warned of the dangers of the drink. You don't need to drink absinthe to enjoy the plant in your garden, where you can admire its lovely looks. The vigorous plant quickly reaches 3 feet (90 cm) tall and wide; cut back its tough stems of feathery foliage occasionally to keep it bushy and compact.

A. ludoviciana (white sage) Palest of them all, this species is known best by three cultivars. 'Silver King' is beautiful but aggressive; its traveling roots will quickly infiltrate your garden. Plant it with other pushy perennials that can hold their own, such as bee balm (*Monarda* spp.), asters, and goldenrods (*Solidago* spp.). 'Silver Queen' is a slightly better behaved cultivar, but it often sprawls over and isn't as pretty. 'Valerie Finnis' is another attempt at taming the takeover tendencies. This upright cultivar has bigger, simpler leaves and is easier to keep in bounds—although still aggressive.

A. 'Powis Castle' This hybrid became instantly popular when it was first introduced in 1972. It is an evergreen—make that "eversilver"—hybrid and is one of the best artemisias for the garden. It stays put, forming a rounded clump of sublime lacy silver leaves. Where winters are mild, it forms woody stems that sprawl outward to a diameter of 4 feet (120 cm). As with other artemisias, don't spare the pruners: Cut this one back hard now and then to keep it dense. It is hardy in Zones 5 to 8, but it tends to "melt," or sprawl outward from the center, in humid areas.

THE BASICS

Artemisias like it hot and dry, but they'll grow well in average garden conditions, too. Keep *A. ludoviciana* in control by rigorously removing roots and shoots that spring up out of bounds. Clip stems of *A. ludoviciana* for dried flower arrangements or wreaths; the leaves retain their silver color. Handle the plant with caution:

Artemisia 'Powis Castle'

Some people are susceptible to a painful skin rash when they touch artemisia. Wear a shirt with long sleeves and a pair of gloves to protect you from contact.

Growing Conditions: Plant in average, well-drained soil, and give them room to grow. Even a tiny plant will reach unbelievable size in just one growing season. Silver plants are noted for drought tolerance, and artemisias are no exception. They need no extra watering, although 'Powis Castle' looks better with an occasional drink during dry spells.

Propagation: Cuttings are easy to root in spring; transplant the traveling roots of *A. ludoviciana*.

▶ **Bloom Time** Summer to fall
▶ **Planting Requirements** Full sun
▶ **Zones** 3 to 8

Aruncus *a-RUN-kus* • goat's beard

Aruncus dioicus

This vigorous plant has stout stems of large leaves and forms a tall clump topped with feathery, creamy spires of fuzzy flowers. Goat's beard, a member of the Rosaceae family, thrives in shade as well as sun, so you can use it to add stature to a shade garden of lower growing hostas and ferns.

Aruncus aethusifolius (dwarf goat's beard, Korean goat's beard) This dwarf perennial reaches 8 inches (20 cm) tall, forming a clump 1 foot (30 cm) wide, which may eventually spread to 3 feet (90 cm) wide. It has dark green, fernlike foliage and creamy spires of tiny flowers in spring.

A. dioicus This American native reaches 3 to 6 feet (90 to 180 cm) tall and 2 to 5 feet (60 to 150 cm) wide. It has compound leaves and flowers in summer. Male and female flowers are carried on different plants; males are showier, and the females form tawny seed heads for fall interest. 'Glasnevin' and 'Zweiweltenkind' (Child of Two Worlds) are smaller cultivars.

THE BASICS

The tall species leans toward the sun, so plant it on the north side of a path or lawn. A single plant is all you need to add a focal point. Transplant young seedlings before the root gets a grip.

Growing Conditions: It thrives in moist soil, grows well in dry soil, and is ideal around ponds or water features. Supply water when rain is scarce until the plant is a year or two old.

Propagation: Try digging up a root and cutting it into sections, making sure each one has a growing point. Females may self-sow.

▸ **Bloom Time** *A. aethusifolius*, spring; *A. dioicus*, summer
▸ **Planting Requirements** Sun to part shade; there are fewer blooms if grown in full shade
▸ **Zones** 3 or 4 to 8

Asclepias *as-KLEE-pee-us* • butterfly weed, butterfly milkweed

Asclepias tuberosa

Clusters of shocking orange flowers—a rare color in the garden—will attract butterflies and make this vibrant plant a delightful choice for the border. Butterfly weed, which is a member of the Asclepiadaceae family, is as tough as nails, so no wonder breeders have been creating more colors of the plant.

Asclepias tuberosa It forms a clump of leafy stems 2 to 3 feet (60 to 90 cm) tall and wide. Starry, spurred orange blossoms are combined in free-form, slightly domed clusters. These are followed by slender seedpods that release feathery parachutes. 'Gay Butterflies' is a mix that adds yellow, salmon, and red shades to the orange.

THE BASICS

Easy to grow, but sometimes short-lived. It is slow to emerge in spring.

Growing Conditions: This adaptable plant grows well in average garden soil, clay, or sand, and in heat and dry conditions. A well-drained site is a must. The plant may develop mildew late in summer; hide it by planting among ornamental grasses or perennials with unsusceptible foliage, such as black-eyed Susan (*Rudbeckia* spp.) Monarch butterfly caterpillars may eat the leaves.

Propagation: Take cuttings before plants bloom. Do not disturb the root. If it self-sows, transplant when there are two sets of leaves, lifting soil with the seedling to protect the taproot.

▸ **Bloom Time** Summer
▸ **Planting Requirements** Full sun
▸ **Zones** 3 to 9

A

Aster AS-ter • aster

These plants fill the summer-to-fall garden with a fresh burst of color, in cool hues that are perfect for the fall foliage around them. Asters, members of the Asteraceae family, vary greatly: Some are tight mounds; others are tall, billowy characters. All are beloved by nectar-seeking insects. With the huge selection of species, cultivars, and hybrids, there's an aster for any garden.

Aster × frikartii Two cultivars to choose from are 'Monch' and 'Wonder of Staffa'. Both are top-notch, trouble-free perennials that bloom nonstop from summer to frost. Big lavender-blue daisies are borne by the relaxed 2- to 3-foot (60- to 90-cm) stems.

A. lateriflorus (calico aster) Countless tiny white daisies smother the branching stems. 'Lady in Black' has moody dark foliage.

A. novae-angliae (New England aster) This tall, rangy species reaches 3 to 6 feet (90 to 180 cm), but it is worth growing in a meadow garden. 'Alma Potschke' has reddish pink flowers on short plants 3 feet (90 cm) tall. Mildew-resistant 'Harrington's Pink' is a 6-foot (180-cm)-tall plant with sprays of pink flowers on arching branches. 'Purple Dome' makes a tightly rounded 2-foot (60-cm) dome.

A. novi-belgii (New York aster, Michaelmas daisy) This species is similar to *A. novae-angliae*, but with prettier cultivars. The 1-foot (30-cm) tall 'Alert' is reddish purple. 'Blue Danube' has big flowers that top the stiff 3 foot (90 cm) stems. 'Eventide' has large, lavender-blue flowers on a 3- to 4-foot (90- to 120-cm)-tall plant. 'Professor Anton Kippenburg' has lavender-blue semidouble flowers and is 1 foot (30 cm) tall.

A. tongolensis (East Indies aster) Lavender flowers on bare stems are held above the creeping foliage; roots spread quickly. Look for 'Wartburg Star' or 'Berggarten', both violet-blue.

A. species (American native species) Among these asters are heart-leaved aster *(A. cordifolius)*, which offers plumes of tiny lavender-blue daisies on arching, wine red stems, and smooth aster *(A. laevis)*, with ethereal lavender-blue flowers. In shady gardens try wood aster *(A. divaricatus)*, with clusters of white flowers, or bigleaf aster *(A. macrophyllus)*, a white- or blue-flowered woodland native.

THE BASICS

Asters are simple to grow. Start with plants, or sow seeds in spring, which will bloom the following year. Some asters slowly spread outward by their roots. A few species remain compact.

Growing Conditions: Plant in average-to-rich, moist but well-drained soil. Fertilize yearly in early spring. Powdery mildew can mar the foliage of *A. novae-angliae* and *A. novi-belgii*; treat with a fungicide. If aster wilt attacks (a plant will suddenly begin to wilt), treat with a fungicide; do not plant another aster in the same spot.

Propagation: Division in early spring; some species will self-sow.

▶ **Bloom Time** Summer to fall, depending on species and cultivars

▶ **Planting Requirements** Most, full sun; *A. divaricatus, A. cordifolius,* and *A. macrophyllus*, part to full shade

▶ **Zones** Depending on species, 3 to 8; *A. × frikartii*, Zones 6 to 8

Aster novae-angliae

Perfect Partners

Ornamental grasses are a natural with asters. For airy grace beside those billows of starry blossoms, try any of your favorites: *Calamagrostis, Cortaderia, Miscanthus, Molinia, Pennisetum,* or *Panicum* grasses. Dark-tinged *Pennisetum* 'Moudry' and reddish *Miscanthus* 'Shenandoah' are especially effective with pink asters, such as 'Alma Potschke'. Hot-colored crocosmia and warm-toned yarrows (*Achillea* spp.), such as 'Marmalade', provide contrast to asters' cool blue hues; so do golden black-eyed Susans (*Rudbeckia hirta*) and sunflowers (*Helianthus* spp.). Add to the blue effect of aster blooms by growing with monkshood (*Aconitum* spp.) or globe thistle (*Echinops* spp.). Plant reddish purple asters near coneflowers (*Echinacea* spp.), which echo their palette. Reddish seed heads of *Sedum* 'Autumn Joy' and gray foliage of mulleins (*Verbascum* spp.) or spiky red-hot poker (*Kniphofia* spp.) are pleasing partners, too.

A

Asters with Artistry

Just when you're ready for a change of scenery in the fall garden, asters come into their own, transforming their bushy clumps into armloads of glorious daisies that proudly say the best is last to come. Clear, rich colors are characteristic of these easy-to-grow asters. Use them to paint your late-season garden with bold strokes of radiant pink, saturated blue-lavender, and dramatic deep purple, or add a fresh splash of pure white or palest pink to the reddening hues of fall foliage. These featured plants offer some of the best colors in the aster rainbow.

◀ *A. × frikartii* 'Monch'

A top-notch, trouble-free perennial that will bloom nonstop from summer to frost. Multitudes of gorgeous lavender-blue daisies, big for an aster at about 2 inches (5 cm), top the relaxed 2- to 3-foot (60- to 90-cm)-tall stems, creating a waterfall of flowers that looks beautiful on a slope, among grasses, or mingling with yarrows (*Achillea* spp.) and other perennials.

▲ *A. amellus*

Purple petals burst from the yellow centers of these exciting flowers, which crowd together in dense clusters on leafy stems above hairy foliage. Expect it to grow about 2 to 2½ feet (60 to 75 cm) tall and as wide as 1 to 2 feet (30 to 60 cm).

▶ *A. novae-angliae* 'Purple Dome'

Its formal, tightly rounded habit means no snipping is necessary. It creates a stunning color among the warm tones of fall. Contrast its controlled posture with the arching form and soft texture of fountain grass (*Pennisetum* spp.).

▼ A. *novae-angliae* 'Harrington's Pink'
Sprays of plentiful pink flowers provide a burst of color in the fall garden, with arching branches covered in blossoms for weeks. Give this one plenty of space; grow through a wire-grid plant support to help keep it from getting too floppy.

▲ A. 'Little Carlow'
This is a hybrid of two American species, *A. cordifolius* and *A. novi-belgii*. It is a lovely fall bloomer that grows to about 2 feet (60 cm) tall and wide. It creates a waterfall effect with a multitude of sky blue flowers with yellow centers. Plant in full sun.

▶ A. *lateriflorus*
An aster of a different color: Instead of blue to purple, calico aster—its common name—is white. As the copious sprays of daisies age, the center disk changes from yellow to red, which has led to the "calico" moniker.

Astilbe a-STILL-bee • astilbe, false spirea

The adaptable astilbe is one of the few perennials that bloom with abandon in shade—and in sun! All astilbes, members of the Saxifragaceae family, have fuzzy plumes of close-packed flowers. The divided foliage looks good even when the plant isn't in bloom, but it's the flowers that are fabulous— a rainbow of white, cream, pink, lavender, or reddish pink. Flower form varies from open and arching plumes to stiffly erect soldiers. With species and cultivars ranging in size from stalwart 5-foot (150-cm)-tall plants to dainty types 1 foot (30 cm) high, astilbes can find a home in any garden.

Astilbe × arendsii Most cultivars belong to this group of hybrids that originated in Germany. 'Fanal' has deep almost-red spires; its leaves are tinged with red, too. 'Amethyst' is a lovely cool lilac-purple; 'Anna Pfeifer' is warm salmon; 'Avalanche' and 'Ellie' are white. Most are 2 to 2½ feet (60 to 75 cm) tall. Don't cut off the finished flowers; they'll turn reddish brown for another interesting touch.

A. chinensis (Chinese astilbe) 'Pumila' is the most well-known of this pink-flowered species' cultivars. It's a low, spreading plant up to 1 foot (30 cm) tall, with dense, glossy, weed-choking foliage that makes it suitable for a ground cover. The tapered spires of flowers are rosy mauve. Experts have reclassified some former cultivars of *A. × arendsii* into this species; 'Finale' (not to be confused with 'Fanal') has soft pink flower spires at least 1 foot (30 cm) long that start blooming in summer and continue into fall; 'Serenade' is deep rosy red; both

reach 1 foot (30 cm) tall. *A. chinensis* var. *taquetii* grows to 4 feet (120 cm).

A. simplicifolia This dwarf reaches 10 inches (25 cm) tall. New leaves are tinged with red or bronze; the flowers are pretty in pink. 'White Sensation' has loose flower clusters.

THE BASICS

Astilbes expand gradually by the roots to form a large clump, so they may take a year or two to reach their full size. They adapt well to light from full sun to shade. You'll see more flowers in sun, but you'll also need to be more careful about moisture there. These cold-hardy plants do best where summers are relatively cool.

Growing Conditions: Plant in moist but well-drained garden soil of average-to-rich fertility. Fertilize in spring. Astilbes are rugged, but they can be finicky, especially in hot, dry conditions. Without regular moisture, their attractive foliage quickly curls and dries; incorporate humus into your soil to help retain moisture. *A. chinensis* is more tolerant of dry soil, but it stays shorter and flowers less. All benefit from a mulch to help retain moisture. As astilbes age, their woody crowns may rise above the soil; cover them with a few scoops of compost or light, humus-rich soil.

Propagation: Divide clumps every few years to keep plants vigorous.

▶ **Bloom Time** Early summer to fall, depending on cultivar

▶ **Planting Requirements** Full sun to part shade; in hot summer areas part shade

▶ **Zones** *A. × arendsii, A. chinensis,* 3 to 8; *A. simplicifolia,* 5 to 8

Astilbe × arendsii cv.

Perfect Partners

In the shade garden, where they'll be paired with foliage plants, astilbe flowers are welcome anytime. Plant them in drifts with bergenia, hostas, speckled lungwort (*Pulmonaria* spp.), late-blooming Japanese anemone (*Anemone × hybrida*), and ferns; add contrasting or complementary colors of annual impatiens (*Impatiens walleriana*) to boost the flower power. In a sunny spot partner with flowers that are simpler and bolder than astilbe's feathery spires. With early bloomers try dramatic iris. Or create a pastel grouping with Shasta daisies (*Leucanthemum × superbum*) and the charming buds and starry blue blooms of balloon flower (*Platycodon* spp.). Later-blooming astilbes add a soft touch to the blooms of hibiscus and the big flowers of 'Stargazer' lilies (*Lilium* 'Stargazer'). Japanese painted fern (*Athyrium niponicum* 'Pictum') will make an elegant partner for dwarf *A. chinensis* 'Pumila'.

A

Athyrium
a-THEER-ee-um • lady fern

Everything we love about ferns is in this genus from the Woodsiaceae family—the delicacy, the grace, and the tough disposition. Lady ferns slip into the shady garden with ease, forming expanding colonies of lacy fronds.

Athyrium filix-femina (lady fern) The delicate, deciduous foliage grows 3 feet (90 cm) tall. Look for the tassled 'Encourage' (also known as 'Vernoniae Cristatum') or 'Fancy Fronds'.

A. niponicum (Japanese lady fern) A lower-growing species with silvery fronds, it is stunning with dark-leaved heucheras and hostas. *A. niponicum pictum* (Japanese painted fern) has silvery fronds lined with a red central

stem and pinkish tinges. 'Apple Court' has crested fronds. 'Burgundy Lace' is purple-red. 'Pewter Lace' is similar, with gunmetal gray fronds.

A. 'Ghost' This hybrid of *A. filix-femina* and *A. niponicum* is a taller, upright fern with pale silvery fronds.

THE BASICS

As long as they have consistently moist soil, lady ferns are easy to grow. Plant them around ponds or streams.

Growing Conditions: Plant in moist-to-wet soil that is rich in humus; compost your fall leaves and add them to the soil to supply acid conditions. Lady ferns spread fast.

Athyrium filix-femina cv.

Propagation: Divide clumps in early spring or fall.

▶ **Bloom Time** No bloom
▶ **Planting Requirements** Full to part shade
▶ **Zones** *A. filix-femina*, 3 to 8; *A. niponicum*, 4 to 8

Aurinia
aw-RIN-ee-uh • basket-of-gold, gold alyssum

An early spring standout, exuberant basket-of-gold spills into bright, sunny bloom just when you're yearning to see some color after a long winter. It's glorious with spring bulbs or draping over a rock wall, where it will self-sow into any nearby crevice. The mat of tiny flowers blooms for a month and is sweetly scented. After bloom, the plant, which is from the Brassicaceae family, forms a mound of gray foliage.

Aurinia saxatilis The species forms a low, spreading mound, about 1 foot (30 cm) tall and 1 to 2 feet (30 to 60 cm) wide. The "unimproved" species is beautiful, but you can also try experimenting with the cultivars. 'Citrinum' (also called 'Sulphurea') is ideal if sulfur yellow suits your garden better than gold; this cultivar leans

toward lemon with no trace of gold. 'Compacta' forms a tidy, more compact ball of foliage and golden flowers to 8 inches (20 cm) tall. The cultivar 'Sunny Border Apricot' has flowers that are an unusual orange-tinted color. 'Dudley Nevill Variegated' has variegated foliage.

THE BASICS

Basket-of-gold is an agreeable plant that needs only an occasional trim to keep it looking good. Avoid crowding it with later perennials; it likes to stay in sunshine. Although short-lived, the plant self-sows.

Growing Conditions: Plant in lean-to-average soil in a well-drained site. Avoid fertilizing; it encourages growth that makes the plants floppy.

Aurinia saxatilis 'Dudley Nevill Variegated'

Cut back hard after flowering to one-third their height.

Propagation: Take cuttings in early spring or fall. Collect and sow seeds. Transplant self-sown seedlings.

▶ **Bloom Time** Spring
▶ **Planting Requirements** Full sun
▶ **Zones** 3 to 8

A

Baptisia *bap-TIZ-ee-uh* • false indigo, wild indigo, baptisia

Baptisia australis

Baptisia resembles a big, shrubby lupine (*Lupinus* spp.), its wilder cousin. The spikes of pealike blossoms aren't as congested as those of cultivated lupines, thus creating a more casual effect. The plant, a member of the Fabaceae family, forms a big, branched mound of stems clothed in cloverlike leaves. In bloom baptisia commands attention with its 1-foot (30-cm)-long spikes of flowers, held like candles above the plant. The foliage has a blue cast to it, which intensifies the effect of the white, yellow, or blue flowers.

You can use this commanding plant to anchor the middle ground of a bed or border. It looks best with other strong-natured neighbors, such as tall phlox (*Phlox maculata, P. paniculata*) or luscious Oriental poppies (*Papaver orientale*), which will glow against the baptisia's cool leaves. Baptisia is deciduous, but its seedpods stay on the stems; these are ideal for using in dried arrangements.

Baptisia alba

Baptisia alba (also known as *B. leucantha*; white false indigo) Erect spikes light up like tapers above this American native plant. Depending on the conditions, it can grow from 3 feet (90 cm) up to as much as 7 feet (2.1 m) tall and 3 feet (90 cm) wide.

B. australis (blue false indigo) The species grows along riverbanks in its native eastern North America. It is a popular species, thanks to its clear blue flowers. It grows to about 3 feet (90 cm) tall and 4 to 5 feet (120 to 150 cm) wide. *B. australis* var. *minor* (also known as *B. minor*) is a smaller version, reaching only about 1½ feet (45 cm) tall.

B. sphaerocarpa (also known as *B. viridis*; yellow false indigo) This species is native from Texas to Missouri, where it dots old pastures. The plant is no shrinking violet—it has intense yellow flowers that shout for attention. Once it's settled into the garden, a single 2-foot (60-cm)-tall plant can produce 100 or more flower spikes, nearly all at once! You can plant blue fescue (*Festuca* spp.), veronicas, or blue hardy geraniums, such as *Geranium* 'Johnson's Blue', in front of it, to step it down to size and help hide its bare bottom stems. It produces cute round "peapods."

THE BASICS

Don't be fooled by the weakling you bring home from the garden center: Baptisia will muscle in like Charles Atlas, although it takes a year or two (or three) to reach full size. Choose a spot for it that has plenty of space.

Disturbing the roots will set back the plant, so make sure its new home is a permanent one—and choose wisely because this is a long-lived plant.

Growing Conditions: Baptisia is widely adaptable to soil and moisture conditions, and thrives in the wild in sand, sun-baked clay, and the moist, humusy soil of woods' edges and riverbanks. Plant in average garden soil with good drainage, then stand back! These tough, long-lived plants are also drought tolerant. Tall species may get floppy; place a wire-grid plant support over them in spring to lend the stems some backbone.

Propagation: The plants are difficult to divide. Collect ripe seeds and soak overnight before planting in moist soil.

▶ **Bloom Time** Early summer
▶ **Planting Requirements** Full sun to part or light shade
▶ **Zones** 3 to 9; *B. sphaerocarpa*, 5 to 9

Bergenia *ber-JEEN-ee-uh* • bergenia

Bergenia is a ground-hugging plant, but it makes a bold statement with its mass of big, rounded, glossy leaves. That foliage is outstanding, whether you grow it as a ground cover, with hostas and heucheras, or crammed into the crevices of a rock wall. Better yet, this tough plant, which is a member of the Saxifragaceae family, is mostly evergreen, so you can enjoy its foliage year-round. In fall the leaves take on burnished bronze or red tints. In spring pretty little nosegays of flowers rise among the leaves. These are pink, but some cultivars have white flowers.

Bergenia cordifolia (heartleaf bergenia) The species forms rosettes of dense, glossy leaves that may be rounded or more heart-shaped; the expanding clump of leaves is about 8 inches (20 cm) high, but the flowers rise above the clump to 12 inches (30 cm). Although the bloom is heaviest in spring, the rosy pink flowers will appear sporadically throughout the season. The foliage takes on a burgundy or bronze cast from fall through winter.

There are many cultivars to choose from. 'Abendglut' (Evening Glow) has outstanding maroon-tinted leaves that are at their most colorful in fall and winter but retain a dark flush all year. Its vivid crimson-magenta semidouble flowers rise to 12 inches (30 cm). Or try 'Bressingham White', with elegant white flowers, for a change of pace. 'Silberlicht' (Silverlight) has white flowers, too, above rounded green leaves. 'Purpurea' has striking reddish purple flowers that are a deeper color. 'Winterglut' (Winter Glow) is larger than most, with spectacular crimson flowers that top stems reaching about 15 inches (38 cm) tall.

***B.* 'Apple Blossom'** Its pale blossoms give this hybrid a different look and make it easier to blend into the garden. The flower stems are reddish and about 18 inches (45 cm) tall, topped with 1½-inch (3.75-cm), pale pink, bell-shaped blossoms. Unlike most other bergenias, it flourishes in areas with hot summers; it is hardy in Zones 4 to 8. 'Baby Doll' is another fine light pink cultivar.

THE BASICS

Bergenias are tough, adaptable plants that can handle neglect. They will look best in climates with cooler summers;

Bergenia cordifolia

however, if planted in the right site, bergenias can flourish despite the thermometer reading.

Growing Conditions: Plant in average, well-drained soil. Bergenias scoff at drought, but summer sun may damage the leaves, causing a faded, sunburned effect. If your summers include stretches of extreme heat, plant bergenias in part-to-full shade, where they'll be sheltered from the brunt of it. The plants are cold hardy, but the leaves may be damaged in cold weather if they're not under a snowy blanket. A mulch of loose fall leaves, such as those of oaks, will give them some protection. Older clumps will often die out near the center; lift and separate them.

Propagation: Division in early spring. Slice through the tough stems with a stout knife, and replant about 1 foot (30 cm) apart.

▶ **Bloom Time** Early spring
▶ **Planting Requirements** Full sun to shade
▶ **Zones** 3 to 9

Perfect Partners

The simple foliage of bergenias invites neighbors with complicated styles. Use the plants as a ground cover with astilbes, or partner with ferns. Plant them along a shady path, backed by lady fern (*Athyrium filix-femina*) or hostas. Or grow them along the top or bottom of a sunny rock wall, or beside an accent rock in the garden. For flowering friends combine bergenia with daffodils (*Narcissus* spp.) and tulips (*Tulipa* spp.), or with Siberian iris (*Iris sibirica*), New Zealand flax (*Phormium* spp.), and other erect, spear-leaved perennials. As a ground cover, bergenia is a beautiful under-pinning for rhododendrons and azaleas (*Rhododendron* spp.). Bergenia looks great in pots in all four seasons.

B

Calamagrostis kal-a-ma-GROS-tis • feather reed grass, calamagrostis

Tall, slender, feather reed grass appears earlier than other ornamental grasses. Use this plant from the Poaceae family to add a vertical accent to a garden bed, or plant a group for a bigger impact. Reed grasses stay in tidy clumps, 1 to 2 feet (30 to 60 cm) wide.

Calamagrostis × acutiflora (feather reed grass) Reed grass forms a tightly erect clump of thin leaves and stems of long, slender, feathery plumes that are pink-tinged in early summer but mellow to tawny gold. In fall the foliage bleaches to tan. 'Karl Foerster' is tall and lean—and it stays erect without staking. The clump may reach 4 feet (120 cm) tall. 'Avalanche' has a white band down the middle of each leaf. Silvery tan plumes rise to 4 feet (120 cm) tall in midsummer. The leaves of 'Eldorado' are broadly streaked with a central golden stripe.

C. brachytricha (fall-blooming feather reed grass, Korean feather reed grass) A graceful beauty, with fine, 2-foot (60-cm)-tall foliage and airy pink fall flowers. It flourishes in sun to shade; in shade it may spill out. It's the ideal grass for hot regions.

THE BASICS

Feather reed grasses need only the minimal maintenance of an annual haircut to look good for years. Except for *C. brachytricha*, they're at their best in areas with cooler summers.

Growing Conditions: Plant in average-to-moist, well-drained soil. Trouble-free. If it is less vigorous after a few years; lift and divide. In a long

Calamagrostis brachytricha

drought the plant will go dormant and turn tan. Cut clumps to the ground in early spring, before new growth.

Propagation: Division.

▶ **Bloom Time** Summer; *C. brachytricha*, fall
▶ **Planting Requirements** Sun to part or light shade; *C. brachytricha*, sun to full shade
▶ **Zones** 4 to 7 and cooler regions of 8; *C. brachytricha*, 5 to 9

Camassia ka-MASS-ee-a • camas, camas lily, quamash

Blue camas blooms when the early summer garden hits its peak. This Hyacinthaceae family member has tufts of slim, pointed leaves and an erect stem bearing dozens of flowers, which open from the bottom up.

Camassia cusickii Ice blue blossoms decorate the 2- to 3-foot (60- to 90-cm) flowering stem.

C. leichtlinii (great camas) Flowering stems stretch to 3 to 4 feet (90 to 120 cm). The blue hue varies from pale to true blue to deep blue-purple. 'Blue Danube' is a stunner with deep blue-purple flowers.

C. quamash (common camas) Flowers of fabulous color, a saturated deep blue, top stems that reach 1 to 2 feet (30 to 60 cm) tall.

THE BASICS

Add a few dozen bulbs to your garden to grow into clumps of color.

Growing Conditions: Plant bulbs in fall, in average-to-moist soil. The plants go dormant after bloom, so they can survive dry summers. Clip off the finished flowering stem, or let the seeds ripen and fall. Trouble-free.

Propagation: Collect ripe seeds and sow in a nursery bed of loose, compost-enriched soil in fall. Water when single-bladed sprouts emerge in late spring; mulch with straw. At the

Camassia leichtlinii

end of the second or third year, dig up the bulbs in fall, and replant.

▶ **Bloom Time** Early summer
▶ **Planting Requirements** Sun to light or part shade
▶ **Zones** Most species 3 to 8; *C. leichtlinii*, 4 to 9

C

Campanula

kam-PAN-yew-la • campanula, bellflower

The gentle lavender-blue color of many campanulas is such a hallmark that other perennials are sometimes described as "campanula blue." This big genus from the Campanulaceae family includes diminutive ground-cover types and stalwart citizens 4 feet (120 cm) tall. All have bell-shaped flowers that may open into stars. Some species hold their blossoms upward and outfacing; on others they dangle demurely.

Campanula carpatica (Carpathian harebell) Neat little tufts of tiny leaves are smothered by large flowers. The popular cultivars 'Blue Clips' and 'White Clips' grow to only 8 inches (20 cm) tall and bloom for a month. Hardy in Zones 3 to 8.

C. cochleariifolia (spiral bellflower, mouse-ear bellflower) One of the smallest-flowered campanulas, this little charmer is perfect creeping around rocks or between pavers. There are plenty of lavender-blue flowers. This is a moderate spreader but never a pest. Hardy in Zones 4 to 8.

C. glomerata (clustered bellflower) Its deep purple flowers are held upright in globe-shaped clusters on stems 1 to 3 feet (30 to 90 cm) tall. The plants spread quickly but aren't aggressive. 'Joan Elliot' is popular, with her rich blue-violet flowers; 'Superba' (also sold as *C. glomerata* var. *superba*) grows to 3 feet (90 cm) in rich soil. Hardy in Zones 3 to 8.

C. lactiflora (milky bellflower) This species often behaves like a biennial: Greenery the first year, flowers the second, and then adieu. Keep it going by letting it sow itself or by planting new seed each year. The stems grow up to 5 feet (150 cm) tall. 'Brantwood' is blue-purple; 'Alba' has white flowers. 'Loddon Anna' forms a large, multi-branched plant covered with pale pink flowers. Hardy in Zones 4 to 7.

C. persicifolia (peach-leaved bellflower) It forms a clump of vertical stems, 2 to 3 feet (60 to 90 cm) tall, with abundant gentle bluish bells that open wide. 'Alba' has white flowers. Cut flowering stems back by one-third after bloom for more flowers later on.

C. poscharskyana (Serbian bellflower) This low creeper travels fast, spreading its mat of trailing stems and starry lavender-blue flowers. If you'd prefer a similar plant that stays mostly in place, try 'Birch Hybrid', a saturated blue-purple campanula.

C. rotundifolia (harebell) A lovely, delicate little wildflower, this species is native to the mountains of the West and Northwest. Wiry stems topped with charming lavender-blue bells arise from a clump of fine, thin basal leaves. It usually grows 8 to 12 inches (20 to 30 cm) tall and is easy to tuck into nooks among rocks.

C. 'Samantha' This low-growing hybrid is cloaked in blue-lilac blooms with cheerful white centers. Unlike most campanulas, this one is sweetly fragrant. It is perfect for edging a bed, or try it in containers.

THE BASICS

Campanula vary greatly in their growth habits. Make sure you read the label to find out whether the plant will fit your needs. A few species are famed for spreading; they're easy to uproot with a trowel.

Campanula lactiflora 'Loddon Anna'

Perfect Partners

Campanulas go well with contrasting flowers, such as daylilies (*Hemerocallis* spp.), yarrows (*Achillea* spp.), and Oriental poppies (*Papaver orientale*). You can add punch with the vertical, deep blue spikes of *Salvia* × *sylvestris* 'Mainacht' (May Night) or 'Caradonna' or bearded iris (*Iris* × *germanica*). In a rock garden partner with pinks (*Dianthus* spp.) or geraniums.

Growing Conditions: Plant in moist but well-drained soil enriched with humus or compost for a lighter texture. Fertilize in spring. In hot summer areas pick a site with some afternoon shade. Some can be short-lived; cutting them back hard after bloom or dividing the clump every year or two helps keep them vigorous.

Propagation: Seed; may self-sow. Division in early spring.

▶ **Bloom Time** Spring or summer; may rebloom

▶ **Planting Requirements** Sun to part shade

▶ **Zones** Hardiness varies depending on species; most, 3 to 7 and cooler parts of Zone 8

Carex KAY-rex • sedge

A soft touch and unusual color are the signature contributions of sedges. These members of the Cyperaceae family resemble ornamental grasses. Their hues of brown, chestnut, bronze, or gold make them stand out, but most species are only 1 to 2 feet (30 to 60 cm) high. Sedge flowers often go unnoticed against their eye-catching foliage; they are borne on stalks in spring or summer. With more than a thousand species and new cultivars rapidly hitting the market, sedges offer enough variety to accent any garden.

Carex buchananii (leatherleaf sedge) Probably one of the most popular and widely available sedges, this oddball is sometimes called "dead sedge" because of its brown color. The exact hue can vary slightly from one plant to another, but it is usually

cinnamon brown. The delicate leaves, which arch up and outward with a graceful curl at the tips, practically beg to be touched. Hardy in Zones 6 to 9.

C. caryophylla 'The Beatles' This is a shaggy mop of dense, arching, slightly curling green foliage, frosted with golden edges. It is a small cultivar, reaching 6 inches (15 cm) high and 10 inches (25 cm) wide. Use it as an accent, or plant it in groups as a ground cover on a shady slope. Hardy in Zones 5 to 9.

C. comans (New Zealand hair sedge) Similar to *C. buchananii,* but it is low and spreading instead of forming an upright fountain. The ultrathin, reddish brown leaves grow to 1 foot (30 cm) tall and form a relaxed, fine-textured mound 2 feet (60 cm) wide. The cultivar 'Bronze' has evergreen, coppery leaves, with more of a soft chestnut hue than its name suggests; the erect flower spikes contrast with the spill of fine sedge leaves. *C. flagellifera* forms an arching mound of brown foliage similar to *C. comans.* Hardy in Zones 7 to 9.

C. elata 'Aurea' (Bowles' golden sedge) A beautiful sedge, native to the United States, it forms a mound of lovely, clear golden leaves. It reaches 15 inches (38 cm) high and 18 inches (45 cm) tall and thrives in full sun to light or part shade; the color is richest in shadier sites. Hardy in Zones 5 to 8.

THE BASICS

Most sedges hail from wet areas in the wild, but they flourish in average garden conditions, too. These plants are tough characters despite their

Carex comans 'Bronze'

fragile looks. They'll thrive for years in the garden or in containers. Check your local nursery for sedges that will flourish in your area.

Growing Conditions: Plant in moist garden soil of average-to-rich fertility. Dig in humus or compost before planting to help hold in moisture. Many sedges can tolerate a moderate amount of drought, but they'll look better with weekly watering during dry times. Brown sedges hold their foliage through winter. Cut back to just above ground level in early spring, or let new leaves emerge among the old, then comb out dead foliage by running your fingers through the clump. Cut back *C. elata* 'Aurea' to just above ground level in fall to make room for the glorious spring foliage. In cold-winter areas grow the more tender brown sedges as annuals, or plant them in pots and bring indoors during winter.

Propagation: Divide in spring.

▶ **Bloom Time** Spring or summer
▶ **Planting Requirements** Part to full shade; also thrive in sun
▶ **Zones** 5 to 9, depending on species

Perfect Partners

Plant three to five sedges in a group to soften even the boldest plants, including bear's-breeches (*Acanthus* spp.). Or try contrasting sedge with silver-gray lavenders (*Lavandula* spp.) or catmint (*Nepeta* spp.). In shady gardens Bowles' golden sedge (*C. elata* 'Aurea') adds highlights among ferns, hostas, and astilbes. This sedge is also beautiful with blue Spanish bluebells (*Hyacinthoides hispanica*). You can use 'The Beatles' sedge to distract the eye from the fading foliage of bleeding heart (*Dicentra* spp.), wood anemone (*Anemone nemorosa*), and other early blooming wildflowers.

C

Centranthus _SEN-tran-thuss_ • Jupiter's beard, red valerian

The Roman god Jupiter was often depicted with a full beard of tight red curls—which is where this perennial gets the common name Jupiter's beard. Only one species of _Centranthus_ from the Valerianaceae family is commonly grown in the garden, but what a species it is! Jupiter's beard is one of the longest-blooming perennials you'll find, with masses of vivid rosy red flowers beginning in midspring and continuing until fall. The fragrant flowers are a beacon for butterflies, bees, and other nectar seekers.

Centranthus ruber This is a Mediterranean native that was naturalized in Europe centuries ago. More recently it's become a common sight in California and the Northwest, where it's leaped from gardens to roadsides and rocky cliffs. Multitudes of tiny flowers in rounded heads grow in branching sprays 3 feet (90 cm) tall, smothering the plant in bloom. The leaves and stems are "glaucous"— covered with a grayish coating that makes them appear gray- to blue-green. The plant clump is 2½ to 3 feet (75 to 90 cm) wide and is attractive in or out of bloom. 'Coccineus' (_C. ruber_ var. _coccineus_) has deep carmine red flowers in big, domed clusters that are a more intense color than the species. The cultivar 'Star' is a mix of pink, medium rosy red, and a deeper rosy red. Create a mixed planting of red and white flowers by adding 'White' (_C. ruber_ var. _albus_)—it will be more eye-catching than the usual red hue alone. The white is often tinted slightly with pink, and it looks best planted with red Jupiter's beard rather than by

itself. Self-sown seedlings may be white, pink, or pinkish red. 'Snow Cloud' is a shorter white cultivar, reaching about 1½ feet (45 cm) tall.

THE BASICS

Once you invite _Centranthus ruber_ into your garden, you can expect to enjoy its color for a long time. Jupiter's beard plants often live only a few years, but that trait is more than made up for by this perennial's habit of enthusiastically self-sowing. In a casual garden that's part of its charm.

Growing Conditions: The highly adaptable Jupiter's beard is well suited to gardens with challenging conditions of soil or drought. Good drainage is a must, but it will bloom well in soils of lean-to-average fertility. It flourishes in stony soils and among niches in

Centranthus ruber 'Coccineus'

rocks, as well as in beds. It adapts well to both acid and more alkaline limestone-rich soils, and also grows well in sandy seaside gardens. In dry areas, such as the eastern Rockies or the Southwest, it's a popular choice for xeric gardens because it needs little or no supplemental watering to survive dry summers. It's also right at home in traditional perennial beds of average garden soil.

For a more compact shape and repeat bloom a few weeks later that will continue to fall, cut back by about one-third after the first round of spring-to-summer flowering. Hand-pull or hoe off unwanted seedlings, or transplant them to another location in your garden. To limit self-sowing, snip off the clusters of faded flowers before they can develop into fluffy seed heads.

Propagation: Easy from seed; self-sows abundantly.

▶ **Bloom Time** Spring through summer; a second round of bloom, late summer to fall

▶ **Planting Requirements** Full sun

▶ **Zones** 4 to 9

Perfect Partners

For a drought-tolerant border partner Jupiter's beard with clumps of yellow yarrows (_Achillea_ spp.), coreopsis (_Coreopsis lanceolata_ and _C. verticillata_), silvery artemisias (_Artemisia_ 'Powis Castle'), blue catmints (_Nepeta_ spp.), and salvias (_Salvia_ × _sylvestris_ 'Mainacht' and 'Caradonna'). Use Jupiter's beard in late-season gardens among asters, gaura (_Gaura lindheimeri_), goldenrods (_Solidago_ spp.), and coneflowers (_Echinacea_ and _Rudbeckia_ spp.). For a simple composition pair it with lavenders (_Lavandula_ spp.) or with pennisetum and switchgrass (_Panicum_ spp.) ornamental grasses.

Cerastium *ser-ASS-tee-um* • snow-in-summer

Cerastium tomentosum

This mat-forming perennial from the Caryophyllaceae family spreads a carpet of white flowers among spring bulbs and blooms through early summer.

Cerastium tomentosum Snow-in-summer spreads fast, with a single plant covering 1 to 2 feet (30 to 60 cm) in a year. At bloom time the mat lifts 6- to 12-inch (15- to 30-cm) branching stems topped by dainty, snowy white flowers. They are so plentiful they look like a snowdrift from a distance. Out of bloom, snow-in-summer forms a tidy, ground-hugging carpet of dense, silvery, narrow leaves. 'Yo-Yo' is slower to spread than the species, and it is a shorter, more compact cultivar. It reaches 6 inches (15 cm) tall in bloom and spreads to 1 foot (30 cm).

THE BASICS

Snow-in-summer is easy to grow if it has good drainage. Older plants often become scraggly or bare. Restore their vigor with an annual trimming to 3 inches (7.5 cm) high after bloom.

Growing Conditions: Plant in well-drained, lean-to-average soil. Avoid fertilizing. Snow-in-summer is drought tolerant. It thrives in sandy and stony soils and in average soil. The plant roots along the stems and may self-sow. In warm, humid summers fungal rot may discolor the foliage; to cure, improve air circulation around the plant, or take healthy divisions and move to a site with better drainage.

Propagation: Division in early spring. Roots easily from stem cuttings in summer.

▶ **Bloom Time** Late spring to early summer
▶ **Planting Requirements** Full sun
▶ **Zones** 3 to 9

Chelone *key-LOW-nee* • turtlehead

Chelone obliqua

Turtlehead has lovely flowers that add color late in the season. Its tolerance for wet soil makes this plant from the Scrophulariaceae family a good choice for problem drainage spots. It has large blossoms held on short, dense-packed spires. The "turtle heads" open first at the bottom of the spire, then progress upward. Finished flowers mature into oval seedpods that add interest in the winter garden.

Chelone glabra (white turtlehead) This American native is robust, with its clump of stems up to 3 feet (90 cm) tall and wide. The flowers are white when in bud. They are white or flushed with pink when mature, often with a darker tinge of pink at the lip of the bloom. It blossoms from July to September. The dark green leaves are slender.

C. lyonii (pink turtlehead) This species has spikes of pink to rosy mauve flowers from late summer to fall. It reaches 2 to 3 feet (60 to 90 cm) tall and 3 to 4 feet (90 to 120 cm) wide. 'Hot Lips' has vivid pink flowers.

C. obliqua (red turtlehead) Rose-colored flowers are held on upright stems, forming a clump up to 3 feet (90 cm) tall and 2 feet (60 cm) wide.

THE BASICS

Turtlehead is a long-lived, easy-to-grow perennial that needs water only in dry times. Allow room for them to mature.

Growing Conditions: Plant in average-to-wet soil. Cut back to just above ground level in spring. If the leaves are ragged, check for caterpillars.

Propagation: Divide in spring.

▶ **Bloom Time** Late summer through fall
▶ **Planting Requirements** Full sun to part or light shade
▶ **Zones** 3 to 8

Chrysanthemum kris-SAN-theh-mum • chrysanthemum, mum

Chrysanthemum × *rubellum* 'Clara Curtis'

There are thousands of chrysanthemum cultivars, from small, humble, flat-faced daisies to gigantic, quilled-petal showpieces bigger than your hand. Only a few decades ago this member of the Asteraceae family was much more popular in the garden than it is today. It's time to start a new push for these pleasing, pretty plants that add so much color to our late-season gardens! All chrysanthemums have pungently aromatic foliage, with flowers in a wide palette of autumnal hues, plus pink, salmon, rosy purple, and creamy white. Try a specialized mail-order supplier if you want to try one of the numerous varieties available beyond the few plants in garden centers.

Perfect Partners

Combine your favorite rustic colors of mums with asters, dahlias, turtlehead (*Chelone* spp.), perennial sunflowers (*Helianthus* spp.), and sneezeweeds (*Helenium* spp.). You can try salmon or coral-pink mums with switchgrass (*Panicum virgatum* 'Shenandoah') to pick up red tones in the grass, or for a cool palette try creamy mums contrasted with steel blue switchgrass (*Panicum virgatum* 'Heavy Metal') and blue fescue (*Festuca* spp.). 'Clara Curtis' and 'Mary Stoker' chrysanthemums are lovely with the flower spikes of salvia (*Salvia* × *sylvestris* 'Mainacht' or 'Caradonna'). For a cottage-style garden grow either of these mums with hollyhocks (*Alcea* spp.), balloon flower (*Platycodon grandiflora*), or geraniums.

Chrysanthemum × *morifolium* (garden mum, florist mum) These hybrids include great possibilities for the garden. Avoid planting florist's mums, which are forced into bloom; buy garden-adapted plants instead.

C. × *rubellum* 'Clara Curtis' (*C. zawadskii* var. *latilobum* 'Clara Curtis'; *Dendranthema zawadskii* 'Clara Curtis') Many gardeners know this dainty pink chrysanthemum simply as "Clara Curtis daisy." If you have room for only one mum, this is the one. It begins blooming early in summer and continues into fall, producing armloads of 2- to 3-inch (5- to 7.5-cm) daisies on a relaxed plant that grows 1 to 3 feet (30 to 90 cm) tall and 2 to 3 feet (60 to 90 cm) wide. 'Mary Stoker' has soft apricot-pink blossoms.

THE BASICS

Mums do best when started from young cutting-grown plants in spring. Those bought as full-grown blooming plants in fall often don't survive the winter, because their roots don't have enough time to get established before the soil freezes. If you can't resist buying a mum in bloom, keep the soil moist around your plant until a heavy freeze and mulch with 4 to 6 inches (10 to 15 cm) of chopped fall leaves around the plant. After the foliage dies, cut back to a few inches from the ground and cover with a blanket of oak leaves or straw, 4 inches (10 cm) deep, or with branches of spruce or fir. Uncover the plant in early spring.

Growing Conditions: Grow mums in moist, well-drained garden soil of average fertility. Fertilizers or rich soil encourage rank, weak growth. Most garden mums need to be kept compact with pinching. Use your thumb and index finger to nip off the top 1 to 2 inches (2.5 to 5 cm) of each stem tip, including those of side branches. Do the first round of pinching when plants are about 8 to 10 inches (20 to 25 cm) tall; pinch again at about 1½ feet (45 cm). Use stakes and plant supports to help hold tall varieties upright.

Mums may be afflicted with aphids, which can be controlled with pyrethrin sprays or insecticidal soap. Spider mites may also infest the plants; cut off and dispose of badly affected parts of the plant. Mums spread quickly to form big clumps that often die out in the center; divide and transplant the pieces every three to four years to keep them robust.

Propagation: Divide in early spring; take cuttings from late spring to early summer.

▶ **Bloom Time** Summer or fall
▶ **Planting Requirements** Full sun
▶ **Zones** 4 to 9

A Cascade of Chrysanthemums

Chrysanthemums come in enough colors to satisfy any gardener when they're in bloom, but it's their wonderful array of form that really sparks the late-season garden. They range from giant "Irregular Incurved" football mums to small, puffy "Pompons." The daisy-shape mums are classed as "Single and Semi-Double"; "Decorative" mums are similar, but their central disk is hidden by petals. Most unusual of all are the "Quilled" and "Spider" classes. With the thousands of cultivars, you're sure to find ones that will suit your tastes.

◀ *C.* **'Grandchild'**
Tickle your favorite grandchild with a bouquet of blooms from this aptly named cultivar. It's an early-blooming "Decorative" type, with flowers that reach 3 to 4 inches (7.5 to 10 cm) wide. Try a trio of fine-textured, steely blue fescue (*Festuca* spp.) in front to accent its color.

▲ *C.* **'Brown Eyes'**
This bronzy orange, early blooming "Pompon" type kicks off the season in late September. Although their 1-inch (2.5-cm)-wide flowers are smaller than other types, pompons are ideal garden cultivars, commanding attention with their tidy balls of petals. Plant it near the front of beds, backed by taller asters or ornamental grasses.

▶ *C.* **'Bullfinch'**
A late bloomer, beginning about mid- to late October, 'Bullfinch' is worth waiting for. The plant is smothered in adorable, 2-inch (5-cm)-wide red daisies with yellow centers. That daisy shape puts this cultivar in the "Single and Semi-Double" class. The display continues for weeks as new buds open to join the show.

▼ *C.* 'Princess'

This "Decorative" type, with fluffy petals that cover the center, is pretty in pink. Try it with an airy waterfall of white or pink gaura (*Gaura lindheimeri*) as a neighbor. 'Princess' is an early bloomer, giving you weeks to enjoy its 3-inch (7.5-cm) blooms before heavy frost stops the show.

▲ *C.* 'Sea Urchin'

Although 'Sea Urchin' looks as spidery as its namesake, it's classed as a "Quill" mum because its petals are straight and open at the tips; "Spider" mums have tubular petals, too, but they hook or coil at the tips. The intriguing blossoms of 'Sea Urchin' can reach 6 inches (15 cm) across. This lively cultivar is an early bloomer.

▶ *C.* 'Vesuvio'

The unusual form of 'Vesuvio' is sure to garner attention in your garden. Its flowers are classed as "Anemone" type because of their cushion center. Plant this midseason bloomer where it can really show off its 2-inch (5-cm) flowers; its vivid color looks great in front of a mass of goldenrods (*Solidago* spp.).

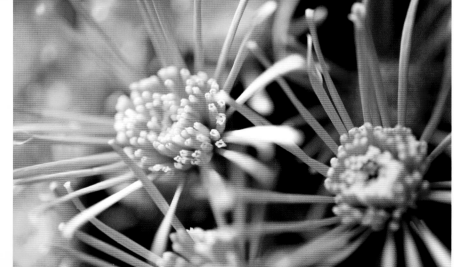

Clematis *KLEM-uh-tis • herbaceous clematis*

Clematis vines, with their showy flowers, are so beloved by gardeners that the herbaceous perennial types of this plant from the Ranunculaceae family are usually left to connoisseurs to seek out. However, once you make their acquaintance, you'll discover they can be just as beautiful, in a more understated way, as their showy hybrid cousins on the trellis. Look for intriguing herbaceous clematis at well-stocked garden centers, or investigate specialized mail-order nurseries.

Clematis heracleifolia (tube clematis) Imagine a "hyacinth bush," and you have the general idea of this species. Sweet-scented blossoms shaped like the individual bells of a hyacinth are held in open clusters on the upper branches of this deciduous shrubby plant. Flower color can vary from pale blue to blue-mauve, and the blossoms are produced for weeks, from late summer to fall. The large, compound leaves are vaguely maple-shaped. It needs no staking. Cut back dead stems to just above ground level in early spring to keep the plant vigorous. It grows to 3 to 4 feet (90 to 120 cm) tall and wide. Hardy in Zones 3 to 9. 'Little Blue', a mini version of the species, reaches only 15 inches (38 cm) tall and 20 inches (50 cm) wide. The gray-green leaves are much smaller than those of its parent species. It has a profusion of pale blue flowers in late summer.

C. heracleifolia var. **davidiana** Named for French missionary Armand David, who collected it in the 1860s in China, this variety spreads by underground rhizomes. It sports clusters of blue, sweet-scented flowers from late summer to fall and reaches about 3 feet (90 cm) tall. Hardy in Zones 4 to 9.

C. integrifolia (solitary clematis) Forms a mound decorated with many elegant blue-purple bells in early summer. The stems reach 2 to 3 feet (60 to 90 cm) long, but the plant tends to be loose and rambling. Let the stems meander beneath roses or through the garden, or corral the plant with neighbors it can lean on, such as iris (*Iris* spp.). Hardy in Zones 4 to 9.

Vining clematis These species and hybrids are vines, but they're not climbers. They lack the twining leaf stems that allow other clematis species to cling to a trellis. Many have charming downward-facing bells instead of the flat, starry, showy flowers of the true climbing hybrids. Let them wander through your garden or scramble upward through a rose, a witch hazel (*Hamamelis* spp.), or other open shrub. They'll lean against other plants or a fence. Or plant them in a container and tie them to a small decorative trellis or obelisk. Cut these species back in spring or throughout the season, as needed.

C. × durandii The 3- to 4-inch (7.5- to 10-cm) flowers of this nonclinging vine—a hybrid with *C. integrifolia* as one parent—are similar to those of the large-flowered climbing hybrids, but the 3- to 5-foot (90-to-150 cm)-long stems of this plant are ramblers, not climbers. The blossoms are rich blue with a tuft of white stamens in the center and bloom from midspring to fall. It is superb

Clematis heracleifolia cv.

with roses or trailing through perennials or yellow-leafed foliage plants. Hardy in Zones 4 to 9.

C. macropetala 'Blue Bird' Nodding blue-purple flowers in abundance, followed by dark silver seed heads, decorate this vine, which reaches 10 to 15 feet (3 to 4.5 m). Attach it to a support with loose strips of garden ties. It blooms from midspring into fall. Hardy in Zones 4 to 9. 'Blue Boy' is similar.

C. tangutica (golden clematis) Clear yellow, bell-shaped blossoms nod on this 8- to 10-foot (2.4- to 3-m) vine for many weeks. Feathery, silvery seed heads that look like loose balls of shining silver follow, lasting into winter. Let this one ramble through your perennial bed. Hardy in Zones 3 to 9. *C. orientalis* is similar, with grayer foliage and golden flowers.

C. texensis 'Etoile Rose' Charming cherry pink bells with a hint of purple are the appeal of this hybrid, which is ideal for scrambling against a silvery conifer or among gray-leaved perennials, such as 'Silver Queen' artemisia. Hardy in Zones 4 to 9.

C. 'Alionushka' A Ukrainian cultivar, it has nodding bells of lovely rose-pink. Its nonclinging stems roam through and over perennials, making a pretty splash of color. 'Heather Herschell' is a pretty pink. Hardy in Zones 4 to 9.

C. 'Arabella' This hybrid has open, starry blue blossoms in such abundance that it will form a lovely solid swathe of color among other perennials. Nonclimbing vines work themselves up and through roses or other tall plants. It's so vigorous that you can use it for a ground cover. Hardy in Zones 4 to 9.

THE BASICS

Herbaceous clematis are much easier to grow than true climbing clematis. They're adaptable plants that flourish in the average perennial garden or in a container. New species and cultivars are being introduced as gardeners embrace these pretty perennials. Experiment with any that catch your eye.

Growing Conditions: Plant in moist but well-drained soil of average-to-rich fertility. Water weekly in dry spells. Cut back to near ground level in early spring to keep them vigorous.

Propagation: You can divide *C. heracleifolia*. Other species are difficult to propagate, but try stem cuttings in early summer, before bloom. Some species may self-sow.

▶ **Bloom Time** Summer; some species, summer to fall
▶ **Planting Requirements** Full sun
▶ **Zones** Hardiness varies, depending on species

Convallaria *kon-vuh-LAIR-ee-uh • lily of the valley*

Old-fashioned romance is yours in an instant with this quaint icon of long-ago lovers. One of the most supremely fragrant plants in the garden, this plant—which is a member of the Convallariaceae family—has dainty white bells hung on slender stems. The intoxicating scent is so beloved that it has been a favorite in perfumes, candles, and scented soaps.

Convallaria majalis A vigorously spreading plant that forms a thick colony of simple, erect leaves. Its blooms last for two weeks in midspring. The foliage turns golden yellow in fall, then dies back for winter. It's ideal as a ground cover in shady gardens, where it combines beautifully with ferns, hostas, and other shade lovers. Sweep visitors to your garden off their feet by planting lily of the valley with equally romantic maidenhair ferns (*Adiantum pedatum*). The species reaches 8 inches (20 cm) tall. Shiny, translucent red berries may follow the flowers. 'Flore Pleno' is a double form, which to some eyes ruins the simplicity of the flowers and to others looks beautiful. 'Rosea' is the famed pink lily of the valley; the color is subtle, not striking bright pink. 'Striata' is a fancy-leaved cultivar, with gold stripes running down the green leaves. 'Albostriata' has leaves striped with creamy white.

THE BASICS

You can buy potted plants of lily of the valley, or start from purchased "pips," or small tubers. Pots of pre-chilled pips are sometimes sold before the Christmas holidays for forcing indoors; enjoy them in your house, then transplant to the garden in spring.

Growing Conditions: Plant in moist, humus-rich soil. It spreads invasively, so choose a site where that won't be a problem, such as beneath trees. In drier sites lily of the valley

Convallaria majalis

spreads more slowly and may even fade out after a few years.

Propagation: Divide the plant in early spring.

▶ **Bloom Time** Spring
▶ **Planting Requirements** Part to full shade
▶ **Zones** 2 to 8

Convolvulus *kon-VOLV-you-lus* • perennial morning glory

The large, lovely morning glories, members of the Convolvulaceae family, are well known to gardeners who grow the annual climbing vines. However, two mounding perennial species offer a different effect for milder climates. The profusion of flowers are the same shape as those of the vines, but they're smaller at 1 inch (2.5 cm) across.

Convolvulus cneorum (silverbush, bush morning glory) A tough shrubby plant, about 2 feet (60 cm) tall and wide, silverbush forms a rounded mound of small, silky, silvery leaves, smothered by white blossoms in early summer. Its buds are flushed with pink. This species is drought tolerant.

C. sabatius (*C. mauritanicus*; ground morning glory) Beautiful, abundant blue-lavender flowers bloom over a long period, from summer to fall. This perennial forms a loose, trailing, low mound 6 inches (15 cm) high and about 1½ to 2 feet (45 to 60 cm) wide. Its stems often root along the ground.

THE BASICS

These perennial morning glories are tough and trouble-free. Keep in mind that both species live up to their name. They bloom in the early part of the day, then close up. If you're not home in the morning, you probably won't see the flowers.

Growing Conditions: These species will do well in hot, sunny sites. Water regularly in the first year; after that, they can tolerate dry conditions. Silverbush is ideal for xeric gardens; its silvery leaves help it conserve water. Ground morning glory needs an occasional watering; once established, it can tolerate weeks of dry conditions. Good drainage is a must for both species; they'll grow in gravelly or stony soils, or in sandy seaside gardens. They are also well adapted to the rain-in-winter/dry-in-summer cycle of much of the western United States.

Propagation: Divide in spring.

▶ **Bloom Time** *C. cneorum*, summer; *C. sabatius*, summer to fall
▶ **Planting Requirements** Full sun
▶ **Zones** 8 to 10

Convolvulus cneorum

Convolvulus sabatius

Perfect Partners

A clump of Spanish lavender (*Lavandula stoechas*) makes a good backdrop for morning glory; its purple flowers will contrast with the white and silver of *Convolvulus cneorum* or coordinate with the lavender-blue of *C. sabatius*. Bright reddish pink Jupiter's beard (*Centranthus ruber*) increases the impact of both species; add pale pink geraniums nearby to soften the scene. Tall spikes of penstemons are a perfect contrast to the form of perennial morning glories.

C

Coreopsis *kor-ee-OP-sis* • coreopsis, tickseed

For a quick splash of sunshine in the garden, you can't beat coreopsis. These mostly North American natives from the Asteraceae family are reliable, and they make a big impact the first year you plant them. With flowers of golden yellow, sulfur yellow, or two-toned yellow-and-rust, they can fit into any color scheme. The pinkish version and dramatic mahogany type are less vigorous than their yellow cousins.

***Coreopsis auriculata* 'Snowberry'** (mouse ear coreopsis) The creamy white daisies in the center have a wine red blotch and an orange eye. It blooms from summer to fall, and it needs no deadheading, because the flowers don't set seed. It slowly spreads into a clump 2 feet (60 cm) tall and wide. Hardy in Zones 6 to 9.

C. grandiflora This central and southeastern native forms a basal clump of lance-shaped leaves with many flowering stems, each topped with a single golden yellow daisy. It reaches 1½ to 3 feet (45 to 90 cm) tall and 1½ feet (45 cm) wide. Although it is often short-lived, it self-sows. It is hardy in Zones 4 to 9. 'Early Sunrise' produces a multitude of fluffy, semi-double, deep yellow flowers; it is a short cultivar, reaching 1½ feet (45 cm) tall in bloom. 'Sunfire' has dramatic wine red centers and fringed petal tips. It blooms from early summer through midfall.

C. lanceolata This species has been cultivated in American gardens longer than any other species. It forms a basal clump of lance-shaped leaves, from which rise a multitude of flowering stems, each bearing a single golden yellow, notched-petaled flower. The leafy clump sprawls open after a few years, but the plant self-sows freely. Hardy in Zones 4 to 9.

***C. rosea* 'Sweet Dreams'** This plant forms a floriferous clump of thread-leaf foliage 15 inches (38 cm) tall; the flowers are dark pink-mauve with lighter petal tips. It may die over winter. Hardy in Zones 4 to 8.

C. verticillata (thread-leaved coreopsis) Totally different foliage and growth habit set this species and its cultivars apart from other coreopsis. It's a multistemmed long-lived perennial, with upright stems clothed in needlelike leaves that create an almost ferny effect as the plant grows into a clump 2 feet (60 cm) tall. The plant spreads into a large, dense clump up to 2 to 3 feet (60 to 90 cm) wide. The profuse flowers are 2 inches (5 cm) across. It is hardy in Zones 4 to 9. 'Zagreb' forms a blanket of rich golden yellow flowers for several weeks; it is drought tolerant.

C. 'Crème Brulee' Luminous yellow flowers that appear above foliage resemble that of threadleaf coreopsis. It grows to 1½ feet (45 cm) tall but often sprawls, forming an open clump 2 feet (60 cm) wide. It is mildew resistant and drought tolerant. Hardy in Zones 5 to 8.

C. 'Limerock Ruby' This hybrid forms a big, airy mound of feathery leaves that is topped with masses of mahogany daisies, but it can die unexpectedly over winter, even in mild climates. Hardy in Zones 7 to 9.

C. 'Pinwheel' A unique hybrid, each light yellow petal is rolled and

Coreopsis verticillata

flared, creating an irresistible effect. The eye of each daisy is deep gold. It grows to 2 feet (60 cm) tall and 2½ feet (75 cm) wide. Hardy in Zones 6 to 8.

THE BASICS

Coreopsis are easy to grow. They adapt well to challenging conditions, as well as to more hospitable sites. Many are easy to grow from seed.

Growing Conditions: Plant in lean-to-average, well-drained soil. Fertilizer may result in floppy plants. Snip off dead flowers for faster repeat bloom. Cut back the plants to just above ground level in late fall. Several afflictions, including mildew, rust, and fungal spots, can disfigure the plants. Avoid problems by allowing room around the plant for air to circulate. Treat with fungicides, if desired.

Propagation: *C. grandiflora* and *C. lanceolata* self-sow. Divide *C. rosea* and *C. verticillata* and their hybrids in early spring, or take root cuttings in early summer, before flower buds form.

▷ **Bloom Time** Summer, often into fall
▷ **Planting Requirements** Full sun
▷ **Zones** Varies, depending on species

Coreopsis for Sunny Spots

Coreopsis were once available only in sunshine shades of golden yellow. Those cheerful blossoms are still immensely valuable for adding a bright splash to your garden in a hurry, but new introductions have added to the color scheme. Look for pink tones and dramatic mahogany, plus softer sulfur yellows, for more possibilities with these easy-to-grow plants. All of the excellent selections featured here thrive in full sun without fading.

◄ *C. lanceolata* **'Walter'**
This popular cultivar grows in a small mound up to 2 feet (60 cm) tall and wide. The showy golden flowers with a red-eye center bloom from late spring through summer. It does well in hot, dry conditions.

▲ *C. verticillata* **'Moonbeam'**
This cultivar produces a mass of sulfur yellow blossoms that will brighten the garden for months, from early summer to fall.

▶ *C. grandiflora* **'Sunray'**
The fluffy, fully double flower heads are a rich, deep yellow. This cultivar grows to 2 to 2½ feet (60 to 75 cm) tall, and the flowers are ideal for cutting. 'Sunburst' is a similar cultivar.

▼ **C. lanceolata 'Sonnenkind' (Baby Sun)**

Here's a cultivar that is smaller and less sprawling than the species, reaching 16 inches (40 cm) tall in bloom. It is more yellow than the semidouble golden orange 'Babygold' cultivar. 'Goldfink' (Goldfinch) is even shorter, reaching only about 10 inches (25 cm).

▲ **C. rosea**

The small flowers on the pink coreopsis are not as showy as some of the other species. They are a dusty mauve, not clear pink, and are best suited as an edging near a walkway, where the flowers can be seen up close.

▶ **C. 'Limerock Ruby'**

This unique coreopsis has rich, velvety red flowers set off by vibrant yellow centers. It forms a bushy mound 1½ feet (45 cm) high and 3 feet (90 cm) wide that blooms from late June until September.

147

Cortaderia *kor-tuh-DAIR-ee-uh* • pampas grass

Pampas grass is a main component of grasslands in Argentina and Uruguay. Towering clumps of silvery plumed pampas grass from the Poaceae family add quick stature to the garden, but these grasses can be invasive and may become pests in and out of the garden.

Cortaderia richardii (New Zealand pampas grass; toe toe) This is a slightly smaller species than the South American native, with a more arching habit. The leaf blades grow to 4 feet (1.2 m) long and form a clump 6 feet (1.8 m) across. The flowering stems rise to 9 feet (2.7 m) tall.

C. selloana (*C. argentea*; pampas grass, Argentine pampas grass) A huge grass, forming a dense clump of mostly evergreen leaf blades 8 feet (2.4 m) long. Silvery, feathery spikes of flowers rise in late summer, often flushed with pink or mauve. They grow 1½ to 3 feet (45 to 90 cm) long, on stems reaching up to 10 feet (3 m).

THE BASICS

Check with your local USDA office, listed in the phone book, to find out if pampas grass causes problems in your area. Do not plant pampas grass in Hawaii, where it is banned. If pampas grass sows itself into your garden, dig out young plants before they get established. Getting rid of an established clump requires repeated applications of herbicide and laborious removal of the deep, tough roots.

Growing Conditions: Choose a permanent site, away from passersby and children—the leaf edges are sharp. Pampas grass thrives in well-drained, average soil. It also grows in stony,

Cortaderia selloana

gravelly, or sandy sites with poor soil and is drought tolerant. The seed heads persist into winter; cut them off after flowering to prevent self-sowing. Remove dead leaves in spring; wear protective gloves and long sleeves.

Propagation: May self-sow.

▶ **Bloom Time** *C. richardii*, early to midsummer; *C. selloana*, late summer to fall
▶ **Planting Requirements** Full sun
▶ **Zones** 7 to 10

Corydalis *ko-RID-uh-lis* • corydalis

Here is a dainty, free-blooming perennial from the Papaveraceae family, which is perfect for a special spot in your garden. The foliage is fine-textured, with evergreen leaflets that stay spring green year-round. It adds a bright spot among hostas, ferns, and other plants in part shade or among pinks (*Dianthus* spp.), geraniums, iris, and other perennials in a sunnier spot. If you look close, you'll see the interesting shape of the blossoms, which have a downward-curving spur.

Corydalis ochroleuca (white corydalis) From late spring to summer, the 1-foot (30-cm) clump is decorated with short spikes of small, drooping, tubular white flowers with yellow tips. It self-sows freely.

THE BASICS

This perennial is easy to grow and quick to multiply. Use it to cover the ground or edge a bed, or place it along a paved or brick walkway or patio.

Growing Conditions: Plant in rich, well-drained soil. Self-sows freely, often popping up in niches; unwanted seedlings are easy to remove.

Propagation: Divide in early spring. Transplant self-sown seedlings

Corydalis ochroleuca

when they are big enough to handle, using a trowel.

▶ **Bloom Time** Spring to summer
▶ **Planting Requirements** Sun to part shade
▶ **Zones** 6 to 8

Crocosmia *kro-KAHS-mee-uh* • crocosmia, montbretia

Crocosmia is one of many popular imports from Africa. This flaming red or orange perennial is a striking presence in the late-summer garden—and is a favorite of all-American hummingbirds. Crocosmias, which are members of the Iridaceae family, grow in an expanding clump because their corms multiply. The foliage is similar to that of Siberian iris (*Iris sibirica*), a dense clump of pointed, slightly arching spears. However, the flower is like none other: Dozens of flaring, funnel-shaped blossoms are borne on each bare, arching flowering stem, and a single clump may produce dozens of stems.

Crocosmia aurea Although the word *aurea* means yellow, pale orange to deep orange flowers are the hallmark of this species. The leafy clump reaches 1½ to 2 feet (45 to 60 cm) tall, with arching flower stems 3 feet (90 cm) long.

C. paniculata This is the giant of the genus, with plants stretching to 5 feet (1.5 m) tall. Large, downward-facing, orange flowers are borne on branching stems.

C. × 'Bressingham Blaze' The brilliant orange-red flowers are 2 to 2½ inches (5 to 6 cm) long. It grows to 2½ to 3 feet (75 to 90 cm) tall.

C. × crocosmiiflora (montbretia) Once classified in its own genus, montbretia now is grouped with crocosmia. This longtime favorite is a vigorous grower that can quickly spread into large clumps and even become invasive. It often survives where old houses once stood or along roadsides. Flowers are orange or yellow, and the plant reaches 2 feet (60 cm).

C. × 'Emberglow' Fabulous deep, rich red flowers can reach 3 inches (7.5 cm) long, among the largest of crocosmias. The flowering stems are branching, multiplying the display.

C. × 'Emily McKenzie' ('Lady McKenzie') This bicolor hybrid has big orange and yellow-orange flowers, marked with maroon in the throat.

C. × 'Golden Fleece' ('Citronella') This floriferous, clear yellow cultivar weaves gracefully into perennial beds, where it's the ideal companion for blue-lavender aster 'Monch'.

C. × 'Lucifer' The base of each upward-facing fiery red bloom has

Perfect Partners

Use the vertical lines of crocosmia to punctuate the mounded or sprawling shapes of other perennials, such as geraniums, balloon flower (*Platycodon grandiflora*), marguerite daisies (*Anthemis tinctoria*), and chrysanthemums. Or let them command a relaxed planting of artemisia or a waterfall of asters. Yellow cultivars mingle sweetly with blue Rozanne or 'Johnson's Blue' geraniums, lavender-blue scabiosa (*Scabiosa* × 'Butterfly Blue'), and with red or blue penstemons and salvias. Incendiary orange-red cultivars are set off by silvery or gray foliage, such as that of lavenders (*Lavandula* spp.), lamb's ears (*Stachys byzantina*), or globe thistle (*Echinops* spp.).

Crocosmia × 'Emily McKenzie'

some orange. It reaches 4 feet (120 cm) tall and is slightly more hardy.

THE BASICS

Buy crocosmia as corms, sold in the fall or spring through catalogs and at garden centers. They'll bloom the same year you put them in the ground. Plant them 3 to 4 inches (7.5 to 10 cm) deep, in groups of at least five corms, or a dozen or more for a bigger splash; they'll multiply quickly. You can also buy potted plants at garden centers and nurseries.

Growing Conditions: Plant in well-drained, average-to-rich soil. Crocosmia also does well in sandy soil and seaside conditions. Although it flourishes in regularly watered gardens, it's also extremely drought tolerant. If your plants spread too fast to suit your garden, use a trowel to uproot the extras.

Propagation: Divide in spring, before new shoots appear.

▶ **Bloom Time** Summer
▶ **Planting Requirements** Full sun
▶ **Zones** 6 to 9

Dahlia *DAL-ee-uh* • dahlia

Dinner-plate dahlias, cactus dahlias, button dahlias, anemone dahlias, orchid dahlias, waterlily dahlias—all originate from a humble wildflower found in the mountains of Mexico and Central America. This member of the Asteraceae family has undergone a lot of fiddling over the years. In 1872 the first collected dahlia tubers were shipped from Mexico to the Netherlands, where they touched off a craze that hasn't stopped. You could fill your garden with nothing but dahlias and have flowers in every color but blue, ranging in height from 1 foot (30 cm) to giants that top out at 6 feet (1.8 m), and with flowers from diminutive bouttoniere size to monsters almost 1 foot (30 cm) across. No wonder the world is filled with dahlia fanciers.

With persistence you can track down a few true dahlia species, such as *Dahlia coccinea* var. *palmeri*, which has bright orange-red flowers, or *D. imperialis*, giant tree dahlia, which in the wild can reach almost 30 feet (9 m) tall. However, there are thousands of gorgeous hybrid cultivars waiting for you to start exploring. Here's a small sampling to whet your appetite for delicious Dahlias.

Dahlia 'Bednall Beauty' Zingy red flowers appear on a 2-foot (60-cm) clump of smoky, dark purple foliage. The deeply cut leaves create an almost ferny effect. This is an early bloomer, kicking off the show in late spring to early summer.

D. 'Bishop of Llandaff' This gem has bronzy red leaves topped with brilliant red daisylike flowers. It begins blooming in midsummer and keeps going until fall. It was named in 1924 to honor Bishop Hughes of Llandaff, which is now Cardiff, Wales. Bishop Hughes of Llandaff may not have known his namesake dahlia was starting a trend, but now there is a group of dark-foliage dahlias known as the "Gardening Diocese" series. 'Bishop of Leicester' is another member of the "Gardening Diocese" series. This hybrid has lavender flowers with orange centers above its moody, dark purple foliage. 'Bishop of York' has golden orange flowers with dark foliage.

D. 'Kiss' One of the "Happy Series" of dahlias with nearly black foliage, this cultivar has cheerful salmon pink flowers with reddish centers.

D. 'Nippon' Breeders have been having a field day with dark foliage, but not all the color combinations with flowers are pleasing to the eye. This pint-sized plant is one of the best, with light yellow, 2-inch (5-cm) flowers highlighting a compact 16-inch (40-cm) mound of somber blackish foliage.

THE BASICS

Taller varieties will need staking. Make sure you push the stakes firmly into the ground before you cover the tubers, so you don't accidentally spear one of your dahlias-to-be.

Growing Conditions: Plant in well-drained, humus-rich soil. For lush, leafy growth apply liquid fertilizer every 10 days to two weeks until midsummer; apply liquid high-potassium fertilizer from midsummer

Dahlia 'Bishop of Llandaff'

to late summer for better flowering. Dahlias will also grow without supplemental fertilizer. Pinch all dahlias by removing the growing tip of each stem to keep them compact and bushy. Deadhead as flowers fade to encourage more buds.

Foliage turns a shocking black when nipped by frost, a sign that it's time to dig the tubers if you live in colder areas. After a frost cut back the stems and carefully dig up the tubers; they'll be a tangled clump. Set them upside down to dry for a few days, then pack them in a box of dry sand and store over winter in a frost-free place. You can dust with fungicide before storage to help prevent problems with rot.

Propagation: Dig and separate tubers in fall. Start stem cuttings in spring.

▶ **Bloom Time** Summer or fall
▶ **Planting Requirements** Full sun
▶ **Zones** 7 to 9

Delphinium *del-FIN-ee-um* • delphinium

These spectacular perennials stand tall, ruling the scene with eye-catching, 4- to 6-foot (1.2 to 1.8 m) spikes of ruffled, spurred blossoms in clear blues and purples, often with a white or dark spot at the center, where small, fuzzy petals form a "bee." Fabulous as they are, delpiniums, members of the Ranunculaceae family, are finicky in some gardens. They demand regular moisture and cool summer nights without high humidity, which puts many of them out of reach for southeastern, southern, and lower Midwest gardeners. A few less familiar species, including red- or orange-flowered species, will thrive in the dry-summer West. Traditional tall delphiniums are mostly hybrids developed by crossing various species. You'll find many choices in every hue of blue, plus pinks, purples, and white.

Delphinium elatum (bee delphinium) The parent of many popular hybrids, this perennial has lobed leaves that form a clump 3 to 4 feet (90 to 120 cm) wide. Spikes of blue-violet flowers stand tall on 5- to 6-foot (1.5 to 1.8-m) stems. Hardy in Zones 2 to 7.

D. grandiflorum (Chinese delphinium) The delphinium for hotter climates, it grows in a loose, branching mound of fine foliage 2 feet (60 cm) tall and wide, and is covered with lovely rich blue flowers. Hardy in Zones 3 to 8. 'Blue Elf' is a small, tidy cultivar that reaches only 1 foot (30 cm) tall. 'Blue Mirror' is a beloved cultivar, thanks to its floriferous habit and deep blue color; it is a short, heat-tolerant cultivar.

D. nudicaule (scarlet larkspur, canyon delphinium) This short-lived orange- to red-flowered delphinium is native to woodland canyons of northern California and the southern Oregon coast; in the garden it can take partial shade to full sun. Unlike most delphiniums, this species has tubular blossoms on wiry stems leaning over the fine foliage, but the color has big impact. 'Laurin' is a fine red cultivar, adored by hummingbirds. Hardy in Zones 5 to 8. The similar but taller *D. cardinale*, also known as scarlet larkspur, is a drought-tolerant native of the Southwest and a good choice for xeric gardens. Hardy in Zones 7 to 9.

D. 'Astolat' This is a popular Pacific hybrid, with gentle lilac-pink flowers that add vertical punctuation to beds of romantic pastels.

D. 'Black Knight' A longtime favorite, this Pacific hybrid has dramatic, deep purple flowers made even more intense by black "bees."

D. 'Blue Bees' A sky blue Belladonna hybrid with an upright, branching flower spike, this plant looks fresh and pretty with white "bees". Other blue varieties include 'Summer Skies', a light blue Pacific hybrid, and 'Blue Fountains', a pale blue Connecticut Yankee hybrid.

D. 'Fanfare' One of the tallest types, the huge, jam-packed stems of this mauve Elatum hybrid can reach 7 feet (2.1 m) tall in good conditions.

D. 'Ivory Towers' You can try this Mid-Century hybrid for a white accent mark, or investigate some of the others: 'Casablanca' is an all-white Belladonna hybrid, 'Percival' is a white

Delphinium hybrids

Pacific hybrid with black bees, and 'Galahad' is all white.

THE BASICS

Delphiniums are best in cooler, wetter regions. If your summers are long and hot, you may get one season of bloom, but the plants will rarely grow into lush, flower-heavy clumps. Unlike many perennials, delphiniums live for only a few years.

Growing Conditions: Choose a site in rich, well-drained soil, and dig in humus before you plant. Fertilize regularly. Most delphiniums are top-heavy and need secure staking to keep them from toppling; attach each flowering stem to a support when buds begin to show color. Cut back the flower spike to just above the leafy part of the stem to promote a second round of bloom. They may self-sow.

Propagation: Easy to grow from seed. Divide clumps in early spring.

▶ **Bloom Time** Summer

▶ **Planting Requirements** Full sun; light to partial shade in hotter areas

▶ **Zones** 3 to 9, depending on species and cultivar

D

Dianthus *dy-AN-thus • pinks, dianthus*

Dianthus gratianopolitanus

These old-fashioned perennials spread fast into mats or tufts of dense needle-like foliage, crowned by fragrant flowers in spring or summer. Most dianthus, which are from the Caryophyllaceae family, are shades of pink, but there are also white, red, and bicolored cultivars.

Dianthus × allwoodii (Allwood pinks) Forming a loose mound 1 to 1½ feet (30 to 45 cm) tall and wide, these clove-scented hybrids come in hues of pink, white, or pinkish purple, and bloom from late spring well into summer. 'Doris' is salmon with a dark center; 'Ian' is a striking scarlet. The species is hardy to Zone 4, but nearly all cultivars are best in Zones 6 to 8.

D. deltoides (maiden pinks) The cultivars of this low-growing species have small blossoms that smother the foliage with vivid color. 'Zing Rose' is cherry red; 'Arctic Rose' is white with a pink center. Hardy in Zones 3 to 9.

D. gratianopolitanus (cheddar pinks) Cheddar pinks form a springy mound of grayish foliage, topped with a profusion of clear rose-pink, fringed blossoms. Magenta 'Firewitch' and white 'Albus' broaden the color choices. 'Tiny Rubies' has small rose-pink flowers. Hardy in Zones 3 to 9.

THE BASICS

Pinks need good drainage. They spread quickly but aren't aggressive. After a few years pinks look weak and ragged; divide and replant the divisions to keep them vigorous. They often self-sow.

Growing Conditions: Plant in well-drained, average garden soil or in gravelly or stony soil. Allow room so that air can circulate. Rust can disfigure the foliage with yellowish spots; apply a sulfur-based preventive. Deadhead to keep new blooms coming.

Propagation: Divide in early spring.

▶ **Bloom Time** Spring or summer
▶ **Planting Requirements** Full sun
▶ **Zones** Varies; many are cold-hardy to Zone 3

Dicentra *dy-SEN-truh • bleeding heart*

Dicentra spectabilis

This charming perennial from the Papaveraceae family includes *Dicentra spectabilis*, a tall, old-fashioned favorite. Other species are shorter and form relaxed mounds of feathery foliage decorated with smaller blooms.

Dicentra eximia (wild bleeding heart) This species forms a lacy, 10- to 18-inch (25- to 45-cm)-tall mound of blue-green leaves with clusters of pink hearts from spring to summer. Hardy in Zones 3 to 9.

D. formosa (Pacific bleeding heart) A familiar wildflower in the Pacific Northwest, it is similar to *D. eximia*, with feathery blue-gray foliage, and blooms from spring through summer. It self-sows and spreads by rhizomatous roots. Rosy red 'Luxuriant' is popular. Hardy in Zones 3 to 8.

D. spectabilis (bleeding heart) The clump expands to 4 feet (120 cm) over the years. The leaves turn yellow and die back after spring flowering except in northern areas. The foliage of 'Gold Heart' emerges golden, then turns yellowish green. Hardy in Zones 2 to 9.

THE BASICS

Bleeding hearts are undemanding, long-lived plants.

Growing Conditions: Plant in loose, moist soil. Water regularly until they go dormant. If your summers are long and hot, give all species part to full shade, especially in the afternoon.

Propagation: Divide in early spring or fall; break the rhizomes into pieces that have at least three buds.

▶ **Bloom Time** Spring to summer
▶ **Planting Requirements** In the North full sun to shade; otherwise, part-to-full shade
▶ **Zones** Varies, depending on species

D

Dictamnus

dik-TAM-nus • gas plant, burning bush, false dittany, fraxinella

The lemony fragrance of the foliage and flowers of gas plant comes from a volatile oil that supposedly turns the plant into a Cherries Jubilee if ignited. Some believe that this Mediterranean native from the Rutacaea family may have spontaneously combusted to create the burning bush of the Bible. Gas plant is one of the few old-fashioned garden favorites that hasn't yet made a comeback in popularity. With its spikes of flowers and elegant leaves, why not start the trend?

Dictamnus albus (burning bush) This plant forms an erect clump of stems 3 to 4 feet (90 to 120 cm) tall and wide, clothed in glossy leaves that look good even when the early summer flowers aren't in bloom.

Spikes of purple-veined pink, mauve, or white flowers have a conspicuous spray of upward-curving stamens.

THE BASICS

It takes a few years for gas plant to get established, but then it is long-lived. The starry seedpods add another decorative touch.

Growing Conditions: Gas plant grows best where summer nights are cool. Choose a permanent site in well-drained, average-to-rich soil. The roots are easily damaged, so be careful when you slide the plant out of its pot; try to keep the soil intact when you settle it into the hole. Water regularly the first year, then leave the plant alone except to sniff its sharp, citrusy aroma.

Dictamnus albus

Propagation: This plant resents root disturbance, so avoid division. It is difficult to start from seed.

▶ **Bloom Time** Early summer
▶ **Planting Requirements** Sun to part shade
▶ **Zones** 3 to 8

Digitalis

dij-ih-TAL-iss • foxglove

This sturdy perennial provides spires of large, bell-shaped flowers that stand erect without staking. Flowers may be pale pink to deep rose, rusty brown, creamy yellow, or pure white, and many are marked with freckles inside the tube. From the Scrophulariaceae family, all foxgloves form a clump of basal leaves, usually large and coarse.

D. grandiflora (yellow foxglove) This long-lived foxglove produces pale primrose yellow flowers on spikes 3 feet (90 cm) tall. The similar *D. lutea* is shorter. Hardy in Zones 3 to 8.

D. × mertonensis (strawberry foxglove) Salmon, apricot, cream, and other hues are found in this hybrid. Hardy in Zones 3 to 8.

D. purpurea (common foxglove, purple foxglove) A popular choice, it has flower spikes 4 to 5 feet (1.2 to 1.5 m) tall. Flower color varies, from rose-pink to deep rose-purple, as well as clear white. It is usually a biennial, growing foliage the first year, flowers the second, and declining or dying the third year. Hardy in Zones 4 to 8. 'Foxy' blooms the first year from seed.

THE BASICS

Foxgloves make a spectacular but short-lived show in shady areas, and you can enjoy them in sunny beds, too.

Growing Conditions: Choose a site that isn't waterlogged in winter. Plant in

Digitalis purpurea

rich, well-drained soil; add humus.

Propagation: Divide *D. grandiflora* in early spring; all species by seed.

▶ **Bloom Time** Summer; occasionally into fall
▶ **Planting Requirements** Sun to shade
▶ **Zones** Varies with species

Dryopteris *dry-OP-ter-iss* • wood fern, shield fern, male fern

Dryopteris erythrosora

Like a Harley rider paired with a ballerina, wood ferns are tough but graceful. From the Dryopteridaceae family, they form a large, outward-arching clump of lacy fronds with a leathery texture, creating a splendid accent in shaded gardens. They're evergreen in mild climates and semievergreen in colder areas. Fancy frilled and ruffled cultivars are available, but the "unimproved" species types are also beautiful.

Dryopteris affinis (golden-scaled male fern) A favorite of plant breeders, this robust species grows 3 to 4 feet (90 to 120 cm) tall, holding its fronds almost upright instead of arching. The stems have shaggy, golden brown scales. If you're a fan of the unusual, seek out varieties with fancy fronds, such as dwarf 'Crispa Gracilis', with a froth of curled tips at the end of each leaflet, or 'Cristata the

Dryopteris filix-mas

King', whose leaflets end in fan-shaped tips. Hardy in Zones 6 to 9.

D. erythrosora (Japanese autumn fern) Colored foliage is a hit with gardeners, and this fern has it in spades. New fronds emerge coppery pink in spring, gradually mellowing to shiny deep green. The color is lovely with pink-flowered epimediums (*Epimedium* spp.), especially in front of evergreens, where the companions can show off against a dark backdrop. Hardy in Zones 5 to 9.

D. filix-mas (male fern) This American and European native provides both yin and yang with its wide vase of tapering, leathery fronds. Consider it a permanent member of your woodland garden, where it will be a significant presence. Plant breeders have created many forms. Look for the gentle giant 'Linearis Polydactyla', a waterfall of 3- to 4-foot (90- to 120-cm)-tall fronds of narrow,

Perfect Partners

Contrast the fine-cut fronds of these stout-hearted ferns with the simple leaves of hostas. Add astilbe for color in summer and Japanese anemones (*Anemone* × *japonica*) for later color in fall. Native American woodland aster species, such as heart-leaved aster (*Aster cordifolium*), make good neighbors, too, as do any woodland wildflowers of your choosing. Create a natural touch by planting your favorite wood ferns of plain or fancy type beside a landscaping rock or beneath a shade tree.

fine-cut leaflets ending in a lacy ruff of curling tips. For a different form try the skinny, ruffly, nearly erect fronds of 'Barnesii'. Hardy in Zones 3 to 9.

THE BASICS

If you don't already have a shade garden, these ferns may be all the inspiration you need to start one. They're among the easiest and most rewarding ferns to grow, and the fancy forms can warm a collector's heart. Once you plant them, you can celebrate their tough character and their beauty for years in your garden.

Growing Conditions: Plant in moist, well-drained, acid soil; work in extra humus at planting time. Mulch with chopped fall leaves. Read the label for the width of your selection so you can allow the plant enough room to freely reach its full glory.

Propagation: Divide young plants, or "offsets," from the outside of the crown of the parent plant.

▶ **Bloom Time** No bloom
▶ **Planting Requirements** Part to full shade
▶ **Zones** Varies, depending on species

Echinacea *ek-in-AY-see-uh* • purple coneflower, coneflower, echinacea

Springing from all-American origins as a wildflower of the prairies, purple coneflower quickly became a must-have when it was introduced to the gardening world a few decades ago. A member of the Asteraceae family, it is a plant that will give you enormous bang for the buck, with its prolific, rosy purple daisies that put on a show for months. As other incentives, it is easy to grow, has an adaptable attitude, and has a magnetic relationship with butterflies and goldfinches—no wonder coneflowers made the leap from the prairies to our backyards.

Echinacea pallida (pale coneflower) Once grown only by dedicated enthusiasts, this species has joined the parade to the garden bed. It has sparse branches and flowers with long, scanty, drooping petals that dangle from the orange-brown cone. Each blossom tops a stem rising 3 to 4 feet (90 to 120 cm) tall. It is listed as threatened in Tennessee and Wisconsin, but it's available as a garden plant. It is hardy in Zones 3 to 8.

E. paradoxa (yellow coneflower) Not to be confused with golden *Rudbeckia* spp. (another plant commonly called coneflower), this species is the parent of many of the exciting warm-colored cultivars that have appeared with much fanfare in recent years. It looks like a relaxed black-eyed Susan, with long, drooping petals hanging from the brown central cone. It is hardy in Zones 4 to 8.

E. purpurea (purple coneflower) The standard-bearer of the bunch, this species has wide, showy daisies of bright rose-pink. The center cone is as pretty as the petals, with a rich orange tint that contrasts with the petals. The plant forms a stout, leafy, clump, 2 to 3 feet (60 to 90 cm) across, with flowers held on mostly bare stems above the foliage. It is hardy in Zones 3 to 8. 'Alba' was the original white cultivar, but others have become more popular. The bright 'White Lustre' is ideal for a moonlight garden.

E. tennesseensis (Tennessee coneflower) Once thought to be extinct, this wildflower was rediscovered in Tennessee in the 1960s. It's still on endangered species lists in the wild, but it's becoming more common in nurseries and garden catalogs. The full wheel of bright pink petals is held wide open; instead of drooping, the petals curl slightly upward at the tips. Its foliage stays low to the ground in a mound. This is another species that has contributed to the parentage of modern hybrids. It is hardy in Zones 5 to 8. 'Rocky Top' has full, flat, bright pink daisies with bold dark centers. Its petals have a slight, uniform upward curl to their tips.

Echinacea purpurea

E. × 'Hope' This hybrid with soft pink flowers has been dedicated to breast cancer survivors, and to the memories of those who have passed away from it. Part of the proceeds from each plant sold will benefit the Susan G. Komen Foundation.

THE BASICS

Prairie plants are tough hombres; they had to be to withstand the drought, wind, wildfires, and winters of the Great Plains. With good looks to match that rugged character, these plants are winners all around.

Growing Conditions: Plant in well-drained, average soil. Let seed heads stand over winter to feed birds and make your garden look more interesting. Cut back plants to just above ground level in early spring. After their first year in the garden, the plants are drought tolerant.

Propagation: Take cuttings of the fleshy taproots in fall.

▶ **Bloom Time** Early summer to fall
▶ **Planting Requirements** Full sun; will bloom in light or part shade but may get leggy
▶ **Zones** Varies, depending on species

Plant Partners

For a long-blooming garden that produces never-ending color, combine purple coneflowers with feathery yarrows (*Achillea* spp.) and threadleaf coreopsis (*Coreopsis verticillata*), red-pink Jupiter's beard (*Centranthus ruber*), and reblooming daylilies, such as sunshine yellow 'Happy Returns' (*Hemerocallis* spp.).

Coneflowers for Constant Color

Many perennials bloom for an all-too-short two weeks, which is why it can be tricky to plan a perennial garden full of continual color. Coneflowers (*Echinacea* spp.) to the rescue! These sturdy perennials begin blooming in early summer and barely pause for breath until well into fall. They're naturally long blooming, but there's also a little trick: Simply snip off the seed heads after the petals fade and are straggly, and you'll have a constant crop of fresh color. Which color? The bouquet of coneflowers on these pages will give you a look at some old and new favorites.

◄ *E. purpurea* **'Fragrant Angel'**
One of the best white cultivars, it has large white flowers with overlapping petals that have tapered tips, creating a shaggy effect.

▲ *E.* × **'Orange Meadowbrite' ('Art's Pride')**
The fabulous color of this deep orange hybrid attracted gardeners when it was introduced. The rugged *E. purpurea* and the lanky *E. paradoxa* are parents to this hybrid, resulting in flowers in a rich, warm hue, but a plant that is not as vigorous as its rugged parents.

▶ *E. purpurea* **'White Swan'**
Try this cultivar in a moonlight garden, where its pale flowers will glow. Or plant scarlet bee balm (*Monarda* spp.) as a dramatic counterpoint to a mass of white coneflowers in the daytime garden. These coneflowers tend to lean toward off-white, with greenish gold cones. One of the most satisfying companions for white cultivars is their pinky purple cousin, *E. purpurea*.

▼ E. purpurea 'Rubinglow'

A shorter cultivar, 'Rubinglow', sometimes labeled 'Rubin's Glow', reaches 24 inches (60 cm). Like many coneflowers, this cultivar's blossoms hold their petals horizontally when fresh, then relax into a drooping attitude. This cultivar shows off a more intense pink-purple color, a perfect contrast of color and form with the plumes of goldenrod (*Solidago* spp.).

▲ E. 'Twilight'

The red cone of this plant from the Big Sky series is surrounded by vivid petals. It has a branching form and grows up to 2 feet (60 cm) tall.

▶ E. 'Summer Sky'

This bicolor coneflower is a first. It's from the Big Sky series, which have flowers up to 5 inches (12.5 cm) across held on stout stems. The flowers are fragrant, and the plant produces plenty of blooms.

157

Echinops *EK-in-ops* • globe thistle

Gardeners are enchanted by the round globes of blue flowers on this unusual perennial—and so are butterflies and bees, which can't seem to get enough of the nectar within the blossoms. However, the prickly, thistlelike leaves, the sometimes ungainly form, and the significant size of these architectural perennials from the Asteraceae family may give gardeners pause. Globe thistles have a strong personality, but their powerful ability to accent a bed or border make these plants stand out among less presumptuous perennials.

Echinops bannaticus 'Blue Globe' Perfectly round, intensely blue globes top this 4-foot (120-cm)-tall plant. It has jagged gray-green foliage. Hardy in Zones 4 to 9. The globe flowers of *E. bannaticus* 'Taplow Blue' are steel blue—an unusual color in the garden.

E. exaltatus (Russian globe thistle) Height can be variable for individual plants of this species, with some staying small—3 feet (90 cm) tall and wide—and others rocketing to as much as 6 to 8 feet (1.8 to 2.4 m) tall and half that wide. The thistlelike foliage can look weedy, so plant it in the back of the bed. It will still rise to glory in summer to late summer, with its clusters of spherical, silvery blue blooms. Hardy in Zones 3 to 9.

E. ritro (globe thistle) The most common garden species, this 2- to 4-foot (60- to 120-cm)-tall plant has stunning blue flowers that retain their color when dried for arrangements. It is a prolific self-sower. 'Veitch's Blue' has deep blue flowers. Hardy in Zones 3 to 9.

E. sphaerocephalus 'Arctic Glow' A smaller white-flowered cultivar, about 2½ to 3 feet (75 to 90 cm) tall, it has brownish red stems and prickly, silvery green foliage. Hardy in Zones 4 to 9.

THE BASICS

Select a site where globe thistle can remain undisturbed. Tap-rooted perennials, such as this one, can take their time settling in, because root disturbance during planting may set them back. Keep in mind that you will want to admire the flowers—and the insects that visit them—but without brushing up against the sharp, prickly foliage.

Growing Conditions: Plant in full sun, in well-drained, average soil. Like the true thistles along our roadsides, globe thistles flourish in poor soil and dry conditions, as long as their roots aren't in soggy soil. They also thrive in sandy soils, but clay may be too waterlogged. The tenacious taproots can withstand drought once established. Be patient after planting; it can take a year or two to see bloom because the taproots need time to settle in. It self-sows freely, and even young plants quickly grow a stubborn taproot; uproot with a dandelion digger. Use caution and wear protective clothing when working around the spiny leaves.

Propagation: Seed; or from root cuttings in spring.

▌ **Bloom Time** Summer

▌ **Planting Requirements** Full sun

▌ **Zones** 3 or 4 to 9

Echinops bannaticus 'Blue Globe'

Perfect Partners

Delicate ornamental grasses, such as switchgrass (*Panicum virgatum*), provide textural contrast to globe thistle; blue fescues (*Festuca* spp.) echo the color of the globe thistle flowers. Choose flower companions that bloom later in the season, as globe thistle does. Lacy sprays of Russian sage flowers (*Perovskia atriplicifolia*) or a spill of asters (*Aster cordifolius* and other spp.) will add soft texture and mirror the color of the blue globes. Add a deeper note with blue-purple monkshood (*Aconitum* spp.). Fire-engine red dahlias are as assertive; contrast them with white-flowered 'Arctic Glow' or steely 'Taplow Blue', along with a clump of miscanthus grass for an oasis of calm. Try neighbors with gray foliage, too, such as a carpet of lamb's ears (*Stachys byzantina*) or a mound of 'Powis Castle' artemisia.

Epimedium

ep-i-MEE-dee-um • barrenwort, fairy wings, epimedium

Epimedium × versicolor

Perennials that will thrive in shade are much more limited than those that do well in sun. The good news is that epimediums from the Berberidaceae family are suitable for shade. These hardy plants have open, branching clusters of dainty flowers, which are often in bloom before the clump of heart-shaped leaves emerges in spring. Fancy, curving sepals and spurs make some of the flowers look almost like tiny orchids. There are dozens of species in cultivation. Most are 1 foot (30 cm) tall and spread to make a ground cover.

Epimedium acuminatum (arrow-leaved barrenwort) This evergreen species was collected in China in 1981 by British plant hunter Roy Lancaster. Stoop down and you'll see that the flowers are purple and white on close inspection; they appear pale purple when viewed while standing. The glossy leaves are elongated, like arrowheads, and have a reddish tint when they first emerge. Hardy in Zones 4 or 5 to 8.

E. alpinum (alpine barrenwort) *Alpinum* indicates an origin from mountainous, or alpine, areas, and that usually translates into cold-hardy plants that can thrive in tough places. This cold-tolerant species has reddish flowers and is deciduous. Hardy in Zones 3 to 8. 'Shrimp Girl' has red-and-yellow flowers that appear shrimp pink from a distance; it grows to 8 inches (20 cm) tall.

E. brachyrrhizum (fairy wings) If epimediums have one flaw, it's that their flowers are tiny. Not this species— its pale rose-pink blooms stretch their spidery spurs to 2 inches (5 cm) across. This newcomer was discovered in China in 1994. New leaves are mottled with dark rose-purple. It grows about 8 inches (20 cm) tall and wide and is semievergreen.

E. franchetii (yellow barrenwort) This recently welcomed Chinese species is a beauty, with large, clear yellow flowers and foliage that emerges with a bronze hue. 'Brimstone Butterfly' has arching stems of spidery, lemon yellow flowers. Hardy in Zones 4 to 8.

E. grandiflorum (long-spurred barrenwort) This species produces sprays of purplish pink flowers with long, thin, downward-curving spurs. New growth is tinted bronzy red. Hardy in Zones 4 to 8. 'Rose Queen' has large, showy, deep pink flowers with long white spurs. The white spidery flowers of 'Saturn' are shown off against unusual foliage—each leaf has a maroon ring around it.

E. × perralchicum (barrenwort) Bronze, heart-shaped evergreen leaves form a mound from which spikes of yellow flowers emerge. 'Frohnleiten' is tinted bronzy red in winter.

E. × versicolor (bicolor barrenwort) This is a ground-cover hybrid with sprays of small, deep yellow flowers. 'Neosulphureum' is pale yellow and 'Sulphureum' is clear sunshine yellow. All look great with blue-flowered pulmonarias or blue wood anemones (*Anemone nemorosa* 'Robinsoniana'). Hardy in Zones 5 to 9.

THE BASICS

All epimediums are valuable, trouble-free perennials. Be aware of their ground-covering tendencies; most will spread at a moderate clip. Species and cultivars may also hybridize in your garden, leading to a surprising new plant every now and then. Evergreen species tend to get weather-worn over the winter; cut back the foliage in early spring to keep the plant looking its best.

Growing Conditions: Avoid a planting site that has soggy soil at any time of year. Plant in moist but well-drained soil of average fertility; dig in some humus at planting time. After that, a once-a-year cutting back is the only care they'll need. Most are moderately drought tolerant after their first year in the ground; they grow well when planted beneath trees. If the plants spread to undesired areas, just dig up the offenders and plant them somewhere else.

Propagation: Division; may self-sow.

▶ **Bloom Time** Spring, often beginning just before leaves emerge

▶ **Planting Requirements** Part to full shade

▶ **Zones** All thrive in at least 5 to 8; some are more cold tolerant

E

Erigeron er-RIJ-er-on • fleabane, erigeron

Fleabanes bring a plethora of daisies to the sunny garden, making a generous show of blue, white, pink, or purple in summer. The flowers of this plant from the Asteraceae family attract butterflies, along with beneficial insects that help keep garden pests under control.

Erigeron karvinskianus (Santa Barbara daisy, Mexican daisy) This ground-hugging daisy starts the spring season of bloom and keeps going into winter in mild climates. It does best in coastal climates; the summer heat of interior gardens may make it stop blooming. A single plant spreads to cover 2 feet (60 cm). It is also highly tolerant of dry conditions, but it may be invasive. Hardy in Zones 6 to 11.

E. speciosus (daisy fleabane, showy fleabane, Oregon fleabane) Here's a western North American native that forms a 2- to 2½-foot (60- to 75-cm) clump, topped with lavender-blue, yellow-eyed daisies. Hardy in Zones 2 to 7. 'Pink Jewel' ('Rose Jewel') has fluffy, rosy pink flowers.

THE BASICS

Fleabanes self-sow freely. To control them, clip off the flowers before they turn to fluffy seeds.

Growing Conditions: Plant in well-drained, average-to-lean soil. Fleabanes thrive in stony and sandy soil, too, and adapt well to seaside gardens. Snip off faded flowers for

Erigeron karvinskianus

more blooms into fall. Plants may be prone to mildew. Disguise affected plants by planting them in the middle of the bed. Or cut back to ground level and discard the clippings in the trash.

Propagation: Divide in spring. Easy to grow from seed.

▶ **Bloom Time** Summer
▶ **Planting Requirements** Full sun
▶ **Zones** *E. karvinskianus*, 7 to 11; *E. speciosus* and its hybrids, 2 to 7

Eryngium er-RIN-jee-um • sea holly

Striking sea holly from the Apiaceae family has leathery foliage that forms a mound of finely cut leaves. Stiff, erect, branching stems rise above them, armed with bluish or silvery leaflike bracts topped by tight-packed globes of tiny blue or white flowers.

Eryngium alpinum (alpine sea holly) Cultivars of this species, such as 'Blue Star' and 'Superbum', both of which boast deep blue flowers, are more commonly available than the species itself, which has steel blue flowers. Hardy in Zones 4 to 8.

E. amethystinum (sea holly) This species is rich blue—blue bracts and blue flowers. It grows to 3 feet (90 cm) tall in flower, forming a clump 2 feet (60 cm) wide. Hardy in Zones 2 to 8.

E. giganteum (Miss Willmott's ghost, giant sea holly) This biennial is simple to grow from seed. In its second year it zooms to 4 to 6 feet (1.2 to 1.8 m), topped with silvery white flower heads set upon a circlet of spiny bracts. Hardy in Zones 4 to 8.

E. 'Sapphire Blue' Every part of this plant—branching stems, leaves, and flowers—is infused with steel blue; it grows to 2 feet (60 cm) high.

THE BASICS

These are tough plants that can take anything, from drought to garden neglect. Use their dynamic architecture to contrast with softer plants.

Growing Conditions: Plant in well-drained, average soil. Sea hollies

Eryngium giganteum

need no fertilizer. They self-sow, often abundantly; transplant seedlings when young, and avoid disturbing the taproot. Cut back dead stems in late fall or early spring.

Propagation: Seed.

▶ **Bloom Time** Summer and early fall
▶ **Planting Requirements** Full sun
▶ **Zones** 5 to 8; some species tolerate more cold

E

Erysimum *ee-REE-see-mum* • wallflower

Sweetly scented wallflowers will nestle into crevices among stone walls and buildings. These short-lived perennials and biennials from the Brassicaceae family are among the earliest flowers to welcome spring. The linear-leaved plants, most 1 to 2 feet (30 to 60 cm) tall and wide, cover themselves in fragrant bloom. Their rounded flower spikes, crowded with small, simple blossoms, come in warm tones of yellow, orange, and rust, as well as in rosy purple.

Erysimum × allionii (Siberian wallflower) This short-lived perennial, formerly classified as *Cheiranthus × allionii*, is a bright orange wallflower when it bursts into bloom. Hardy in Zones 3 to 7.

E. cheiri (formerly *Cheiranthus cheiri*; wallflower) A rainbow of cultivars in warm oranges, yellows, reds, and creamy white, plus some bicolors, are more common than the

Erysimum cheiri

saffron-orange species. It is usually grown as a biennial.

***E. cheiri* 'Bedder Series'** Fill your spring with color from cultivars such as 'Orange Bedder', 'Blood Red', or 'Brilliant Bedder', an extravagant mix of warm hues.

***E. cheiri* 'Fair Lady Series'** Bushy plants produce a splendid display of gold, cream, pink, purple, and rust flowers, perfect for filling containers.

***E.* 'Bowles Mauve'** One of the best hybrids, this sturdy plant has an erect, shrubby habit, with long spikes of rose-purple flowers that begin blooming in winter and last into summer. It rarely lives for more than two to three years. Hardy in Zones 6 to 10.

***E.* 'John Codrington'** The buds are bronzy red, for a lovely multicolored effect; blushing pink cheeks tint the creamy yellow flowers as they age.

***E.* 'Wenlock Beauty'** Dark and moody, with hints of purple, maroon, copper, and tangerine, this spectacular cultivar looks perfect when paired with vivid red, orange, or golden flowers.

THE BASICS

Wallflowers have a short life in the garden, but they'll reward you with prolific, fragrant flowers in early spring. And they'll sow a crop of babies for the following years.

Growing Conditions: Plant in well-drained, poor-to-rich soil; they can adapt to any kind of soil except a waterlogged one. Remove finished flower heads, and cut back the plant by about one-quarter after flowering to keep it compact and to extend its life:

Erysimum 'Bowles Mauve'

Wallflowers may prematurely die after setting seeds. They may be troubled by mildew and other fungal problems; treat with a fungicide if you want.

Propagation: Sow seed in fall.

▸ **Bloom Time** Spring to early summer
▸ **Planting Requirements** Full sun
▸ **Zones** 5 to 8 unless otherwise noted, or grow as bedding annuals in any zone

Perfect Partners

Wallflower hues are gorgeous with coordinating or contrasting tulips (*Tulipa* spp.). Try orange *Erysimum × allionii* or orange-flowered cultivars with 'Prinses Irene' tulip, which has deep orange flowers with purplish flames. Combine yellow wallflowers with pure white tulips, or with those flamed in red and yellow. Wallflowers bloom for a long period, so use earlier-blooming perennials, such as coreopsis and columbines (*Aquilegia* spp.), to play off their colors, too.

E

Eupatorium *you-puh-TOR-ee-um* • Joe Pye weed, boneset, eupatorium

Eupatorium maculatum

The best-known eupatoriums are a pair of towering, rugged plants topped with huge mops of fuzzy mauve flowers, known as Joe Pye weed (*E. maculatum* and *E. purpureum*)— named after a Native American doctor who purportedly used the medicinal herb. Eupatoriums, which are from the Asteraceae family, are excellent plants if you like butterflies. Most of those in cultivation in the United States, including the plants described here, are hardy, adaptable American natives.

Eupatorium coelestinum (mistflower, hardy ageratum) This enthusiastic grower, which spreads to form colonies, bears plentiful stems of fuzzy blue-lavender flowers that provide pleasing color from late summer into fall. The aromatic plants grow 2 to 3 feet (60 to 90 cm) tall and spread to 3 feet (90 cm) or more. Hardy in Zones 3 to 7.

E. maculatum (*E. purpureum* ssp. *maculatum*; spotted Joe Pye weed) This is the smaller of the Joe Pye weeds, but the multistemmed clump grows 4 to 7 feet (1.2 to 2.1 m) tall! Purplish red freckles mark the green stems. Rosy pink to mauve-purple flower heads bloom from midsummer to early fall. Hardy in Zones 3 to 8. 'Bartered Bride', a 3- to 4-foot (90- to 120-cm) cultivar, has dark greenish brown leaves topped with white flowers. 'Gateway', also reaching 3 to 4 feet (90 to 120 cm) tall, has fluffy flowers in muted lavender-purple.

E. purpureum (Joe Pye weed) The most well-known species, this plant forms a multistemmed clump that can tower to 10 feet (3 m), but in most gardens it stays at a more manageable 5- to 7-foot (1.5- to 2.1-m) height. The foliage is large and coarse; its reddish stems contrast with the green foliage and the giant clumps of fuzzy mauve flowers. Hardy in Zones 3 to 9. 'Atropurpureum' is a tall cultivar with wine red stems and intense purplish red flowers.

E. rugosum (white snakeroot) This species is common in fall along the edges of eastern and midwestern woodlands. The white flowers turn dirty white as they age, so this species is best suited for the wild garden. However, dark-foliaged cultivars are valuable among other fall flowers in the garden. Both species and cultivars can be invasive; dig out strays to keep the clump in control. Hardy in Zones 4 to 9. 'Chocolate' has glossy, reddish brown foliage and purple stems that form a clump 4 feet high (120 cm) by 3 feet (90 cm) wide. The cloud of bright snow white flowers stand out against the dark foliage. The young foliage of 'Braunlaub' is also tinged with a brownish hue.

THE BASICS

Eupatoriums are stalwart, adaptable plants, but they will require room. Clump-forming *E. maculatum* and *E. purpureum* are big, towering plants that can overpower a small garden; *E. coelestinum* and *E. rugosum* will spread by running roots.

Growing Conditions: Plant in moist soil of average-to-rich fertility; except for *E. rugosum,* all species listed also thrive in wet soil. Fertilizer will increase height. No staking will be necessary. Cut back all species to ground level by early spring.

Propagation: Divide in spring or fall.

- **Bloom Time** Summer to early fall
- **Planting Requirements** Full sun for all; *E. coelestinum*, also light-to-part shade; *E. rugosum*, also part-to-full shade
- **Zones** Hardiness varies, depending on species

Perfect Partners

In the summer-into-fall garden, eupatoriums add height to the relaxed forms of asters and other fall bloomers. Enjoy the soft blue color of *E. coelestinum* with yellow or white mums (*Chrysanthemum* spp.), and with the yellow fall foliage of balloon flower (*Platycodon grandiflora*). Let Joe Pye weeds (*E. maculatum* and *E. purpureum*) stand tall among ornamental grasses (*Miscanthus, Panicum,* and *Pennisetum* spp.); plant a swath of purple coneflowers (*Echinacea* spp.) in front. Try *E. maculatum* 'Bartered Bride' with bright, tall bulbs, such as gladiolus and cannas. Pink neighbors will perk up the dark-tinted foliage of *E. rugosum* 'Chocolate'; plant with pink asters, dahlias, and chrysanthemums.

E

Euphorbia *you-FOR-bee-uh* • spurge, euphorbia

This is a huge and diverse group of plants from the Euphorbiaceae family, with a striking, different look than most perennials. Many look like desert plants, with smooth, gray, succulent leaves, and most have abundant yellow or red flowers in showy clusters.

Euphorbia amygdaloides (wood spurge) This creeping evergreen is topped with clusters of greenish yellow bracts from midspring to early summer. 'Purpurea' has dark reddish purple foliage that stands out against the bracts. Hardy in Zones 6 to 9.

E. characias Along with its subspecies and cultivars, this popular species grows 4 feet (120 cm) tall and wide. It forms an upright, evergreen clump of gray-green foliage with a spectacular show of yellow-green bracts, borne from early spring to early summer. It may be short-lived, lasting only a few years in the garden. Hardy in Zones 7 to 10.

E. griffithii Erect, leafy stems 3 feet (90 cm) tall are topped by large yellow-red, almost orange, clusters of flowers and bracts in early summer. This euphorbia spreads by means of rhizomatous roots and can border on invasive. 'Dixter' has deep green foliage with a hint of burnished copper. 'Fireglow' has red stems of red-tinged green leaves topped with orange bracts that glow like a Yule log. Hardy in Zones 4 to 9.

E. myrsinites (myrtle spurge) The prostrate stems are clothed in intriguing circlets of succulent gray leaves. Stems sprawl outward along the ground from the center of the 1-foot (30-cm) clump, providing an evergreen accent of texture and form. In spring the stems are tipped with a generous burst of bright yellowish green bracts. Hardy in Zones 5 to 8.

E. polychroma (cushion spurge) A neat, tidy mound of dark green leaves, often tinged with red, form a backdrop when the plant is in bloom. It reaches 1 to 1½ feet (30 to 45 cm) tall and 1 to 2 feet (30 to 60 cm) wide. 'Candy' ('Purpurea') adds deep purple foliage during the growing season. 'Emerald Jade' provides a generous display of bright green bracts on red stems. Hardy in Zones 4 to 9.

E. schillingii This 3-foot (90-cm)-tall species has cool gray-green leaves with a noticeable white midrib, topped by yellow flowers in early summer. Hardy in Zones 7 to 9.

E. sikkimensis A striking species, this euphorbia offers bright pink new shoots in winter and early spring. The pink is retained in the midrib and veining of the mature leaves. Its lime green flowers bloom in late summer. You'll see another color show in fall, when the 3- to 4-foot (90- to 120-cm)-tall clump of foliage turns yellow tinted with red. Hardy in Zones 6 to 9.

THE BASICS

Well-drained soil is a must for euphorbias, which will quickly die in soggy sites. All have milky sap that can cause severe gastric distress if eaten and severe skin irritation if touched; some sensitive people may even have effects from brushing against the plants. Play it safe and wear gloves and long sleeves when working around them.

Euphorbia sikkimensis

Growing Conditions: Plant in well-drained soil of lean-to-average fertility. Fertilize for vigorous growth. Euphorbias thrive on challenging soil, including poor, stony or gravelly soils. Most are long-lived members of the garden; *E. characias* is the exception, but it self-sows. Species with succulent leaves are tolerant of dry conditions and are good for xeric gardens as well as average conditions; those with green foliage flourish in moist-to-average soil, but they can also withstand long periods of drought. Only *E. griffithii* requires regularly moist soil. Wait until late winter or early spring to cut back the plants, removing dead stems and bracts. If the plant self-sows, transplant seedlings to a better site, if you prefer.

Propagation: Divide in early spring; take tip cuttings of stems in summer. Wear gloves to protect your skin from contact with the sap.

▶ **Bloom Time** Varies from early spring to midspring or early summer, but all last for many weeks

▶ **Planting Requirements** Full sun

▶ **Zones** Hardiness varies, depending on species

Euphorbias for Long-Lasting Effects

The most popular euphorbias are bushy or sprawling plants with showy, super-long-lasting flowers, suitable as specimens that will add an unusual touch to your garden. Euphorbia "flowers" are actually tiny clusters in the center of bright-colored bracts, creating the effect of a bouquet of blossoms. Long after the true flowers turn to seed, the bracts remain ornamental on many species, especially those with an upright habit. But flowers aren't the only reason to grow euphorbias—their foliage provides a long-lasting show, too. Deciduous species have warm fall color, outstanding with the mellow tones of ornamental grasses; evergreen types offer something to admire even in winter, with their deep green or gray foliage.

◀ *E. myrsinites*

Myrtle spurge may sound like a character's name in an old novel, but this species is a valuable performer for a demanding position. It flourishes in dry, sandy, or stony soils, so it's perfect in niches of walls or in rock gardens, as well as in more hospitable well-drained sites.

▲ *E. polychroma*

An outstanding, long-lasting display of yellow bracts and flowers are borne from midspring to midsummer. You'll get a bonus in fall, when the plant turns a glorious mix of red, purple, and yellow.

▶ *E. characias* subsp. *wulfenii*

This subspecies has large, dense, rounded spikes of eye-catching chartreuse yellow bracts that crown the plant for months. One of the earliest bloomers in the garden, it makes a superb companion for daffodils. Try it with white 'Mount Hood' or 'Ice Follies' daffodils, fronted with a drift of snowy white candytuft (*Iberis* spp.).

▼ E. schillingii

This robust species forms 3-foot (90-cm)-wide and tall clump of leafy stems. The deep green leaves are striped with a white vein. Stems branch near the top and finish in a climax of yellowish green bracts from midsummer to midfall.

▲ E. griffithii

Orange is an unusual color in the garden. In summer the abundant bracts and flowers add a finial of warm orange to each stem. Fall foliage is just as colorful as the flowers, turning warm red and yellow in fall.

▶ E. amygdaloides

This creeping evergreen wood spurge has matte, dark green leaves borne on red stems, which look good even when the bracts are no longer in bloom.

Festuca *fess-TOO-kuh* • blue fescue

There are more than 300 species of fescue grass in the Poaceae family, but only a few are ornamental enough to earn a place in the garden. Those few, however, are among the most valuable and versatile grasses for a perennial bed or border. Their endearing tussock of stiff, fine leaves, their dwarf size, and their lovely blue-hued color make them ideal partners for flowering perennials.

The threadlike leaf blades of fescues and their delicate stems of flowers bow easily before the wind, then spring back without lasting damage. That trait makes them a good choice for seaside or midwestern gardens, or in any other area where windy conditions are frequent.

Festuca amethystina (large blue fescue, tufted fescue) An evergreen species, it grows a dense, bristly-looking tuft of gray-green leaves that roll inward on themselves to create a fine-bladed texture. Although it's named "large," the 10-inch (25-cm)-tall tuft is a dwarf compared to tall ornamental grasses such as miscanthus.

Narrow sprays of purplish green flowers appear in late spring to summer, on upright stems that rise above the foliage to 18 inches (45 cm) tall. Stems and seed heads quickly mature, turning tan. 'Bronzeglanz' (Bronze Luster) sports narrow leaves gilded with bronze. 'Superba' has outstanding blue-gray foliage, as fine as thread, in a relaxed tuft that spills outward at the edges. The erect, slightly arching flower heads are rosy red with reddish stems when fresh. They soon turn tan, contrasting with the foliage.

F. glauca (*F. ovina* var. *glauca*; blue fescue) The parent of most of today's most cherished cultivars, it is an excellent plant in its own right. It is the bluest of dwarf grasses and forms dense, semiupright tufts. In early summer tall stems of flowers emerge, ripening into tan spikelets of seeds. The blue foliage color, which is retained year-round, is most intense in dry conditions.

Many cultivars are available, most with only subtle differences. 'Blaufink' (Blue Finch), one of the smallest cultivars, is a tidy tuft of fine leaves that reaches only 6 to 8 inches (15 to 25 cm) tall. It's a charmer for a rock garden or a flowerpot. 'Blauglut' (Blue Glow) has spiky, threadlike foliage in an icy silver-blue shade and reaches 8 to 10 inches (20 to 25 cm) tall and wide. 'Boulder Blue' forms a compact, spiky mound of intensely blue foliage topped by tall seed heads that soon turn golden tan. 'Elijah Blue' is a bristly, chalky blue grass, but it is surprisingly delightful to touch.

THE BASICS

These fescues are usually carefree garden plants, tolerating drought, heat, humidity, and cold. Some gardeners consider the seed heads decorative; others prefer to remove them after bloom to avoid interrupting the blue effect of the foliage.

Growing Conditions: Plant in well-drained, average soil 8 inches (20 cm) apart for a ground cover, or 12 to 15 inches (30 to 38 cm) apart to emphasize the individual tussocky form of each plant in the group.

Festuca glauca 'Elijah Blue'

Comb through the plant with your fingers in winter to remove dead foliage. If you notice your fescue is marred by spots or looking generally unhealthy, cut it down to ground level and dispose of the clippings in the trash. It should come back in good health.

Propagation: Divide in spring.

▸ **Flowering Time** Early summer
▸ **Planting Requirements** Full sun
▸ **Zones** 4 to 9

Perfect Partners

Plant blue fescue to contrast with lamb's ears (*Stachys byzantina*), Corsican hellebore (*Helleborus argutifolius*), New Zealand flax (*Phormium* spp.), sedums, or heucheras. For flower companions, try bright pinks (*Dianthus* spp.) or the reddish pink of Jupiter's beard (*Centranthus ruber*). Use blue fescue to accent sunny coreopsis, snow-white shasta daisies (*Leucanthemum superbum*), and purple coneflowers (*Echinacea purpurea*).

F

Filipendula *fil-ih-PEN-dew-luh* • meadowsweet

These large, rugged plants from the Rosaceae family have a casual attitude, with open, branching sprays of tiny, fluffy flowers. The fragrant flowers range from warm, deep pink to rosy purple to white. The stout, toothed, maplelike leaves contribute eye appeal.

Filipendula palmata (Siberian meadowsweet) In midsummer white or pale pink flowers appear on this 6- to 10-foot (1.8- to 3-m)-tall plant. 'Nana' reaches only 2 feet (60 cm) tall.

F. rubra (queen of the prairie) This American native with pink flowers grows 6 to 8 feet (1.8 to 2.4 m) tall and 4 feet (1.2 m) wide.

F. ulmaria (queen of the meadow) This 2- to 3-foot (60- to 90-cm)-tall species has dense clusters of creamy flowers in summer. Fancy-leaved cultivars include the yellow 'Aurea' and yellow-striped 'Variegata'.

F. vulgaris (dropwort) A basal rosette of foliage forms, from which stems with white blooms arise. It reaches 2 feet (60 cm) tall and 1½ feet (45 cm) wide and prefers a sunny site. 'Multiplex' ('Flore Pleno') boasts double, creamy white flowers.

THE BASICS

Meadowsweets need plenty of room. They're tough, long-lived plants that spread by creeping roots; most adapt well to sun or shade.

Growing Conditions: Plant in moist soil with added humus, in a sheltered site where the large leaves

Filipendula ulmaria

won't get battered by wind. Mulch to retain soil moisture, and water weekly in dry periods. Clip off any damaged foliage, and it will quickly regrow.

Propagation: Divide in spring.

▶ **Bloom Time** Summer
▶ **Planting Requirements** Sun to shade; *F. vulgaris*, sun
▶ **Zones** 3 to 9; *F. palmata*, 4 to 8

Gaillardia *gay-LAR-dee-uh* • gaillardia, blanket flower, Indian blanket

Festive daisies in striking two-tone colors and warm hues are the hallmark of free-blooming gaillardias. The vivid daisies are produced continually for months, covering the clump of hairy foliage with red and yellow. Most gaillardia, from the Asteraceae family, grow about 2 feet (60 cm) tall and are in bloom from midsummer on.

Gaillardia × grandiflora This hybrid combines the traits of *G. aristata*, a yellow perennial wildflower, with *G. pulchella*, an annual with yellow-tipped red petals and a reddish brown center. Because of that annual parentage, most are short-lived in the garden, petering out in only two to three short years,

but they'll give you plenty of firepower while they last. You'll find a fiesta of exciting cultivars to explore, in red-and-yellow combinations or in single colors. Here's a sampling of the best.

'Burgunder' has a more formal effect, thanks to its uniform, deep wine red flowers. It grows to 2 feet (60 cm) tall. 'Dazzler' draws the eye like a magnet, with a wide band of yellow edging the deep red flowers; it grows to only 8 to 12 inches (20 to 30 cm) tall. 'Fanfare' is a bicolor, with tangerine orange petals tipped in yellow, and has flowers of an entirely unique shape. The orange part of each petal is rolled into a

Gaillardia × grandiflora 'Fanfare'

tube, flaring outward at the yellow tip like a golden trumpet. It begins blooming early in late spring and never slackens until fall. More than 100 blossoms can cover the compact plant, which reaches about 14 inches (35 cm) high and 18 inches (45 cm) wide. 'Kobold' (Goblin) shows off the traditional two-tone color, with red petals tipped with yellow, but its form is improved. It makes a neat mound of foliage that stays compact at 1 foot (30 cm) tall and wide. You won't see that foliage for long, though, once its firecracker flowers open. 'Goldkobold' (Golden Goblin) has the same tidy form and floriferousness, but it's solid golden yellow.

THE BASICS

Gaillardias grow best in dry, lean, light soils. Too much kindness, in the form of generous water or fertilizer, can lead to an early death for these tough plants. They're ideal for your hottest, driest location, such as among rocks, on a hillside, or against a masonry wall. Dwarf cultivars are ideal for windy conditions, such as in a seaside garden. The fuzzy centers of the flowers are a favorite target of nectar-seeking butterflies.

Growing Conditions: Gaillardias thrive in poor soils, but they become floppy in rich, moist soils. Plant in light, well-drained soil. Amend clay soil with a generous amount of sand. Expect the plants to live only two to three years; many self-sow to ensure a continued supply, but the progeny may not look like the parent. The fuzzy, bristly seed heads have their own appeal, but keep them clipped off to encourage fresh blooms.

Propagation: Divide plants in spring; also grow from seed.

> ❚ **Bloom Time** Summer to fall
> ❚ **Planting Requirements** Full sun
> ❚ **Zones** 4 to 8

G

Gaura *GAW-ruh* • gaura, appleblossom grass

Slender, nearly bare stems form an arching clump dotted with dainty flowers. The unusual form and long-lasting color demand attention, but this delicate plant is also wonderful as a bridge between bold plants. Only one species of this plant from the Onagraceae family is cultivated.

Gaura lindheimeri Long, slim flowering stems emerge from the basal foliage and form a loose clump 3 to 5 feet (90 to 150 cm) tall and 2 to 4 feet (60 to 120 cm) wide. New flowers open from early summer until frost. 'Pink Cloud' forms a clump 2½ feet to 3 feet (75 to 90 cm) tall and 2 to 3 feet (60 to 90 cm) wide, with wine-colored stems and buds, maroon-mottled foliage, and pink flowers. 'Bijou Butterflies' has variegated foliage. 'Siskiyou Pink' has foliage, stems, and buds tinged with maroon-red and rosy pink flowers; it grows 2 to 3 feet (60 to 90 cm) tall and wide. 'Crimson Butterflies' grows to 1½ feet (45 cm), with rosy red flowers.

THE BASICS

Gaura grows from a deep taproot, so it can survive drought. In an extended drought the plant may go dormant; it quickly resprouts once water returns.

Growing Conditions: Plant in well-drained soil of poor-to-rich fertility; it adapts well to sandy, stony, and clay soils, as well as garden loam. Cut stems back to near ground level in early spring, avoiding the taproot.

Gaura lindheimeri

Propagation: Transplant self-sown seedlings when young.

> ❚ **Bloom Time** Summer through fall
> ❚ **Planting Requirements** Sun
> ❚ **Zones** 6 to 9

Geranium jer-AY-nee-um • hardy geranium, cranesbill

When most gardeners hear the word "geranium," we typically think of tidy red flowers in window boxes or strongly scented plants for the herb garden. British gardeners, however, know "geraniums" as beloved, versatile perennials that bear no relation to those strident red potted plants. American "geraniums" are actually *Pelargonium* species; they're part of the Geranium family, Geraniaceae, but they're a completely different plant from the species we refer to as "hardy geraniums."

Keep your tender geraniums for containers or the scented garden, and focus on the hardy perennial species for your garden. These valuable, easy-to-grow plants come in every hue of pink, from shocking magenta to blush to rose, as well as beautiful blues and clear white. With dozens of fabulous cultivars to choose from, you're sure to find the perfect fit for your garden.

Geranium species The geranium world is a large one, with dozens of species in cultivation, along with scores of their cultivars. Collectors take pride in exploring the many species, tracking down the plants from specialty nurseries. However, typical gardeners usually focus on a handful of the most adaptable, most popular, and most easily available, including those species (and their cultivars) profiled on pages 170 and 171. These include the bloody cranesbills—the species *G. sanguineum* and its cultivars—which are among the most popular garden plants of this genus. They

spread nicely, weaving their deeply toothed leaves among other perennials. Pale rose-pink flowers with darker veins decorate the plant all summer.

Many geranium species are hardy in Zones 4 or 5 to 8, although some tender species, such as Madeira geranium (*Geranium maderense*, Zones 8 to 9), are cold-sensitive and suitable for growing only in areas with mild winters.

G. hybrids Crosses between geranium species have led to the creation of some wonderful hybrids. You'll find some of the best at your local garden center or nursery, and many others in specialty catalogs. 'Wargrave Pink' is an old reliable with bright pink flowers. 'Johnson's Blue', a breathtaking blue hybrid, often reblooms a second or third time. The dwarf 'Kate' (which is also known as 'Kate Folkard') is a charmer that forms a mat dotted with small pale pink flowers.

One of the newest geranium hybrids, Rozanne ('Gerwat'), is an outstanding plant that forms a tumbling mass of mouthwatering blue flowers that are simply scrumptious. Even better, it seems to bloom forever, producing prolific blossoms even in the heat of midsummer. Hardiness varies, as do growth habit and adaptability to sun or part shade, so check the label or catalog description to make sure the cultivar you choose is the right one for your garden.

THE BASICS

You'll enjoy weeks of colorful bloom from these reliable perennials. In areas

Geranium sanguineum cv.

with cooler summers, geraniums can bloom for months. Unfortunately, in areas with extreme heat, hardy geraniums often take a break from blooming. However, even if the blooming period is shortened in your area, you'll still appreciate the rich red color that the foliage takes on in fall. Pick a few of the plant's fall leaves to accent a small bouquet for your kitchen table.

Growing Conditions: Plant in well-drained, humus-rich soil. Mulch around the plants to retain soil moisture. Geraniums are moderately drought tolerant, but the plants will look better if watered weekly when rain is scarce. Trim back the plant by about one-third after the first flush of bloom to keep a more compact shape and encourage a later round of bloom.

Propagation: Divide in early spring.

▶ **Bloom Time** Early to late summer
▶ **Planting Requirements** Sun to part or light shade
▶ **Zones** Hardiness varies, depending on species; most are hardy in Zones 4 to 9

G

Easygoing Geraniums

Now you, too, can see why gardeners everywhere rave about geraniums. This sampler of hardy geraniums includes species and cultivars that will thrive in many gardens, in average garden soil. All that most of them ask for is a regular drink of water. If you keep your garden on the dry side, investigate *Geranium renardiii*, which flourishes in a niche among rocks or in a stone wall.

◀ *G. phaeum* **'Samobor'**
The petals of this cultivar bend backward, or "reflex," so that the prolific purple flowers look like butterflies above the 20-inch (50-cm)-wide clump of foliage. The maplelike leaves have a splotch of deep burgundy. It grows well in sun or shade and blooms from late spring into fall. Hardy in Zones 4 to 9.

▲ *G. sanguineum* **'Lancastriense'**
This cultivar's foliage turns red in fall. Some consider this plant a variety, *G. sanguineum* var. *lancastriense* or *G. sanguineum* var. *striatum*, not a cultivar. Hardy in Zones 4 to 8.

▶ *G. maculatum*
A beloved spring wildflower of the eastern woodlands, you can admire it for three full seasons in the garden. It produces soft pink-purple flowers in late spring to midsummer. In fall the upright mound of foliage takes on a rich red glow. It can reach 2½ feet (75 cm) tall in moist soil; if the clump of foliage flops open after bloom, cut it off at the base and it will quickly regrow. It adapts well to a sunny spot in the garden and thrives in shade. Hardy in Zones 4 to 8.

▼ G. himalayense

The color may vary from one plant to another, but the midblue to violet-blue flowers are stunning. Small white centers add an extra punch. This sprawler makes a good ground cover in a sunny spot, spreading to 2 feet (60 cm) across. It blooms strongly in early summer, then produces occasional flowers into fall. Hardy in Zones 4 to 7.

▲ G. renardii

This unusual geranium has become much easier to acquire, thanks to the advent of Internet searching. It's worth seeking because of its unusual grayish foliage. The dainty leaves are velvety gray-green and wrinkled, with pretty scalloped edges. The pale flowers can be few and far between, but the 12-inch (30-cm) mound of foliage will catch the eye. Hardy in Zones 4 to 8.

▶ G. psilostemon

This upright grower forms a clump of lobed leaves that arise tinted red in spring, turn green, then go back to red in fall. Its shocking bright magenta flowers, accented with black veins and stamens, are impossible to overlook when they ignite the garden in summer. This large species usually grows to about 2 feet (60 cm) tall, but it can reach 4 feet (120 cm) in rich soil. Hardy in Zones 5 to 8.

171

Geum *JEE-um* • geum, avens

Geum coccineum

Because its flowers are reminiscent of the simple beauty of a wild rose, geum was once known as "Grecian rose." These perennials from the Rosaceae family bring a bright spot to the garden. Their prolific flowers are only 2 inches (5 cm) across, but their eye-catching reds, oranges, and yellows make them ideal accent plants. Newer cultivars broaden the palette with luscious tropical tones, such as apricot and mango. The graceful flowering stems rise well above the basal clump of fuzzy leaves, so you can plant geum in the front of your beds, and perennials in the background will still show easily through its stems.

Geum chiloense (Chilean avens) The most familiar geum, this species offers a bouquet of slender, branching stems, crowned with loose clusters of bright flowers. 'Mrs. J. Bradshaw' has splendid bright scarlet, semidouble flowers that are hard to resist. 'Lady Stratheden' is semidouble, too, but has clear yellow flowers. The loose clump of flowers reaches 1½ to 2 feet (45 to 60 cm) tall and wide. Hardy in Zones 4 to 7.

G. coccineum (scarlet avens) A shorter species, this geum tops out at 1 foot (30 cm). As with other geums, the branches of flowers are held above the low clump of foliage, where the red flowers can really show off. 'Borisii' and 'Red Wings' are striking red-orange cultivars. Hardy in Zones 4 to 7.

G. 'Beech House Apricot' This small-scale hybrid has warm, peachy yellow flowers streaked with red. It forms a dense clump of divided leaves topped by many stems of nodding flowers. It reaches 8 inches (20 cm) high and wide. Hardy in Zone 5 to 7.

G. 'Mango Lassi' One of the most roselike of the geums, this hybrid has flowers that look soft orange from a distance. Up close, they're a double-petaled parfait of warm orange and coral mingled with golden yellow; the buds are reddish purple. It grows to 1 foot (30 cm) tall and wide. Hardy in Zones 5 to 7.

THE BASICS

Geum is a garden stalwart in cooler climates, but in hot or dry conditions it may peter out quickly or fall prey to problems. Some of the most popular cultivars are short-lived, lasting only a few years in the garden. Yet they remain perennial favorites, thanks to that punch of color. Give them a try, and see how they liven up the summer scene.

Growing Conditions: Plant in moist but well-drained soil, and mulch to help retain moisture. If your summers are hot, geum will do best where they're in shade during the intense afternoon sun. Spider mites may move in during a dry spell and disfigure the foliage. Check the undersides of the leaves for the spider mites' webbing, and dislodge with a strong spray of water from the hose.

Propagation: Divide in early spring or fall.

▶ **Bloom Time** Midspring to summer
▶ **Planting Requirements** Full sun to light or part shade
▶ **Zones** Hardiness varies, depending on species

Perfect Partners

Because geums bloom at the peak of the early summer season, your choices for partners are practically unlimited. Look for those that offer contrasting form, texture, or color. For an elegant effect, plant 'Mrs. J. Bradshaw' or another red geum in front of white bearded or Siberian iris (*Iris* spp.). Add a clump of stately blue delphiniums for even more impact.

Campanulas, especially creeping or low species, such as *Campanula poscharskyana* and *C. carpatica,* provide contrasting cool color as well as a change of form. Hardy geraniums create old-fashioned cottage-garden romance with geum of any color. For garden romance with a modern slant, try a group of luscious 'Mango Lassi' geum with brown sedges, such as New Zealand hair sedge (*Carex comans*) or leatherleaf sedge (*C. buchanii*).

Gypsophila *jip-SOFF-ill-uh* • baby's breath

Baby's breath is as airy as its name. This dainty perennial, a member of the Caryophyllaceae family, forms a soft cloud of tiny white or pink flowers. However, for all of its softness, baby's breath is one of the toughest kids on the block when it comes to challenging conditions. It thrives in poor soil and shrugs off extended drought. Give this old-fashioned species room to breathe in a good-sized garden, or nestle in the miniature version (*Gypsophila repens*) where space is more restricted.

Gypsophila paniculata (baby's breath) The unassuming foliage of this ground-hugging rosette of smooth, narrow, gray-green leaves doesn't look able to host such an outstanding cloud of flowers. Yet, when the branching flowering stems arise from that little clump of leaves, this plant reaches shrub size of 3 to 4 feet (90 to 120 cm) tall and almost as wide. The species has white single flowers. 'Bristol Fairy' reaches 3 feet (90 cm) and forms a froth of fluffy double flowers. 'Schneeflocke' (Snowflake) blooms a few weeks before others. Pale pink 'Pink Star' grows to about 18 inches (45 cm) tall and wide; 'Pink Fairy' is a clear light pink and about the same size. 'Red Sea' is a deeper rose, with double flowers.

G. repens (creeping baby's breath) This miniature version of big, billowy baby's breath is an outstanding edger for walks, patios, or anywhere else you need a soft touch. Plant it in groups to make an instant sweep of soft pink, or let a single plant spread naturally by creeping stems to form a solid mat.

The flowering stems reach 6 inches (15 cm) tall, while the trailing stems reach out to several feet over time. The species is pale pink. 'Rosea' is a deeper pink cultivar. 'Alba' has white flowers.

THE BASICS

Baby's breath is easy to grow. It is extremely cold-hardy, but it tends to falter in humid heat, where it is usually short-lived. In some parts of the West and Midwest, especially dry areas with open land, baby's breath has made the leap from gardens to wild places, where it can quickly become invasive

Gypsophila paniculata 'Festival White'

because it sows itself. It's prohibited in California. Check with your USDA extension agent, listed in the Federal Government section of your telephone book, to see if it's unwelcome in your area. If not, you can safely enjoy its soft presence in your summer garden.

Growing Conditions: Plant in well-drained soil of lean-to-average fertility. Baby's breath grows from a taproot, which allows it to reach deep for water and to tolerate drought, once established. The roots resent being disturbed, so select a permanent home for it before you plant. It may self-sow. Clip back finished flowering stems for a second round of bloom. Cut back flowering stems to ground level in fall.

Propagation: Transplant self-sown seedlings when young, keeping as much soil as possible around the roots to avoid disturbing them.

▶ **Bloom Time** Summer
▶ **Planting Requirements** Full sun
▶ **Zones** 4 to 9

Perfect Partners

White- or pink-flowered baby's breath will look beautiful with silvery or blue-green foliage, such as that of globe thistle (*Echinops* spp.), artemisia, or lamb's ears (*Stachys byzantina*). Anchor a cloud of baby's breath with perennial flowers of stronger shape, such as the fringed daisies of pinks (*Dianthus* spp.), the bells of campanula (*Campanula carpatica* 'Blue Clips', 'White Clips', and other spp.), or the rounded faces of hardy geraniums. For an easy, eye-catching quartet, plant white baby's breath (*Gypsophila paniculata*) behind a loose, sprawling mass of pink hardy geranium (*Geranium sanguineum*); add a plant of creeping pink baby's breath (*G. repens*), and accent the group with the deep burgundy blooms and purplish black foliage of *Geranium phaeum* 'Samobor'.

Hakonechloa

hack-oh-nee-CLOE-uh • Japanese forest grass, Hakone grass

Hakonechloa will give you instant appreciation for the beauty of foliage plants. The best ornamental grass for shade, this plant from the Poaceae family forms a waterfall of ribbonlike leaves, providing the beauty of bamboo without the aggressive tendencies.

Hakonechloa comes from the Hakone region of Japan, probably the most famous Japanese national park, where volcanic mountains, hot springs, and a fantastic view of Mount Fuji across the water of Lake Ashi draw visitors from near and far. On forested cliffs, hakonechloa grass draws the eye with its incomparable grace—exactly as it will do in your own partly shady garden. In late summer spikelets of greenish yellow flowers appear, but they're inconspicuous against that foliage.

Hakonechloa macra The species form of Hakone grass is hard to find at nurseries, because its all-green foliage has been overshadowed by the spectacular effects of more colorful cultivars. Lovely 'Aureola' is the oldest cultivar on the scene, and it still serves as most gardeners' introduction to hakonechloa. Its abundance of green leaves are subtly striped with golden green, chartreuse, and even cream. In fall its leaves add a red flush to their palette. Like other cultivars, it forms a lush clump, about 10 inches (25 cm) high and 18 inches (45 cm) wide. 'All Gold', just as its name promises, gleams like the golden hour of the sun. Its leaves are broader than other cultivars, and its cascading form is slightly more erect, but it's still the epitome of grace—and that color is impossible to overlook. 'Albolineata' (variegated hakonechloa) has green leaves striped with cream. It tolerates more sun than others and flourishes in light shade or under the shifting leaves of a birch or Japanese maple.

THE BASICS

Hakonechloa stays in a well-behaved clump, gradually expanding with age as its rhizomes slowly spread. This grass is one of the more expensive perennials, but it's strong enough to plant as a single specimen if that's what your budget allows. It's also gorgeous in groups. Many gardeners in colder regions beyond Zone 6 have had it survive in their gardens for years, perhaps because of less extreme winters in some years. If you're enamored by the plant and live north of its usual hardiness range, it's worth a try, even for a single season or two of beauty.

Growing Conditions: Plant in moist but well-drained soil. Add a generous helping of humus to the soil at planting time. Its color is best in partial shade, but the cultivars will grow in sun. Plant in a site that's shaded during the worst of the afternoon sun in hot-summer areas. It is untroubled by diseases or insects. Cut back to ground level in early spring, or leave dead foliage in place as a natural mulch.

Propagation: Divide in spring.

▶ **Bloom Time** Late summer
▶ **Planting Requirements** Part or light shade
▶ **Zones** 6 to 9; may survive in colder zones

Hakonechloa macra 'Aureola'

Perfect Partners

The texture and color of hakonechloa make it a superb companion for other shade plants with larger, bolder leaves, such as hostas, ferns, or heucheras. Hostas with green or golden-variegated leaves are perfect for golden cultivars of this grass; hostas splashed or striped with white or cream are better with variegated hakonechloa, whose foliage echoes those hues. Purplish heucheras, such as 'Palace Purple' or 'Black Beauty', are stunning with any hakonechloa. For an arrangement that honors this plant's heritage, plant it beneath Japanese maples or conifers, such as Japanese black pine (*Pinus thunbergii*).

Helenium · hel-EN-ee-um · helenium, sneezeweed

Just when the late-summer garden needs a boost of fresh energy, heleniums burst into bloom. These tall plants from the Asteraceae family are crowned with a multitude of perky daisylike flowers in rich autumnal shades of russet red and gold. They're a treat for the last of the butterflies, and a treat for gardeners hungry for fresh color. The flowers bloom over a long period, producing new buds that keep the show going well into fall. The legendarily beautiful Helen of Troy, from whom helenium gets its name, was supposedly gathering these flowers when she was abducted by Paris of Troy, which set off the Trojan War.

Helenium autumnale (sneezeweed) Feel free to sniff those blossoms: Sneezeweeds get their name from the long-ago use of the powdered root as snuff, not as an allergen. This species is native across nearly the entire United States, though you might not recognize its wild form, which is variable and much less striking than the garden cultivars and hybrids developed from it. The species is an authentic touch for a prairie garden, where it grows 3 to 5 feet (90 to 150 cm) tall, with yellow blossoms. It spreads by roots to form a large patch. Hybrids of this species are much more floriferous, in a wide range of mouthwatering fall colors, and grow in a clump rather than a colony. A planting of mixed colors is an arresting sight.

H. 'Bruno' Tall and erect, 'Bruno' holds court over the garden with stiff stems topped with abundant deep crimson to reddish brown flowers

from late summer through early fall. 'Bruno' is a big boy, standing about 4 feet (120 cm) tall and at least 2 feet (60 cm) wide.

H. 'Butterpat' Butter yellow blooms in abundance are the crowning glory of this robust cultivar, which grows to 4 feet (120 cm) tall in bloom and 2 feet (60 cm) wide. It blooms from mid- to late summer.

H. 'Coppelia' The coppery red flowers of this sturdy cultivar add instant zing to a tired late-summer garden. It's shorter than most cultivars, topping out at 3 feet (90 cm) when in bloom and 18 inches (45 cm) wide.

H. 'Mardi Gras' This festive cultivar has oodles of golden daisies streaked and splashed with red, mahogany, and yellow. Plants are vigorous, bushy, and compact. The sturdy 3-foot (90-cm)-tall stems are topped with large, rounded clusters of 2-inch (5-cm) daisies for months, beginning weeks earlier than other cultivars and lasting into midfall. Thanks to its vigor, cold-hardiness, and long-lasting flower show, it was named as a "Tough & Terrific" perennial in 2004 by the University of Minnesota.

H. 'Moerheim Beauty' Brick red petals around a darker center disk make this cultivar a standout in the garden. Pair it with a cascade of blue asters, or choose a pink aster cultivar, such as 'Harrington's Pink', for an unusual color combo.

H. 'Zimbelstern' (Cymbal Star) This cultivar has large flowers, about 3 inches (7.5 cm) across. They're a rich

Helenium 'Moerheim Beauty'

golden brown, with darker brown centers, and bloom from mid- to late summer. It grows to 4 feet (120 cm) tall and 2 feet (60 cm) wide.

THE BASICS

Sneezeweeds are tough, hardy plants that are ideal for the back or middle of your beds and borders, where they will quickly give your garden that long-established look. Heleniums require patience: They're just a leafy clump until late in the season, when they transform themselves into beauties.

Growing Conditions: Plant in average, well-drained garden soil. Snip off spent flowers to encourage new blooms. Lift and divide the clump every two to three years to keep the plant vigorous. Helenium has strong stems, but if your garden is in a windy area, stake taller cultivars. Some may self-sow, but the progeny may not look like the parent.

Propagation: Divide in spring.

▶ **Bloom Time** Summer to fall
▶ **Planting Requirements** Full sun
▶ **Zones** 3 to 8

H

Helianthemum
hee-lee-AN-thih-mum • sun rose, rock rose

Helianthemum 'Henfield Brilliant'

Crepe-paper flowers in sherbert colors, along with some spectacular brights, smother these pretty perennials for a long period from late spring through midsummer. The 1- to 2-inch (2.5- to 5-cm) flowers are shaped like wild roses, but these plants from the Cistaceae family are low and sprawling, with nary a thorn to be seen. They demand excellent drainage and full sun, so they're well suited to south-facing slopes or a rock garden of alpine plants.

The evergreen, silvery or gray-green foliage remains attractive when the flowers aren't in bloom. Even the clusters of drooping, pointed buds are decorative. Nearly all garden sun roses are hybrids that combine the best traits of wild species, such as *Helianthemum apenninum* and *H. nummularium,* and add hybrid vigor with a lot of flowers. Most grow to about 8 inches (20 cm) tall and 18 inches (45 cm) wide.

Helianthemum '**Cheviot**' Dainty peach blossoms blanket the gray foliage of this cultivar. They keep going strong for about two months, bridging the garden calendar from late tulips through the peak of June bloom.

H. '**Fire Dragon**' One of the most vivid cultivars, this orange-red bloomer is spectacular planted in a mass or a group of three. Like other cultivars, it blooms for six to eight weeks without stopping. The foliage is gray-green and looks good all winter.

H. '**Henfield Brilliant**' The splendid flowers of this cultivar have a delicate texture, but their rusty red color hollers for attention. The small, silvery leaves retain their color all year.

H. '**Wisley Pink**' This reliable pastel pink cultivar is excellent for dotting among rocks, which will provide a strong textural contrast to its silvery leaves and soft color.

H. '**Wisley Primrose**' The softest of yellows, this gratifying perennial is one of the longest blooming of the sun roses. Its form is low and spreading, so it works well as a ground cover when planted in groups on a sunny slope.

H. '**Wisley White**' Not snow white but pale cream, this elegant cultivar dresses up the garden with a low mound of blossoms from May to July. For a whiter-than-white cultivar, try the pristine elegance of 'St. Mary'.

Perfect Partners

Choose blue catmints (*Nepeta* spp.), bright rose-red Jupiter's beard (*Centranthus ruber*), or lavenders (*Lavandula* spp.) for companions; like the sun rose, they flourish in hot, dry conditions. Let sun roses show off their feminine side with ornamental oreganos (*Origanum* spp.), such as 'Amethyst Falls' or 'Kent Beauty'. Try helianthemums among late-blooming tulips, too—'Blushing Lady', a tall, lily-flowered tulip, is striking behind pink, yellow, or peach sun roses; the rusty orange 'Henfield Brilliant' sun rose is spectacular with a sweep of near-black 'Queen of Night' tulips. Include euphorbias nearby; their red-tinged stems and foliage and their spikes of unusual flowers will provide an interesting contrast to the delicacy of sun roses.

THE BASICS

Sun roses are one of those rare plants that you can kill with kindness. They flourish under adversity in dry areas, poor soil, baking heat, and even in seaside gardens. In moist, rich loam, they aren't as floriferous and may become weak and straggly.

Growing Conditions: Plant in well-drained soil of lean-to-average fertility. They will grow in a variety of soils, including sand, but sulk in clay; if you have clay soil, dig in plenty of sand and humus at planting time to lighten the texture and increase drainage. Sun roses are drought tolerant after their first year in the garden. After flowering, clip back the plants by about one-third to maintain a more compact shape.

Propagation: Do not divide; all those sprawling stems go back to a single stem or to several woody stems that resent being disturbed. Take cuttings of soft, pliable stems in late spring or early summer.

▶ **Bloom Time** Late spring to midsummer
▶ **Planting Requirements** Full sun
▶ **Zones** 4 to 8

Helianthus *hee-lee-AN-thus* • sunflower

The perennial species of sunflower all have buttery yellow blossoms. Most perennial species, from the Asteraceae family, are tall, vigorous plants. The species listed here do not spread by running roots, so they're easier to keep in bounds than some other species.

Helianthus angustifolius (narrow-leaved sunflower, swamp sunflower) The clump of branching stems crowned with golden daisies in fall grows 8 feet (2.4 m) high and 5 feet (1.5 m) wide. It self-sows. 'First Light' is only 4 feet (120 cm) tall. Hardy in Zones 6 to 9.

H. maximiliani (Maximilian's sunflower) This species can grow to 12 feet (3.6 m) tall. The golden daisies bloom from early to late fall. Hardy in Zones 4 to 9.

H. mollis (soft sunflower) Clusters of furred buds are just as attractive as the daisies that bloom in late summer. It grows 3 to 4 feet (90 to 120 cm) tall and wide. Hardy in Zones 4 to 9.

THE BASICS

Perennial sunflowers are big, pushy plants that need plenty of space, so think twice before planting them.

Growing Conditions: Plant in average, well-drained garden soil; *H. angustifolius* also grows well in wet soil. All thrive in clay, as well as looser soils. They are drought tolerant after the first year. Cut off finished flowers to prevent self-sowing, or leave the seed heads to attract birds; cut back to ground level in early spring.

Helianthus angustifolius

Propagation: Divide in spring; transplant self-sown seedlings.

▶ **Bloom Time** Late summer to fall
▶ **Planting Requirements** Full sun
▶ **Zones** Hardiness varies, depending on species

Heliopsis *hee-lee-OP-sis* • heliopsis, false sunflower, ox eye

This late-blooming daisy forms a stout, coarse-leaved clump. The bright flowers look a lot like those of the perennial sunflower species, but bloom begins weeks earlier and can last for three months. This reliable, long-lived perennial from the Asteraceae family thrives for decades in the garden.

Heliopsis helianthoides This American native forms a vigorous, leafy clump 3 to 5 feet (90 to 150 cm) tall and 3 feet (90 cm) wide in shade or sun. The dense, branching stems are tipped with buttery yellow daisies. 'Sommersonne' (Summer Sun) has an abundance of deep, golden yellow flowers. 'Karat' has clear yellow flowers; 'Mars' is yellow-orange.

Cultivars with double flowers include 'Gold Greenheart', with green centers; 'Incomparibilis', with orange-yellow flowers; frilly 'Patula', a semidouble golden yellow. 'Halban' has white leaves veined in green.

THE BASICS

This plant is a "plant it and forget it" type, needing only an occasional drink of water in its first year.

Growing Conditions: Plant in average-to-rich, well-drained soil. Support with a loose wire or string to prevent the plant from flopping open at bloom time. Snip off faded flowers to limit self-sowing. Cut back the plant to ground level in early spring.

Heliopsis helianthoides 'Sommersonne'

Propagation: Divide in spring. Transplant self-sown seedlings.

▶ **Bloom Time** Summer to early fall
▶ **Planting Requirements** All cultivars and the species, full sun; the species also grows in part to light shade
▶ **Zones** 3 to 8

H

Helleborus hell-e-BOR-us • hellebore, Christmas rose, Lenten rose

Helleborus argutifolius

Being the first perennial flower to bloom makes hellebores, from the Ranunculaceae family, endearing to any gardener's heart. The nodding, waxy flowers are held at the top of the stems that rise from the center of a clump of large, lobed leaves. The flowers may be white, pink, green, or maroon; each blossom lasts for weeks, often changing color to a deeper hue as it ages. The large leathery, glossy foliage is striking.

Helleborus argutifolius (Corsican hellebore) This species has glaucous gray-green, toothed leaves and green flowers. It thrives in sun or shade, forming a clump up to 4 feet (120 cm) high and 3 feet (90 cm) wide.

H. foetidus (stinking hellebore, bear-claw hellebore) This plant only smells bad if the foliage is crushed. It has fans of toothy, lobed leaves and grows in sun or shade. The flowers are pale green, often with a purple edge. It forms a clump 2½ feet (75 cm) tall and 1½ feet (45 cm) wide. The leaves of 'Golden Showers' are streaked and mottled with yellow. 'Piccadilly' has narrow, almost black-green foliage and red marks on leaf and flower stems.

H. niger (Christmas rose) In early winter white blooms appear and keep coming into early spring. They turn pink as they age. The plant grows to 12 inches (30 cm) tall and 18 inches (45 cm) wide. Hardy in Zones 4 to 8.

H. orientalis (Lenten rose) This adaptable species begins flowering in midwinter and continues to midspring. The white or greenish white flowers turn pinkish. Hardy in Zones 4 to 9.

H. 'Brandywine Strain' Every color in the hellebore rainbow is reflected in this group of hybrids, including white, cream, chartreuse, yellow, reddish pink, and maroon.

H. 'Citron' This hybrid offers primrose yellow flowers to warm up the late winter garden. 'Yellow Button' has small, deep yellow flowers.

H. 'Double Queen Strain' These fluffy, double-petaled flowers come in a mix of shades. Greens, yellow, pinks, and maroons may show up, many marked with a splash of freckles.

H. 'Peggy Ballard' The large, reddish pink to maroon flowers and maroon flower stems of this hybrid provide unusual color in the garden.

H. 'Pink Beauty' This unusual hybrid has gray-green leaves, topped with clusters of pink flowers. The blossoms open cream and pale pink, then darken to dusty pink as they age.

Perfect Partners

A mass planting of hellebores looks beautiful under spring-blooming trees and shrubs, as well as under shade trees, where they will slowly spread into a significant patch. Combine them with early spring bulbs, such as snowdrops (*Galanthus* spp.) and with daffodils. Use the lobed leaves to add texture and contrast with other foliage plants, such as heucheras, ferns, and hostas. In a sunny spot anchor a bed along a walk with the fantastic foliage of Corsican hellebore, partnered with dwarf conifers that will have the visual heft to stand up to the hellebore's bold leaves.

THE BASICS

Plant your hellebores where you'll notice them when in bloom, such as near a walk or steps. The foliage is evergreen in milder winters, but it may look shabby by springtime. New leaves quickly emerge to surround the flowers.

Growing Conditions: Plant in well-drained, average-to-rich soil. Choose a site that's sheltered from strong winds, which can damage the foliage. Snip off tattered or dead leaves in spring to make room for fresh foliage. After a year in the ground, hellebores are tolerant of drought; overwatering can cause them to wilt in slow-draining soil. Avoid disturbing the rhizomatous roots. It often self-sows, although the progeny of hybrids may not look like the parent.

Propagation: Transplant self-sown seedlings. Division can be tricky because the plants are often slow to reestablish if the roots are disturbed.

▶ **Bloom Time** Winter to spring
▶ **Planting Requirements** Part to full shade, unless noted otherwise
▶ **Zones** 6 to 9, unless noted otherwise

Hemerocallis hem-er-oh-KAL-iss • daylily

Next time you pass a swathe of rusty orange daylilies *(Hemerocallis fulva)* growing wild along a roadside, take a minute to consider how far those plants traveled to reach that humble ditch. Those rusty orange daylilies are one of a handful of daylily species native to China and Japan, where they were once an honored member of the emperors' gardens, cultivated for thousands of years. When Western explorers reached the Orient, daylily roots were slipped into their packs and brought to other parts of the world. By the 1500s, daylilies had reached Europe. Only a few centuries later the cast-iron-tough tawny daylily was spreading across North America, carried by settlers to their new homesteads.

Daylilies, which are members of the Hemerocallidaceae family, are still a great choice for a dependable perennial. Nearly all of the luscious daylilies in today's gardens are hybrids developed from *H. fulva,* as well as from a few other species native to China, Japan, and Korea. Each blossom lasts only a day, but new buds open day after day for weeks of bloom. You'll find a variety of flower forms and sizes, from ruffled or spidery giants to dainty midgets, and every hue of the rainbow except green and blue.

Hemerocallis fulva (tawny daylily) One of the oldest plants in garden cultivation, this species is rugged and practically indestructible. Dig up extras and throw them on the compost pile, and before you know it, they've reached into the compost and begun growing again. The rusty orange flowers, which open for weeks, are held on 3-foot (90-cm)-tall, bare stems, branched at the top. Foliage is dense and semievergreen. 'Flore Pleno' is an old cultivar that is still valued for its thick double flowers.

H. lilioasphodelus (*H. flava*; lemon lily) Another ancient species still worth growing, this daylily has narrow leaves and clear lemon yellow flowers with a delicious fragrance. This is a "nocturnal" species: The flowers open in late afternoon, bloom all night, and wither away by about midday, soon to be replaced by the next afternoon's flowers.

THE BASICS

These undemanding plants multiply quickly to form a splash of color in the summer garden. Some are evergreen or semievergreen; others die back in winter. Cultivars bloom at various times, so you can enjoy daylilies for months. Rebloomers, or "remontant" daylilies, extend the season with a second round of bloom in the fall.

Growing Conditions: Plant in average-to-fertile, well-drained soil. All stand up well to winter extremes, but many fade in intense sun. Reds and purples are particularly prone to fading, but even orange, melon, and pink hues may change color in bright sun. If your summer days are long and hot, plant them where they'll be protected from intense afternoon sun. Daylilies are usually vigorous, but they can fall prey to thrips, which deform the buds, as well as to aphids, spider mites, and rust or crown rot. If yours look sickly, identify the problem and apply a specific remedy.

Propagation: Divide in spring; evergreen types in spring or early fall.

▷ **Bloom Time** Late spring to late summer; some have a smaller show in fall

▷ **Planting Requirements** Sun to light or part shade; usually fewer flowers in shade

▷ **Zones** 3 to 10

Hemerocallis fulva

Perfect Partners

Pair daylilies with garden phlox (*Phlox paniculata* and *P. maculata*), hollyhocks (*Alcea* spp.), and red-hot poker (*Kniphofia* spp.). The strappy leaves and bold flower form give satisfying contrast to finer-textured perennials, such as yarrows (*Achillea* spp.). Red-flowered cultivars look great with blue companions, such as scabiosa, campanulas, or salvias, and with golden or sulfur-yellow coreopsis. Miniature daylilies, such as 'Little Grapette' or 'Happy Returns', slip easily into a space among perennials with smaller flowers, such as veronicas and hardy geraniums (*Geranium* spp.).

Daylilies of Distinction

The daylily universe is an enormous one, with more than 30,000 named cultivars to choose from! With all that variety of color, size, and flower form, it's a mystery why so many plantings depend on *Hemerocallis* 'Stella d'Oro', a small-flowered, reblooming daylily, whose brassy orange is difficult to combine with other colors. Why not step away from Stella and explore a wider selection of colors and forms? These pages are just a small sampling of what awaits in the wide, wide world of daylilies.

◀ *H.* '**Paper Butterfly**'
The 6-inch (15-cm) flowers of this delightful peach hybrid are splotched with a reddish violet that attracts the eye. The blossoms are big, but the deciduous plant is relatively small, reaching only 1½ to 2 feet (45 to 60 cm) tall and wide. This Tetraploid hybrid is an indefatigable bloomer, sending up new flowers from late spring through fall. It's as pretty in a pot as it is in the garden.

▲ *H.* '**Chicago Sunrise**'
Vigorous Tetraploid hybrids have bigger leaves, thicker stems, and bigger flowers than nontetraploid daylilies. This robust hybrid forms a clump of evergreen foliage 2½ feet (75 cm) tall and wide, and blooms in sun or part shade. The flowers open in the morning and stay open until late afternoon. Its main flush of flowers comes in midseason; a smaller round of rebloom appears in late summer.

▶ *H.* '**Indian Paintbrush**'
Thick clusters of stunning tangerine flowers with a hint of sienna and burnt orange veining are a standout in the summer garden. Look deep into the throat of these 5-inch (12.5-cm) blossoms, and you'll see a deeper orange that brightens to gold. Each petal has a narrow flounce of ruffles around the edge. A midseason bloomer, 'Indian Paintbrush' forms a clump about 2½ feet (75 cm) tall. The foliage goes dormant in fall, which makes this cultivar a fine choice for gardeners in cold-winter areas.

▼ *H.* 'Sunstar'

The American Daylily Society listed 528 registered spider cultivars in 2007, a small fraction of the thousands of named daylilies available. 'Sunstar' was registered way back in 1954, and it's still shining in gardens more than half a century later. The spidery, bright yellow blooms rise above the 2- to 3-foot (60- to 90-cm) clump of foliage. The plant goes dormant in winter.

▲ *H.* 'Yabba Dabba Doo'

"*Yabba dabba doo!*" may be your reaction when you see the 10-inch (25-cm) flowers of this spectacular spider hybrid, which is medium purple with a contrasting chartreuse throat. It's a nocturnal type, so the blossoms open in early evening and wither away by midday. The semievergreen foliage reaches 30 inches (75 cm) tall. This is a late bloomer that keeps producing new flowers into fall. Could it be the finale of your daylily extravaganza?

▶ *H.* 'Sammy Russell Red'

This is an excellent choice for a garden: It multiplies fast enough to make a good ground cover on a south-facing slope. The hybrid is a late bloomer, extending the season of your daylily collection. The starry, almost spidery, brick-red blossoms measure only 3 to 4 inches (7.5 to 10 cm) across, but they're held on tall stems. The plant grows into a dense clump 2½ to 3 feet (75 to 90 cm) tall and wide. The arching foliage is dormant over winter.

Hepatica *he-PAT-ih-ka* • hepatica

Hepatica americana

Those who wander the woodlands know this sweet little plant as a welcome wildflower of spring. Its cupped or starry flowers form a charming nosegay of lavender-blue, pink, or pure white, brightening the brown leafy floor of the spring forest beneath beeches, oaks, and other trees. Each flower is centered with a spray of yellow stamens. Lobed leaves, glossy and reddish bronze in winter, surround the flowers, setting off their simple beauty. Hepatica, which is from the Ranunculaceae family, moves easily from the wild woods to the shady garden, where it will nestle in and gradually sow itself to form a small colony of springtime cheer.

In olden days it was believed that hepatica could cure liver ailments. However, hepatica can be poisonous in large doses, so keep it out of the medicine cabinet and in your shade garden, where the lift it will give your spirits in spring is benefit enough.

Hepatica acutiloba (sharp-lobed hepatica) Three-lobed leaves with pointed tips are the trademark of this eastern and midwestern native, which blooms in early spring. In bloom the plant is only 3 inches (7.5 cm) high; out of bloom its leaves hug the ground, forming a clump 6 inches (15 cm) across. The bare, fuzzy, flowering stems are topped with adorable round buds that open into blue-lilac to lavender flowers, and sometimes pink or white.

H. americana (round-lobed hepatica) More common than the sharp-lobed species in the northern part of the country, but often growing nearby it, this pretty perennial is a little bigger than its cousin *H. acutiloba*. Its rosette of leaves persists all winter, even if it is buried by snow. In early spring the furry stems of blue-lavender, lavender, or occasionally white or pink flowers emerge, soon followed by new foliage that stands more erect than older leaves at first, then relaxes into a clump 8 inches (20 cm) across. The small but eye-catching flowers open their petals wide as sunlight filters through the bare trees overhead, then close up again each night.

THE BASICS

Hepaticas may bloom as early as February or as late as May, depending on the climate in your area. As soon as the first sunny days appear, check for those unfurling buds rising up from the remains of winter leaves. As your collection expands, whether by purchase or by self-sowing, you'll notice flowers of different colors and shapes cropping up. Even double flowers may occur naturally.

Growing Conditions: Plant in average-to-rich, moist soil. *H. acutiloba* flourishes in limestone soils as well as acid soils. Choose a site beneath deciduous trees that allow sunlight to draw forth the early spring blossoms, but which shield the plant from sun in summer. Snip off shabby leaves before the flowers emerge, or let them remain and die off naturally. It often self-sows; seedlings are slow-growing and take a few years to bloom.

Propagation: Divide in spring, after new leaves begin to mature; dig up the entire clump and gently pull apart sections, then replant.

> **Bloom Time** Early spring
> **Planting Requirements** Light to full shade; seasonal shade beneath deciduous trees
> **Zones** 3 to 8

Perfect Partners

The dainty flowers of hepatica look best when allowed to naturally push up in scattered clumps through dead leaves. They're also ideal in a shaded rock garden or tucked against a tree trunk or a large, exposed tree root. Delicate Himalayan maidenhair fern (*Adiantum venustum*) or other maidenhairs that retain their foliage over winter are appealing neighbors. For a flowering partner, plant early blooming pulmonaria nearby, but allow 6 to 12 inches (15 to 30 cm) of open space between it and the hepaticas so that the plants don't visually compete.

Heuchera

HEW-ker-uh • heuchera, coral bells

Not so long ago, heucheras were known as coral bells and grown mainly for their flowers. Then the big-leaved, dramatically dark 'Palace Purple' came along in 1986 and shifted the spotlight from flowers to foliage. Nowadays, you'll still find many charming cultivars of coral bells—a member of the Saxifragaceae family—to grow for their flowers. However, you'll also find a superb selection of plants with fabulous foliage that overshadows the flowers by a mile. Ruffles and flourishes in stunning foliage colors of maroon, purple, pewter, silver, apricot, gold, and lime green expand the contributions of "coral bells" and make them one of the most sought-after perennials today.

You'll find enough choice cultivars to fill practically an entire garden all by themselves, but these superb plants are irresistible when combined with other perennials in any situation. Most thrive in shady situations as well as in sun, and they are as at home in a container as in the garden. With these perennials the possibilities are limited only by your imagination.

Heuchera × brizoides (hybrid coral bells) Drawing their traits from *H. sanguinea* and various other species that have been crossed, these hybrids are floriferous and hardy. The plants bloom for weeks on end, from late spring through late summer. They vary in size from 12 to 18 inches (30 to 45 cm) tall when in bloom and form a tidy clump 12 to 15 inches (30 to 38 cm) wide. 'Leuchtkäfer' (Firefly) is a knockout, with an explosion of vermilion flowers and a pleasant fragrance. 'June Bride' is dressed in white, with larger flowers than most cultivars. 'Rosamund' is coral pink. Hardy in Zones 3 to 8.

H. sanguinea (coral bells) This native of the Southwest is the original "coral bells," from which many hybrids have been developed. The plant produces a slowly spreading clump of green foliage, from which emerge many taller bare stems that are lined with tiny, tubular, red or red-pink flowers. Although the individual flowers are extremely small, their color is bright enough to make a splash. Hummingbirds find them irresistible. The species has now been superseded by more popular modern hybrids, although it's still worth a spot in your garden. Hardy in Zones 3 to 8.

H. hybrids This group of modern hybrids was developed to focus attention more on the foliage than the flowers. Large, rugged 'Palace Purple' was the first, but it's been superseded by many other selections developed with more refined form and other appealing colors.

THE BASICS

Heucheras are trouble-free plants, whether you grow them for foliage or flowers. Plant them in groups of at least three for a bigger impact, or use a single plant of those with striking foliage as an accent or container plant. They can be relatively short-lived in the garden, but a little extra care to keep their roots covered will help them live long and prosper.

Heuchera sanguinea

Growing Conditions: Plant in rich, moist, well-drained soil. The tough, woody rootstock will tend to lift itself out of the soil once the plant has been in the ground for a year or two, so you should cover it with a shovelful of compost or mulch for better longevity.

Or lift the plant in late summer and replant at a deeper depth, being careful not to bury the growing points on the crown where the leaves emerge.

Propagation: You can carefully divide established plants in early fall.

▶ **Bloom Time** Late spring to summer
▶ **Planting Requirements** Adapts to almost any light conditions, from full shade to full sun; flowering is diminished in full shade
▶ **Zones** 4 to 8

Heucheras for Fancy Foliage

Heucheras are hot, hot, hot in today's gardens, thanks to the huge range of delicious colors and textures in modern hybrids. These handsome plants are traffic-stoppers, a far cry from the neat green mounds of older coral bells, which barely rate a second glance. All have amazing foliage colors, from cool silver to warm peach and gold, as well as green leaves speckled or splashed with white. Use them to perk up your shade garden, or plant them in sunnier spots to partner perennial flowers or roses. They're also ideal for growing in raised containers, closer to eye level. You'll find dozens of cultivars to choose from, with more being introduced all the time. All are hardy in Zones 4 to 9.

◀ *H.* **'Obsidian'**
A dramatic partner for any other color or form of fancy-leaved heuchera, this cultivar has simple leaves that set off a neighbor's frills and flourishes. It grows to about 16 inches (40 cm) wide and looks best when companion heucheras or other plants interweave their brighter-colored leaves among its somber foliage.

▲ *H.* **'Crimson Curls'**
This scrumptious selection has ultra-curly leaf edges that create a mass of fascinating texture. And it boasts unusual color, too. New leaves emerge deep red, then pale to silvery green in summer, with dark crimson undersides that flash among the mass of curls. Stems of creamy flowers arise in midsummer. The plant reaches 12 to 18 inches (30 to 45 cm) tall and wide. Plant this heuchera where you can reach out and tousle its red head, at the front of a bed or in a container.

▶ *H.* **'Lime Rickey'**
Jazz up your shade garden with this outrageously ruffled, vivid chartreuse cultivar, named for a gin-and-lime-juice drink that was popular decades ago (today's mojito is a variation that uses rum instead of gin). Sip your beverage while admiring the tight 18-inch (45-cm)-wide mound of yellow-green leaves or the abundant stems of white spring flowers.

▼ *H.* 'Peach Flambé'

This fabulous plant begins with bright peach leaves that mellow into a soft peach tinged with red as they mature and turn plum in fall. 'Marmalade' and 'Amber Waves' have colors in the same spectrum, but this cultivar offers larger, smoother leaves. Plant this gem in a raised container on your doorstep.

▲ *H.* 'Pewter Veil'

One of the earlier fancy-foliage heucheras, this cultivar has luscious silver-burgundy leaves traced with dark veins. New leaves have a soft gleam with pink undersides that deepen as they age. This is a gorgeous companion for dark-leaved heucheras.

▶ *H.* 'Midnight Rose'

This cultivar adds pink freckles to the mix. The leaves brighten slightly as the speckles and occasional splotches become lighter pink against the maroon-black background. It grows well in sun to part shade and forms a mound about 16 inches (40 cm) wide.

Hibiscus *hi-BIS-kus* • hibiscus, rose mallow

The oversized pink, white, or rose-red blooms of shrublike rose mallow hybrids are familiar in gardens, but other hibiscus with smaller flowers and different habits deserve attention, too—you can expect them to be one of the stars of summer. Let the shrub-size plants, from the Malvaceae family, stand in winter, when bare stems and chunky seedpods will add character to your sleeping garden.

Hibiscus acetosella (African rose mallow) This spectacular red-foliaged hibiscus is so fast growing that within weeks it is 2 to 5 feet (60 to 150 cm) tall and 3 feet (90 cm) wide. The plant needs a long, hot summer to produce single, 3-inch (7.5-cm) yellow or reddish purple blossoms in fall. 'Red Shield' ('Coppertone') is the most available version of this plant, with stunning maroon red leaves and stems. Hardy in Zones 10 to 11.

H. coccineus (scarlet rose mallow) The bright red flowers of this species are stunning. This shrubby American native grows 6 to 8 feet (1.8 to 2.4 m) tall and 5 feet (1.5 m) wide and is studded with 6-inch (15-cm) blooms from midsummer to fall. It has thin, deeply lobed foliage, like a fancy Japanese maple. Its see-through foliage will let you place it in the middle or toward the front of your beds. It thrives in wet soil, as well as average conditions, so you can plant it in bog gardens or beside a water feature. 'Davis Creek' is a deep pink-flowered version. Hardy in Zones 6 to 9.

H. moscheutos hybrids (rose mallow, common rose mallow) While the species is low-key, with rose-centered white blossoms, its hybrids are anything but. You'll find a spectrum of stupendous flowers in shades of pink, rose-red, and pure white, on shrub-size, multistemmed plants that reach 4 to 6 feet (1.2 to 1.8 m) tall and 3 feet (90 cm) wide. Leaves are either simple and coarse, like those of *H. moscheutos,* or lobed and maplelike, depending on the parentage of the hybrid. 'Lord Baltimore' is vivid crimson; 'Lady Baltimore' is pink with a red center. 'Disco Belle Mix' comes in a variety of shades. Shorter 'Southern Belle' grows to 3 feet (90 cm), with white flowers washed with red and pink. For maplelike foliage instead of the typical coarse leaves, try 'Kopper King', white with a reddish center and bronze foliage; 'Plum Crazy', a pinkish purple; or 'Anne Arundel', a pretty clear pink. Hardy in Zones 5 to 10.

Perfect Partners

Choose neighbors that can stand up to hibiscus without getting swamped, such as red-hot poker (*Kniphofia* spp.) or New Zealand flax (*Phormium* spp.). Extra-large dahlia flowers can do the trick, too; choose those with cactus or spider shapes to contrast with the rounded hibiscus blossoms. A clump of miscanthus, or a trio of switchgrass (*Panicum* spp.) or fountain grass (*Pennisetum* spp.), will not only hold its own but will smooth the transition to smaller perennials. One of the best partners for heavyweight hibiscus is dainty baby's breath (*Gypsophila paniculata*).

Hibiscus 'Lord Baltimore'

THE BASICS

Easy-to-grow hibiscus can be shorter-lived than other perennials, but what a show they provide. Their fast growth and substantial size will quickly give a long-established feel to your yard. Choose a site that allows enough space for the plant to reach full size.

Growing Conditions: Plant hibiscus in moist, average-to-rich soil. *H. moscheutos* and *H. coccineus* are native to damp sites and don't mind occasional wet soil. Japanese beetles may attack the leaves; tap the beetles into a jar of ammonia early in the morning when they're slow to fly. Cut down old stalks in early spring; new shoots are slow to emerge. The plant may self-sow.

Propagation: Collect or purchase seeds and start inside in late winter in pots. 'Disco Belle Mix' and other strains of *H. moscheutos* hybrids often bloom the first year from seed.

▸ **Bloom Time** Summer

▸ **Planting Requirements** Full sun

▸ **Zones** Hardiness varies, depending on species; *H. moscheutos* hybrids, Zones 5 to 10

Hosta HOSS-tuh • hosta

It's no wonder that hostas have a host of fans. These reliable perennials are indispensable in the shady garden, where they add appealing form and beautiful foliage in an array of colors, shapes, and textures. Leaf colors include every shade of green you could ever imagine: spring greens, deep greens, grays, blues, even bright gold. Add edgings or centers of white or yellow to those colors, and you get an almost infinite variety of possibilities.

Hostas, which are members of the Hostaceae family, also supply textural accents with leaves that may be wavy, smooth, ruffled, curled, or as puckered as a seersucker suit. Whether a stout or slender plant, they all have a tidy, clump-forming habit. And we haven't even mentioned hosta flowers! White or lilac trumpets arise on bare stems in summer, many of them spreading fragrance throughout the garden.

Hosta fortunei A sturdy species (some authorities consider it a hybrid) that multiplies quickly, this hosta has deeply veined green to gray-green leaves on long stems. In summer it produces generous lilac mauve flowers. It reaches 1 to 2 feet (30 to 60 cm) tall. Look for yellow-leafed cultivars, such as 'Aurea' ('Albopicta Aurea') and 'Gold Standard'. For colored leaf margins, try gold-edged 'Albopicta' ('Aureomaculata') or white-margined 'Albomarginata'. Fresh-looking white-edged 'Francee' grows as well in nearly full sun as it does in shade and multiplies fast; it makes an ideal ground cover.

H. plantaginea (August lily) Here's a hosta to plant for fragrance when its spikes of large white bells bloom in late summer. This is a big plant, reaching nearly 3 feet (90 cm) tall and wide. The big, heart-shaped leaves are a fresh midgreen. 'Aphrodite' has double flowers. The vigorous 'Royal Standard' grows well in sun or shade.

H. sieboldiana Another hosta of substance, this species and its cultivars grow into a beautiful clump 2½ to 3 feet (75 to 90 cm) tall and wide. The heart-shaped leaves are broad and blue-green, and are topped with stems of pale purple flowers in summer. 'Elegans' has an intriguing seersucker texture; its leaves are blue-gray in sun and blue-green in shade. 'Frances Williams' has rounded, cupped, gray-green leaves with broad, deep yellow margins. 'Kabitan' is a downsized cultivar, reaching only 12 to 18 inches (30 to 45 cm) tall; its narrow, ruffled, gold-trimmed leaves are deep green, and it spreads fast by rhizomes to make a good edger or ground cover.

H. venusta A tiny dwarf by hosta standards, this species grows 4 inches (10 cm) tall and 8 inches (20 cm) wide. 'Variegata' has white edges on the green leaves.

H. hybrids Hostas have been bred for thousands of years. The parentage of cultivars can be confusing, so most cultivars are identified simply as hosta hybrids. You'll find dozens of plants in this group, with the full complement of hosta color, form, and texture. Enjoy your explorations!

THE BASICS

Hostas live for decades, but most take a few years to reach full size. Choose

Hosta fortunei cv.

a site with enough room for the full-grown plant, and fill in with annuals or ground covers while you wait. Hostas vary in their tolerance for sun; read the label before you buy to make sure the plant is right for your site. Gray, blue, or golden cultivars achieve their best color in part sun to light shade; greens are generally best in shade. Keep cultivars with white-splashed leaves out of direct sun, which can damage their foliage.

Growing Conditions: Plant in moist but well-drained soil of average-to-rich fertility. Regular fertilizing increases the size and speed of growth. Slugs and snails will devour leaves; control them with traps or other products, or hand-pick them. Hostas do not tolerate extended dry periods; mulch around the plant to preserve soil moisture, and water weekly when rain is scarce.

Propagation: Divide in spring.

▶ **Bloom Time** Summer
▶ **Planting Requirements** Full shade to part sun, depending on cultivar
▶ **Zones** 3 to 8

Handsome Hostas

Hosta cultivars can satisfy any taste, with their huge diversity of leaf color, leaf texture, and size. You'll find diminutive plants perfect for edging, midsize types that make good ground covers, and knee-high giants that can hold center stage by themselves. Use variegated and yellow-green hostas to bring light to shadier areas of your yard. Cultivars with simpler, cooler blue-green or blue-gray leaves are perfect for setting off other perennials.

◀ *H. 'Kabitan'*
One of the smaller hostas, this charmer forms a clump of narrow leaves 10 inches (25 cm) tall and 15 inches (38 cm) wide. Use it to edge a path in part sun to light shade, or try planting beneath shrubs or trees for a splash of color.

▲ *H. 'Midwest Magic'*
This 1999 introduction has dimpled, golden yellow-green leaves with an irregular green margin. In shade the yellow tones are understated; in a sunnier site the yellow is more pronounced, contrasting strongly with the deep green margins. The leaves are slightly shiny on top, and their quilted texture also helps to catch the light, making this medium-to-large cultivar look almost luminescent. The clump of striking foliage reaches about 4 feet (120 cm) wide but stays below 1½ to 2 feet (45 to 60 cm) in height. The tubular, pale lavender flowers bloom in mid- to late summer.

▶ *H. 'Snowdon'*
Snowdon is the highest mountain in Wales, and a popular hiking destination from which Ireland, Northern Ireland, and England can all be seen on a clear day. Like the mountain, this hosta hybrid is visible from a long way away. It matures into a clump about 3 feet (90 cm) tall and wide, making it an outstanding choice for an accent. The immense blue heart-shaped leaves measure about 14 inches (35 cm) long when the plant is mature. White flowers on sturdy stems bloom in midsummer.

▼ *H.* 'Sum and Substance'

A perennially popular cultivar, this large hosta forms an impressive clump that reaches 3 feet (90 cm) wide at maturity. Each gigantic, strongly textured leaf can grow to about 18 inches (45 cm) long. The chartreuse color adds to the show-stopping effect. Use this big guy as a specimen or focal point in your partly shady garden; the foliage tends to bleach in full sun.

▲ *H.* 'Wide Brim'

A versatile, medium-sized hosta, this pretty cultivar grows equally well in sun to shade. The white edging of the leaves gradually takes on a yellowish tint as the foliage matures. In summer stalks of lavender flowers tempt hummingbirds.

▶ *H.* 'Fire and Ice'

Green flames around the edges of the leaves lead to a glacial heart in this medium-sized, slow-growing hosta, which reaches about 1½ feet (45 cm) tall and 2½ feet (75 cm) wide. The twisting leaves give a sense of movement to this showy cultivar, which offers a bonus of lavender flowers in summer. One of the delights of hostas is noticing how two different plants can show coloring that's almost the exact reverse of one another. The leaves of 'Fire and Ice' are the reverse image of green-leaved, white-margined 'Patriot', a cultivar chosen as Hosta of the Year in 1997.

189

Iberis *eye-BEER-iss* • candytuft

One of the whitest whites in the garden, candytuft is an invaluable companion for spring bulbs and other early bloomers. Although more than one species of perennial candytuft from the Brassicaceae family is available, only a single species, *Iberis sempervirens,* is so popular that it graces a multitude of gardens. That's because it is one of the first perennials to bloom in spring. And it's a pretty one, spreading a snowy cloth of bright white flowers among other plants or draping over a wall. Lesser known species are worth investigating, too.

Iberis saxatilis (perennial candytuft) This plant shares the same common name as *I. sempervirens* and some of the same traits, but it has its differences. Its stems are erect instead of trailing, and its small white flowers emerge from pink-tinged buds and take on a purple tinge as they age. Its

dark green evergreen leaves form a mat 6 inches (15 cm) tall and 1 foot (30 cm) wide. Hardy in Zones 7 to 9.

I. semperflorens Even earlier to bloom than other candytufts, this tender species kicks into gear in late winter. Its clusters of fragrant flowers can reach 2 inches (5 cm) across and are held erect above the foliage. The evergreen plant, actually a tiny shrub of narrow spoon-shaped leaves, grows to 1 foot (30 cm) high and twice as wide. *Semperflorens* means "ever flowering," and this shrubby little plant lives up to the name; flowers appear nearly throughout the year. It's native to southern Italy and Sicily, and is perfect for a rock garden in mild climates. Hardy in Zones 8 to 9.

I. sempervirens (perennial candytuft) Its low, spreading mat of intertwined trailing stems, densely cloaked in narrow, dark green leaves, reaches 6 to 12 inches (15 to 30 cm) tall and spreads up to 2 feet (60 cm) wide. The foliage is evergreen, so this species contributes texture and color even when it's not blooming. You'll appreciate the calming color of the foliage among bright summer flowers or in the winter season. However, the mat of foliage will be a background player when the mass of tiny white clustered flowers appears. For such small flowers, this plant packs a punch. Several excellent cultivars are available. Try 'Purity' or 'Schneeflocke' (Snowflake) for long bloom and a lot of it. 'Nana' and 'Weisser Zwerg' (Little Gem) are smaller versions with tiny leaves, reaching only 6 inches (15 cm) tall. If you like the thought

Iberis sempervirens

of spring flowers in fall, plant 'Autumn Snow', which blooms twice, once in early spring and a second time in fall. Hardy in Zones 4 to 9.

THE BASICS

Candytuft needs only minimal care to give you years of reliable bloom. In a large garden plant in drifts for a calm effect. Or use candytuft to border paths, top walls, or nestle beside landscaping rocks, where it can draw attention to the design of your garden.

Growing Conditions: Plant in well-drained soil of lean-to-average fertility. Candytuft also grows well in poor soils, including stony or sandy sites and in crevices in a rock wall. Shear back the plant by about one-third after bloom to help keep it dense and compact.

Propagation: Root cuttings of soft green stems in late spring.

▶ **Bloom Time** Early to late spring
▶ **Planting Requirements** Full sun
▶ **Zones** Hardiness varies, depending on species

Perfect Partners

A drift of candytuft draws the eye and makes other colors really stand out. Early bright red tulips, such as 'Red Riding Hood', are a can't-miss combo with snowy candytuft; pastel tulips, such as 'Apricot Beauty', will give a more romantic look. Dwarf irises (*Iris reticulata*), including pure blue 'Harmony', are a beautiful match, too. The reddened stems and foliage of euphorbias will glow behind a drift of white candytuft. Add golden chartreuse 'Angelina' sedum (*Sedum rupestre* 'Angelina') to highlight the flowers when euphorbia bloom.

I

Iris *EYE-riss • iris*

A garden without iris is unimaginable, given the huge impact of these plants. This genus from the Iridaceae family includes plants that have added color, fragrance, and form to gardens for many years. Every color of the rainbow can be found, plus copper, brown, and bicolors. The leaves are long and pointed, and often evergreen or semievergreen, maintaining a presence after the flowers fade. The blossoms have six petals—three that form an upright "standard" and three that "fall" below. The shape may be simple or have crests, horns, pleats, or ruffles.

Iris cristata (crested iris) This little iris forms a clump 6 inches (15 cm) tall and 1 to 2 feet (30 to 60 cm) wide. The sky blue flowers appear in spring. 'Alba' is white. Hardy in Zones 3 to 9.

I. douglasiana (Pacific Coast iris) It forms a clump of evergreen foliage to 3 feet (90 cm) tall, topped by

Perfect Partners

Irises add a puctuation point to your garden, contrasting with mounding or sprawling perennials. Pair dwarf irises (*Iris reticulata*) with miniature daffodils and other spring bulbs, and with early blooming perennials, such as basket-of-gold (*Aurinia saxatilis*) and candytuft (*Iberis sempervirens*). Try planting bearded iris among coordinating or contrasting colors of columbines (*Aquilegia* spp.), yarrows (*Achillea* spp.), pinks (*Dianthus* spp.), and 'Clara Curtis' chrysanthemum (*Chrysanthemum × rubellum* 'Clara Curtis').

flowers in blues, reddish purple, and white. Hardy in Zones 7 to 9.

I. × louisiana (Louisiana iris hybrids) This group of hybrids brings new hues of warm reds to the palette. 'Cajun Love' is a blend of reddish purple and copper. Height varies from 3 to 5 feet (90 to 150 cm) tall and wide. Hardy in Zones 6 to 10.

I. pseudacorus (yellow flag) This species thrives in wet places, but it will also perform in consistently moist garden soil. The upright leaves form a clump 3 to 4 feet (90 to 120 cm) tall and wide. Clear yellow flowers appear in spring. Hardy in Zones 4 to 9.

I. reticulata (dwarf iris) This little iris is an early spring bloomer. It bears blue or purple flowers and has leaves in small tufts 4 to 6 inches (10 to 15 cm) tall. Hardy in Zones 5 to 9.

I. sibirica (Siberian iris) A cold-hardy species, it is long-lived and trouble-free. It forms a clump of foliage 2 to 4 feet (60 to 120 cm) tall. Blue, purple, reddish purple, white, yellow, or bicolor flowers bloom in summer. Hardy in Zones 3 to 9.

THE BASICS

All irises are easy to grow and long-lived. Most spread at moderate speed and benefit from division. Give each species the moisture conditions that it does best in, and you'll be rewarded with years of fabulous flowers.

Growing Conditions: For bearded iris (see page 193) dig a hole deep enough for the thin roots, but leave the tops of the rhizomes slightly exposed. It can tolerate drought in summer, but its foliage looks better if you

Iris reticulata

occasionally water it. Iris borer can be a problem; look for skinny trails in the leaves where the pests have fed, and remove and destroy infected plants.

Plant Siberian iris in average-to-moist garden soil, covering the roots to the crown of the plant. Divide every few years for best flowering. Plant bulbs of dwarf iris in well-drained soil. Dwarf iris go dormant after their foliage ripens, so they can tolerate periods of summer dryness.

Plant water-hungry *I. ensata, I. pseudacorus,* and *I. × louisiana* in moisture-retentive soil; dig in extra humus at planting time and mulch well to help keep the soil from drying out. Water these species weekly when rain is scarce. Or plant these species in wet soil, such as in a bog garden or at the edge of a pond. Japanese iris does best when soil is moist in spring and summer, but drier in winter.

Propagation: Divide in spring.

▶ **Bloom Time** Spring or summer
▶ **Planting Requirements** Full sun; Pacific Coast hybrids, yellow flag (*I. pseudacorus*), and Louisiana hybrids adapt to light or part shade
▶ **Zones** Hardiness varies depending on species

I

Easy, Elegant Irises

Irises have been gracing our gardens for centuries. Their beauty belies their workhorse character: These plants are easy to grow, dependable, and extremely long-lived. Today, the palette of possibilities has expanded to include new hybrids that draw from American natives, as well as reblooming types that supply a second show of flowers in late summer or fall. Whichever iris you choose, you'll enjoy its good-natured grace for years to come.

◀ *I. ensata*
If you can supply the moist-to-wet soil these Japanese irises demand, you'll be rewarded with huge fantastic flowers. This is one of the most beautiful varieties of the iris clan, and also one of the tallest, with some cultivars topping 5 feet (150 cm). Many cultivars are available in shades of blue, purple, and white, including blue-purple 'Electric Glow'; 'Sorcerer's Triumph', with purple standards and white falls veined with purple; and double-flowered 'Double Delight'. Hardy in Zones 5 to 9.

▲ **Pacific Coast hybrid**
Bred from native American wildflowers, these irises have delicate flowers. Many reach 18 inches (45 cm) tall and form a clump 2 to 3 feet (60 to 90 cm) wide; however, height and spread as well as foliage can vary widely. Hardy in Zones 6 to 9.

▶ *Iris pallida* '**Variegata**'
Variegated foliage makes a strong accent in the garden, especially when it's a clump of vertical spears, as with this iris. The purple flowers are similar to those of bearded iris, but it's the leaf appeal that earns these irises a place of honor in the garden. Hardy in Zones 4 to 8.

▼ *I.* × *louisiana* 'Black Gamecock'

Louisiana irises are becoming more mainstream, thanks to new introductions such as magnificent 'Black Gamecock'. It requires moist soil and is ideal for water gardens. The extremely vigorous plant reaches 2 to 3 feet (60 to 90 cm) tall and blooms in midspring.

▲ Bearded irises

Most bearded irises are known as "iris hybrids." These are easy to grow and there are hundreds of cultivars, from 1 to 3 feet (30 to 90 cm) tall or more. Each part of the flower, including the fuzzy beards, adds to a rainbow effect. Flaming orange beards add a dab of heat to the cool elegance of the white blooms of cultivars such as the reblooming 'Knock-Out' and 'Frost and Flame'. Some bearded irises are scented, such as 'Cantina', Mary Frances', and 'Pacific Mist'. Hardy in Zones 4 to 10.

▶ *I. sibirica* 'Caesar's Brother'

Dependable, durable, and delightful, in or out of bloom: That's 'Caesar's Brother', probably the most popular cultivar of Siberian iris. It forms a dense, vertical clump of narrow, pointed leaves, topped with an abundant display of deep blue-purple flowers in late spring or early summer. The plants reach about 3 to 4 feet (90 to 120 cm) tall in bloom. Hardy in Zones 3 to 8.

Kniphofia *nip-HO-fee-uh* • red-hot poker

Even though red-hot poker hails from South Africa, hummingbirds are quick to discover the bounty of nectar inside the tubular flowers that make up the showy spikes. These tough plants from the Asphodelaceae family are ideal for dry gardens, where they bloom madly with no additional water. They're also ideal for igniting a bed of perennials in less demanding conditions, too. Their stout stalks are a valuable vertical accent among perennials of rounded, bushy, or sprawling shapes, and their blazing color draws the eye like a living flame. The basal mound of long, narrow, longitudinally folded leaves are also strong garden accents, even when the plant is out of bloom.

In recent years these plants have received more attention from plant breeders and gardeners. Dozens of cultivars, mostly hybrids, are available, with torches that range from traditional red-and-yellow to plain orange-red and soft yellow.

Kniphofia rooperi Adorably plump-bellied flower spikes top the 4-foot (120-cm)-tall stems of this late bloomer, which puts on its show from early-to-late fall. It's a robust grower with dark green foliage. Hardy in Zones 6 to 9.

K. uvaria The parent of many modern hybrids, this species is a beautiful performer in its own right. This is the classic red-hot poker, with the flowering spikes colored like a flame—red at the top, yellow at the bottom. The effect is created by the aging of the blossoms: They open fiery red, then pale to orange and finally to yellow. The plants reach about 4 feet (120 cm) tall in bloom, with a grassy foliage clump about 2 feet (60 cm) across.

K. hybrids Although the stunning *Kniphofia* genus includes more than 60 species, most garden plants are hybrids that have been bred for improved flowering or form. You'll find an array of flower colors from just-out-of-the-fire red to cool yellow, green, and ivory. They bloom in spring or summer, depending on the cultivar you choose, so be sure to read the label. Hummingbirds will give them the seal of approval in any season. Most grow into a clump of foliage about 2 to 3 feet (60 to 90 cm) tall, and about 4 feet (120 cm) wide. The "pokers" easily stretch 4 to 6 feet (1.2 to 1.8 m) tall. Most are reliably hardy in Zones 6 to 9; some are hardy in Zones 5 to 9.

THE BASICS

Red-hot pokers are undemanding plants that require only once-a-year maintenance to look good for years. A single plant quickly grows into a substantial clump.

Growing Conditions: Plant in well-drained, poor-to-average soil. These tough plants also thrive in sand, and their flowering stalks are sturdy enough to stand tall without staking, so they're good in windy or seaside gardens, too. Red-hot pokers are ideal for xeric gardens: Their roots go deep, which helps them flourish in dry conditions; their grayish leaves also help them shrug off drought and extreme heat. Cut off finished flowering stalks near the base. To keep the plant looking its best, cut back the foliage to the ground in late fall or early spring. In mild-winter areas the foliage is evergreen, but it may look shabby by spring. Cutting it back entirely in early spring is the easiest course of action unless you have the patience to snip out the stragglers.

Propagation: Divide in spring; be careful to keep as many of the fleshy, breakable roots intact as you can.

▶ **Bloom Time** Spring or summer, depending on cultivar; may rebloom
▶ **Planting Requirements** Full sun
▶ **Zones** Hardiness varies; most thrive in Zones 6 to 9

Kniphofia uvaria

Perfect Partners

Partner cultivars with pale yellow or green flowers with neighbors of deep red foliage, such as 'Bishop of Llandaff' dahlia, or make them part of a pastel planting of pale pink hardy geraniums (*Geranium* spp.), lilac blue campanulas (*Campanula persicifolia* and other spp.), and white or yellow yarrow (*Achillea* 'Moonshine' and other spp.).

K

Lavandula la-VAN-dew-luh • lavender

Romantic lavenders are dear to every gardener's heart. The queen of fragrant perennials, lavender is a bushy "subshrub" that forms a 2- to 3-foot (60- to 90-cm) mound of woody stems clothed in narrow gray-green leaves. In early summer the prized flowering stalks elongate to bring their namesake color and signature scent wafting across the garden.

These plants from the Lamiaceae family are easiest to grow in climates that resemble their Mediterranean or European homelands: mild, rainy winters and nonhumid summers, such as in the West and Northwest. Still, some species and hybrids are adaptable, bringing the pleasures of fragrant lavender to gardeners across the country. Selecting the right lavender for your region is vital for success with these lovely plants.

Lavandula angustifolia (English lavender) One of the most popular lavenders, this sturdy species and its cultivars are adaptable to wide-ranging conditions and climate. 'Hidcote' has gorgeous deep blue-lavender flowers; 'Munstead' is lavender blue. 'Grosso' has particularly plump spikes of flowers. 'Jean Davis' offers pale pink flowers. 'Lady' is ideal in regions where other species don't survive; it's easy to grow as an annual, so you can still indulge in the legendary pleasures of lavender. Most reach 2 feet (60 cm) tall. Hardy in Zones 5 to 9.

L. dentata (French lavender) The most fragrant species, this tender lavender has soft, gray-green leaves that are sticky to the touch. It blooms nearly year-round. Hardy in Zone 9.

L. × intermedia (lavandin) This vigorous hybrid is a hardy plant that blooms later than other species, but when it does, you'll discover that it has perhaps the sweetest fragrance of them all. 'Alba' and 'Caty Blanc' have white flowers. Hardy in Zones 5 to 9.

L. stoechas (Spanish lavender) This astonishingly vigorous plant quickly grows into a bush 4 to 5 feet (120 to 150 cm) wide and 3 feet (90 cm) tall. The flowers are unlike those of other lavenders; they have colored petal-like bracts that form a tuft of "bunny ears." The flowers are reddish purple. The prolific blossoms of 'Otto Quast' lean a bit more toward blue-purple. Hardy in Zones 8 to 9; it may live for years in Zone 7 until a hard winter.

THE BASICS

Lavenders grow best in regions that have dry rather than humid summers. Plant them in groups or as hedges, where their evergreen foliage will be delightful to brush by year-round.

Growing Conditions: Plant in fast-draining, light-to-ordinary-textured soil. It thrives in sandy or gravelly soil. In heavier soil make a mound and place the plant so that its crown is higher than surrounding areas, which will help prevent it from becoming waterlogged, especially in winter. In clay soil add a generous amount of humus and sand or gravel at planting time to improve drainage.

Cutting back lavenders requires some caution. In mild-winter areas you can cut back the plant at any time of the year. In other regions cut back in early spring or soon after flowering;

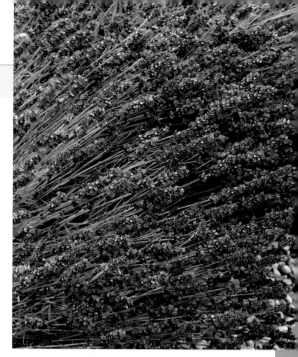

Lavandula angustifolia 'Hidcote'

avoid pruning after midsummer, or the new growth encouraged by pruning will be killed by the coming cold. It's important to restrain yourself with those pruners when you're cutting back lavenders; "a little off the top and sides" is the best approach for the health of the plant. Remove only one-third of the plant during its annual or semiannual haircut to encourage the stems to produce side branches and bushier form. If the plant has become open and bare, cut it back by about half to encourage interior branches. Many gardeners have made the mistake of cutting back a lavender plant to the ground, only to find that the plant quickly gives up the ghost instead of sprouting new stems.

Propagation: Start cuttings from the tips of stems in late summer to early fall.

▸ **Bloom Time** Summer
▸ **Planting Requirements** Full sun
▸ **Zones** Hardiness varies, depending on species

Easy Red-Hot Pokers

South Africa is the source for some of our most valuable garden plants, including red-hot pokers. Interestingly, red-hot pokers were relegated to the greenhouse when they were first introduced to England from Africa in the early 1700s. Not until more than a century later was the innate hardiness of red-hot pokers discovered. Today, these trusty specimens are just as beloved for their garden toughness as for their exotic blooms. You'll find dozens of cultivars worthy of your own plant exploration.

▲ *K.* 'Sunningdale Yellow'

This regal hybrid produces an impressive display of bright yellow flowers. Its candles stretch to 3 feet (90 cm) tall or more. The show begins in midsummer and lasts several weeks, into late summer. Hummingbirds find it just as appealing as orange- or red-flowered cultivars, and the color may be easier to slip into your garden. Hardy in Zones 6 to 9.

▶ *K.* 'Erecta'

Most red-hot pokers taper toward the tip, but 'Erecta' takes another tack: The blossoms bunch out at the top as bloom moves upward, while spent flowers, still brightly colored, turn upward and hug the stem. Some consider this a separate species, *K. erecta*. Hardy in Zones 6 to 9.

K. 'Ice Queen'

The staunchly erect, creamy white-green flowers of this easy-to-grow cultivar make it a great companion for other perennials of more relaxed form. It reaches 2 to 3 feet (60 to 90 cm) tall and blooms in midsummer. Hardy in Zones 6 to 9.

K. 'Apricot'

The luscious color of this midsize hybrid combines easily with bright or pastel neighbors, and it is luminescent against neighboring plants with dark foliage. It reaches about 3 feet (90 cm) tall and 2 feet (60 cm) wide and blooms in summer. Hardy in Zones 6 to 9.

K. 'Alcazar'

This splendid hybrid offers bronzed stems topped with chartreuse buds that open into warm terra-cotta blossoms, which age to a delicious salmon-orange. Its bloom spans the season from midsummer to early fall. The flowering spikes reach 3½ feet (105 cm) above the 18-inch (45-cm) mound of leaves. Less cold-hardy than most hybrids, it is best in Zones 7 to 9.

Leucanthemum *lew-KAN-thih-mum* • Shasta daisy, oxeye daisy

Leucanthemum vulgare

A daisy has such a simple, classic shape that it's the first flower kids learn to draw. The fresh faces of snowy white daisies from the Asteraceae family bring simple charm to the garden, where they combine easily with perennials of other flower forms. Unlike trendy flowers that wax and wane in popularity, daisies have been a consistently welcome presence for centuries in flower beds and fields. Whether you choose one of the many cultivars of the reliable Shasta daisy (*Leucanthemum × superbum*), or go for the casual style of oxeyes (*L. vulgare*), you'll find daisies delightful.

Leucanthemum × superbum (Shasta daisy) In 1901 American plant breeder Luther Burbank successfully crossed four species to create this big, bold daisy, named for Mount Shasta in northern California. He was inspired by wild oxeye daisies (*L. vulgare*) from his boyhood home in New England and spent 17 years experimenting with crosses of that species with wild species from England (*L. maximum*), Portugal (*L. lacustre*), and Japan (*L. nipponicum*). Burbank introduced an unbelievable 800 plant varieties, including vegetables, grains, fruit, and flowers. Burbank's hybrid daisy, along with many other cultivars created from it, have been popular from the moment they were introduced. Most reach about 2 to 3 feet (60 to 90 cm) tall and wide, although the height varies, depending on the cultivar, as does the size of the flowers, which ranges from 3 to 4 inches (7.5 to 10 cm) across. They're stout plants, with glossy, deep green

foliage and strong stems to support the long-blooming, floriferous display. 'Little Miss Muffet' and 'Snow Lady' are tidy dwarf forms, forming a neat mound that reaches 12 to 15 inches (30 to 38 cm) tall. Flowers vary from a simple shape ('Alaska', 'Becky', 'Northern Lights', and 'Mount Everest', among many others) to those with tufted centers and frilled or double petals ('Ice Star', 'Christine Hageman', 'Marconi', and others). The prolific blossoms of 'Broadway Lights', a breakthrough yellow Shasta introduced in 2006, open light canary yellow, then whiten with age. Hardiness varies according to cultivar, so read the label.

L. vulgare (oxeye daisy) The graceful white daisies that sprinkle American roadsides and meadows seem like native wildflowers, but they're European immigrants that followed the footsteps of early settlers. Their casual charm makes them ideal for a cottage-style garden, among annual poppies (*Papaver rhoeas*), bachelor's buttons (*Centaurea cyanus*), and other easygoing flowers, where their habit of self-sowing will be welcome. Oxeye daisies usually reach 12 to 18 inches (30 to 45 cm) tall. The plants form a clump of dark green foliage, from which arise many slender, bare stems crowned by solitary daisies. They bloom from late spring to early summer and self-sow freely.

THE BASICS

Shasta daisies are one of the most rewarding perennials in the garden. Success is practically guaranteed, and care is minimal. Their only drawback

is a tendency to die out within a few years, but frequent division—an easy process because of their dense, fibrous roots—will ensure a constant supply of cheerful flowers on vigorous plants. Plant them in groups, or dot them among your other perennials for a splash of white that boosts the effect of neighboring plants.

Growing Conditions: Plant in well-drained, average-to-rich soil. Established clumps can shrug off a few weeks of drought. Mulch the plants to help retain soil moisture, and give them a drink when rain is scarce. To keep your collection thriving, dig up the entire clump in spring every two to three years, divide with a sharp shovel, and replant the most vigorous sections. Snip off faded flowers to encourage new buds and blooms. Cut back the entire clump to just above ground level in late fall. Some cultivars may self-sow, but the seedlings may not resemble the parent plant.

Propagation: Divide in early spring.

▶ **Bloom Time** Early to midsummer
▶ **Planting Requirements** Full sun
▶ **Zones** 4 to 8 for most Shastas (*L. × superbum*); Zones 2 to 10 for oxeyes (*L. vulgare*)

Liatris *lee-AY-tris* • blazing star, gayfeather

These unusual perennials form spikes of eye-catching fuzzy blossoms that bloom for weeks. Unlike most flowers that grow on spikes, blazing stars, from the Asteraceae family, open first at the top of the stem and move downward. The multitude of tubular red-purple blossoms are beloved by butterflies, and the seeds attract goldfinches. Blazing stars have thin, narrow leaves, almost grasslike, and mostly in a basal tuft. You'll find excellent cultivars, as well as a good selection of species.

Liatris aspera (rough blazing star, button gayfeather) This species has fewer flowers than others, but it grows to 4 to 6 feet (1.2 to 1.8 m), adding height without blocking the view of plants behind it. The flowers are clustered in "buttons"; color varies from pale purple to rosy pink.

Liatris pycnostachya

L. pycnostachya (Kansas blazing star, cattail gayfeather) Statuesque flowering stems, 3 to 5 feet (90 to 150 cm) tall, arise from the clump of slender leaves. These sturdy stems are leafy at the bottom, then packed along the top 1½ to 2 feet (45 to 60 cm) with magenta flowers. *L. pycnostachya* var. *alba* ('Alba') is a white variety.

L. scariosa (Eastern blazing star, tall blazing star, tall gayfeather) Other species tower over this 2½- to 3-foot (75- to 90-cm)-tall plant. It produces pale reddish purple flowers and is a late bloomer, with flowers from late summer into early fall. 'September Glory' has reliable, rich purple-red color. 'White Spire', an off white flower, looks good with gray-toned grasses and blue fescues (*Festuca* spp.).

L. spicata (spike gayfeather) The bottlebrush flowering stalks of this species and its cultivars are popular

Perfect Partners

Plant blazing star with purple coneflower (*Echinacea purpurea*), goldenrod (*Solidago* spp.), and switchgrass (*Panicum virgatum*) to create a prairie vignette. Or use them with tea roses (*Rosa* spp.), baby's breath (*Gypsophila* spp.), and hardy geraniums (*Geranium* spp.) to add an American accent to an English-style garden. For a fall composition you can combine late-blooming *L. scariosa* with lavender blue asters, russet mums (*Chrysanthemum* spp.), and the casual golden daisies of black-eye Susan (*Rudbeckia* spp).

Liatris spicata 'Kobold'

in gardens. Free-blooming, magenta 'Kobold' is only 2 to 2½ feet (60 to 75 cm) tall in bloom; 'Floristan Violet' holds long wands of intense purple; 'Floristan White' is densely packed with white flowers in late summer.

THE BASICS

Blazing stars grow equally well from inexpensive corms, sold as summer bulbs, as they do from higher-priced potted plants. Plant this free spirit in generous groups of a dozen or so corms so that its vertical spikes don't look like isolated exclamation marks.

Growing Conditions: Plant in average-to-moist but well-drained soil; plant *L. aspera* and *L. pycnostachya* in drier soil of lean to average fertility, so that they don't grow too tall and keel over. Blazing stars flourish in sandy soil, too, and are highly tolerant of dry conditions. Many self-sow freely, so be careful that you don't mistake them for grass and weed them out.

Propagation: Divide clumps in early spring. Transplant self-sown seedlings in spring.

▶ **Bloom Time** Summer; *L. scariosa*, early fall
▶ **Planting Requirements** Full sun
▶ **Zones** 3 to 10

Lilium LIL-ee-um • lily

Lilies are among the greatest glories of the garden. Their tall stalks, crowned by large trumpets or decked with tiers of charming, back-curved blossoms, steal the show in summer. Fashions in lilies, from the Liliaceae family, have changed over the years. A couple of generations of gardeners ago, it was the Madonna lily *(Lilium candidum)* and the tiger lily *(L. lancifolium)* that dominated the scene; many of those plants still thrive at old homesteads, attesting to their hardy nature. As more and more lily species joined the array, and as plant breeders got their hands on these spectacular flowers, the field has broadened. Today we can choose from hundreds of hybrid lilies, nearly all of them priced at less than a cup of specialty coffee.

To make sense of so much variety, plant authorities have grouped lilies into eight divisions of hybrid cultivars, plus Division IX, which includes all true species of lilies. The most popular lily cultivars belong to Division I, Asiatic hybrids; Division VI, Trumpet and Aurelian hybrids; and Division VII, Oriental hybrids. Their big, colorful, long-lasting blooms are a hit with gardeners and florists alike.

Once you fall under the spell of these fantastic flowers, the biggest problem will be finding more space for yet another lily. The best news? Most are as easy to grow as daffodils!

***Lilium* Asiatic hybrids** These plants, derived from *L. bulbiferum, L. davidii, L. lancifolium,* and other species, are vigorous growers with a cluster of usually unscented flowers, many in bold red, orange, and other strong, clear colors. The blossoms of many cultivars face upward or outward, making a big splash at summer bloom time. Some cultivars show their tiger lily *(L. lancifolium)* heritage with stems of nodding, recurved blossoms. Hardy in Zones 3 to 9.

***L.* Oriental hybrids** This group of lilies includes crimson-and-white 'Star Gazer', as well as the white 'Casa Blanca'. Oriental hybrids originated from *L. japonicum, L. henryi,* and other East Asian species. They bloom from mid- to late summer, and many are scented. Hardy in Zones 4 to 8.

***L.* Trumpet and Aurelian hybrids** Look for giant-flowered, sweet-scented cultivars in this group derived from the royalty of lilies, including *L. auratum, L. regale,* and others. Some are huge flaring trumpets; others are wide open or tightly recurved. 'African Queen' is a superb light orange cultivar. Hardy in Zones 4 to 8.

THE BASICS

Lilies are long-lived plants that grow from bulbs. The least expensive way to fill your garden is to buy dormant bulbs, sold with other summer bloomers, such as gladiolus. You'll find them in garden centers and nurseries, as well as through many mail-order sources. Potted lilies in bloom are also sold as florist plants; if you receive one as a gift, transplant it to the garden after the flowers are finished.

Growing Conditions: Plant in well-drained soil of average-to-rich fertility; dig in humus or compost at planting time. Mark the location of lily bulbs to prevent accidentally slicing

Lilium (Trumpet type) 'African Queen'

into them. In spring protect emerging lily shoots from cold snaps and freezes by covering them with a flowerpot or other shelter. Slugs can devour young lily shoots overnight; use beer traps, handpicking, or other control methods. The bright red European lily leaf beetle—both the adult and the sluglike larvae—can devastate plants in some areas, particularly New England. Vigilance in handpicking is the best control. After the lily's leafy flowering stems have gone dormant and turned tan, cut them back to about an inch (2.5 cm) above ground level.

Propagation: Some lilies self-sow. Others produce tiny bulbils in the leaf axils, which you can detach easily when ripe. You can also carefully dig up a lily bulb after the plant has gone dormant and peel off several scales of the bulb. Plant seeds, bulbils, or scales in a nursery bed, where they can safely grow to blooming size in a few years.

▶ **Bloom Time** Early to late summer, depending on species

▶ **Planting Requirements** Full sun unless otherwise noted

▶ **Zones** Hardiness varies, depending on species

Limonium *li-MOE-nee-um • sea lavender, statice*

Limonium sinuatum Sunburst Series

These plants from the Plumbaginaceae family are perfect fillers in the garden, where their papery flowers in brights or pastels weave among other plants. Two species are commonly grown.

Limonium platyphyllum (*L. latifolium*; sea lavender) This species forms a ground-hugging basal rosette of oval leaves. Flowering stems arise in late summer, growing into a rounded, 2-foot (60-cm) cloud of tiny lavender flowers. 'Blue Cloud' is more blue. Hardy in Zones 4 to 9.

L. sinuatum (statice) Because it is hardy in only Zones 8 to 9, it is often planted as an annual. Its tiny flowers are held within colorful papery calyxes.

Cultivars are available in primary to pastel hues, often as easy-to-grow seeds. All form a basal rosette of lobed, wavy leaves, but the flowering stems are 12 to 30 inches (30 to 75 cm) tall in bloom. Look for cultivars from the Fortress, Sunburst, and Art Shades series.

THE BASICS

Limonium thrives in sand and gravelly or stony sites and is impervious to drought. The stiff stems or airy ball of flowers shrug off windy conditions, making them ideal for seaside gardens. They also thrive in salty conditions.

Growing Conditions: Plant in well-drained soil of lean-to-rich fertility. Clip off finished flowering stems to ground level. May self-sow.

Propagation: Transplant self-sown seedlings without disturbing the roots.

▶ **Bloom Time** Summer to early fall
▶ **Planting Requirements** Full sun
▶ **Zones** *L. platyphyllum*, 4 to 9; *L. sinuatum*, 8 to 9, or grow as an annual

Lobelia *lo-BEE-lee-uh • perennial lobelia, cardinal flower, great blue lobelia*

Think "lobelia," and chances are your mind turns to those brilliant blue annuals used in containers. But the genus is also represented by two striking hardy perennials. You can give cardinal flower (*Lobelia cardinalis*) and great blue lobelia (*L. siphilitica*)—native American wildflowers from the Campanulaceae family—a place of honor in the garden. You will also find fancy-colored hybrids, which are more readily available than the species.

Lobelia cardinalis (cardinal flower) This species shows off tall, tapering spires of pure red flowers that light up the garden like a living flame. It blooms for weeks from late summer into fall, with flowers opening from the bottom of the 2- to 4-foot

(60- to 120-cm)-tall stem and moving upward. Hardy in Zones 3 to 9.

L. siphilitica (great blue lobelia) A chunkier plant than the cardinal flower, this species reaches up to 2 feet (60 cm) tall, with multiple flowering stems packed thickly with tubular blue blossoms. The blossoms don't have the "wings" of cardinal flower. 'Alba' and 'White Candles' are white-flowered cultivars. Hardy in Zones 4 to 8.

THE BASICS

Cardinal flower is striking enough to plant singly, as an accent plant. You'll get more oohs and aahs over great blue lobelia and hybrid cultivars if you plant them in groups of three.

Growing Conditions: Plant in average-to-rich moist soil. Clip back

Lobelia cardinalis

flowering spikes below the bottom flowers or seeds when most flowers have finished; new bloom stems may sprout as side branches.

Propagation: Divide in spring.

▶ **Bloom Time** Summer to early fall
▶ **Planting Requirements** *L. cardinalis* and *L. siphilitica*, sun to light or part shade
▶ **Zones** Varies, depending on species

Lupinus *loo-PIE-nus* • lupine

With their fat candles of colorful flowers, lupines are gorgeous garden plants. These members of the Papilionaceae family form good-sized clumps to shrub-size specimens of pretty, palmate leaves. But it's the steeples of bloom that draw the eye. The sweetpea-shaped blossoms come in clear bright colors, icy white, and every pastel in between, as well as eye-catching bicolors. Planted in groups of single or mixed colors, the Russell Hybrids and other hybrid cultivars are true standouts. If you explore further afield than the garden hybrids, you'll find American native species that also adapt to garden life.

Lupinus perennis (wild lupine) This usually blue-flowered species is native in New England. It has an erect habit, reaching about 2 feet (60 cm) tall in bloom—and half that height is the flower spikes! Its casual attitude makes it a good choice for meadow gardens. Hardy in Zones 4 to 9.

L. polyphyllus One of the parents of many hybrid cultivars, this western native reaches a considerable height of about 4 feet (120 cm), with abundant spikes of blue-lilac flowers. It's a tough plant that thrives in difficult places in the wild, such as along roadsides or in empty lots. Soften it with marguerite daisies *(Anthemis kelwayi)* and yarrow *(Achillea* spp.) in your garden. Hardy in Zones 7 to 9.

***L.* hybrids** Unless you shop at native-plant specialists, you'll most often come across hybrid lupines offered for sale. The first group of hybrids were bred by James Kelway of England in the 1890s; the most famous, the Russell hybrids and the improved Russell hybrids, grew from the work of George Russell, who crossed several species, including annuals with perennials, to create irresistible colors and prolific bloom. Hybrid lupines are available in a huge variety of colors; here's a sampling.

***L.* Russell hybrids** This fabulous mix offers vivid colors of blue, red, and pink shades, and white, in heights about 2½ to 3 feet (75 to 90 cm) tall. Both solids and bicolors are in the mix, which makes an incredible mass planting. Plant in groups of at least three for the most bang. Hardy in Zones 4 to 7, Zone 8 in the West.

***L.* 'Manhattan Lights'** Elegant spires of bicolored gold and purple create a rhythm in the garden. These shorties reach about 12 inches (30 cm) and look best in groups. Hardy in Zones 4 to 7, Zone 8 in the West.

***L.* 'Moonraker'** Lemon yellow spires reach for the sky in this 3-foot (90-cm) cultivar. Plant it at the back of your beds, against a dark background of hedge or fence. 'Chandelier' has white-and-yellow flowers. Hardy in Zones 5 to 7, Zone 8 in the West.

***L.* 'The Governor'** A classic combination of marine blue-and-white bicolored flowers, this 3-foot (90-cm) hybrid is a dramatic presence in the back of borders. Hardy in Zones 4 to 7, Zone 8 in the West.

THE BASICS

The vertical flower spikes of these perennials are spectacular in bloom, especially when planted in masses. However, the beautiful and popular

Lupinus Russell hybrid

hybrids are short-lived; they may give you flowers for only a year or two.

Growing Conditions: Plant hybrids in moist, rich, well-drained, acid soil, and water weekly when rain is scarce. Choose a location where the flower spikes will be sheltered from hot summer wind. If you've had difficulty growing lupines, grow your own from seeds; it's simple to do, and many bloom the first year. Or buy gallon-size potted plants, which have well-developed roots. Try to keep as much soil around the roots as you can when transplanting to the garden. Most self-sow, so you'll have a ready crop of replacements, but the colors may not match the parent. A variety of diseases, including mildew, can affect lupines.

Propagation: Do not disturb roots of established plants. Before planting, soak the seeds for 24 hours. Transplant self-sown seedlings carefully when 3 to 6 inches (7.5 to 15 cm) tall.

▶ **Bloom Time** Late spring to early summer
▶ **Planting Requirements** Full sun
▶ **Zones** Varies, depending on species; most hybrids grow well in Zones 4 or 5 to 7, and in the western part of Zone 8

L

Lychnis *LIK-niss* • campion, catchfly, Maltese cross

Campions are leafy, mounding plants with clusters of small but showy flowers. The most famous campion is Maltese cross *(Lychnis chalcedonica)*, a fiery red fellow that ignites the early summer garden and blooms for weeks. Rose campion *(L. coronaria)*, another eye-catcher, is not rose at all, but vivid magenta. If you're not ready to go for the bold, other species and cultivars of this member of the Caryophyllaceae family offer gentler colors that may be easier to weave into your own garden.

Lychnis chalcedonica (Maltese cross, Jerusalem cross) The hot color of this species seems made for today's bolder color schemes, but it's a longtime favorite. Its common name originates in the story that it was introduced to Europe during the

Crusades by the Knights of Malta. It's been spreading through American gardens for centuries; Thomas Jefferson sowed it at Monticello in 1807. Few perennials can match its intense orange-red color, which is absolute manna to hummingbirds. Abundant 3- to 4-inch (7.5- to 10-cm)-wide flower clusters, made up of cross-shaped flowers with four deeply notched petals, stand out against the leafy green stems.

L. coronaria (rose campion) Best considered a biennial, this short-lived plant forms a basal rosette of woolly, silvery-white leaves, from which arise openly branching stems topped with simple flowers of blazing magenta. In its second year the plant can reach 3 feet (90 cm) tall and wide, but it rapidly declines thereafter. In the right spot the combination of bright flowers, ghostly stems, and velvety silver leaves is beautiful. 'Angel's Blush' offers ivory flowers with a deep pink eye; 'Alba' is pure white. Cut back the flowering stems to ground level when they're finished. Rose campion self-sows prolifically. Keep the plant toward the middle or back of your beds to prevent it from seeding your lawn.

L. viscaria (German catchfly) The common name "catchfly" comes from the sticky sap exuded by the stems of some species, an adaptation that helps prevent insects that are too small to pollinate the flowers from reaching their nectar. This species forms a tuft of long, thin green leaves, topped by 12-inch (30-cm)-tall stems holding bouquets of bright rosy pink flowers with wide petals and a frilled

Lychnis chalcedonica

center that gives them a slightly fluffy look. It blooms from late spring to early summer.

THE BASICS

Campions are endearing plants with prolific flowers and strong color. Plant them in groups of three for best effect. They can be short-lived, so nurture some of the self-sown seedlings.

Growing Conditions: Plant in average-to-rich, well-drained soil. Fertilize *L. chalcedonica* in spring. *L. coronaria* and *L. viscaria* are highly tolerant of extended dry periods. Deadhead all species to encourage more bloom, which can last for months. Many self-sow; *L. coronaria* is a prolific self-sower. To prevent self-sowing, snip off faded flowers before the seed capsules mature.

Propagation: Transplant self-sown seedlings. Divide *L. chalcedonica* and *L. coronaria* in early spring.

▷ **Bloom Time** Late spring or early summer
▷ **Planting Requirements** Sun; plant *L. chalcedonica* in afternoon shade where summer heat is intense
▷ **Zones** 3 to 9

Perfect Partners

All campions work well among bolder early summer perennials, such as delphiniums and Shasta daisies (*Leucanthemum* × *superbum*). Their flower clusters offer contrast to softer-textured perennials, too; pale pink, white, or light yellow yarrows (*Achillea* spp.) and pink or white pinks (*Dianthus* spp.) are appealing partners. Vivid Maltese cross (*L. chalcedonica*) shows off with partners in other primary colors, including blue veronicas and campanula. It also makes an ideal companion for the dainty nodding flowers of equally red *Lilium pumilum*, or for Asiatic hybrid lilies (*Lilium* hybrids) in yellow, orange-red, or pure white.

L

Meconopsis *me-ko-NOP-sis* • meconopsis, Himalayan blue poppy

With an intense, almost turquoise blue unlike that of any other flower in the garden, the Himalayan blue poppy was the Holy Grail for gardeners in the recent past. It is from the Papaveraceae family, and it is also famed for growing to heights of 4 feet (120 cm) or more. Unfortunately, it's also a daunting challenge to grow. For most American home gardeners, it seems impossible to grow from seed, although evidence from England attested that the plants self-sow with ease. Only within the last decade have plants become more widely available.

For most American gardeners, the blue poppy may still be an impossible dream. Thus far, the plants are known to thrive only in the Pacific Northwest. In other areas, a purchased plant will probably give you just a taste of that fabled color before the plant declines, rarely to return for a second year. Don't give up, though: With the wider availability of plants, the poppy is being tried out in all kinds of conditions and climates. It may turn out to be happily at home in other areas, too.

Meconopsis betonicifolia (Tibetan blue poppy) Look for this plant on your next trek to the high alpine meadows of the Himalayas—or in the parentage of that hybrid in the nursery. Like other blue poppies in this genus, it forms a clump of basal leaves that point upward. The leaves also clothe the bottom part of the flowering stems. The flowers are the hallmark *Meconopsis* blue. When the plant feels at home, it can reach 4 feet (120 cm) tall in bloom.

M. grandis (Himalayan blue poppy) Another parent for hybrids, this species was once, and perhaps still is, grown for its oil-rich seeds by shepherds in mountains in the eastern Himalayas. It is similar to *M. betonicifolia,* bearing one to four flowers per stem. It grows 3 to 4 feet (90 to 120 cm) tall in suitable conditions.

M. × sheldonii (Himalayan blue poppy hybrids) Plants available in western cultivation are almost always hybrids of this cross between *M. betonicifolia* and *M. grandis.* The plants were first bred in Surrey, England, in 1937, and today they fill many famed British gardens, where they grow like—sorry, American wannabes—weeds. Hybrids reach 4 to 5 feet (1.2 to 1.5 m) tall in hospitable conditions.

Perfect Partners

The color of the Himalayan blue poppy is an attention-getter. Surround it with simple foliage plants in a shady garden, so it can stand regally in the spotlight. Plain green hostas and ferns are ideal companions, because they won't compete with the color. Variegated hostas may create a busy rather than a restful picture. The lacy foliage of lady fern (*Athyrium* spp.) offers a pleasing contrast to the blue poppy's tuft of simple leaves. Dark-toned foliage plants that lean more toward red than purple make a satisfying match. For a flowering friend, try white corydalis (*Corydalis ochroleucha*); it blooms at the same time.

Meconopsis grandis

THE BASICS

In summer the alpine elevations at which Himalayan blue poppies thrive in the Himalayas get soaked with monsoons that bring high amounts of rain. That climate heritage causes these perennials to grow best in cooler, wetter regions than in those with warm or dry weather. Keep your plants well watered and sheltered from strong sun.

Growing Conditions: Plant in moist but well-drained soil; dig in humus at planting time. Allow space around the plant so that it isn't crowded. Choose a site that is sheltered from cold or hot winds. Water regularly so that the plant gets an inch of water a week from rainfall and/or watering, and mulch around it to conserve soil moisture.

Propagation: Buy plants; seed is difficult to germinate successfully.

▶ **Bloom Time** Summer
▶ **Planting Requirements** Dappled shade is best; avoid planting close to trees, which will compete for moisture
▶ **Zones** 7 to 8 is the general rule, but it also thrives in Quebec's Gaspé region; much is yet to be learned about the plant's cultivation

Miscanthus *mis-KAN-thuss* • miscanthus, eulalia grass

Long before ornamental grasses hit the scene with a splash a few decades ago, "eulalia grass" *(Miscanthus sinensis)* was adding its handsome, statuesque presence to public and private gardens. A garden stalwart since the Victorian days, miscanthus grasses have returned to the hit parade, thanks to a spate of cultivars introduced by Kurt Bluemel and popularized by landscape architects Wolfgang Oehme and James van Sweden. With good looks and utter reliability, these large grasses from the Poaceae family are four-season players in the garden.

Most form an arching waterfall of long, slender leaf blades 4 to 7 feet (1.2 to 1.9 m) tall. In late summer or fall a crowd of tall, bare flowering stems emerge, topped by long-fingered reddish pink sprays that soon mature into fluffy, pinkish silver plumes. These grasses bleach to warm blond in late fall and retain their foliage through winter. Winter winds often bow the persisting plumes and leaf blades. Snow adds another dimension, crowning the curly, fluffy seed heads with white caps. Many excellent cultivars and related species, including wide-bladed and variegated types, are available to add the perfect note of grace to your garden.

Miscanthus sacchariflorus (silver banner grass) This species has stiff, flat, blue-green leaves marked by silvery midribs. Fans of silken, then fuzzy flowers bloom in summer to early fall. It grows to 5 to 7 feet (1.5 to 2.1 m) tall and about 4 feet (1.2 m) wide. Hardy in Zones 8 to 9.

M. sinensis (miscanthus, eulalia grass) The origins of this plant's common name have been obscured by time, but this most popular miscanthus species has a long and honored history. In its native Japan, where fields of this silken-plumed grass shimmer in the moonlight, it's an object of beauty as well as utility. More than a thousand years ago it was extolled as one of "the seven grasses of fall" in the *Manyoshu*, the earliest collection of Japanese poetry (A.D. 600–759). Probably just as long, it's been a souce of fodder and roof thatch in Japan, where it's known as *obana*, or "tail feather grass." Today it's even grown commercially on farms as a renewable biomass fuel. The species can reach 12 feet (3.6 m) tall, but you'll rarely find it at nurseries; most plants today are cultivars that reach about 4 feet (1.2 m) tall and about 3 feet (90 cm) wide. Purplish flower spikelets arise in fall, softening into feathery, pink-silver plumes that curl as they mature. 'Super Stripe' has superb gold bands on its leaves. Hardy in Zones 4 to 9.

M. yakushimensis (Yakushima silver grass) This stiffer, shorter species has narrow leaves marked with silvery pink midribs and slender, silvery plumes in late summer to early fall. It reaches only 2 to 2½ feet (60 to 75 cm) tall and wide. Hardy in Zones 5 to 9.

THE BASICS

Miscanthus grasses are long-lived and trouble free. Choose a permanent location before you plant; once these grasses get a grip, their thick, tenacious roots make them difficult to remove.

Miscanthus sinensis 'Super Stripe'

Use them as specimens, where they will be the main focal point, or blend them into the garden for foliage effects and fall flowers.

Growing Conditions: Plant in well-drained, average-to-rich soil. Allow plenty of open space around that unprepossessing young plant; in just a year or two it may quadruple in size. Some cultivars may become open and floppy, especially if subjected to wind; support them with a discreet corral of stakes and garden twine or bendable hoops. Cut back dead foliage in late winter, before new growth begins.

Propagation: It's nearly impossible to get a shovel through the roots of an established clump of miscanthus and difficult to even remove a small piece from the edge. Slice, hack, or wrestle a section from the edge of the plant in very early spring. Sharpen the blade of your shovel before you begin.

▶ **Bloom Time** Late summer or fall, depending on cultivar
▶ **Planting Requirements** Sun
▶ **Zones** Hardiness varies, depending on species; most *M. sinensis* cultivars, Zones 4 to 9

M

Miscanthus in Motion

Miscanthus grass is invaluable as a fast-growing focal point, but it brings other, more subtle benefits, too. These large ornamental grasses add movement and gentle rustling music to your garden year-round. The long leaf blades sway and shimmy at the slightest touch of a breeze. Even after the grass has bleached to winter tan, it still adds a sense of life to the landscape. Here are some fine choices to add a touch of music and motion to your own garden.

◄ *M. sinensis* **'Silberfeder' (Silver Feather)**

This excellent cultivar from Germany forms a clump that's taller than wide. It reaches 6 to 8 feet (1.8 to 2.4 m) high, and about 4 feet (1.2 m) across. The leaves are plain green, but height alone would make it a focal point—and then there are those flowers! The huge, fluffy white plumes begin blooming in late summer, which is relatively early by the miscanthus calendar. That early blooming habit, combined with excellent cold hardiness, makes this cultivar a good choice for regions with shorter growing seasons and harsh winters.

▲ *M. sinensis* **'Morning Light'**

This popular and widely available miscanthus cultivar has fine-textured, extremely narrow leaves with white margins that give the plant a silvery sheen. Perfect for smaller gardens, it tops out at about 4 feet (1.2 m) tall. The flower plumes emerge crimson red, then mature into soft tan sprays. 'Gracillimus' is similar, with a white midrib down the center of each leaf blade.

▶ *M. sinensis* **'Strictus'**

Commonly called "porcupine grass," this 6- to 7-foot (1.8-m to 2.1-m) cultivar adds spiky, upright architecture to your garden. A fast grower, it quickly forms a clump of at least 5 feet (1.5 m) wide. The leaves are boldly striped horizontally with golden yellow bands. If you have the space, try a group of three for real punch. Bronze plumes, fading to pink-tinged silvery white, arise in late summer and persist all winter. Hardy in Zones 5 to 9. Shorter 'Zebrinus' has look-alike foliage but an arching habit.

▼ *M. sinensis* var. *condensatus* 'Cabaret'

Self-sowing can be a problem with miscanthus because the fluffy seeds go airborne and sprout far from home. This cultivar solves the problem by producing sterile seeds. It's a stout grass, with blades more than an inch wide, with a bold, creamy stripe down the center. Combine this 6-foot (1.8-m) clump with dramatic, dark-leaved cannas for tropical flair. It flowers very late, with plumes topping 9 feet (2.7 m) tall.

▲ *M. sinensis* 'Zebrinus'

"Zebra grass," as this cultivar is commonly called, is horizontally striped with yellow-gold. New leaf blades emerge plain green but soon acquire the distinctive pattern. It reaches 5 to 8 feet (1.5 to 2.4 m) in height. The plant tends to flop open; stake the clump with a loop of garden twine or linking metal supports to help keep it erect. Coppery pink blooms emerge in late summer to early fall; they mature to silvery white plumes.

▶ *M. sinensis* 'Variegatus'

Wider foliage forms a stiff but arching fountain in this cultivar. It reaches 4 to 6 feet (1.2 to 1.8 m) tall, forming a clump of about equal width. Plant this one in part shade to prevent the sun from damaging the creamy white-striped leaves. Plumes that are 12 to 24 inches (30 to 60 cm) tall appear in late summer to early fall.

Monarda *mo-NAR-duh • bee balm*

Only a single perennial species of bee balm (*M. didyma*) is commonly grown in perennial beds, but this longtime favorite from the Lamiaceae family is indispensable for its burst of bloom in summer—and its magnetic attraction to hummingbirds. Dozens of pretty cultivars provide red, pink, purple, and white flowers, all with intriguing whorled clusters of blooms carried atop their strong, stiff stems. Each cluster is made up of dozens of tubular flowers. For a meadow or prairie garden consider *M. fistulosa,* a taller, less showy species with flowers of soft pink or pink-purple.

Monarda didyma (bee balm, Oswego tea) Bee balm has only been in cultivation since John Bartram, a Quaker farmer called the "Father of American Botany," observed Oswego Indians using it for tea in the 18th century. The leaves have a pleasant citrus-mint scent, and you can use them for tea. Dependable moisture is important. Cultivars are best suited to sun. They form dense clumps that spread rapidly by creeping underground stems. For bright, clear red, try 'Cambridge Scarlet', 'Jacob Kline'—a midew-resistant type— and 'Gardenview Scarlet'. Deeper wine reds include 'Mahogany' and 'Raspberry Wine'. 'Marshall's Delight' is also mildew-resistant. One of the most popular pinks is a 1934 cultivar, 'Croftway Pink'; other pinks include 'Aquarius' and 'Melissa'. For purplish flowers investigate 'Blue Stocking', 'Scorpio', 'Sunset', 'Vintage Wine', and others. 'Snow Maiden' ('Snow White') is creamy white.

M. fistulosa (wild bergamot) Another American native, this one is found in old fields and alongside roads in its native range in the East. It's taller and rangier than the more compact *M. didyma* cultivars, reaching 4 to 5 feet (1.2 to 1.5 m) high, and doesn't form such a dense clump. Blooms are often double-decker, with the second bossom cluster held atop a short stem growing out of the lower one. It blooms in late summer.

THE BASICS

Bee balm is easy to grow—maybe a bit too easy. Its underground stems travel fast in loose, rich soil. Luckily, the strays are easy to uproot and transplant elsewhere. Look for cultivars that are labeled mildew-

Monarda didyma

resistant to minimize the possibility of foliage becoming disfigured by that disease.

Growing Conditions: Plant *M. didyma* in moist, average-to-rich soil. Allow several inches of open space between bee balm and its neighbors to encourage air circulation that may help ward off mildew. Cut plants back by one-third after bloom to encourage another round of flowers. If mildew affects the plant, apply your favorite remedy and consider replacing it with a more resistant cultivar. Plant *M. fistulosa* in well drained, lean-to-average soil; it's highly resistant to drought, as well as to mildew. For fuller plants with more bloom, pinch out the growing tip of each stem when the plants are 1 foot (30 cm) tall.

Propagation: Divide in early spring. Dig and replant strays from traveling roots anytime. Cuttings root easily in moist soil.

▶ **Bloom Time** *M. didyma,* summer; *M. fistulosa,* late summer
▶ **Planting Requirements** Sun; the species form of *M. didyma* also in light-to-part shade
▶ **Zones** *M. didyma,* 4 to 8; *M. fistulosa,* 3 to 9

Perfect Partners

Bee balm (*M. didyma*) blooms at the height of the summer perennial show, and its unusual flowers and upright form offer excellent contrast to other perennials. Combine red cultivars with Shasta daisies (*Leucanthemum × superbum*), white phlox (*Phlox paniculata* 'David'), and a softening mound of blue hardy geraniums (*Geranium* 'Johnson's Blue'). Try pink bee balm with yellow, pink, or rose yarrows (*Achillea* spp.), blue or pink veronicas, and blue fescues (*Festuca* spp.). Plant *M. fistulosa* in naturalistic gardens, where it can wander among ornamental grasses, asters, turtlehead (*Chelone* spp.), and other late-summer bloomers.

Nepeta *NEP-eh-tuh* • catmint

Soft blue is a valuable, versatile color in the garden, and catmints are one of the best for soft blue flowers that bloom for months. No matter what palette you choose for your beds, you'll find plenty of uses for this member of the Lamiaceae family. Siberian catmint (*Nepeta sibirica*) is an upright grower, but the more popular blue catmint (*N. × faassenii*) and its cultivars form a billow of blue that's beautiful along sidewalks or stepping stones. Honeybees, butterflies, and hummingbirds will visit the flowers. Cats approve of the tangy foliage of *N. × faassenii*; they're not interested in *N. siberica*.

Nepeta × faassenii (blue catmint) Catmint is finally coming into its own in American gardens. It looks like a lavender that didn't know when to quit, with a myriad of blue flower spikes that arch outward and upward. The blue is not a harsh electric blue, but is softened with a purplish tinge to create a gentle hue. Plants of the species form reach 12 inches (30 cm) tall and 18 inches (45 cm) wide, but the flowers can spill outward to cover an area 2 feet (60 cm) across or more. Cultivars and hybrids vary in size. Small, scallop-edged, gray-green leaves form a dense mound of aromatic foliage before the flowers arise. The profuse flowers start the show in late spring to early summer and keep going for weeks. When they get tired, just shear back the plant and you'll get another round. Repeat until you run out of growing season.

'Walker's Low' is taller than the species, reaching 2 to 3 feet (60 to 90 cm) high and 3 feet (90 cm) wide in bloom. Each spike of flowers—and there are many spikes—is 8 inches (20 cm) long, creating an incredible show. 'Six Hills Giant' is a free-flowering cultivar that grows to 3 feet (90 cm) tall and wide in bloom. It's an outstanding plant for your garden, with a long bloom season that you can easily extend by shearing back after the first round of flowers fade.

N. sibirica (Siberian catmint) This vigorous species forms erect, multistemmed clumps, with wands of blue-lavender flowers arranged in widely spaced whorls. It spreads by underground running stems. Siberian catmint begins to bloom later than its cousins, from midsummer into fall. It grows to 3 feet (90 cm) tall.

Nepeta × faassenii 'Walker's Low'

THE BASICS

Aromatic catmints are easy to grow, easy to care for, and untroubled by pests or disease. All they need is an occasional haircut to encourage more flowers and an annual cutting back to the ground.

Growing Conditions: Plant in lean-to-fertile, well-drained soil. *N. × faassenii* thrives in dry sites, as well as soil of average moisture. It also flourishes in sandy or stony soil. Established plants sometimes spill out from the center, leaving an open space; clip them back by half to encourage denser growth. The plants regrow quickly, so don't be afraid to wield your pruners to shear off faded flowers or to shape the plant. Cut the entire plant back to the ground in late winter.

Propagation: Divide in early spring. Low-lying stems often root where they touch the ground; slice them off and replant.

▸ **Bloom Time** Early summer to fall
▸ **Planting Requirements** Sun to part shade
▸ **Zones** *N. × faassenii*, Zones 4 to 8; *N. sibirica*, Zones 3 to 8

Perfect Partners

Plant blue catmint (*N. × faassenii*) with coreopsis, pinks (*Dianthus* spp.), foxgloves (*Digitalis* spp.), 'Mainacht' or 'Caradonna' salvia (*Salvia × sylvestris*), and marguerite daisies (*Anthemis tinctoria*). It's a good contrast for the bold flowers of lilies (*Lilium* spp.) and daylilies (*Hemerocallis* spp.). On a sunny slope or in other dry sites, choose companions that are also tolerant of the conditions, such as ornamental oreganos (*Origanum* spp.), pink evening primroses (*Oenothera speciosa*), and lavenders (*Lavandula* spp.). Erect clumps of Siberian catmint (*N. sibirica*) give a controlled look to sprawling hardy geraniums (*Geranium* spp.) or yarrows (*Achillea* spp.).

Oenothera *ee-no-THEER-uh* • evening primrose, sundrops

If you have a big plot to fill or need a reliable performer for an unloved strip, the perennial evening primroses are a good bet. Many of these ground-covering plants from the Onagraceae family spread fast, soon staking their claim to their share of garden space. Most evening primroses fall into the "sundrops" category. They bloom during the daytime, rather than at night. In fall their foliage becomes a burnished red hue that is beautiful with ornamental grasses or blue asters.

Oenothera fruticosa (*O. tetragona, O. linearis*; sundrops) You may find these perennials labeled with other scientific names. This sunny charmer has leafy, reddish stems topped with deep yellow, four-petaled flowers 2 inches (5 cm) wide, usually in a cluster of at least three blooms at the same time. The pointed buds, often red-tinged, open over a few weeks, from late spring to early summer. The plant reaches 1 to 2 feet tall (30 to 60 cm) and 1 foot (30 cm)

Oenothera macrocarpa

wide. The species is less common than the cultivar 'Youngii', which spreads fast to form a dense colony. A few other cultivars are available, including 'Sonnenwende' (Summer Solstice), an extra-long bloomer, and 'Yellow River', which has bigger flowers.

O. macrocarpa (*O. missouriensis*; Ozark sundrops) This vigorous plant can be an aggressive spreader, but it's a beauty. It has a trailing habit and blooms for a long time, from late spring to early fall. The large golden yellow blossoms, up to 5 inches (12.5 cm) across, are borne singly and stay open during the day. It reaches about 6 inches (15 cm) tall and is an eye-catcher in a rock garden.

O. speciosa (pink evening primrose) It will quickly colonize an ever expanding area until you stop it with a shovel. The delicate flushed pink blossoms are open during the day and bloom from early summer to early fall. It grows well in average garden conditions but is also a great candidate for a hot, dry niche—but be careful near sidewalks, where it will work its way into the cracks. It is about 1 foot (30 cm) tall in bloom. The species form is usually white, with a pink tinge as the blooms age, but 'Rosea' and 'Siskiyou' are a lovely pink right from the start.

O. versicolor '**Sunset Boulevard**' This recent addition to the gardening scene is an erect plant about 2 feet (60 cm) tall in bloom, with a similar habit to the wild yellow primroses along roadsides. Its warm, rusty orange flowers are held in a spike atop the leafy stem. The plant is often short-

Oenothera speciosa

lived but self-sows. However, the seedlings may not be the same color as the parent. It does not spread by roots and is easy to grow from seed.

THE BASICS

Some gardeners find the spreading habit of most evening primroses to be too much of an annoyance to tolerate, while others are pleased with how quickly they fill a space and how beautiful they are in bloom. All species are simple to grow.

Growing Conditions: Plant in well-drained, lean-to-average soil. Deadhead 'Sunset Boulevard' to prevent self-sowing and encourage rebloom. Cut back all species by about one-third after bloom to keep plants compact and tidy. Pull out unwanted plants as needed to keep them in bounds.

Propagation: Divide all but *O. versicolor* in early spring.

▶ **Bloom Time** Late spring to late summer, depending on species

▶ **Planting Requirements** Full sun

▶ **Zones** 5 to 8; *O. fruticosa*, 4 to 8

Origanum oh-RIG-uh-num • oregano

Traditional oregano (*Origanum vulgare*) and its cultivars are still an excellent choice to cover ground in the perennial garden, especially in a dry situation. But its cousins—all of which belong to the Lamiaceae family—offer showier flowers that are just as eye-catching as other perennials that don't have their roots in the pizza parlor.

Origanum laevigatum (flowering oregano) This species has given rise to a whole new appetite for oregano, thanks to the knockout flowers of its cultivars. 'Herrenhausen' forms neat mounds of red-stemmed foliage, about 1 foot (30 cm) high and 2 to 3 feet (60 to 90 cm) wide, topped in late summer with crowded clusters of tiny reddish purple flowers. 'Hopley's Purple' has thin-stemmed sprays of purplish flowers, borne from summer into fall, and reaches about 2 feet (60 cm) tall; cut it back when it gets lanky. 'Pilgrim' grows to 18 inches (45 cm) in bloom.

O. vulgare (common oregano) This mat-forming species is the familiar herb used in many Italian dishes. In the perennial garden it makes a good ground cover along a sun-baked walkway or patio. The clusters of tiny, rosy pink-purple flowers are a boon to butterflies. Fancy-leaved cultivars up the ante, adding a hem of golden yellow or bronze foliage in front of taller perennials. Try 'Aureum', a 4- to 6-inch (10- to 15-cm)-tall ground cover with beautiful golden leaves; 'Variegata', with leaves marked by golden green; or 'Dark Leaf', which has dark bronze new foliage that often pales in summer sun.

O. hybrids (hybrid flowering oregano) Watch for new hybrids of ornamental oregano, now that the plants have been embraced by gardeners. 'Kent Beauty' is a beauty, forming a mound of foliage that grows about 8 inches (20 cm) high and 12 inches (30 cm) wide. Its hopslike bracts, a beautiful rosy pink, are much larger than those of ordinary oreganos; each pendant cluster reaches 2 to 3 inches (5 to 7.5 cm) long. They begin as purple but warm to rosy pink as they dry, holding their warm color for months and begging to be snipped for dried bouquets. 'Santa

Origanum vulgare

Cruz' also has dangling clusters of flowers within bracts; it's a soft dusty rose and is much bigger, forming a mound 1½ to 2 feet (45 to 60 cm) tall and 3 feet (90 cm) wide.

THE BASICS

Common oregano is an aggressive spreader, but other types expand with more decorum. Allow some room around the plants to avoid crowding neighbors. Plant ornamental flowering types atop or along a masonry wall or in a window box, where they won't falter if you forget to water them.

Growing Conditions: Plant in lean-to-average, well-drained soil. Pull up stray rooting stems of any oregano to keep it within its determined bounds. Shear common oregano after flowering. Cut back all species to ground level in late winter.

Propagation: Cuttings root like lightning. Or divide in early spring.

▶ **Bloom Time** Summer; *O. hybrids*, summer to fall
▶ **Planting Requirements** Full sun
▶ **Zones** *O. vulgare*, 3 to 9; *O. laevigatum* and *O. hybrids*, 4–6 to 9

Perfect Partners

Heat-loving oreganos need partners that flourish in similar conditions. The long-lasting flower spikes and red-tinged stems of euphorbias (*Euphorbia characias* and other spp.) are a good foil for *O. vulgare* 'Dark Leaf' or any of the *O. laevigatum* cultivars. Use penstemons to add contrasting height and supportive color behind oreganos. Experiment with sedums of any sort and size. The sprawling, chartreuse and red 'Angelina' sedum looks great with 'Kent Beauty' and other oregano hybrids; tall 'Autumn Joy' sedum is perfect with the pink bracts of 'Santa Cruz'. Gray-leaved sedums, such as *S. spathulifolium* 'Cape Blanco', are a dramatic partner to 'Dark Leaf' oregano. With golden oregano (*O. vulgare* 'Aureum'), try a reddish or purplish sedum.

O

Osmunda *oz-MUN-duh* • cinnamon fern, interrupted fern, royal fern

Osmunda regalis

These big, handsome ferns add stature to shady places in your garden and also flourish in sunny spots, as long as the soil is moist. Among the most vigorous members of the Osmunaceae family, they form regal clumps of upright fronds. Established plants easily reach 3 to 5 feet (90 to 150 cm) tall and 3 feet (90 cm) wide. They're beautiful planted singly or in masses, as a backdrop or companion for other foliage and flowering shade plants, or as a softening touch along walls or fences. Water features are also a natural companion for these lovers of moist soil. All species form dense mats of wiry roots, which often rise above the soil in long-established colonies.

Osmunda cinnamomea (cinnamon fern) This statuesque beauty, a native of the eastern United States, has been popular in gardens since great-grandma's day. Its clump of lacy fronds forms a 3- to 5-foot (90- to 150-cm)-tall vase shape, arching slightly outward. Narrow plumes of showy, cinnamon-colored spore-bearing fronds emerge in spring for a dramatic addition to the display. The cinnamon sprays die back in summer, yielding the stage to the leafy green fronds, which are covered with furry, cinnamon-colored fibers at the bottoms of their stems. In fall the foliage turns yellow, then bronze, before dying back for winter. Hardy in Zones 3 to 10.

O. claytoniania (interrupted fern) Ferns reproduce by spores, which are produced on "fertile" fronds; the spores are those small, often rusty tan bumps that you'll usually spot on the backside of fern fronds. Non-spore-bearing fronds, or sterile fronds, are plain green and lack the bumpy spore cases. Like other ferns, this 3- to 4-foot (90- to 120-cm)-tall American native fern produces both fertile and sterile fronds. The "interruption" of this unusual fern is caused by its unique arrangement of spore-bearing leaflets on the fertile fronds. The dark brown spore-bearing leaflets—or *pinnae* in fern lingo—are packed closely on a small section of the stem, interrupting the flow of sterile green pinnae on the same frond. In midsummer the fertile pinnae fall off, leaving a bare section on the frond. Hardy in Zones 3 to 8.

O. regalis (royal fern) This species looks nothing like its cousins. Its open, lacy fronds are not arranged with leaflets two-by-two up the stem; instead, the main stem of each frond has pairs of side stems lined with opposite pairs of pinnae. From a distance it's a graceful effect, especially when this beautiful, slightly blue-green fern reaches its potential height of 4 to 6 feet (120 to 180 cm) tall and 3 to 5 feet (90 to 150 cm) wide. In most gardens royal fern remains at a smaller size unless you plant it in a bog garden, where it can get the moisture it needs to achieve its top height. Hardy in Zones 3 to 10.

THE BASICS

Osmunda ferns are rewarding to grow, but like hostas, they require patience. They will produce fronds when newly planted, but they take a few years to settle in and reach substantial size. They do best in cooler regions, where they shrug off brutal winters without a shiver. In areas warmer than Zone 7 or in less moisture-retentive soils, they may be smaller in size, but they are still worth a place in the shade garden.

Growing Conditions: Dig in an abundant amount of humus or composted leaf litter to increase the moisture-holding ability of the soil before planting. Choose a permanent location, since the mass of tangled roots can be difficult to lift once it's settled in. Plant in moist-to-wet, acid soil. *O. regalis* and *O. cinnamomea* also grow in wet soil and in shallow water. Water generously and regularly; if the soil dries out, the ferns may go dormant. Fronds die back and collapse in winter; you can let them remain in place as a natural mulch or remove them for a tidy look.

Propagation: Use a sharp shovel to slice through the tough, matted roots to take a division in early spring.

▶ **Bloom Time** Fertile fronds emerge in spring
▶ **Planting Requirements** Shade to sun (with consistently moist soil)
▶ **Zones** Hardiness varies, depending on species

Paeonia *pay-OH-nee-uh* • peony

For pure ruffled romance it's hard to beat a peony. These members of the Paeoniaceae family are long-lived and can brighten a garden for a hundred years or more. There are herbaceous kinds that die back to the ground in fall, and tree peonies—these are shrubby plants, not trees—with woody stems that persist in winter. All peonies have big, blowsy blooms with a fat cushion of yellow stamens in the center. There are simple, single-petaled flowers or heavy-headed double blossoms.

Experts disagree on the botanical classification of peonies. Keep it simple and follow the American Peony Society's guidelines to choose your plants by flower type and bloom season. Early bloomers begin in late spring, usually early May (late March or April in the South); midseason types begin about two weeks later; late bloomers follow up two to three weeks afterward. Flower types include the self-explanatory single; Japanese, which lack the yellow pollen in the center, or have a tuft of tiny curled petals in the center ("anemone-flowered"); semidouble, which retain some yellow stamens but add more petals; and double, a thick, fluffy mass of petals.

Paeonia lactiflora (Chinese peony) Single white or pink flowers are borne on this late-blooming herbaceous species, which reaches 1½ to 3 feet (45 to 90 cm) tall and 2 to 3 feet (60 to 90 cm) wide. 'Bowl of Beauty' has fragrant rose petals.

P. suffruticosa (tree peony) This upright, deciduous shrub has given birth to many cultivars. It reaches 5 to 6 feet (150 to 180 cm) tall and wide. It has huge flowers, whose petals are often crinkled like crepe paper. Hardy in Zones 5 to 8.

P. tenuifolia (fernleaf peony) This plant veers away from other species by having delicate, feathery foliage and blooming in spring. It forms a mound 1 to 1½ feet (30 to 45 cm) tall and wide, topped with single, deep red flowers. Hardy in Zones 3 to 8.

P. **hybrids** (herbaceous types) Most cultivars of herbaceous peonies are hybrids; the species forms are difficult to find. You'll discover many possibilities, in every color of the peony rainbow. Most reach 2½ to 3 feet (75 to 90 cm) high and wide, with flowers 4 inches (10 cm) across. Read the label to check the details of plant and flower size before you buy. Many have sweet fragrance that adds to their charms. Hardy in Zones 3 to 8.

P. 'Krinkled White', a single white herbaceous hybrid, is an early bloomer with great heat tolerance for southern gardens. It grows to 2 feet (60 cm) tall. 'Scarlet O'Hara' is a single red belle that also flourishes in southern heat. 'Félix Crousse' has large, double carmine flowers. 'Coral Charm' has flowers in an unusual light coral-apricot. Hardy in Zones 4 to 8.

THE BASICS

Peonies grow best in areas with cold winters. While many peonies have thrived for years with no problems, others are afflicted by a host of diseases and other frustrating problems, such as failure to bloom.

Growing Conditions: Choose a permanent location; peonies usually

Paeonia lactiflora 'Bowl of Beauty'

don't like having their roots disturbed. Select a site that isn't exposed to strong winds. Plant in well-drained, fertile soil. Place the "eyes" on the fleshy roots 1 to 2 inches (2.5 to 5 cm) below the surface. Rain can cause the top-heavy flowering stems of herbaceous types to keel over, so staking is a must. Surround the plant with hoops to keep them more upright; they'll still lean, but they'll stay clean. Cut back herbaceous peonies to the ground in fall. Verticillium wilt, botrytis blight, tip blight, leaf blotch, and other diseases may occur; diagnose and treat appropriately. Thrips and Japanese beetles can cause problems, too; use control methods as needed.

Propagation: Divide herbaceous peonies in early fall, lifting the entire root clump and slicing it into sections, each containing several "eyes." Replant as described above. Take tree peony cuttings in summer.

▷ **Bloom Time** Summer
▷ **Planting Requirements** Sun to part shade
▷ **Zones** Hardiness varies, depending on species

Peonies of Stupendous Size

Tree peonies (*Paeonia suffruticosa* and hybrids) are the royalty of the peony genus. Long revered in China and other parts of the East, these vigorous, hardy shrubs boast blossoms of unbelievable size—almost a foot across in some cultivars and at least saucer size in the "smaller" types. Any tree peony will knock your socks off when those fat buds unfold into multipetaled blooms, so choose your favorite at the nursery. Here's a sample of what you might find.

◀ *P.* **'Black Pirate'**
Arthur P. Saunders, a pioneer in American peony breeding in the early 1900s, raised more than 17,000 seedlings—and deemed only 300 of them worth naming. 'Black Pirate' was one of them, and it has remained a favorite. The deep maroon blossoms are semidouble, with a black blotch at the base. This fast-growing cultivar grows 4 to 5 feet (1.2 to 1.5 m) tall. It makes an ideal focal point paired with yellow-flowered perennials, such as yarrow (*Achillea* spp.).

▲ *P. suffruticosa* **'Joseph Rock'**
(Paeonia rockii)
A treasure for peony collectors, this plant is argued over by experts as far as its botanical classification. No argument from gardeners, though, many of whom are besotted when they lay eyes on those enormous white flowers—which can reach 1 foot (30 cm) across! This tree peony was named for Joseph Rock, an 18th-century American plant hunter who found it in China and introduced it to the West. The single or semidouble flowers are white with a rosy blush, marked with purple-red spots at the base; some plants have pinkish purple flowers. The fast-growing shrubby plant can reach as much as 7 feet (2.1 m) tall.

▶ *P. suffruticosa*
'Godaishu'
This tree peony has elegant, snow white flowers with ragged-edged petals that give it a slightly shaggy look. The humungous blossoms that light up the 4- to 5-foot (1.2- to 1.5-m)-tall plant can reach 10 inches (25 cm) across.

▼ *P. suffruticosa* 'Rimpo'

This cultivar, also known as 'Bird of Imagination', looks like no avian species on earth. Its deep purple blossoms are fully double, crammed full of petals with a tuft of bright yellow stamens at the center. Each fantastic flower can be as much as 10 inches (25 cm) across—a single blossom is all you need for a bouquet.

▲ *P.* 'High Noon'

One of the most popular tree peonies, this rugged hybrid has showy, clear yellow flowers that glow like the sun across the garden. Peek inside one of those bountiful blossoms to see the red markings at the center. The plant grows to about 5 feet (1.5 m) tall, and occasionally will surprise you with a flower or two later in summer.

▶ *P. suffruticosa* 'Hana-Kisoi'

Huge, silky flowers of clear cherry blossom pink glow against the fresh foliage of this popular tree peony cultivar, whose name means "Champion of Flowers." The blossoms are semidouble, with slightly curled petals. This vigorous cultivar quickly grows to 4 to 5 feet (1.2 to 1.5 m) tall.

Panicum *PAN-ih-kum* • switchgrass

Panicum virgatum 'Häense Herms'

From out of the prairie, switchgrass has easily made the transition to the garden. *Panicum virgatum* is the most popular species of this member of the Poaceae family, and it has fathered a host of cultivars. Switchgrass grows to 3 to 4 feet (90 to 120 cm) tall, but its fine texture and narrowly upright form keep it from overwhelming nearby plants. In late summer to early fall, branching stems decked with tiny flowers burgeon forth in an airy mass, transforming the grassy clump of foliage into a heavenly cloud. It's one of the best-behaved ornamental grasses. The plant stays in a controlled clump, so you can use it among other perennials without worrying about neighboring plants being smothered or shouldered aside. In fall switchgrass adds another element to its repertoire—the foliage mellows to golden, reddish, or bright yellow, depending on the cultivar.

Panicum virgatum (switchgrass) Switchgrass was one of the main components of the once vast Midwest prairie. You may also find it growing wild in fields and along roadsides in just about every state except for Washington, Oregon, and California. Wild plants are variable in form and size; they can be as short as 2 feet (60 cm) or as tall as 5 feet (150 cm). Switchgrass blooms in late summer to fall and turns golden tan in late fall. The species type is a valuable plant for prairie or meadow gardens.

Today's garden cultivars are several steps removed from their wild parent: Their growth habit is more controlled, and their foliage colors add outstanding variety. Most reach 3 to 4 feet (90 to 120 cm) tall. Perhaps the most popular is 'Heavy Metal', an upright grower that boasts beautiful blue-gray foliage that turns golden in fall. Another blue-tinged choice is 'Prairie Sky'; its leaf blades are wider than those of 'Heavy Metal'. Giant blue switchgrass, which is the cultivar 'Cloud Nine', also has a strong gray-blue color, but it's much taller, soaring to 6 or 7 feet (1.8 to 2.1 m). Red switchgrass, or 'Rotstrahlbusch', has green leaves tinged with varying amounts of red. 'Shenandoah' also has a touch of red on the tips of its leaves; it has pinkish flowers. 'Hänse Herms' forms a fountain of green leaves that take on reddish-to-purple tints in fall. The most tightly vertical cultivar is

'Strictum', which adds a bright yellow gleam to the garden when it takes on its fall foliage color.

THE BASICS

Switchgrass is easy to grow. Just give it an annual cutting back and a helping hand to prevent it from flopping. Plant as single specimens, as a group of three, or as a mass planting.

Growing Conditions: Plant in lean-to-average soil; rich soil will encourage lusher growth that may need support to stay erect. Established clumps are drought tolerant. 'Cloud Nine' can get weak-kneed, especially in moist soil or windy sites; surround it with supportive hoops to help it stay upright. Let the plants stand to provide food and shelter for birds but cut back to ground level when the foliage begins to shatter in late winter.

Propagation: Division can be difficult. Use a sharp shovel to slice off a section in early spring.

▶ **Bloom Time** Late summer to fall
▶ **Planting Requirements** Sun
▶ **Zones** 3 to 9

Perfect Partners

The blue-gray switchgrass cultivars add a color other than green to the scene. Try 'Cloud Nine' or 'Heavy Metal' with phlox (*Phlox paniculata*) in coral or crimson shades, such as 'Starfire' or 'Orange Perfection'; they also provide a calm partner for sprightly bicolored phlox, such as 'Bright Eyes' or 'Peppermint Twist'. Mulleins (*Verbascum* spp.) or yarrows (*Achillea* spp.) make a pretty partner for switchgrasses, too. Plant imposing 'Cloud Nine' with hollyhocks (*Alcea* spp.) of any color. Plan ahead for fall, when switchgrass's clouds of flowers and ripening foliage will set off late-blooming neighbors, such as asters, sunflowers (*Helianthus* spp.), and black-eyed Susans (*Rudbeckia* spp.).

Papaver *pap-AY-ver* • poppy

Poppy flowers open from fat, hairy buds that split open to allow the tightly crinkled petals to expand into silken cups; intriguing seedpods follow. This member of the Papaveraceae family includes one of the all-time favorite perennials, the stunning Oriental poppy (*Papaver orientale*). Perennial poppies form basal clumps of bristly-haired foliage from which tall, bare stems topped by a single flower bud emerge. Their blooming season is short, but the show is spectacular.

Papaver alpinum (alpine poppy) Plants from mountain regions are often smaller and can stand up to extremes of wind and weather, and the alpine poppy is no exception. This short-lived species forms a 4-inch (10-cm)-wide tuft of gray-green leaves, topped with wiry stems that bear flowers in clear yellow, orange, red, or white. It reaches 6 inches (15 cm) tall when it blooms in summer. Hardy in Zones 5 to 8.

P. nudicaule (*P. croceum*, Iceland poppy) Iceland poppies make a colorful splash in the early summer garden, with their 3-inch (7.5-cm) crepe-paper blooms in strong, clear colors. Whether you plant a mix en masse or dot single colors here and there, you'll find these single-petaled yellow, orange, red, salmon, and pink flowers will lift your spirits. Their hairy, gray-green leaves form a casual mound 6 inches (15 cm) across, while the flowers rise on bare stems to 1 foot (30 cm). Snip off finished flowering stems for continued bloom. The plants are often short-lived, but are easy to grow from seed. These poppies are hardy in Zones 2 to 8.

Many cultivars are available. They're grown from seed, so you'll find they include a mix of colors. 'Sparkling Bubbles' reaches 15 inches (38 cm); 'Champagne Bubbles' includes many pastels plus some brights on 18-inch (45-cm) stems. Hardy in Zones 2 to 8.

P. orientale (Oriental poppy) This superb plant has big, bold flowers. The species has vivid red-orange flowers. Each bloom is 4 to 6 inches (10 to 15 cm) across, and many have a contrasting purplish black blotch at the base of the petals. The plant forms a clump of large, bristly leaves, each about 12 inches (30 cm) long. The stout flowering stems, also bristly, stretch to 2 to 3 feet (60 to 90 cm) tall,

Papaver orientale

each one topped by a single stunning flower. Hardy in Zones 2 to 7.

Dozens of cultivars are available. 'Bonfire', 'Brilliant', and giant-sized 4-foot (120-cm) 'Goliath' are a few of the reds. 'Queen Alexander' is salmon with a black center. 'Lighthouse' is light pink with a wide, dark blotch. All reach 2 to 3 feet (60 to 90 cm) wide.

THE BASICS

Oriental poppies have an unusual growth habit—the foliage dies back after flowering, usually by midsummer, leaving a hole in the garden. Disguise the hole by planting other summer-blooming perennials nearby, but don't crowd the poppy's place; the foliage reemerges in late summer to fall.

Growing Conditions: Plant in well-drained soil of average-to-rich fertility. To maintain vigor, lift the entire clump in early fall, when new leaves emerge, and slice into sections.

Propagation: Snip off pencil-thick roots for cuttings in early fall.

▸ **Bloom Time** Early summer
▸ **Planting Requirements** Full sun
▸ **Zones** Hardiness varies, depending on species

Perfect Partners

Look to early summer bloomers for poppy partners, such as indefatigable blue catmint (*Nepeta* × *faassennii*), whose continuing show will help disguise the hole left when the poppy dies back after flowering. Asiatic lilies (*Lilium* spp.) can hold their own in the bold department: Choose colors that contrast with your poppies for the most pleasing effect. Red or orange Asiatic lilies with white poppies, and vice versa, is a foolproof combo. Snowy Shasta daisies (*Leucanthemum* × *superbum*) are another fail-safe choice; add blue veronicas (*Veronica* spp.) to complete the garden scene. Creeping or mounding campanulas (*Campanula* spp.) are beautiful with pink or salmon poppies.

Treasures of the Orient

Spectacular poppies are in bloom for only about two weeks, but what a centerpiece they make for any garden! A single plant is enough to garner attention all by itself; a group of three is simply magnificent. Mix and match colors, or plant a group of the same kind. The original red-orange is hard to beat, but fabulous cultivars, such as those shown here, add white, salmon, pink, and even purple to the possibilities.

◀ *P. orientale* **'Watermelon'**
Luscious is the only word to describe this juicy watermelon pink Oriental poppy. The ruffled flowers, with a dramatic black heart, top a compact plant that reaches 2 feet (60 cm) tall in bloom. Why not plant a group of three to create a mouthwatering "watermelon patch" in your early summer garden bed or border?

▲ *P. orientale* **'Allegro'**
Giant flowers, 5 to 6 inches (12.5 to 15 cm) across, on a downsized plant are the attraction of 'Allegro', a fabulous red-orange cultivar that will steal the show in bloom. Plant this poppy in the front of your perennial bed, where it will draw the eye like a magnet from hundreds of feet away. The smaller-than-usual plants grow to only about 20 inches (50 cm) tall, so they visually fade into the background once the spectacular flowers are finished.

▶ *P. orientale* **'Royal Wedding'**
Get ready to curtsey to this outstanding cultivar, with its immense bowl-shaped blossoms that can reach 5 to 8 inches (12.5 to 20 cm) —yes, 8 inches (20 cm)!— across. The snow-white cup of petals is accented inside with five small black blotches, as if someone dipped a fingertip in ink, then dabbed the flower. 'Royal Wedding' is a tall cultivar, checking in at 3 to 3½ feet (90 to 105 cm) in bloom.

218

◄ *P. orientale* 'Patty's Plum'

Add unusual color to your garden with this purple-pink cultivar, a beauty that was supposedly discovered sprouting in a compost pile. A taller cultivar, this plant reaches about 2½ feet (75 cm) in bloom. Black markings decorate the petals near their base. Highlight the dusky grape hue of 'Patty's Plum' with pristine white companions, such as white bearded or Japanese iris (*Iris* cvs.), 'White Clips' campanula (*Campanula carpatica* 'White Clips'), and a collar of snow-in-summer (*Cerastium tomentosum*).

▼ *P. orientale* 'Picotee'

If your perennial garden leans toward warm, spicy colors, 'Picotee' will fit right in. The huge, double, creamy white flowers are edged with delicious apricot-peach tones. In bloom, this poppy reaches 2 to 2½ feet (60 to 75 cm) tall. Pair it with yarrow cultivars (*Achillea* hybrids) in equally warm tones, such as 'Paprika' or 'Terracotta', or contrast its spicy shade with blue bearded irises (*Iris* hybrids).

► *P. orientale* 'Helen Elizabeth'

Pure romance in the June garden, 'Helen Elizabeth' is a clear salmon-pink, with no dark blotch to distract the eye from her pretty frilled petals. This cultivar is an especially generous bloomer, so you'll get a gratifying display with just a single 2½-foot (75-cm)-tall clump. Highlight the lovely color by planting lavender-blue campanulas (*Campanula persicifolia* and other spp.) and catmints (*Nepeta* × *faasenii* 'Walker's Low' or 'Six Hills Giant') as partners.

Penstemon PEN-ste-mon • penstemon, beardtongue

Penstemon digitalis

Penstemon spires add color to your garden—and attract hummingbirds. Many species of this Scrophulariaceae family member are native wildflowers in the West and Southwest, and they transition easily into garden plants in those regions. However, these western species fail to flourish in the South, Midwest, and East. Unfortunately, many species (and their cultivars) are naturally adapted to dry, low-humidity summers, such as that of the western United States. They decline and rot when there's abundant summer moisture in the soil or in the air. If muggy summers are de rigueur for your region, only plant penstemons that thrive in your conditions.

Penstemon barbatus (common beardtongue, beardlip penstemon) The tubular blossoms of this western native have yellow beards on the bottom lip, but you'll be distracted by the showy pink-to-carmine flowers. This tall species raises spires to 6 feet (180 cm) tall from a basal clump of foliage 12 to 18 inches (30 to 45 cm) across. 'Elfin Pink' is 12 inches (30 cm) tall, with clear pink blooms. Hardy in Zones 4 to 9; not for humid regions.

P. digitalis (foxglove penstemon, showy beardtongue) This species is reason to celebrate if you have humid conditions. Native from Maine to South Dakota and down to the Gulf of Mexico, it forms dense clumps with 2- to 4-foot (60- to 120-cm) spikes of 1-inch (2.5-cm) white flowers in early summer. The species is related to turtlehead *(Chelone glabra)*, a host plant for the caterpillars of the Baltimore checkerspot butterfly; the caterpillars may also nibble on this penstemon. Hardy in Zones 3 to 9. 'Husker Red' is more familiar than the species; it has red-tinged leaves that contrast strongly with the white blossoms. 'Ruby Tuesday' has even darker red foliage and white flowers with a bluish blush. Smooth beardtongue or Eastern beardtongue *(P. laevigatus)* is similar to *P. digitalis*. Both species may show a purplish flush at the base of the flowers.

P. eatonii (firecracker penstemon) Tops for attracting hummingbirds, this species throws up flares of 1-inch (2.5-cm) scarlet flowers to catch their eye. Plants of this Southwest and California native vary in height, from 1 to 3 feet (30 to 90 cm). Hardy in Zones 4 to 9; not for humid regions.

P. fruticosus (shrubby penstemon) A familiar species to those who like to hike in western mountains, this low grower carpets gravelly slopes with a spreading mat of evergreen foliage, topped in summer with short spikes of prolific purplish blue flowers. It is hardy in Zones 4 to 9; not for humid regions. Cardwell's penstemon *(P. cardwellii)* is similar but hardy in only Zones 6 to 9; its cultivar 'Roseus' has rosy pink blooms.

P. heterophyllus (foothill penstemon) Incredible true blue flowers are the trademark of this western native. Cultivars include 'Blue of Zurich', 20 inches (50 cm) tall and wide, and 'True Blue', about 16 inches (40 cm) tall and wide. Hardy in Zones 7 to 10; not for humid regions.

P. hirsutus (hairy beardtongue) This native of the eastern United States has 1- to 3-foot (30- to 90-cm) stems of white-to-lavender flowers. It blooms in midsummer. In fertile, moist soil it grows taller than in average, less watered sites. Hardy in Zones 4 to 8.

P. pinifolius *Pinifolius* refers to the needlelike leaves of this southwestern species, which is 16 inches (40 cm) tall in bloom and about 10 inches (25 cm) wide. The small, tubular blossoms are bright red. 'Mersea Yellow' has soft, sulfur yellow flowers. Hardy in Zones 4 to 10; not for humid regions.

P. smallii (Small's beardtongue) A species for gardeners in humid areas, this 1- to 2-foot (30- to 60-cm) native hails from the mountains of Tennessee, the Carolinas, and Georgia, where it grows in light shade. In the garden it thrives in sun or part shade. The purple-veined leaves and stems give rise to purple flowers, which may vary from mauve-pink to bright magenta. It's short-lived but self-sows freely. Hardy in Zones 5 to 9.

THE BASICS

Plant both dry-summer and humid-summer penstemons in the places that supply the same conditions they prefer in the wild. In the western part of the country, that means dry, sunny, super-fast-draining sites; in the East, Midwest, or South, typical moist garden conditions will suit your plants just fine.

Growing Conditions: West (also including Southwest and Northwest): Plant in lean-to-average, fast-draining soil; most will also thrive in rocky ground, which contributes to good drainage. East, Midwest, or South: Plant *P. digitalis* in moist, average-to-rich soil; it also thrives in clay. Plant *P. smallii* in well-drained, even sandy soil. Seed heads can be decorative and contribute to self-sown progeny, but if you prefer, in all regions cut back flowering stems when finished. Many species are evergreen; clip tattered or dead foliage as necessary to tidy the plant.

Propagation: Seed. Also try cuttings in early summer; divide humid-region species in early spring.

▶ **Bloom Time** Spring, summer
▶ **Planting Requirements** Sun
▶ **Zones** Hardiness varies, depending on species

Perovskia *per-ROF-skee-uh* • Russian sage

A relative newcomer to the gardening scene, Russian sage was an instant hit when it became available in the late 1980s to early 1990s. This 4-foot (120-cm)-tall subshrub is from the Lamiaceae family, which is the same family that mint belongs to. It is a plant of substantial size, but it's not a heavy-handed dominating type.

Plant Partners

Contrast the delicacy of Russian sage with large, simple blooms, such as those of daylilies (*Hemerocallis* spp.) of any color, or with Trumpet and Aurelian or Oriental lilies (*Lilium* spp.). The huge blossoms of hibiscus are also a great backup for that fine-textured spill of blue. Coneflowers of any color (*Echinacea* spp. and *Rudbeckia* spp.) are rugged companions, too. In a dry garden try 'Autumn Joy' and other taller sedums, coral-pink 'Desert Sunrise' or other drought-tolerant agastaches, and 'Red Rocks', 'Garnet', or other bright penstemons. In early fall partner with goldenrods (*Solidago* spp.) and sneezeweed (*Helenium* spp.).

Instead, it steals the scene with softness: light and airy form, small silvery leaves and ghostly stems, and a fantastic fountain of gentle blue flowers. Butterflies, particularly monarchs, find it irresistible.

Perovskia atriplicifolia (Russian sage) Russian sage is not a sage at all (those plants belong to the *Salvia* genus), but it does have Russian roots. The enormous land mass known as the former Soviet Union has given the world many popular garden plants, such as Siberian squill (*Scilla siberica*), Siberian iris (*Iris sibirica*), bergenia (*Bergenia crassifolia*), and baby's breath (*Gypsophila paniculata*), among hundreds of others. Russian sage makes a stunning specimen and is glorious in groups of three. Several cultivars are now available, including 'Blue Spire', with darker blue flowers than the species; 'Filigran', which has finely cut foliage and remains more upright than the species; 'Little Spire', a compact, 2-foot (60-cm)-tall plant; and 'Longin', with simpler leaves and a narrower, upright habit, growing 3 to 4 feet (90 to 120 cm) tall but only 1½ to 2 feet (45 to 60 cm) wide.

Perovskia atriplicifolia

THE BASICS

Out of bloom it's a valuable foliage plant. In bloom, well, see for yourself. It adapts easily to a range of climates and conditions, including dry sites.

Growing Conditions: Plant in well-drained, lean-to-fertile soil. Cut back to just above the lowest bud on the stems in early spring, before new growth begins.

Propagation: Cuttings.

▶ **Bloom Time** Midsummer through early fall
▶ **Planting Requirements** Full sun
▶ **Zones** 3 to 8; 'Longin', 4 to 9

P

Penstemons for Long Blooms

Penstemon collectors take pride in growing the species forms, which offer a variety of habit, form, and superb color. But for a long bloom season you can't beat the hybrids, which provide plentiful flowers for months, from early summer to fall. They're also less demanding than species types, easily adjusting to life in average garden conditions. Pick your favorite color from the selection on these pages, and keep your eyes open for exciting new hybrids that enter the scene.

◀ *P.* **'Crushed Grapes'**

A penstemon on the small side, this purplish flowered cultivar forms a mound only 12 inches (30 cm) tall. It's best for areas with hot, dry, nonhumid summers because it's more finicky than other cultivars. 'Crushed Grapes' requires excellent drainage. Avoid fertilizer and additional watering; this pretty little plant prefers life on the lean and dry side. Hardy in Zones 6 to 9.

▲ *P.* **'Garnet'**

This hybrid will amaze you by rapidly achieving the size of a small shrub, at least 2½ feet (75 cm) tall and wide—and it's evergreen in mild winter areas. Hummingbirds make it a favorite destination, lingering at the spectacular pink-red flowers. It blooms from early summer well into fall, even without deadheading. Don't be afraid to cut back to keep the plant compact or in bounds—it'll quickly regrow, better than ever. Hardy in Zones 7 to 9.

▶ *P.* **'Apple Blossom'**

This evergreen hybrid forms a 1- to 2-foot (30- to 60-cm)-wide multistemmed clump about 1 to 1½ feet (30 to 45 cm) tall. In early summer the unprepossessing plant is transformed by an explosion of showy pink flower spikes that stretch more than 1 foot (30 cm) above the foliage. Their bright, warm color combines beautifully with other perennials in nearly any hue. For an elegant combination try partners with silver-gray foliage or white flowers. Hardy in Zones 6 to 9.

▲ *P.* 'Firebird'

Many penstemon hybrids are vigorous plants, but this one may be the most robust and fastest growing of all. A small plant can easily reach 3 to 4 feet (90 to 120 cm) tall and wide in a single season, producing an unbelievable show of carmine red flowers. The blooms just keep on coming, even after a light frost. Cut back to near ground level in spring to renew vigor and keep the plant dense. Hardy in Zones 7 to 9.

▶ *P.* 'Sour Grapes'

This cultivar boasts unusual color—exactly like that of a glass of fresh grape juice. It blooms abundantly from early summer into fall, attracting bees and hummingbirds. 'Sour Grapes' forms an evergreen clump about 2 feet (60 cm) tall and wide. Cut back to about 1 foot (30 cm) in early spring to keep the plant bushy and compact. Hardy in Zones 7 to 9.

▲ *P.* 'Catherine de la Mare'

Breathtaking as a bluebird, this gorgeous hybrid looks clear blue from a distance but holds subtle tints of pink on its buds when you take a closer look. Use the lovely "Catherine of the Sea" to beautify a difficult hot, dry strip along a sidewalk.

Phlox *flox · phlox*

These hearty, hardy plants bloom year after year. Tall, sweet-smelling phlox (*Phlox paniculata*) persists for decades. Creeping phlox (*P. subulata*) offers ground-covering mats covered in spring blossoms. In between the two you'll find several other species, all from the Polemoniaceae family, that are worth investigating. All have clusters of small, simple flowers in white, pink, or blue-purple, with a contrasting center "eye."

Phlox carolina (Carolina phlox) This species and its cultivars are well suited for the steamy summers of the Southeast and South. It's a bright, deep pink and an upright grower to 4 feet (120 cm) tall. The shorter pink 'Bill Baker' reaches 18 inches (45 cm). Hardy in Zones 4 to 8.

P. divaricata (wild sweet William) This ground-cover species forms mats of semievergreen leaves topped with slender-stemmed clusters of bluish blossoms in spring. In bloom it reaches 12 to 14 inches (30 to 35 cm). Flowers are in shades of blue-lavender. 'Fuller's White' has snowy flowers. Hardy in Zones 4 to 8.

P. maculata (meadow phlox) This summer-blooming, 3-foot (90-cm)-tall species is more resistant to powdery mildew than *P. paniculata*. The bright pinkish purple flowers are fragrant and attract butterflies. Unlike *P. paniculata,* this species flowers well in light or part shade. 'Rosalinde' is deep pink; 'Miss Lingard' has blossoms as white as a June bride's gown. 'Flower Power' is an ethereal pearly pink. Zones 4 to 8.

P. paniculata (garden phlox, tall garden phlox) Experts disagree on the classification of tall phlox, with some assigning cultivars to this species and others arguing for *P. maculata* or a combination of the two. The plants bloom in the summer for many weeks. Many cultivars self-sow; but these often revert to the cultivar's pinkish purple parent. Most cultivars grow 3 to 4 feet (90 to 120 cm) tall and 2 to 3 feet (60 to 90 cm) wide. Mildew-resistant 'David' has huge heads with pure white blossoms; 'David's Lavender' shares the disease-resistant trait. 'Orange Perfection' is an unusual rich salmon shade. Spectacular 'Starfire' has crimson flowers. 'Blue Paradise' is close to true blue, with the flowers taking on a purplish cast as they age. Mildew-resistant 'Eva Cullum' is only 2½ feet (75 cm) tall but prolific, with rosy pink flowers dotted by purple eyes. 'Peppermint Twist' has deep pink flowers pinwheeled with white stripes. Hardy in Zones 4 to 8.

P. subulata (creeping phlox, moss phlox) This species and its cultivars hug the ground along the edges or atop walls. It forms a dense mat of needlelike leaves hidden by a solid mass of white, pink to crimson, or lavender blossoms in late spring. Each plant spreads to 20 inches (50 cm). 'Emerald Blue' is pale blue-lilac; 'G. F. Wilson' is lavender-blue. 'Red Wings' is crimson; 'White Delight', snow white. Hardy in Zones 3 to 8.

THE BASICS

You can ignore phlox once they're established, and they'll still bloom for decades. Use taller types to fill out a new garden; they make agreeable partners for almost all other perennials.

Phlox paniculata 'Starfire'

Growing Conditions: Plant in moist soil of average-to-rich fertility. An annual application of fertilizer will result in lusher plants. *P. subulata* is drought tolerant; other species appreciate regular water and a layer of mulch to conserve soil moisture. Pinch out the tips of each stem of tall varieties when 12 to 18 inches (30 to 45 cm) tall to encourage side branches with additional flowers; cut back by half when flowers fade for another round of bloom. Powdery mildew is the most common affliction; rust, stem canker, and leaf spots may also occur. Avoid crowding tall phlox so that air can circulate and help ward off mildew. Cut back tall varieties to the ground in fall or early spring.

Propagation: Divide in early spring. Transplant self-sown seedlings in spring. Take nonflowering cuttings of *P. divaricata* and *P. subulata* in early spring.

▶ **Bloom Time** *P. divaricata*, *P. subulata*, late spring; taller types, summer

▶ **Planting Requirements** Most taller types and *P. subulata*, full sun; *P. divaricata*, shade to sun

▶ **Zones** Varies, depending on species

P

Phormium FOR-mee-um • New Zealand flax, phormium

Foliage is the reason these plants have so many fans; the tall, open spikes of tubular yellow-green or dull red flowers that arise in summer are just a bonus compared to the year-round effects of that giant clump of colorful spears. Only two species of this genus exist, but they've given rise to some garden gems. These New Zealand natives are from the Phormiaceae family, and like agave, they're ideal for dry gardens in mild climates. These evergreen plants form statuesque clumps of stiff, linear leaves, growing substantially up to 6 feet (1.8 m) tall and 10 feet (3 m) wide. You'll find cultivars with maroon leaves, striped yellow-and-green leaves, pink-tinted leaves, and leaves as glorious as a sunset.

Perfect Partners

Silvery gray artemisia, lavender (*Lavandula* spp.), and lamb's ears (*Stachys byzantina*) are appealing against the somber hues of 'Dazzler', 'Maori Chief', and other dark-toned cultivars. A group of pink, salmon, or terra-cotta yarrow (*Achillea* spp.) will increase the warmth of 'Dazzler' or 'Sundowner' phormium; yellow yarrows look great with *P. tenax* 'Variegatum' or *P. cookianum* subp. *hookeri* 'Cream Delight' or 'Tricolor'. The flowers of daylilies (*Hemerocallis* spp.) or Asiatic lilies (*Lilium* spp.) stand out against New Zealand flax; choose a flax leaf color to complement the flowers. For later-season color in a hot, dry site, plant gaillardia or orange or scarlet dahlias with New Zealand flax.

Phormium cookianum (mountain flax) Cultivars and hybrids of this species are often available; the species itself requires a dedicated hunt. The broad, strappy leaves arch outward at the tips and can grow to 6 feet (1.8 m) tall and 10 feet (3 m) wide under good conditions. *P. cookianum* subsp. *hookeri* 'Cream Delight' has multiple stripes of pale yellow; 'Tricolor' is marked with pale yellow and red margins.

P. tenax (New Zealand flax) The cultivars and hybrids of this species are grown more often that the dark green-leaved species. 'Variegatum' is green with pale yellow edges; 'Veitchianum' has bold, creamy stripes.

P. hybrids Many popular cultivars of New Zealand flax are hybrids of mixed parentage, which creates a variety of form—some arching, like *P. cookianum*; some upright, like *P. tenax*—and size. 'Yellow Wave' has arching, mostly yellowish green foliage with a darker green stripe down the middle; this giant towers up to 12 feet (3.6 m) tall. 'Aurora' is an arching plant that reaches 4 feet (1.2 m) tall and wide, with striking bronze, salmon, red, and yellow leaves. 'Dazzler' has similar colors and arching habit but is only 3 feet (1 m) tall. Dwarf 'Bronze Baby' is a small fry, at 2 feet (60 cm) tall and wide; its drooping tips give it a graceful attitude. 'Maori Chief' has striking bronze leaves streaked with pink and red; 'Maori Sunrise' has narrow leaves of apricot to pink, bordered by bronze edges. 'Sundowner' reaches 6 feet (1.8 m) tall and wide, with broad, upright, bronze-tinted leaves with deep pink along the edges.

Phormium tenax

THE BASICS

If you live where New Zealand flax survives the winters, it will be an easy plant for adding colorful, contrasting form to beds or for planting as an accent at the corner of your potting shed or the foot of your driveway. Otherwise, you can enjoy it as a temporary garden character or plant it in large pots.

Growing Conditions: Plant in well-drained, average-to-lean soil. Fertilizing will help the plant grow more quickly, a process that usually takes a few years. Established plants are drought tolerant. New Zealand flax flourishes in coastal gardens. If you plant outside of Zone 9 or 10, give it a deep mulch in fall to help the roots survive, even if the top growth is killed by cold. Cut off any winter-damaged foliage in spring.

Propagation: Divide in spring with a sharp shovel.

▶ **Bloom Time** Summer, but secondary to the year-round leaf color

▶ **Planting Requirements** Full sun

▶ **Zones** 9 to 10; may survive in Zone 8 or even Zone 7 until a particularly cold winter

P

Phlox to Fit Any Garden

All phloxes have clustered flowers of a similar shape—a thin tube that flares out into five petals. However, these sturdy perennials come in a huge variety of colors, sizes, and habits. From ground-hugging creepers to stately beauties, the members of this genus supply enough flower power to decorate a garden of any style. Try those featured here, or explore the many other phlox that are waiting for you to find them.

◀ *Phlox* × **'Chattahoochee'**
A sweetheart for the spring wildflower garden, this pretty cultivar is probably a hybrid between two species (*P. divaricatus* and *P. pilosa*). It's lovely beneath spring-flowering trees, where it can enjoy morning sun and shade in the afternoon. It forms a low, semievergreen mound not quite 1 foot (30 cm) across, covered with fragrant, magenta-eyed blue flowers. It tends to be short-lived. Hardy in Zones 5 to 9.

▲ *P. carolina* **'Bill Baker'**
Carolina phlox have a wilder, looser habit than the familiar tall garden type, which makes them easy to blend into perennial beds for extra color. Pink-flowered 'Bill Baker' reaches 1 to 1½ feet (30 to 45 cm) tall in bloom; it spreads moderately. It shows good resistance to mildew.

▶ *P. paniculata* **'Peppermint Twist'**
This oddball cultivar has pink petals boldly striped with white. It's a short one, at only 16 inches (40 cm) tall. Plant in groups of three for best effect, or let a single plant spice up subdued characters in your garden. A recent introduction, it's said to be fairly resistant to mildew. Hardy in Zones 4 to 8.

▼ *P. paniculata* 'Eva Cullum'

A particularly long bloomer, this dark-eyed pink phlox is in flower from summer into fall. That's good news for butterflies, which are frequent visitors to the showy flowers. The plant forms a multistemmed clump 2 to 2½ feet (60 to 75 cm) tall and wide and thrives in full sun to part shade. Hardy in Zones 4 to 8.

▲ *P. maculata* 'Alpha'

Spires laden with lilac-pink blossoms crown this tall phlox, which reaches 3 to 4 feet (90 to 120 cm) tall. It blooms from early to midsummer with a sweet fragrance and attracts butterflies. Cultivars of *P. maculata* tend to be more mildew-resistant than those of similar *P. paniculata*. Hardy in Zones 4 to 8.

▶ *P. stolonifera* 'Blue Ridge'

This charming phlox is a wildflower that can work wonders in your shady-to-part-shade naturalistic garden or perennial beds. In spring the low mound of semievergreen foliage becomes a cloud of beautiful, pleasantly scented, soft blue blossoms. "Stolonifera" refers to stolons, the creeping underground stems that cause plants to spread. This easy, graceful phlox is fairly quick to expand its territory, but few gardeners ever complain; plus, it's easy to uproot to keep in bounds. Hardy in Zones 3 to 8.

227

Physostegia fy-so-STEE-gee-uh • obedient plant

Physostegia virginiana

"Obedient"? Not when it comes to the behavior of this pretty plant in the garden: A member of the Lamiaceae—or mint—family, this perennial can be an aggressive spreader. However, obedient plant is valuable for bridging the gap between the early summer extravaganza of irises, poppies, and other June bloomers and the late-season show of asters and grasses. Its erect, flower-packed candles of rose, purplish, pink, or white brighten the scene from midsummer to fall.

Physostegia virginiana The word *virginiana*—"from Virginia"—is the clue that this plant hails from the eastern part of North America. In the wild it thrives in wet, sunny places, along stream banks, beside ponds and swamps, and in roadside ditches or wet grasslands. In the garden it does equally well in average, moist, or waterlogged soil, making it a prime choice for heavy clay soil. Wherever you grow it, you're likely to forget all about obedient plant as it bides its time during the rush of earlier summer perennials. But as those peak performers fade away, you'll be grateful for the fresh color of this plant. Creeping underground stems soon grow into a dense, ever-expanding clump with narrow, pointed leaves. The plant has an unusual orderly look, thanks to the opposite pairs of leaves and the eye-catching calyxes that hold the buds and flowers.

There are a number of cultivars of this species, showing plenty of variation, with flowers ranging from mauve to pink to white. It reaches 3 to 4 feet (90 to 120 cm) tall and at least that wide; over the years it may send those creeping roots outward until it forms a large colony. It's much easier to keep in control than other members of its family, such as the notorious mints; just pull up those trespassing new shoots. Or plant white-flowered 'Miss Manners', which stays in a clump instead of spreading; white 'Summer Snow' is also better behaved. Other cultivars include bright rosy 'Vivid' and pink 'Bouquet'. 'Variegata' offers white-edged leaves to make the clump of foliage more interesting while you're waiting for those blooms.

THE BASICS

Long-lived and trouble-free, obedient plant is a "plant it and forget it" perennial. It will flourish for many years, requiring nothing more than an annual cutting-back. The interesting flowers, which attract the attention of butterflies and hummingbirds, are long-lasting in an indoor bouquet.

Growing Conditions: Plant in lean-to-rich garden soil. Obedient plant is highly adaptable to soil moisture: It flourishes in conditions from average, occasionally watered soil to moisture-holding clay. It spreads more quickly in loose, moist soil. Rich soil leads to taller growth and weaker stems, so you may need to stake the plants. For more compact growth less prone to toppling, pinch back the tips of the stems once or twice before buds form. Seedpods are decorative, so you can let them stand as long as you like. Cut back the entire plant to ground level in early spring. Pinch each stem before it buds, when the plant is 1 foot (30 cm) tall, then again at 2 feet (60 cm) to keep it compact.

Propagation: Pull up running roots and transplant in spring.

▶ **Bloom Time** Late summer to early fall
▶ **Planting Requirements** Sun to part shade
▶ **Zones** 2 to 9

Perfect Partners

Use the vertical spikes of obedient plant to contrast with the rounded heads of tall garden phlox (*Phlox paniculata*, *P. maculata*), long-blooming yarrows (*Achillea* spp.), and the soft spill of asters. Or combine it with native prairie plants that share its late-blooming habit, such as perennial sunflowers (*Helianthus* spp.), goldenrods (*Solidago* spp.), black-eyed Susans (*Rudbeckia* spp.), and Joe Pye weed (*Eupatorium* spp.). You can also use them in a shadier spot to accent the simpler form of fall-blooming anemones (*Anemone japonica* and other spp.).

Platycodon *pla-tee-KO-dun* • balloon flower

Only a single species of this genus is commonly found in gardens, but it's a beauty that gardeners have known well for hundreds of years. However, it got lost for a while in the rush toward newer, "better" perennials a few decades ago. In recent years more plant lovers are rediscovering this long-lived perennial of the Campanulaceae family, with its lovely blue flowers and oddball inflated buds.

Platycodon grandiflorus (balloon flower) *Platycodon* comes from Greek words that mean "broad bell," but anyone who's ever seen a hot-air balloon knows that "balloon flower" is a more apt description—the inflated flower buds look exactly like a flock of hot-air balloons. They open into a generous display of wide blue-violet stars that catch the eye of anyone strolling the late-summer garden. Flowering time will last for about a month or longer—especially if you snip off the seedpods when the

Platycodon grandiflorus 'Apoyama'

blossoms fade. The species can reach 3 feet (90 cm) tall.

Platycodon grandiflorus var. *mariesii*, which is a more compact plant, reaching about 1½ to 2 feet (45 to 60 cm), is the plant usually stocked at nurseries. The Fuji Series includes a mixture of blue, pink, and white. 'Shell Pink' is another good pink. For dramatic deep blue-violet, why not try 'Apoyama'. *Platycodon grandiflorus* var. *albus* is a pristine white.

THE BASICS

Balloon flower is simple to grow, as long as you avoid disturbing its sensitive roots. Give it a permanent home, and the plant will be happy. The unusual and beautiful flowers are perfect in a vase; sear the base of the stem with a match as soon as you snip it to keep the flowers fresh in water.

Growing Conditions: Plant in poor-to-fertile, well-drained soil. Balloon flower thrives in tough

Perfect Partners

All colors of balloon flower will make agreeable companions for smaller-flowered perennials, such as salvias, asters, and yarrows (*Achillea* spp.), and with bold orange or rust-colored daylilies (*Hemerocallis* spp.). A group of balloon flowers are also beautiful against a soft backdrop of silvery artemisia (*Artemisia* 'Silver Queen' and others), or with a collar of velvety lamb's ears (*Stachys byzantina*).

Platycodon grandiflorus

conditions, including sandy or stony soils and clay; once established, it is drought tolerant. The strong stems need no staking. The foliage turns clear yellow in fall, and the interesting seedpods are a good winter accent in the sleeping garden. Cut back to ground level in early spring. Remember where you planted this perennial; new growth is very late to emerge in spring.

Propagation: Root division in spring or fall, when plants are dormant; work carefully to avoid breaking the roots of the parent plant. Often self-sows; learn to recognize seedlings so that you can transplant them carefully when they're young. They will bloom the second year after sprouting.

▶ **Bloom Time** Late summer
▶ **Planting Requirements** Sun to part shade
▶ **Zones** 3 to 8

Polemonium
po-lee-MO-nee-um • Jacob's ladder

Polemonium reptans 'Blue Pearl'

Cheerful blue spring flowers that keep coming for weeks are the calling card of this mounding perennial. A few species are available, plus an array of cultivars, including pink- and white-flowered varieties and some with striking variegated leaves. These plants are in the Polemoniaceae family, which also includes phlox; like phlox, they are generous with their ½-inch (12-mm) flowers. The foliage, which looks good long after the flowers have faded away, makes these plants an excellent, lighter-textured companion for hostas.

Polemonium caeruleum (Jacob's ladder) Most well known of the clan and most widely available, this species raises erect, leafy stems, topped with clusters of small, nodding flowers, from the dense mound of foliage. It forms a leafy mound 1½ to 2 feet (45 to 60 cm) tall and wide. If you prefer snow white rather than sky blue, look for *P. caeruleum* var. *lacteum* (also called var. *album*). If fancy leaves suit your fancy, consider white-edged 'Snow and Sapphires' (or *P. reptans* 'Stairway to Heaven'). Some gardeners think the variegated foliage distracts from the flowers, while others find it appealing. Hardy in Zones 3 to 7.

P. carneum (pink Jacob's ladder) Jacob's ladders grow across much of the country, but the species that you will encounter in the wild vary from one region to another. Their distinctive paired leaves make them easy to recognize as Jacob's ladder, no matter which species you're admiring. This pretty, pale salmon pink species is found from Washington to California. Its early summer flowers may be up to 1 inch (2.5 cm) wide. Available from native plant specialists, it forms a clump 8 inches (20 cm) across, and is 12 inches (30 cm) tall in bloom. Hardy in Zones 4 to 9.

P. pauciflorum This is the Southwestern representative. It has long, narrowly tubular flowers that dangle downward; they are soft straw-yellow with an occasional red blush, and self-sow. Hardy in Zones 7 to 9.

P. reptans (creeping Jacob's ladder, Greek valerian) Jacob's angels would have had a hard time getting off the ground using the "ladders" of this species, which stays lower than others, reaching only 8 to 12 inches (20 to 30 cm) tall and slightly taller in bloom. This American native grows wild across much of the eastern half of the country, joining the spring wildflower show in deciduous woodlands or at their edges. Unlike other spring wildflowers, it keeps its foliage for months after the flowers are finished. In the wild or in your shady garden, it may slowly expand into a good-sized colony, with individual plants knitting together as their slow-to-moderately-spreading roots reach out. It may also self-sow, a welcome trait for a plant as pretty as this one.

The free-flowering blue species needs no improvement, but cultivars do exist. 'Blue Pearl' has bright blue flowers. 'Lambrook Mauve' ('Lambrook Manor') has lilac-tinged flowers. 'Stairway to Heaven' has striking variegated foliage, edged with broad white margins; in hot summers the leaves may turn green. Hardy in Zones 2 to 9.

THE BASICS
Remember that Jacob's ladder hails from habitats that get at least some shade, and plan its place accordingly. These easy-to-grow perennials will survive in sun, but they live longer if protected from all-day rays. The free-blooming flowers flourish in a shadier nook, such as beneath spring-blooming trees or snuggled against the large, exposed roots of maples.

Growing Conditions: Plant in moist, average-to-fertile soil loosened with a generous helping of humus. Slugs crave the foliage, so use your favorite methods to keep them at bay. Cut back to ground level in early spring, being careful not to damage newly emerging leaves. Or let the dead leaves stay in place to serve as a living mulch for the plants.

Propagation: Transplant self-sown seedlings in spring. Divide *P. reptans* in early spring.

▶ **Bloom Time** Late spring to early summer
▶ **Planting Requirements** Part shade; also sun, in cooler zones
▶ **Zones** Varies, depending on species

Primula *PRIM-yew-luh* • primrose

Primula vulgaris

Many Americans know primroses best for adding an instant splash to the early spring garden, but they are forgotten as soon as other flowers bloom. However, many British gardeners cherish these bright, pretty plants. What makes the difference? Climate. Few regions in North America have the moist, cool climate that the "instant color" types crave, so nursery owners concentrate on longer-lived perennials of other genera. However, these members of the Primulaceae family include some excellent garden plants suitable for many regions. All form a low rosette of foliage, from which bare stems rise up crowned with clusters of flowers, some of which are fragrant.

Primula auricula (bear's-ear primrose, auricula primrose) These evergreen plants produce a tidy rosette of gray-green leaves, from which clusters of sunny yellow flowers rise up in late spring. Try this native of the Alps in a rock garden, which will provide the excellent drainage it requires. Give it full sun in coastal areas, where it does well, or part shade in other areas. Specialty catalogs include many cultivars and hybrids, such as 'Blossom', which has red flowers with gold centers, and near-black 'Lovebird'. Hardy in Zones 3 to 7 and in cooler regions of Zone 8.

P. denticulata (drumstick primrose) Its tight-packed balls of flowers are just as eye-catching as they are in the Himalayas, from which it hails. The species has purple flowers with a yellow eye. 'Rubra' is reddish purple; var. *alba* is snow white. One of the larger species, it forms a clump of ground-hugging foliage 18 inches (45 cm) across, with 18-inch (45-cm) stems of flowers rising above it. Plant in part shade in loose, rich, humusy soil, and keep moist. Hardy in Zones 2 to 7 and in cooler regions of Zone 8.

P. japonica (Japanese primrose, candelabra primrose) This robust plant is an adaptable type that produces abundant reddish purple, pink, or white flowers held in whorls along the stems. Like most species, it does best in moist soil in a shady place. It self-sows to form a loose colony. 'Miller's Crimson' has striking color; 'Postford White' is cheerful, with white flowers dotted with red eyes. Hardy in Zones 3 to 7 and in cooler regions of Zone 8.

P. veris (cowslip) This is a native wildflower in the British Isles, dotting meadows with nodding yellow flowers that smell sublime. Add a British accent to your own shady lawn with this European species, which grows to about 12 inches (30 cm) tall in bloom. Hardy in Zones 4 to 8.

P. vialii This species has short spikes of flowers that are purple at the bottom, contrasted with red buds at the top. It rarely lasts more than a few years. Hardy in Zones 4 to 8.

P. vulgaris (English primrose) This is the wild primrose of the British Isles, from which *P.* × *polyantha* (Polyanthus Group; polyanthus primroses) have been bred. These are the bright-colored primroses sold at every garden center in late winter to early spring, when gardeners are hungry for color. Pop them into your garden or that pot by your front door, but don't expect a long life; most peter out in a few years. Irrestible colors include blue, bright red, wine, purple, orange, yellow, white, and pink. Hardy in Zones 6 to 8 and in any Zone as annuals.

THE BASICS

Primroses can be challenging, but it's mostly a matter of meeting their needs. Moist soil and a partly shady setting are the trick to growing them. The plants quickly decline and die out if the soil is too dry, and they suffer in hot, humid summers. If your conditions are not right, you'll have to enjoy primroses as an annual.

Growing Conditions: Plant in moist, humus-rich, fertile soil. Mulch with chopped, composted fall leaves to retain soil moisture. Snip off flowering stems near the base when finished. Slugs may eat leaves or flowers; control with your favored method.

Propagation: Divide or transplant self-sown seedlings in early spring.

▶ **Bloom Time** Spring
▶ **Planting Requirements** Part shade
▶ **Zones** Varies, depending on species

P

Pulmonaria *pul-mon-AIR-ee-uh* • lungwort, pulmonaria

Pulmonaria saccharata 'Highdown'

These easy perennials offer some of the first flowers of the new season. Pulmonarias are members of the Boraginaceae family; if you grow the herb borage, you may notice that these plants share the similar trait of blue flowers that open pink at first. Pink, purple, and white flowers are available, too. There are numerous cultivars and hybrids with a variety of leaf shapes and colors, including splotches or ghostly silver-white leaves. The handsome foliage, in most species forming a loose clump about 1½ feet (45 cm) across and 1 foot (30 cm) high, contributes to the beauty of your garden long after the flowers are gone.

Pulmonaria angustifolia (blue lungwort, blue cowslip) This species has a mound of plain green leaves serving as a backdrop for the heavenly blue flowers. Like most other species, this one has been used as a parent of hybrids, such as 'Beth's Pink'.

P. longifolia (longleaf lungwort) A dense clump of silvery-spotted leaves supports the long-lasting clear blue flowers of this European species, which is ideal in the hot, humid weather of the southern United States. The leaves are longer and narrower than those of other lungworts, especially in the deep blue cultivar 'Bertram Anderson'. 'Little Star' is similar but more vigorous.

P. officinalis (spotted dog, soldiers-and-sailors) This is a species with white-spotted leaves and flowers that open pink, then change to blue. 'Cambridge Blue' has pale blue blooms; 'Sissinghurst White' offers pink buds opening to white flowers. Hardy in Zones 4 to 8.

P. saccharata (Bethlehem sage) This broad-leaved species is the parent of many cultivars. Species plants may be reddish purple, violet-blue, or white, but the cultivars vary. 'Bielefeld', 'Dora Bielefeld', and 'Pierre's Pure Pink' are pink-flowered; 'Leopard' is reddish pink; 'Mrs. Moon' opens pink, then turns to lavender; 'Highdown' is blue. The foliage of Bethlehem sage is spotted with silver. The Argentea Group of cultivars developed from this species has striking leaves that are almost completely silver, a beautiful backdrop to the reddish purple flowers.

P. hybrids New hybrid cultivars of pretty pulmonarias are appearing in such numbers that it's hard to keep up with the latest and greatest. You can select those that suit your style or sample some of these modern choices.

P. 'Dark Vader' boasts deep green leaves spangled with silvery dots, with flowers that open pink, then change to blue-purple. It's a vigorous grower, as well as a beauty. P. 'Excalibur' has totally silver leaves, with a green-edge accent that makes this plant a living highlight in any shady garden. Try it with ferns for contrasting texture as well as fantastic color. P. 'Samurai' has extra-long, extra-silvery leaves, with narrow green, rippled edges and a green midvein, which give this plant pure elegance, producing a low mound of cascading foliage. The cobalt blue flowers are beautiful, too. This one stands up to heat and humidity. P. 'Trevi Fountain' is a recent introduction and sports heavily spotted leaves that form a large, 2-foot (60-cm) clump with masses of blue spring flowers. It's a great ground cover choice in a shady or wooded garden, and like many other hybrids, it keeps looking fresh even in heat and humidity.

THE BASICS

Pulmonarias are easy to grow, but they are often underused in gardens because they are such early bloomers. By the time most gardeners head for the nursery, their prime time for flowers is already past and the leaves are a little ragged. Seek them out, plant them in a shady niche, and they'll turn into true garden gems.

Growing Conditions: Plant in moist, humus-rich soil of average-to-rich fertility. Water weekly when rain is scarce for lush growth. Snip off dead leaves in late winter, before new foliage begins to emerge.

Propagation: Divide in early spring.

▶ **Bloom Time** Early spring flowers; foliage into fall

▶ **Planting Requirements** Part to full shade

▶ **Zones** 4 to 8; *P. officinalis*, Zones 6 to 8

Rudbeckia *rood-BEK-ee-uh* • rudbeckia, black-eyed Susan, coneflower

Black-eyed Susans have such a friendly look that it's no wonder they're so popular. Knee-high plants with the classic brownish black central cone are best known, but these sturdy plants of the Asteraceae family offer species of varying heights, some up to 4 feet (120 cm) or more. Flowers range from fluffy doubles, whose petals hide the cone, to green-domed daisies.

Rudbeckia fulgida (black-eyed Susan) This American native is best known by its German cultivar, 'Goldsturm' (*Rudbeckia fulgida* var. *sullivantii* 'Goldsturm'). The cultivar quickly fills out to form a 2- to 3-foot (60- to 90-cm)-wide mound of toothed leaves topped with a multitude of black-eyed Susans 3 inches (7.5 cm)

across; it blooms for months. Hardy in Zones 4 to 9.

R. hirta (gloriosa daisy) This plant is a biennial, not a true perennial; it forms a rosette of hairy leaves its first year, flowers its second year, and usually dies that fall—but you may get another year if you cut it back before it sets seeds. The big, colorful daisies are 6 inches (15 cm) across in gold, russet, and bicolor hues, with dark central cones. Many cultivars are available, in both single colors and color mixes. The strain called Gloriosa Daisy Mixed reaches 3 feet (90 cm) tall with autumnal hues; 'Rustic Dwarfs' provides the same hues but on plants 2 feet (60 cm) tall. 'Becky Mixed' supplies a rustic mix on plants 1 foot (30 cm) tall. Hardy in Zones 3 to 9.

R. laciniata (coneflower) This native of the American prairies is tall. Unlike most black-eyed Susans, its leaves are smooth instead of bristly. It forms a stout clump of foliage from which arise leafy stems crowned by 3- to 6-inch (7.5- to 15-cm), pale yellow daisies with greenish central cones. Plants reach 5 to 10 feet (1.5 to 3 m) tall, and the roots spread to form a large clump. Hardy in Zones 3 to 9.

R. triloba (brown-eyed Susan) This self-sowing species is also a biennial; it blooms in shade and sun. In bloom it's 3 to 4 feet (90 to 120 cm) tall and 3 feet (90 cm) wide. Hardy in Zones 4 to 7.

THE BASICS

Use these sturdy growers to supply plenty of color, carrying the garden through the early summer perennials into dahlias, asters, and ornamental

Rudbeckia fulgida var. *sullivantii* 'Goldsturm'

grasses. All are easy to grow, even in drought, clay soil, and hard winters.

Growing Conditions: Plant in well-drained, lean-to-average soil. Rudbeckias adapt to challenging conditions; they thrive in clay soil, as well as in stony soil. Rich soil or fertilizing can cause the plants to grow tall and floppy and encourages the invasive tendencies of 'Goldsturm' and *R. laciniata* 'Golden Glow'. These perennials survive moderate drought, but regular watering is best. Loosely stake tall species to keep them from toppling when their heads become heavy with flowers. Let the intriguing cone-topped stalks stand in winter to attract birds and for winter interest; cut back to ground level in spring or when they begin to shatter.

Propagation: Divide in spring. Transplant self-sown seedlings of *R. hirta* or *R. triloba* in spring, or let them multiply into a loose colony.

▶ **Bloom Time** Summer to fall
▶ **Planting Requirements** Full sun; *R. laciniata* and *R. triloba* also in part-to-light shade
▶ **Zones** Varies, depending on species

Perfect Partners

Rudbeckias are long blooming, so they will supply reliable color while other perennials come and go around them. All are beautiful with blue or purple neighbors, including catmints (*Nepeta* spp.), Russian sage (*Perovskia atriplicifolia*), anise hyssop (*Agastache* spp.), asters, and penstemon hybrids, such as 'Blue Midnight' or 'Sour Grapes'. Their size sets off more delicate neighbors, such as salvias (*Salvia* × *sylvestris* for earlier bloom; *S. greggii* and many other spp. for late-season color), and their leafy form is good contrast to strappy or spiky foliage, such as that of daylilies (*Hemerocallis* spp.), red-hot poker (*Kniphofia* spp.), or bearded irises.

Reach for the Sun with Rudbeckias

When you explore rudbeckias, you'll find a whole clan of cheerful daisies to add several hues of sunshine to your summer-to-fall garden. On these pages you'll meet the original black-eyed Susan and get to know her sisters—including a green-eyed beauty, a burnished redhead, and a towering giant that goldfinches can't get enough of.

▲ R. hirta

At first glance, they all look alike, but this wildflower includes several subspecies, as well as regional variations, so there's a lot of variety in height and habit. Some plants behave as annuals, others as biennials, while many are perennial. They reach from 18 inches (45 cm) to 3 feet (90 cm) tall or more. The dark-eyed daisies are instantly recognizable. This species is simple to grow from seed scattered in a sunny spot; the plants will bloom their first or second year, depending on their parentage, and will flower prolifically. Many cultivars are available. Hardy in Zones 3 to 9.

▶ R. maxima

This prairie wildflower with gray-green leaves is best suited for a naturalistic or prairie garden. In late summer the plant is topped by an open collection of outward-leaning stems topped with yellow, short-petaled daisies with exaggeratedly tall brown cones. It grows 5 to 6 feet (1.5 to 1.8 m) tall in bloom. Hardy in Zones 4 to 9.

▼ *R. triloba*

The flowers of this rudbeckia are small compared to other species, but in bloom it's a showstopper. The branching stems, 3 to 5 feet (90 to 150 cm) tall and 3 to 4 feet (90 to 120 cm) wide, create a huge billow of sunny blossoms. The display lasts for more than a month, from late summer well into fall. Known as brown-eyed Susan, this species has central cones that start out black, then fade to brown. It tends to be short-lived, but self-sows. Hardy in Zones 4 to 7.

▲ *R.* 'Herbstsonne' (Autumn Sun)

The German name of this hybrid is more widely known than its English translation. This is a big one, forming a stout clump 6 feet (180 cm) tall and 3 feet (90 cm) wide, with hundreds (maybe—you count them!) of bright yellow flowers with slightly drooping petals and raised green center cones. The cones turn brown as the flowers age. Let the dead stalks stand over winter to catch the snow and add some architecture to the sleeping garden. Hardy in Zones 3 to 9.

▶ *R. hirta* 'Irish Eyes'

This cultivar is a new take on its black-eyed Susan parent. Usually short-lived, 'Irish Eyes' ('Green Eyes') has green center cones with bright yellow petals. It's easy to start from seed, and it self-sows, so those eyes will keep on smiling. Hardy in Zones 3 to 9.

235

Salvia *SAL-vee-uh* • salvia, sage

You'll find salvias for any condition, from boggy soils to desert heat, in a patriotic palette of red, blue, and white, plus every gradation of those hues. The abundant, tubular flowers are borne on upright spikes. Most plants have aromatic foliage and square stems, clues to their Lamiaceae—or mint—family heritage. Form varies widely, with some stretching into tall clumps to 5 feet (1.5 m), others growing into woody shrubs, and many forming tidy mounds or clumps that fit easily into perennial beds. No matter what their habit or color, all salvias share the trait of extra-long bloom—and every one will attract hummingbirds.

Salvia argentea (silver sage) This biennial produces a rosette of huge, velvety silver leaves its first year; plant at the front of your border as an irresistible touch. Hardy in Zones 5 to 9; not for humid-summer regions.

S. elegans (pineapple sage) Deliciously fragrant foliage on a plant that can reach 3 feet (90 cm) tall and wide in a single season. Cardinal red flowers bloom in fall. Hardy in Zones 8 to 11; grow as an annual elsewhere.

S. greggii (Texas sage) This small-flowered, shrubby native reaches about 2 feet (60 cm) tall and wide. Look for cultivars in many colors. Hardy in Zones 7 to 9.

S. leucantha A native species that, along with its cultivars 'Midnight' and 'Santa Barbara', is a large 4-foot (1.2-m) plant, ideal for late-season purple color. Hardy in Zones 8 to 11.

S. × sylvestris Popular cultivars include 'Blaukönigin' (Blue Queen), 'Caradonna', and 'Rosenwein', with upright spikes to 1½ feet (45 cm), packed with small blossoms. Hardy in Zones 5 to 9. Deep purple 'Mainacht' (May Night) is floriferous and reliable.

S. uliginosa (marsh sage) A tall species—it grows to 3 to 7 feet (90 cm to 2.1 m)—it has intense pale blue flowers in late summer. It needs regular watering but is a good back-of-the-border plant. Hardy in Zones 6 to 10.

THE BASICS

Many salvias are adaptable to average garden conditions, which generally means well-drained soil of medium fertility. Many also thrive in difficult conditions, such as dry soil, lean soil, sandy soil, or even wet soil, as well as in seaside conditions, xeric gardens, summer humidity, or extra-cold winters. Read the label or catalog description to make sure the site you have in mind is suitable for the salvia that has caught your attention.

Growing Conditions: Most species do well in average soil of average fertility. Plant *S. uliginosa* in moist or boggy soil, and water regularly when rain is scant. Supply regular water to *S. elegans,* too, but avoid waterlogged soil. Plant salvias with hairy or woolly leaves, such as *S. argentea,* in well-drained soil that also drains quickly in winter; they rot in too much soil moisture. For most other salvias, err on the side of too little water than too much; most are drought tolerant. If your plants look wilted or paler-leaved during a dry period, they'll recover after a watering.

A spring application of fertilizer, repeated every six weeks thereafter,

Salvia × sylvestris 'Blaukönigin'

will result in lusher, leafier growth and often increased height. For denser, more compact growth, cut back branching types by one-third in late spring to early summer, when the plant is leafed out but buds haven't yet formed. Taller, branching salvias respond quickly to pruning, sending out a flurry of new side branches and shoots; snip them back anytime during the growing season for improved shape. Clip off finished flowers to encourage repeat bloom. Cut back nonwoody plants to ground level in late winter to early spring. Cut back woody plants to about half their size in late winter. Whiteflies, aphids, mealybugs, or spider mites may move in on the plant; remove affected branches or apply appropriate controls.

Propagation: Divide clump-forming types in early spring. Take cuttings of green stems of all types in spring to early summer.

▶ **Bloom Time** Most species, summer to fall; some begin blooming in fall

▶ **Planting Requirements** Sun

▶ **Zones** Varies, depending on species

Scabiosa *skab-ee-O-suh* • scabiosa, pincushion flower

Pincushion flowers are free flowering and long blooming. Each blossom is held atop a slender, graceful bare stem, and each mound of basal foliage produces dozens of flowers at once. Most scabiosas are soft blue-lilac, but pink and white forms are available. As the flowers fade, each bloom ages into a hairy round tuffet of soon-to-be seeds. These plants from the Dipsacaceae family are short-lived, but their prolific flowers make them a must-have.

Scabiosa caucasica The big blossoms, up to 3 inches (7.5 cm) across, are the temptation of this easy-to-grow perennial, which has grayish green foliage. The flowers are pale blue to lavender-blue and are produced from midsummer to fall. In bloom,

Scabiosa caucasica

a single plant of this species covers an area 2 feet (60 cm) tall and wide. 'Fama' is sky blue. House hybrids have especially large flowers that can reach 4 inches (10 cm) across, creating a lovely patch of cool blue-lavender or white. 'Perfecta Blue' is a reliable blue-lavender; 'Perfecta Alba' is white.

S. columbaria (small scabiosa) Smaller than *S. caucasica*, this species and its cultivars are still big garden performers. The blue-lilac blossoms, about 1½ inches (3.75 cm) across, dance above the leaves from early summer into fall. The species reaches 1½ to 2 feet (45 to 60 cm) tall and wide. The cultivars 'Butterfly Blue' or 'Pink Mist' ('Butterfly Pink') are popular. Cultivars are smaller plants, forming a tidy mound about 16 inches (40 cm) tall and wide.

THE BASICS

Pincushion flowers are easy to care for, usually pest- and disease-free. Butterflies and bees visit these flowers, so pick a site depending on how closely you want to see butterflies or how strongly you prefer to avoid bees.

Growing Conditions: Plant in average-to-fertile, well-drained soil. Fertilize in spring and again in early summer for lusher growth, if desired. The plants can tolerate some drought, but bloom may slow down without a drink of water about every 10 days. Snip off dead flowers as soon as you spot them to encourage the plant to keep producing buds. To prolong the life of these plants, divide them every two to three years. They often self-sow, although the seedlings may not look

Scabiosa columbaria

exactly like the parent if they're the progeny of a cultivar.

Propagation: Easy to grow from collected or purchased seed. Divide plants in spring. Transplant self-sown seedlings in spring.

▶ **Bloom Time** Summer to fall
▶ **Planting Requirements** Sun
▶ **Zones** *S. caucasica*, 4 to 7, plus cooler parts of Zone 8; *S. columbaria*, Zones 3 to 7, plus cooler parts of Zone 8

Perfect Partners

The soft color of scabiosa makes these plants ideal partners for many summer perennials, including lilies (*Lilium* spp.), daylilies (*Hemerocallis* spp.), tall phlox (*Phlox paniculata*, *P. maculata*), bee balm (*Monarda* spp.), and yarrows (*Achillea* spp.). Plant blue scabiosas in groups of three to provide a sweep of cooling color with bright gaillardias or vivid coneflower hybrids (*Echinacea* 'Big Sky Series'). Let their flowers mingle with salvias or dahlias; pink, blue, or white cultivars are great accents for dark-foliaged dahlias or purple-gray sage (*Salvia officinalis* 'Purpurascens'). Pink or white cultivars will provide contrasting form for veronicas in any hue.

S

Salvias for Late-Season Color

A hundred years ago the only widely grown perennial salvia was *Salvia officinalis,* familiar for its fragrant, gray sage leaves that are still used as a culinary seasoning. Today salvias are some of the hottest plants of the new millennium. Nurseries and breeders have been investigating and introducing new species, cultivars, and hybrids in such numbers that it seems we find a new one every time we visit the garden center. Here are just a few of them.

◀ *S. guaranitica*
"Anise sage" is the common name for this species, and although its leaves are aromatic when crushed, they smell nothing like licorice. Its beautiful blue flowers appear from summer to fall, and as with all salvias, they're a big hit with hummingbirds and butterflies. The large, shrubby plant grows 3 to 5 feet (90 to 150 cm) tall and wide. Hardy in Zones 7 to 11.

▲ *S. patens* 'Cambridge Blue'
Light blue flowers decorate this salvia, which grows 2 to 3 feet (60 to 90 cm) tall. It blooms from summer to fall. Hardy in Zones 8 to 9.

▶ *S.* × *sylvestris* 'Mainacht' (May Night)
The blue-violet flowers repeatedly bloom from late spring to early summer and will attract bees. This is a drought-tolerant plant, making it suitable for xeriscaping.

▼ S. 'Indigo Spires'

The outstanding blue of this recent cultivar has made it popular with gardeners who have a winter climate on the milder side. It grows 2 to 3 feet (60 to 90 cm) tall, forming a multistemmed clump. The flowers begin in summer and keep on going well into fall. Hummingbirds visit often. Hardy in Zones 7 to 10.

▲ S. uliginosa

This species is commonly named "bog sage," but you don't need a bog to grow it. While it will thrive in wet soil, it also flourishes in average garden conditions and can even take some drought. This is a big salvia, forming a shrub-size plant 3 to 7 feet (90 cm to 2.1 m) tall and about 5 feet (1.5 m) wide. From summer into fall, it produces abundant light blue flowers that are attended by bees. Hardy in Zones 6 to 10.

▶ S. elegans

Crush a leaf of this plant to reveal a delicious pineapple fragrance that gives it the common name of "pineapple sage." The plant is frost-tender, but it grows superfast and can reach 3 feet (90 cm) tall and wide in a single season. Cardinal red flowers bloom in fall. Hardy in Zones 8 to 11; however, you can grow it as annual elsewhere.

Sedum *SEE-dum • sedum, stonecrop*

These unusual plants are ideal for a hot, dry spot in your yard, such as a wall with chinks in the stonework, a rock garden, or a gravelly slope that cries out for ground cover. Sedums, from the Crassulaceae family, are succulents, so their leaves and stems are filled with water ready for use in times of need. A waxy coating keeps the water locked in. These plants vary in size, color, and form. Their fleshy leaves may be shaped like spoons, spiky and needlelike, or little nubbles.

Sedums are spectacular in bloom. Even the smallest species boast showy clusters of starry flowers. Larger species, including live-forever *(Sedum spectabile)* and its offspring, the hybrid 'Autumn Joy', are true standouts in bloom. Butterflies flock to the flowers.

Sedum acre (golden moss, golden acre) This mat-forming species is smothered in small yellow flowers in spring. It's pretty out of bloom, too, with tiny, overlapping midgreen leaves forming a solid carpet. 'Aureum' has bright yellow leaves; it is only 2 inches (5 cm) high, but it keeps spreading indefinitely. Hardy in Zones 4 to 9.

S. kamtschaticum (Kamtschatka stonecrop) This pretty yellow-flowered perennial grows about 4 inches (10 cm) tall and 1 foot (30 cm) wide. Its leaves are glossy and spoon-shaped, with leafy stems topped by tight clusters of starry flowers from late summer into fall. 'Variegatum' has white-edged leaves, often with a pink tinge. 'Rosy Glow' has lovely pinkish blue leaves and pink flowers. Hardy in Zones 4 to 9.

S. spathulifolium A native of the American West, it grows abundantly on rocky cliffs. It forms a ground- (or rock-) hugging mat of stems clothed in plump, rounded, gray-green leaves. In summer stems crowned with yellow flowers add to its beauty. It thrives in light shade and full-strength sun. 'Cape Blanco' is ghostly whitish silver. 'Purpureum' has dark, reddish purple leaves. Hardy in Zones 5 to 9.

S. spectabile (live-forever, showy sedum, showy stonecrop) One of the largest, this species forms a clump of erect, fleshy stems with grayish to midgreen, spoon-shaped leaves. In late summer the stems are topped with flat packed clusters of pink flowers to 6 inches (15 cm) wide. It reaches about 1½ feet (45 cm) tall and wide. 'Iceberg' has pale leaves and white flowers. Experts disagree on the classification of some of this species' offspring, such as 'Autumn Joy' and 'Brilliant'. Some place them in the species; others call them hybrids. Hardy in Zones 4 to 9.

S. telephium A clump-forming sedum that spreads by rhizomes, it has erect, 2-foot (60-cm)-tall stems with gray-green leaves and 5-inch (12.5-cm) clusters of purplish pink flowers from late summer to early fall. *S. telephium* ssp. *maximum* 'Atropurpureum' is deep reddish purple, covered with a grayish bloom, and has smaller pink flowers. 'Munstead Dark Red' has purplish red flowers. Hardy in Zones 4 to 9.

THE BASICS

Taller sedums flourish in a perennial bed among other flowers; ground-huggers do best in a rock garden, atop or in a wall, or in other well-drained nooks. Most sedums are vigorous

Sedum spectabile 'Autumn Joy'

growers that live for many years. If your plants fail to thrive, it is often because the soil is too moist (although some cultivars may be weaker in habit). Transplant them to a drier site, or start new plants from cuttings.

Growing Conditions: Plant in lean-to-average, well-drained-to-dry soil. Fertilizer can cause tall sedums to become floppy and require staking. Cut off flowering stems of low-growing varieties when they begin to dry up after blooming. Let seed heads of taller varieties stand all fall and for winter interest as they age to russet and then brown. Cut back tall sedums to about 1 inch (2.5 cm) above ground level in late winter, being careful not to damage any newly emerging shoots.

Propagation: They root swiftly and easily from cuttings stuck directly in the ground. Even individual leaves of large species will grow roots and become new plants. You can also divide plants of any species in spring.

▷ **Bloom Time** Summer; many to fall
▷ **Planting Requirements** Sun
▷ **Zones** Varies, depending on species

Solidago *sol-lih-DAY-go* • goldenrod

Goldenrods are one of the most common wildflowers in North America, with more than 30 species splashing sunny color along roads and in fields across a large part of the country. Take a moment to imagine what those abundant sprays of gold can do for your late-summer garden, and you may join the growing crowd of fans of these adaptable, easy perennials of the Asteraceae family. Well-behaved cultivars that stay in a clump are widely available, and native species are easily found at many specialty nurseries. Butterflies adore the tiny blossoms that make up the plumes, as do many other pollinators, including beneficial parasitic wasps that prey on garden pests.

Solidago canadensis (Canada goldenrod) Large, tapering plumes top the leafy, 2- to 5-foot (60- to 150-cm)

stems of this vigorous species. This is a fast-growing invasive species, so plant it where its aggressive rhizomes have room to spread outward to form a colony—in a meadow garden, perhaps, or along a fence, or against the garage. Dwarf 'Cloth of Gold', which reaches about 2 feet (60 cm), is less invasive. Hardy in Zones 3 to 8.

S. odora (sweet goldenrod) This species has a licorice scent. It was once known as "Blue Mountain tea" because of its Appalachian use as an herbal cure (for flatulence and other maladies) and a warming drink. It grows to 2 to 5 feet (60 to 150 cm) tall and forms a clump 1 to 2 feet (30 to 60 cm) wide. The flowers are open, fingerlike sprays atop the stems. Variation is a constant with the *Solidago* genus, and many species are difficult to tell apart except by experts. This stalwart, highly adaptable native is hardy in Zones 3 to 9.

S. rugosa (rough-stemmed goldenrod) Wide, fingerlike sprays that arch outward are the crowning glory of this 2- to 4-foot (60- to 120-cm) species, which is fairly well behaved and tends to stay in a clump. 'Fireworks' is a popular cultivar. Hardy in Zones 4 to 9.

S. sempervirens (seaside goldenrod) One of the most beautiful species, this clump-forming goldenrod has larger-than-usual individual blossoms tightly crammed into generous plumes. As the common name says, this 2- to 4-foot (60- to 120-cm) species is ideal for coastal gardens, although it thrives in average gardens, too. Hardy in Zones 4 to 9.

Solidago odora

THE BASICS

All goldenrods are easy to grow. Choose a species and planting site with care. Some goldenrods (including *S. canadensis*) are prolific spreaders, by roots and/or by seeds. Read the label or catalog description so that you can keep the roguish types in an area where you won't mind if they push the boundaries.

Growing Conditions: Plant in lean-to-fertile, well-drained soil. Seaside goldenrod thrives in pure sand as well as in garden soil. Control spreading types by carefully pulling up and removing the running roots that extend the colony. Cut back after flowers fade to reduce the possibility of self-sowing. Or let the plants stand throughout winter to provide shelter and seeds for sparrows, juncos, and other songbirds. Cut back to ground level in late winter or early spring.

Propagation: Divide in early spring.

▶ **Bloom Time** Late summer to fall
▶ **Planting Requirements** Sun; some also in part shade
▶ **Zones** Varies, depending on species

Perfect Partners

Goldenrods herald the end of the gardening season with an eye-catching fanfare. Pair them with other late bloomers, including blue or purple asters, autumnal hues of chrysanthemums, and russet or maroon sneezeweeds (*Helenium* spp.). Harken to their wild heritage with other native plants, such as Joe Pye weed (*Eupatorium purpureum*, *E. maculatum*), blue mistflower (*E. coelestinum*), coneflowers (*Echinacea* spp. and *Rudbeckia* spp.), and perennial sunflowers (*Helianthus* spp.), as well as with *Panicum*, *Miscanthus*, and other grasses.

S

Sedums for Color

Many plants are chosen for the garden based on their blossoms, but many of these succulents are selected for their attractive foliage—their flowers are a bonus. Their leaves come in all kinds of shapes, textures, sizes, and colors, but here is a selection of a few sedums noted for their foliage to get you started. There are dark-leaved types to choose from, as well as other types, including one species with foliage that forms a dense white-silver mat.

▲ S. 'Vera Jameson'

This lovely hybrid adds color even when it's not in bloom. Its clump of burgundy-purple leaves emerge blue-green in spring, then gradually take on wine tones. Named for an English gardener who found the original plant in her own yard, 'Vera Jameson' has sprays of rosy flowers from late summer to early fall. She's appealing against gray rocks or a pebbled path. Hardy in Zones 4 to 9.

▶ S. spathulifolium 'Purpureum'

This pretty plant has fleshy red-purple leaves with a powder of silvery white, especially at the stem tips. In summer the low-growing mat of foliage is transformed by a burst of yellow flowers. Hardy in Zones 5 to 9.

▼ *S. telephium* ssp. *maximum* **'Atropurpureum'**

The popularity of plants with dark foliage has caused a boom in dark-leaved sedums like this cultivar. 'Atropurpureum' forms a clump 1½ feet (45 cm) tall, but it's a floppy character. Plant it along a paved walk or behind a low rock onto which it can sprawl. Pinch the stem tips in spring to encourage a denser habit. 'Atropurpureum' has dusty pink flowers from late summer into fall. Hardy in Zones 4 to 9.

▲ **S. 'Ruby Glow'**

Gardeners adore this easy sedum in summer, with its abundant rich reddish flower clusters against bright green foliage. Older flower clusters mellow to a deep chestnut brown as new clusters continue opening. 'Ruby Glow' forms a mound 8 inches (20 cm) high, the perfect size for the front of a bed. Hardy in Zones 4 to 9.

◀ *S. spathulifolium* **'Cape Blanco'**

This species grows abundantly on rocky cliffs. Its nubbly foliage is ghostly white-silver and forms a dense, ground-hugging mat that creeps into crevices of rocks or spills over stones. It has stems of starry yellow flowers. Hardy in Zones 5 to 9.

Stachys
STAY-kiss • lamb's ears, hedge nettle, betony

Stachys macrantha

Sweet, soft lamb's ears with velvety silver leaves are the best-known *Stachys,* but the genus also includes some stellar, taller characters. They're simple to grow and thrive in difficult conditions. All share the tubular flowers of the Lamiaceae family, and most spread via underground stems. Hummingbirds and butterflies will visit the blooms.

Stachys byzantina (lamb's ears) An ideal ground cover for a sunny spot, this fast grower has rosettes of silvery 3- to 4-inch (7.5- to 10-cm)-long leaves that form a spreading carpet. A single small plant or division can grow 1½ to 2 feet (45 to 60 cm) wide in one year. This low grower reaches only 6 inches (15 cm) tall. Erect stems studded with whorls of rosy pink blossoms give it a different look in bloom. The woolly white stems grow 15 to 18 inches (38 to 45 cm) high. If you consider the flowers an interruption to the effect, choose a sparsely flowering or rarely blooming cultivar, such as 'Silver Carpet', which has silvery, almost whitish foliage. 'Big Ears' ('Countess Helene von Stein') offers supersized leaves and a tolerance for humidity. For a little extra zing try 'Primrose Heron', a beauty with soft chartreuse-yellow foliage. Hardy in Zones 4 to 8.

S. coccinea (scarlet hedge nettle, Texas betony) This American native has profuse spikes of small but brilliant flowers from summer into fall. Although it tolerates some drought, it grows best with regular watering. It reaches about 1½ feet (45 cm) tall and wide. The slightly fuzzy foliage is dark green. In climates milder than Zone 7 the plant often remains evergreen all year; in colder areas, it dies back to the ground, then regrows the following year. It's easy to grow from seed. Hardy in Zones 4 to 9.

S. macrantha (betony, big betony) This species produces a rosette of pretty heart-shaped, scalloped-edged green leaves, about 5 inches (12.5 cm) long and textured with wrinkles. The flowers, on stems that can reach 2 feet (60 cm), vary from reddish violet to pale rosy purple or pink. It blooms in summer and often produces additional flowers into fall. For more reliable color and incredibly prolific spikes of flowers that keep going into fall, consider purple 'Robusta' or pink-purple 'Superba'. 'Alba' has white flowers. Hardy in Zones 4 to 8.

THE BASICS

Lamb's ears are a reliable staple in the garden, except in areas with humid or rainy summers. Other species do well in wetter climates. Most spread by stems that reach out under- or above ground to root new plants.

Growing Conditions: Plant in well-drained, lean-to-average soil. Plants also grow well in sandy soil. Mulch *S. coccinea* to reduce the need for watering. Cut back lamb's ears to ground level if it becomes unsightly from too much water or humidity; divide if older plants become open and sprawling. In mild climates (Zone 8 and 9) let *S. coccinea* stand in winter; it is often evergreen. Cut back dead foliage and flowering stems of all species in fall or early spring. Monitor the spreading of these plants; remove any unwanted strays before they get established. All species may self-sow.

Propagation: Divide in spring or fall. Transplant self-sown seedlings in spring.

▶ **Bloom Time** *S. byzantina,* late spring to early summer; *S. coccinea* and *S. macrantha,* summer to fall

▶ **Planting Requirements** Sun to light or part shade

▶ **Zones** Varies, depending on species

Perfect Partners

Plant lamb's ears (*S. byzantina*) as a contrast with vertical forms, such as the veronicas, salvias (*Salvia* × *sylvestris* 'Mainacht'), and irises. The silver foliage will look terrific with pink or rose yarrows (*Achillea* spp.), mahogany or pink daylilies (*Hemerocallis* spp.), and white or pink lilies (*Lilium* 'Casablanca', 'Star Gazer', and others). Yellowish 'Primrose Heron' is superb with blue campanulas (*Campanula carpatica* 'Blue Clips' and many others) or creeping blue veronicas (*Veronica peduncularis* 'Georgia Blue' and others).

S

Tradescantia *tra-des-KANT-ee-uh* • spiderwort

Long-lived spiderworts come in a wide array of colors. These perennials are in the Commelinaceae family, and each blossom lasts only a day. However, there will be plenty of buds to take its place. The clump of spidery leaves often dies back after flowering is over.

Tradescantia × andersoniana (common spiderwort, spiderwort) This is the group that encompasses nearly all garden spiderworts. Most grow 1 to 2 feet (30 to 60 cm) tall and wide, forming a clump of long, skinny leaves. The three-petaled blossoms top clusters of decorative green buds. There are many cultivars, such as compact 'Concord Grape'; sky blue 'J. C. Weguelin'; maroon 'Red Cloud'; and 'Pauline', a happy pink.

***T. pallida* 'Purpurea'** (purple queen; purple wandering Jew) This trailing perennial is sold for use in summer containers or as a fast-growing ground-cover annual. It quickly forms a mat of dark violet-purple leaves, with rose-pink flowers. It's suitable for year-round use in Zones 9 to 11, where it will be evergreen and may bloom all winter.

THE BASICS

Spiderworts adapt well to sun or part shade. The foliage of all but purple queen (*T. pallida* 'Purpurea') will start to look ratty after flowering; cut back to the ground.

Growing Conditions: Plant in average-to-rich soil. Mulch to help

Tradescantia × andersoniana 'J. C. Weguelin'

retain soil moisture. Purple queen tolerates dry sites and humid heat.

Propagation: Divide *T. × andersoniana* in early spring; root stem cuttings of *T. pallida* 'Purpurea' by pushing them into moist soil.

▸ **Bloom Time** Late spring to summer
▸ **Planting Requirements** Sun to part shade
▸ **Zones** 4 to 9 unless otherwise noted

Verbascum *ver-BAS-kum* • mullein

Statuesque flowering spikes arise from a silvery-leafed rosette, making a beautiful accent in dry, difficult conditions. New hybrids offer a more petite form, bigger flowers, and delicious colors, such as copper, pink, and peach. Mulleins are from the Scrophulariaceae family, and some species act as biennials, blooming the second year, then dying back.

Verbascum olympicum (Olympic mullein) This species forms a 3-foot (90-cm)-wide mound of woolly gray leaves, topped with spikes of golden flowers. It can reach 6 feet (180 cm) tall. Hardy in Zones 5 to 9.

V. thapsus (common mullein, Indian flannel, many other common names) The long-appreciated form, its

flowering spikes are 3 to 6 feet (90 to 180 cm) tall. Hardy in Zones 3 to 10.

V. hybrids (hybrid mulleins) Warm-colored mulleins are 2 feet (60 cm) tall in bloom, forming a clump 1 to 2 feet (30 to 60 cm) wide. 'Helen Johnson' has copper-pink flowers; 'Jackie' is a brighter peach to apricot. Hardy in Zones 5 to 8; Zone 9 in the West.

THE BASICS

Use these plants as vertical accents. Allow space around the plant.

Growing Conditions: Plant in well-drained, lean-to-rich soil. For additional flowers, especially on hybrids, cut back flowering spikes to ground level when only the top third of the spike is still in

Verbascum thapsus

bloom. Often self-sows; seedlings of hybrids will not look like the parent.

Propagation: Easy to grow from seed. Take root cuttings in early spring.

▸ **Bloom Time** Summer
▸ **Planting Requirements** Full sun
▸ **Zones** Varies, depending on species

Verbena *ver-BEE-nuh* • verbena, vervain

Verbena × *hybrida*

These engaging plants are covered with bright blooms for months. The tiny flowers appear in clusters at the tips of the stems. Most of the popular garden species from this member of the Verbenaceae family are low plants that cover ground fast, but Brazilian verbena (*Verbena bonariensis*) grows upright. There are other tall species, often known by the common name vervain. You'll find cultivars in soft pastels as well as strong, clear colors, in most shades, except yellow.

Verbena bonariensis (Brazilian verbena, Brazilian vervain) The stiff, hairy foliage is held in an open tangled clump 2 feet (60 cm) wide. Bare, slender flowering stems are 3 to 4 feet (90 to 120 cm) tall. The stems branch at the top to present a multitude of tiny purplish flowers. This is a tall plant, but it has an open, airy feel and form, so you can plant it in the front of garden beds, as well as in the middle or the back. It self-sows generously. Hardy in Zones 7 to 9.

V. canadensis (rose verbena) Usually short-lived, this native of the Southeast and South Central states has rosy pink flowers in its wild form and a host of progeny that add other color choices to the mix. It stays low, usually 8 to 16 inches (20 to 40 cm), but covers an area 2 feet (60 cm) wide. The leafy mound supports an amazing display of flowers. Hardy in Zones 5 to 10. This species is a parent of many popular hybrids, including the renowned 'Homestead Purple'.

V. hastata (blue vervain) Best suited to natural gardens or a meadow or prairie planting, this species has tiny but lovely blue-violet blossoms. It forms a clump of foliage 2 feet (60 cm) across, with flowering stems to 5 feet (150 cm) tall. This species flourishes in wet soil, as well as in average garden conditions. Hardy in Zones 3 to 7.

V. × hybrida (hybrid verbena) Many verbenas at the garden center belong to this group. You'll find dozens of colors, including many with a white eye. They'll quickly grow into low mounds 8 to 18 inches (20 to 45 cm) tall and wide. Many are sold as hardy in Zones 7 to 10, but they often die over winter. They often last only one growing season in the ground.

V. 'Homestead Purple' Its abundant flowers are a rich purple, and the plant is resistant to mildew, an unsightly disease that can affect verbenas. Hardy in Zones 7 to 10.

Perfect Partners

Use low-growing verbena hybrids, including 'Homestead Purple' and *V.* × *hybrida* cultivars, in front of daylilies (*Hemerocallis* spp.), baby's breath (*Gypsophila paniculata*), and coneflowers (*Echinacea* spp.) to anchor them together. Punctuate the same perennials with tall *V. bonariensis*. Try a solid sweep of rich blue verbena hybrids at the foot of goldenrod (*Solidago* spp.) for a spectacular effect. Combine hot-colored verbena hybrids with ornamental grasses, such as fountain grass (*Pennisetum* spp.); pink or carmine verbenas will glow against the black-toned plumes of 'Moudry' fountain grass.

THE BASICS

Hybrid verbenas are simple to grow, producing a big splash of color in a hurry. All verbenas thrive in punishing heat and in dry conditions, as well as in less extreme gardens. Their short life span will allow you to play with new colors when the old ones die.

Growing Conditions: Plant in well-drained, average-to-fertile soil or in sandy soil. Fertilize two or three times during the growing year. *V. bonariensis* is drought tolerant; water hybrids occasionally. Mildew may disfigure the foliage; apply controls as needed. Trim back hybrid plants to keep them compact and to reinvigorate them. Cut back to just above ground level after cold kills the foliage.

Propagation: Divide in spring. Take stem cuttings in late summer. Stems often root where they touch the ground; sever and transplant. *V. bonariensis* may self-sow; transplant seedlings in spring.

▸ **Bloom Time** Summer to fall
▸ **Planting Requirements** Sun
▸ **Zones** Varies, depending on species

V

Veronica *ve-RON-ih-kuh* • veronica, speedwell

Veronicas are true blue, easy-to-grow plants that will live in your garden for decades. The plants fall into two categories: ground-cover types that form a blanket of blue blossoms and taller types, with tall, upright spikes of flowers. You can use these flowers of the Scrophulariaceae family to cushion a wall, accent a rock garden, or spike up your perennial beds. Choose mat-forming veronicas for spring bloom or taller types for a summer show, often lasting well into late summer. Pink and white cultivars, and a few with silvery foliage, increase the choice.

Veronica austriaca ssp. teucrium (*V. teucrium*) This species forms a mat of scalloped foliage 2 feet (30 cm) wide. In summer dozens of 4- to 6-inch (10- to 15-cm) spikes of bright blue flowers rise from the stem tips, lasting for several weeks. Bright blue 'Crater Lake Blue' reaches 12 to

Veronica spicata 'Heidekind'

18 inches (30 to 45 cm) in bloom. 'Shirley Blue' is also bright blue but smaller in size, at 10 inches (25 cm); 'Royal Blue' reaches 12 to 15 inches (30 to 38 cm). Hardy in Zones 3 to 8.

V. peduncularis One of the fastest-growing mat-formers of the species, it has dainty leaves and a multitude of blue flowers in loose clusters. In bloom it's only 4 inches (10 cm) tall, and it quickly spreads to 2 feet (60 cm). 'Georgia Blue' is a vigorous cultivar, smothered in flowers from spring to early summer. Hardy in Zones 5 to 9.

V. prostrata (prostrate speedwell) Another low grower, this species bears short spikes of blue flowers in early summer. It grows to 18 inches (45 cm) across and reaches 6 inches (15 cm) tall in bloom. 'Heavenly Blue' is a spring bloomer and 3 inches (7.5 cm) tall. 'Aztec Gold' has eye-catching yellow foliage. Hardy in Zones 5 to 8.

V. spicata (spike speedwell) A tall and clump-forming plant, it forms into a mound 18 inches (45 cm) wide and reaches 1 to 2 feet (30 to 60 cm) in bloom. The flowers are long, graceful, pointed spires, bright blue in the species but with shades of pink, many variations on blue, and icy white in the cultivars. 'Blue Peter' is deepest blue; 'Goodness Grows' is also dark blue; 'Blue Charm' is pale campanula blue; 'Caerulea' is sky blue. Pink forms include 'Erica', 'Heidekind', 'Rotfuchs' (Red Fox), and 'Barcarolle'. 'Icicle' ('White Icicle') is as pristine as new snow; 'Noah Williams' has white flowers and a bonus of white-edged leaves. Hardy in Zones 3 to 8; however,

Veronica austriaca ssp. *teucrium*

hardiness may vary—check the label or catalog description.

V. 'Sunny Border Blue' One of the most popular tall veronicas for the garden, this fine hybrid has glossy foliage in a clump 1 foot (30 cm) wide, topped with erect spikes of rich blue flowers that last from early summer to late fall. It reaches about 18 inches (45 cm) tall in bloom. Hardy in Zones 4 to 8.

THE BASICS

Veronicas are easy to grow. Generally, they are trouble-free and long-lived.

Growing Conditions: Plant in well-drained, lean-to-fertile soil. Fertilize taller types in spring. Apply controls as desired if plants become discolored by mildew. Cut back after blooming to remove dead flower spikes and keep the plants compact. Cut back taller types to just above ground level in late fall or early spring.

Propagation: Divide in early spring.

▶ **Bloom Time** Spring or summer

▶ **Planting Requirements** Sun; many taller cultivars also tolerate part shade

▶ **Zones** Hardiness varies, depending on species

Resources

MAIL-ORDER PLANTS

Buying plants in person at a garden center or nursery is your best option because you can examine the plants and pick the healthiest specimen. You can also buy perennials through mail-order suppliers, most of which have online catalogs. As with nurseries, mail-order catalog offerings vary, depending on availability.

Brent and Becky's Bulbs
A superb source for perennial bulbs.
7900 Daffodil Lane
Gloucester, VA 23061
(804) 693-3966
Web site: www.brentandbeckysbulbs.com

Carroll Gardens, Inc.
A wide variety of perennial plants.
444 East Main Street
Westminster, MD 21157
(410) 848-5422
Web site: www.carrollgardens.com

Digging Dog Nursery
Interesting, inspiring catalog featuring many unique and unusual perennials.
P.O. Box 471
Albion, CA 95410
(707) 937-1130
Web site: www.diggingdog.com

Forestfarm
Perennials, grasses, and foliage plants in smaller sizes that establish quickly in the garden.
990 Tetherow Road
Williams, OR 97544-9599
(541) 846-7269
Web site: www.forestfarm.com

Joy Creek Nursery
Inspiring selection of popular as well as more unusual perennials.
20300 NW Watson Road
Scappoose, OR 97056
(503) 543-7474
www.joycreek.com

Park Seed Company
A selection of popular perennial plants.
1 Parkton Avenue
Greenwood, SC 29647
(800) 213-0076
Web site: www.parkseed.com

Plant Delights Nursery, Inc.
A wide variety of interesting perennial plants, including many unusual cultivars and foliage plants.
Plant Delights Nursery, Inc.
9241 Sauls Road
Raleigh, NC 27603
(919) 772-4794
Web site: www.plantdelights.com

Prairie Nursery, Inc.
Specializes in American native prairie plants and other natives.

P.O. Box 306
Westfield, WI 53964
(800) 476-9453
Web site: www.prairienursery.com

Sequim Rare Plants
Unusual, enticing perennial plants.
500 N. Sequim Avenue
Sequim, WA 98382
(360) 683-6244
Web site: www.sequimrareplants.com

Sunlight Gardens
Many perennials; specializes in American natives, including native prairie plants.
174 Golden Lane
Andersonville, TN 37705
(800) 272-7396 or (865) 494-8237
Web site: www.sunlightgardens.com

W. Atlee Burpee & Co.
Offers a wide variety of perennials, bulbs, and also seeds.
300 Park Avenue
Warminster, PA 18974
(800) 333-5808
Web site: www.burpee.com

White Flower Farm
A variety of perennials, bulbs, and grasses.
P.O. Box 50
Route 63
Litchfield, CT 06759
(800) 503-9624
Web site: www.whiteflowerfarm.com

In Canada

Spring Garden Canada
Mail-order provider of perennials.
P.O. Box 123, Station Main
Oakville, ON L6J 4ZN
(800) 917-2852
Web site: springgardencanada.com/

PERENNIAL SEEDS

If you can't find seeds in your local garden center, the following sources offer seeds for perennials. Burpee and Park Seed (see above) sell seeds as well as plants.

Swallowtail Garden Seeds
Variety of unusual perennial seeds.
122 Calistoga Road, #178
Santa Rosa, CA 95409
(707) 538-3585
Web site:
www.swallowtailgardenseeds.com

Thompson & Morgan Seedsmen, Inc.
Jam-packed catalog with seeds for old favorites and new and unusual perennials.
220 Faraday Avenue
Jackson, NJ 08527
(800) 274-7333
Web site:
seeds.thompson-morgan.com/us

In Canada

Halifax Seed Company
Canada's oldest seed company; also supplies other gardening products.

5860 Kane Street
P.O. Box 8026, Stn. "A"
Halifax, NS
B3K 5L8
Phone: 902-454-7456
Web site: shop2.itnweb.com/halifaxseed/

BOTANICAL GARDENS

Visiting public gardens will provide ideas when it comes to choosing plants for your own garden. Listed here are some of the popular botanical gardens—these often are involved in the conservation of plants and education about them—but also visit estate and other large gardens.

Atlanta Botanic Gardens
Half of this 30-acre garden is dedicated to landscape gardens, the other to a forest.
1345 Piedmont Avenue
Atlanta, GA 30309
(404) 876-5859
Web site:
www.atlantabotanicalgarden.org

Brooklyn Botanic Gardens
Plant collections and specialty gardens displayed over 5 acres.
1000 Washington Avenue
Brooklyn, NY 11225
(718) 623-7200
Web site: www.bbg.org/

Chicago Botanic Garden
A botanic garden with 26 gardens, displaying plants native to the area.
1000 Lake Cook Road
Glenco, IL 60022
(847) 835-5440
Web site: www.chicago-botanic.org/

Cleveland Botanical Garden
Different display gardens are spread among landscaped grounds.
11030 East Boulevard
Cleveland, OH 44106
(216) 721-1600
Web site:
www.cbgarden.org/Visit/Gardens.html

Dallas Arboretum and Botanical Garden
Landscaped grounds include an English-style perennial garden and a garden with thousands of chrysanthemums in the fall.
8617 Garland Road
Dallas, TX 75218
(214) 515-6500
Web site: www.dallasarboretum.org/

Denver Botanic Garden
This botanic garden has a spectacular 23-acre artistic garden.
1005 York Street
Denver, CO 80206
(720) 865-3500
Web site: www.botanicgardens.org/pageinpage/home.cfm

Fort Worth Botanic Garden
The grounds include a perennial garden, and over 2,500 native and exotic species.
3220 Botanic Garden Boulevard
Fort Worth, TX 76107

(817) 871-7686
Web site: www.fwbg.org/

The State Botanical Garden of Georgia
Contains theme gardens, special collections, and a tropical conservatory.
2450 South Milledge Avenue
Athens, GA 30605
(706) 542-6195
Web site: www.uga.edu/botgarden/

The Huntington Botanical Gardens
Landscaped grounds display plants from around the world.
1151 Oxford Road
San Marino, CA 91108
(818) 405-2141
Web site: www.huntington.org/

Memphis Botanic Garden
Over 96 acres of horticultural attractions, including display gardens.
750 Cherry Road
Memphis, TN 38117
(901) 576-4100
Web site:
www.memphisbotanicgarden.com

Minnesota Landscape Arboretum
Features more than 1,000 acres of gardens, model landscapes, and natural areas, with plants hardy in the north.
3675 Arboretum Drive
Chanhassen, MN 55317
(952) 443-1400
Web site: www.arboretum.umn.edu/

Missouri Botanical Gardens
Home to a greenhouse displaying tropical frain forest species, as well as a large Japanese garden, Chinese garden, and demonstration gardens.
4344 Shaw Boulevard
St. Louis, MO 063110
(800) 642-8842
Web site: www.mobot.org/

North Carolina Botanical Garden
A leader in native plant conservation in the southeastern United States.
Chapel Hill, NC 27599
(919) 962-0522
Web site: www.ncbg.unc.edu/

In Canada

Montréal Botanical Garden
A Chinese-style garden and more than 20,000 plant species, as well as an insectarium, are among the attractions.
4104 Sherbrooke Street East
Montréal, Quebec PQ HIX 2B2
(514) 872-1400
Web site:
www2.ville.montreal.qc.ca/jardin/en/propos/propos.htm

Royal Botanical Gardens
Untamed and cultivated landscapes make up Canada's largest botanical garden.
680 Plains Road West
Hamilton/Burlington, Ontario L7T 4H4
(905) 527-1158
Web site: www.rbg.ca/

Index

Note: Page references in **boldface** indicate illustrations or photographs.

Acknowledgments and Photo Credits

PHOTO CREDITS

Abbreviations: T = Top; M = Middle; B = Bottom; L = Left; R = Right

Front Cover: **Garden Picture Library** Howard Price (TR); Pernilla Bergdahl (ML); **Neil Hepworth** (BL); **Gardeners Monthly** (BR); **Courtesy of ItSaul Plants** (BM).

Back Cover: **Alamy Images** M. A. Battilana (TM); Ian Armitage (BM), (BR)

Alamy Images David Chapman 2–3, 61 (MR); Bjanka Kadic 64 (BM), 65 (BL), 69 (BR); M. A, Battilana 177 (TR); Peter Titmuss 194; Mike Booth 196 (LM); Holmes Garden Photos/Neil Holmes 209; Garden World Images Ltd./Philip Smith 223 (RM); Garden World Images Ltd./Liz Cole 239 (RM)

Ian Armitage 17 (TL), 26 (BR), 36, 37 (BL), 46 (TLM), 51, 98 (BL), 153 (T), 158, 160 (BR), 163, 177 (BR), 203

Chailey Iris Garden 103

Clive Nichols Garden Photography Clive Nichols 68–69, 68 (BR), 69 (TR), 69 (BL), 70 (BR), 108–9, 218 (TR), 226 (LM), 237 (BL)

Corbis Hal Horwitz 220

Jane Courtier 15 (BL), 15 (BLM), 15 (BRM), 15 (BR), 113 (B), 171 (TL), 178, 184 (LM)

Dorling Kindersley Peter Anderson 77 (TL)

Derek Fell 48 (BL)

FLPA Jurgen & Christine Sohns 172, 183; Alan & Linda Detrick 188 (TR); M Szadzuik and R. Zinck 189 (RM); Alan and Linda Detrick 190; Nigel Catlin 210 (BL); Primrose Peacock 223 (TL)

GAP Photos Adrian Bloom 22; Vision 65 (BM); Richard Bloom 147 (B)

Garden Picture Library Suzie Gibbons 5; Lynn Keddie 6 (TR); Lynn Keddie 9 (BL); John Glover 9 (BR); Marie O'Hara 12 (TL); Jason Ingram 12 (TLM); Clive Nichols 12 (TRM); Howard Rice 13; J. S. Sira 14 (T); Mark Boulton 15 (T); Jason Ingram 16; J. S. Sira 17 (BR); Noel Kavanagh 19 (BL); John Glover 19 (BR); Stephen Henderson 20; Clive Nichols 21 (T); Steven Wooster 21 (B); Juliet Greene 23 (T); Ron Evans 23 (B); Clive Nichols 24 (T); Marie O'Hara 24 (B); Sunniva Harte 25 (T); Suzie Gibbons 27; Animals Animals/Earth Sciences 28–29; Brigitte Thomas 30; Howard Rice 31 (T); Clive Nichols 32 (T), 34; Pernilla Bergdahl 37 (L); Mark Boulton 38 (B); Michael Davis 39 (TL); Ron Sutherland 40 (BR); Sunniva Harte 41; Clive Nichols 43; Steven Wooster 44; Lynn Keddie 45; Animals Animals/Earth Sciences 46 (TL); Garden Picture Library 46 (TRM); Georgia Glynn Smith 46 (TR); David Dixon 47; Clive Nichols 48 (BR); Mark Boulton 49; Georgia Glynn Smith 50; Animals Animals/Earth Science 54–55; Chris Burrows 60 (BL); Michelle Lamontage 60 (BR); Howard Rice 61 (TR); Ron Evans 61 (TRB); Aaron McCoy 62 (TR); Ron Evans 62 (BL); Howard Rice 62 (BR); Clive Nichols 64–65; J. S. Sira 64 (BL); Steven Wooster 66 (TR); Howard Rice 66 (BL), 66 (BR); Christi Carter 69 (MR); J. S. Sira 70 (TR); Clive Nichols 70 (BL); Mark Bolton 72 (TR); Brigitte Thomas 73; Mark Winwood 74; John Swithinbank 80 (BL); Howard Price 86–87; Steve Wooster 89 (TR); Alec Scaresbrook 91; Mark Bolton 92 (BL); Howard Price 92 (BR); Mel Watson 95 (BR); Botanica/Deering William 98 (BR); J. S. Sira 106 (BL); Botanica 106 (BR); Howard Price 107; Lynn Keddie 112 (T); John Glover 112 (LM); Mark Bolton 113 (TL); Richard Bloom 113 (MR); Jerry Pavia 115 (B); Christie Carter 119 (TR); Lynn Keddie 121 (T); Suzie Gibbons 121 (B); Neil Holmes 124; Steven Wooster 126 (T); Lynn Keddie 127; Mark Bolton 128 (T); Anne Green-Amytage 129 (BR); Richard Bloom 132 (T); Animals Animals/Earth Science/Maresa Pryor 132 (B); Anne Green-Amytage 134 (T); David England 134 (B); Francois De Heel 136; John Glover 137; Sunniva Harte 138 (B); Didier Willery 139; Clive Nichols 140 (TR); Joan Dear 140 (LM); John Glover 140 (BR), 141 (TL), 141 (RM); Pernilla Bergdahl 141 (BR); John Glover 142; Botanica 144 (T); Sunniva Harte 144 (B); Andrea Jones 145; Ruth Brown 146 (BR); Jerry Pavia 147 (TL); Linda Burgess 147 (RM); Howard Rice 148 (B); David Dixon 150; Milse Milse/Mauritius Die Bildagentur Gmbh 152 (T); Brian L. Carter 154 (T); Suzie Gibbons 154 (B); Richard Bloom 156 (LM); J. S. Sira 156 (BR); Pernilla Bergdahl 157 (RM); J. S. Sira 159; Mark Bolton 161 (TR); Friedrich Strauss 161 (BL); Richard Bloom 164 (TR); Mark Bolton 166 (TR); John Glover 167 (TR); Stuart Blyth 176; Botanica 182; J. S. Sira 191; Michele Lamontage 192 (TR); Jacquin Hurst 192 (LM); Richard Bloom 192 (BR); John Glover 195; Clive Nichols 197 (TL); Mark Boulton 197 (RM); J. S. Sira 197 (BR); Howard Rice 201 (TR); Georgina Glynn Smith 201 (BR); Mark Bolton 206 (TR); Jerry Pavia 206 (LM); Jason Ingram 207 (BR); Mark Bolton 211; Howard Rice 212; Chris Burrows 218 (LM); Neil Holmes 218 (BR); John Glover 219 (TL); Neil Holmes 222 (BR); Pernilla Bergdahl 226 (TR); Didier Willery 227 (TL); David Askham 228; David Dixon 229 (TR); Hemant Jariwala 229 (BL); J. S. Sira 230; 232; Christopher Fairweather Ltd. 235 (BR); John Glover 238 (TR); Howard Rice 238 (LM); Ron Evans 238 (BR); Lynn Keddie 239 (TL); Mark Boulton 239 (BR); Neil Homes 242 (R); Clive Nichols 243 (TL); Brian Carter 243 (BR); Jacqui Hurst 244; Christopher Fairweather Ltd. 247 (BL)

Gardens Monthly 75 (TR), 128 (LM), 128 (BR), 129 (TL), 129 (RM), 164 (LM), 164 (BR), 165 (TL), 165 (RM), 165 (BR), 169, 170 (TR), 170 (LM), 170 (BR), 171 (RM), 171 (BR), 174; 180 (LM), 180 (BL), 181 (BR), 187, 188 (LM), 188 (BR), 189 (BR), 200, 204, 213, 223 (BR)

Hayloft Plants Ltd. 226 (BR)

Neil Hepworth 7 (TR), 12 (TR), 14 (BR), 18, 25 (BR), 26 (BL), 31 (B), 33 (TR), 35 (T), 35 (B), 38 (T), 38 (M), 40 (TL), 42, 112, 118, 122 (B), 125, 126 (B), 131 (T), 135, 146 (TR), 146 (LM), 167 (BR), 168, 173, 175, 180 (TR), 181 (TL), 181 (RM), 189 (TL), 199 (TR), 205, 225, 236

Courtesy of ItSaul Plants 7 (BL), 157 (TL), 157 (B); Andrea Jones 10–11; Andrew Lawson 68 (BL), 206 (BR), 207 (TL), 207 (RM), 214 (LM), 214 (BR), 219 (RM), 221, 222 (LM), 227 (RM), 227 (BR), 234 (BR), 235 (TL), 235 (RM), 242 (LM), 243 (RM)

Photos Horticultural 61 (BL), 64 (BR), 65 (MR), 131 (B), 214 (TR,) 216

Schreiner's Iris Gardens 193 (RM)

Shutterstock Zina Seletskaya 1; Jakez 6 (BL); Jerry Higkang Chan 8 (BL); Jakez 33 (B); Malle 37 (T); Svetlana Tikhonova 39 (BL); Michael Rosenberg 39 (TL); Michael Rosenberg 52; Patrick Hermans 53; Rainbow 56; Jeff Krushinski 57; Sergey Chushkin 58; Romeo Koitmäe 59, 60 (BM); Sally Scott 61 (BR); Denis Aleksandrouch Kotov 65 (TR); Lijuan Guo 72 (TL); Sally Scott 72 (TLM); Ladanov Sergey Valentinovich 72 (TRM); Theresa Martinez 78 (B); Wheatley 78 (BR); North Georgia Media 82 (TR); Ryan Kelm 83 (BR); Paul-André Belle-Isle 85; Pixelman 97; Jean Schweitzer 101 (TR); Sergey Ladanova 101 (BL); Malle 104 (BM); Alan James 110; Sergey Chushkin 111 (T); Steve Mcwilliam 111 (B); Breiholz 114 (T); Rob Huntley 115 (T); Michael Thompson 116; Michael Rosenburg 117 (T); Luis César Tejo 117 (B); Trevor Allen 119 (B); Marilyn Barbone 120; Michaela Steininger 122 (T); Craig Ruaux 123 (T), 123 (B); Scott Pehrson 130; Malle 133; Shutterstock 138 (T); Sergey Chushkin 143; Steve McWilliam 148 (T); Malle (149); Verga Bogaerts 151; Jerry Hinkang Chan 152 (B); Jean Ann Fitzhugh 153 (B); Zina Seletskaya 155; Malle 160 (TR); Sharon R. Haynes 162; Dogmar Schneider 179; John Teate 186; Theresa Martinez 193 (TL); Jill Lang 198; Douglas Greenwald 199 (BL); C. Rene Ammundsen 202; Tootles 208; Michael J. Thompson 210 (TR); Cassiopedia 217; Alexy Obukhov 224; Frank Podgorsek 231; Melissa Dockstader 233; Andrey Khrolenok 234 (LM); 237 (TR); Kuehdi 240; Dagmar Schneider 241; Alexey Obukhev 245 (TR); Rob Huntley 245 (BR); Shutterstock 246; Nikita Tiunov 247 (TR)

Terra Nova Nurseries Inc. 8 (BR), 156 (TR), 184 (BR), 184 (TR), 185 (TL), 185 (RM), 185 (BR), 222 (TR)

Photo Courtesy of White Flower Farm 215 (TL), 215 (RM), 215 (BR)

Mark Winwood 75 (BL), 75 (BM), 75 (BR), 76, 77 (TR), 77 (MR), 77 (BR), 81 (TR), 81 (TM), 81 (TL), 82 (BL), 84, 88, 89 (BL), 90 (BL), 90 (BM), 94 (BL), 94 (BR), 95 (TR), 99 (TR), 99 (MR), 99 (BR), 100 (BL), 100 (BM), 100 (BR), 101 (BR), 102 (BL), 102 (BM), 102 (BR), 104 (TL), 104 (LM)

ACKNOWLEDGMENTS

Toucan Books would like to thank the following for their assistance in the preparation of this book:

Liz Dobbs and the staff at *Gardens Monthly*
Justin Wilson
Robert Sackville West
Knole (a National Trust property)

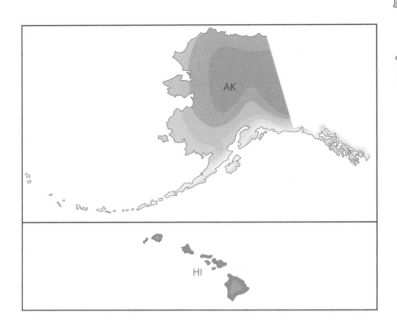

NORTH AMERICAN ZONE MAP

Hardiness across North America

Plants that survive freezing winters are called hardy, while those that succumb to cold weather are called tender. The plants in this book are rated according to the coldest temperatures they can survive. Summer heat and humidity, and lack of winter chilling in warmer climates may limit the ability of some plants to thrive. Because of this, and the fact that within each zone there are microclimates that can be colder or warmer, we suggest that you use the zones as a guide, but feel free to experiment with plants rated marginally hardy in your area.

Zones in North America are based on average minimum temperatures, with Zone 11 rated warmest and Zone 1 coldest. Each zone can grow plants from lower numbered zones. For example, if you live in Zone 4, you can include plants from Zones 3, 2, and 1 in your garden.

A note to our Canadian readers: This zone map was generated by the U.S. Department of Agriculture (USDA) and differs slightly from the zone map developed by Agriculture Canada. Hardiness ratings for all of the plants in this book are based on the USDA map. To judge the suitability of a particular plant for your garden, refer to the zone information given here for your area.